The Impact of Evolutionary Theory:
A Christian View

The Impact of Evolutionary Theory:
A Christian View

by

Russell Maatman

Copyright 1993 by
Dordt College Press

ISBN: 0-932-914-28-4

Printed in the United States of America

Table of Contents

Chapter   Page

    Foreword i
    Preface iii
1. Introduction 1
2. Background 5
3. Design 22
4. Objections to Design 37
5. Scientific Consensus: The Scenario 52
6. Analysis: From Inert Matter to Cells 76
7. Analysis: From Cells to Humans 98
8. Revelation 121
9. Science 143
10. Genesis 162
11. Human Origin and the Evolutionary Paradigm ... 186
12. Human Behavior 208
13. Progress 230
14. Consequences 251
    Notes and References 271
    Indexes 297

Foreword

In 1988 Russell Maatman, professor of chemistry, was appointed to the Dordt College Studies Institute. Approaching his proposed project, Maatman believed that much of modern academic thought was driven by the assumption that all phenomena can be understood in terms of evolutionary theory.

It was clear from the beginning that Maatman was dealing with a subject of current interest, since questions about various origins theories were and are receiving universal attention. The origin of the human race has rated a cover story in several secular news magazines. Public schools have become embroiled in the creation/evolution controversy, begun primarily by the "creation-science" movement. The American Scientific Affiliation, an association of evanglical academicians, has for decades given considerable attention to this question. And it is an issue that has been debated in most church and church-related institutions of higher education in North America.

Recognizing the wide-spread interest in the question of origins, Maatman was concerned, first, to discover if and to what extent evolutionary assumptions have influenced the various academic disciplines. Therefore, while gathering literature on the subject and consulting with others knowledgeable in the field, he interviewed Dordt faculty in the divisions of Humanities, Natural Science, and Social Science as to the effect of evolutionary thinking in the various disciplines.

Second, in dealing with this controversy, Maatman wanted to look beneath the surface. How do scientists do science? What is the proper way to carry out scientific activity? More specifically, Maatman sought answers—not necessarily final answers—to two questions: "What does a *Reformed* worldview lead to in understanding how scientific activity should be carried out? And how does a reformational understanding help reveal the impact of evolutionary though on modern life?

Foreword

During his tenure in the Studies Institute, Maatman indicated his willingness to share with us the material he was gathering for the writing of a book. The response in the Studies Institute was positive. Following his retirement in 1990, Maatman did precisely what he had suggested, i.e., used his research in the development of a book, and the result was the manuscript for *The Impact of Evolutionary Theory: A Christian View*.

When Maatman had completed his writing, he submitted the manuscript for publication to the Dordt Press Committee. I was pleased when, following extensive review and evaluation, the committee decided to publish this book. It reflects Maatman's knowledge of the subject and his intense desire to evaluate evolutionary theory from a Reformed, Christian viewpoint. This book also serves to demonstrate the commitment of the entire Dordt College community, including the Studies Institute and the Dordt College Press, to openly confront these sensitive, important issues from a biblical, reformational perspective.

Dr. Maatman has written about these issues before. *The Bible, Natural Science, and Evolution* appeared in 1969, and *The Unity in Creation* was published in 1978. I trust that this most recent publication will provide the Christian community with further insight and direction in seeking to understand God's world in the light of God's Word.

John B. Hulst
President, Dordt College

Preface

Often the debate on creation and evolution centers on only one aspect of the question. Sometimes that aspect is a part of biology or of another natural science. At other times the focus is on certain theological considerations or particular philosophical propositions. At still other times the principal interest might be the effect of evolutionary thinking on the sciences outside the natural sciences.

I am certainly not the first person to bring several aspects of the creation-and-evolution question into a single discussion. Yet it seemed to me before I began this book that those aspects needed to be brought together by one who is committed to the Reformed, Christian perspective. After all, it is the essence of a Reformed approach that no single aspect of this large question be isolated: life is of one piece.

I decided to relate the unity of life to the creation-and-evolution question for both scholars and nonscholars. Although this book rests on the work of scholars in several fields, it is addressed to the reading Christian public. It is an attempt to demonstrate how one Reformed Christian brings together the various aspects of this very large question.

To write such a book I needed special kinds of help. I want to acknowledge the help I received.

First of all, I thank Dordt College for allowing me to be a part of the Dordt College Studies Institute in order to write this book. Dr. J.B. Hulst, President of Dordt College, and Dr. Rockne McCarthy, Director of the Institute, gave me needed encouragement. Rev. B.J. Haan, President Emeritus of Dordt College, also urged me on as I worked in the Institute.

The Institute provided an unusual opportunity for a multidisciplinary project. In a somewhat formal setting, I discussed my questions about evolutionary thinking with faculty colleagues from a variety of disciplines. From them I learned where evolutionary thinking has made an impact and where

Preface

it has not. Because of these discussions, I accessed key books and articles I might not have seen. In addition, some colleagues read parts of the text.

In appropriate places I acknowledge specific contributions of certain colleagues. In addition, others who helped either by discussion or reading parts of the manuscript are Charles Adams, Kenneth Bussema, Karen De Mol, Henry Duitman, Richard Eigenbrood, George Faber, Edwin Geels, Joan Heifner, Beryl Hugen, Calvin Jongsma, Donald King, Wayne Kobes, John Kok, Jasper Lesage, James Mahaffy, Aaldert Mennega, Paul Moes, Paulo Ribeiro, Marian Vander Ark, Daryl Vander Kooi, John Vander Stelt, Thomas Visker, John Visser, Ron Vos, and John Zwart.

My membership on the Creation-Science Study Committee formed by the 1988 Synod of the Christian Reformed Church also helped me address the issues of this book. During the three-year life of the Committee, its nine other members—theologians, philosophers of science, and natural scientists—brought to my attention many ideas concerning origins and the nature of scientific activity. I am grateful to them for our many long and helpful discussions.

But no one else should be held responsible for what I have written. Errors and mistakes in judgment are mine alone.

I thank *Pro Rege*, the Dordt College faculty quarterly, for granting me permission to use parts of my article, "The Origin of the Human Family," which appeared in the March, 1990 (Vol. 19, No. 3) issue, in Chapter 11.

My wife, Jean, had considerable patience during the preparation of this manuscript. We both thank our daughter Becky for helping with the manuscript. Finally, I thank the Dordt College Press for providing the excellent editorial assistance of Kim Rylaarsdam.

Except where noted, the New International Version is the source of biblical quotations.

My prayer is that this work will help some readers to glorify the Lord. If this book helps them perceive that the Lord is the Creator and the Sustainer of all that he has made, then my purpose will have been accomplished.

                        Russell Maatman
                        Sioux Center, Iowa

Chapter One
Introduction

For several generations the Christian church has discussed origins. This book surveys questions concerning origins: origins of living and nonliving things, the origin of Creation itself. It looks again at the "creation versus evolution" question.

Not everyone is convinced that such a discussion is worthwhile—worthwhile for the Christian community or the world in which Christians witness. Those against continuing the discussion say it is only a debate on *how* God created, a subject on which Christians may be allowed to differ. Instead, they argue, Christians should address contemporary issues such as the endangered environment, abortion, and the treacherous technological-political situation that could lead to a nuclear winter. With such Satanic influences loose in the world, they argue, Christians shouldn't quibble over how the Lord made the world.

The issue is not merely how God did something. The subject of origins is actually an important part of a much larger picture, and so a restatement of the question of origins needs to show its significance. The following five questions indicate the dimensions of the problem:

(1) Given that both Creation and the Bible reveal God, how are these two modes of revelation related to the various sciences?
(2) What is the Christian way to study science?
(3) In what way does a Christian understanding of science differ from the commonly held view of science?
(4) How do these different understandings of science result from different worldviews?
(5) How do worldviews influence questions of origins and, therefore, one's understanding of the world today?

In the popular mind the fifth question, rephrased as creation versus evolution, looms important. But the question of origins is influenced by the answers to the previous questions. This book broadens the discussion to that of all five questions, a necessary approach to the popular question of origins. The bottom-line issues in this debate are one's perception of the relationship between creational and Scriptural revelation and how a Christian should study science.

The question about creation and evolution is therefore worth examining, even though it exhibits Christians in serious disagreement with one another. The Christian church has adopted many important doctrines through struggle. By nature such debates happen within the church. No doubt the spirit of the present origins debate is often unChristian. However, new and better positions are often hammered out among people with strong, but differing, opinions.

The nagging question of priority remains. One might concede that the question of origins is important, that it is related to how Christians understand science, and that an intense struggle is unavoidable. But do we not see a world in flames? Can't we at least put out some of the fire before attempting to come to a Christian consensus on creation and evolution?

Obviously, the Christian community works on many matters simultaneously. Halting the origins discussion would not likely solve other pressing problems. But an origins discussion is, in fact, crucial. Beliefs in creation and in evolution stem from different worldviews. If opposing worldviews exist side by side in the Christian community, then presumably the consequences of those worldviews can also co-exist. In this book I will show that evolutionary theorizing affects not only biology but also the so-called human sciences. Perhaps problems such as pollution and abortion derive from a misleading worldview, a worldview which also leads to an evolutionary understanding of origins. Perhaps a broad discussion of issues relating to creation versus evolution will also be relevant to contemporary problems some deem more important.

Following secular scientific leaders uncritically is dangerous in the matter under discussion. We should not accept claims made by scientists whose claims have little support. After all, we do not accept uncritically the advice of secular professionals in other matters, such as pedagogy and child psychology. We must help each other recognize the false claims of those who at first seem to advocate only the acceptance of hard scientific evidence, but who actually have an unChristian philosophical agenda. On the other hand, Christians should warn against those who claim great biblical and scientific knowledge, when, in fact, their knowledge is shallow. Such persons can also lead many astray.

In this book I contend that how we study science has shaped the present discussion. In Chapter 2, I trace the history of ideas concerning the nature of science and how those ideas bear on the present origins discussion. Complementing this historical sketch, Chapters 3 and 4 provide a discussion of design in Creation.

Introduction

Chapter 5 describes the scientific consensus concerning physical and biological evolution, the "scientific scenario." I do not want us to reject this scenario completely. But I do suggest some serious scientific problems with the scenario in Chapters 6 and 7.

Given this evolutionary scenario and the scientific problems it poses, how should Christians respond? My answer to that question has four parts, described in Chapters 8-11. In Chapter 8 I discuss the relationship between Scriptural and creational revelation. In Chapter 9 I describe the nature of Christian scientific activity, a response to creational revelation.

In Chapter 10 I focus on the Bible, with particular emphasis on passages that speak of origins. I also discuss the lack of symmetry in our interactions with the two kinds of revelation: in both cases we can have control beliefs that determine our answers to many problems, but only the study of Scriptural revelation leads to control beliefs that are nonnegotiable. In Chapter 11 I discuss the origin of the human family. Here the concept of a nonnegotiable control belief becomes especially important.

Evolutionary theory has not only greatly impacted the natural science but also subjects outside the natural sciences. After all, for good or bad, this is the scientific age—the *natural* scientific age. Natural scientific results and the popular understanding of the natural scientific method shape the modern mind. The role that evolutionary thinking plays in the human disciplines and sciences is the subject of Chapters 12, 13, and 14. In the human sciences it is easy to see the consequences of abandoning the Christian belief that human beings are unique. I consider some of the disciplines in which evolutionary theory has made an impact: psychology, sociology, religion, economics, and the arts.

A central problem is that human response to Creation and human response to Scriptural revelation were assigned separate domains by some natural scientists at the beginning of the scientific era. The Bible could not address natural scientific activity. Eventually general evolutionary theory appeared. This theory reached outside the natural sciences as it shaped an evolutionary model for the human sciences and disciplines; everything "spiritual" then became other-worldly. Everything worth explaining has been or will be explained using evolutionary theory.

I generally define key terms as they appear in the text. But allow an initial clarification.

I use *evolution* to denote change over time. Some claims for evolution are justified; others are not. In this book, my use of the word evolution is not in itself judgmental. Where possible, the context will indicate the validity of a particular claim for evolution.

What about *evolutionism?* To add *ism* to a word usually implies absolutization of the idea. Thus, *communism* and *capitalism* usually refer to the absolutization of a certain economic philosophy and the consequent subservience of every other aspect of life to that philosophy. The *ism* becomes a god. Evolutionism certainly qualifies. It is my claim that evolution does in innumerable ways intrude upon our lives and has, for many, become a god. Yet I use the word evolutionism sparingly. My reason is that I attempt to analyze the beliefs of others, and usually people avoid admitting that their perception of truth is subservient to their belief in evolution. Therefore, it prejudices the argument to describe a person's acceptance of evolution as evolutionism.

Chapter Two
Background

What gave rise to the concept of evolution in the nineteenth century? Ideas appear on the scene for a reason. They have a background. Of course, natural scientists and other scholars sometimes receive flashes of insight for reasons that seem to have no cause. But such new ideas arise in a context, a context that is like a set of concentric circles: the smallest circle, the scholar's day-to-day experience; the next circle, a project of which the scholar's work is only a part; the next, the culture in which the scholar finds himself or herself; and the largest circles, the history of that society and of civilization.

To understand most scientific ideas it is not necessary to go back thousands of years. But for an idea that leads to a scientific revolution, the local context is not enough. Certainly this is especially true for the set of ideas which, when lumped together, constituted the evolutionary revolution. After all, evolutionary ideas have been incorporated—albeit often altered—into much of natural science and have significantly affected not only various aspects of Western culture but also other cultures. To grasp nineteenth-century evolutionary ideas and the worldwide impact of those ideas by the end of the twentieth century, we must indeed go back thousands of years to countries far from North America.

The purpose of this chapter is to trace key ideas in the history of science by showing how one idea led to another. The history of ideas did not take an accidental turn in a particular direction in the middle of the nineteenth century with the scholarship of Charles Darwin (1809-1882). A very long sequence of events has brought evolution's impact on modern society.

To claim that Darwin's ideas have a history is not to say that we must give credit to someone other than Charles Darwin for the key evolution ideas as evolution was understood after he published his landmark books. Science historian Peter Bowler correctly criticized all attempts to show that someone before Charles Darwin propounded the key ideas.[1] What is important in tracing the history of ideas that led up to Darwin, said Bowler, is to avoid taking remarks or discoveries of Darwin's predecessors out of context. The Darwinian revolution happened; no one before Darwin articulated the key ideas of that revolution.

Following is a brief sketch, beginning with ancient times, of ideas that led not only to the dominant scientific ideas Darwin used but also to modern science.

A Brief Survey
Ancient Period. In 1800 B.C. Ahmes, an obscure Egyptian scribe, copied a table of numbers which had been formulated about 2000 B.C.[2] Ahmes gave his reason for copying: this table provided "the entrance into the knowledge of all existing things and all obscure secrets." What was the table? It was a table of fractions. Evidently Ahmes meant that when a person can handle numbers, the key to all knowledge is at hand. As we shall see, Ahmes's desire to explain everything, especially in terms of numbers, has been expressed many times.

Eventually the center of learning in what is now the Western world passed to Greece. Ionian philosophers of the sixth century B.C. said that facts had causes which they could investigate. Thales of Miletus, one of the "Seven Wise Men of Ancient Greece," is often credited as the founder of science because he accepted causes to be natural. No longer were the gods responsible for causes.[3] Aristotle (384-322 B.C.), probably the most important scientist (in physics, astronomy, and biology) of the ancient world, made important suggestions concerning causality. He said that the world is a living organism and a final "cause" draws it toward its goal.[4] Aristotle's ideas influenced thinking even two thousand years after he died.

Greek scientists made specific suggestions about the origin of living things. Anaximander of Miletus said that life came from sea slime. Empedocles, Epicurus, and Democritus postulated a never-ending flux of matter, which generated by chance a large number of objects. Objects that were not monsters would survive. People did not need the gods.[5] The hierarchical linking of the simplest inorganic matter to the most complex life can be traced to ancient Greece.[6]

Ancient Greek thinkers also had ideas on the origin of the universe. Plato (427-347 B.C.) taught that matter was co-eternal (has always existed) with God, although God did fabricate the present world, including living things.[7] Aristotle said that the world has neither beginning nor end and that God has no knowledge of that world. Aristotle did not teach that God fabricated the world. The universe is independent and does not need God.

Mathematics was to play an important role in the search for the ultimate nature of things. The Ionian philosophers used mathematics in their investigation of causality. Pythagoras, a Greek who migrated to Italy, had learned the Ionian approach and founded a derivative school of thought. He taught that the first cause of all things—musical harmonies, movements of the stars, and even the nature of the gods—lies in numbers.[8] The Pythagorean school developed a branch of mathematics.[9] Euclid, a Greek of Alexandria, developed another branch of mathematics by systematizing plane geometry about 300 B.C.[10]

Although there were many practical inventions in the ancient period, the development of new theories became more important: they become stepping-stones toward newer, better theories. For example, in the second century A.D. Ptolemy, an Egyptian, included in his compilation of scientific knowledge the idea that the planets move around the earth in circles built upon circles.[11] Fifteen centuries later the Ptolemaic system was replaced by the sun-centered, or heliocentric, system. This replacement was a necessary step in the development of modern astronomy.

Medieval Period. As the Christian religion spread and interacted with pagan ideas in the first centuries after Christ, it encountered the teachings of both Plato and Aristotle. For the present discussion, Augustine (354-430) is the most important Christian theologian of that period. He taught—unlike Plato and Aristotle—that God created the entire world by divine fiat in a single instant. After that beginning God ordered and developed what had already been called into being.

Augustine discussed both the works of God and the understanding of human investigators:

> For the Christian, it is enough to believe that the cause of all created things, whether in heaven or on earth, whether visible or invisible, is nothing other than the goodness of the Creator, who is the one and true God.[12]
>
> ... [I]t is a disgraceful and dangerous thing for an infidel to hear a Christian, presumably giving the meaning of Holy Scripture, talking nonsense on [astronomy, living things, stones, etc.]; and we should take all means to prevent such an embarrassing situation, in which people show up vast ignorance in a Christian and laugh it to scorn.[13]

These two passages may suggest that a tension between God-is-the-cause and the-cause-is-within-Creation existed in Augustine. When considering the cause of an event, is it always sufficient to hold that God is the cause? Or must the cause come from within Creation? Yet there is no doubt about Augustine's starting point: Creation is one integrated, comprehensive, and all-encompassing work of God.

After Augustine, there were significant changes in thinking about the nature of the world. The new ideas harked back to the pre-Christian era, in particular, to Greek philosophy. Theological conclusions could not, according to some scholars, reveal anything about the nature of the cosmos. Thus, for William of Conches (ca. 1080-ca. 1154) and others of his period, physical laws took precedence over those that the church taught. He complained that the church did not want people to look into the cause of things. Appealing to God's omnipotence or a biblical passage to explain phenomena amounted to a confession of ignorance. The Bible, including the creation account in Genesis, had to be interpreted according to the teachings of science. Scholars came to investigate nature for its own sake. But this attitude was to lead to serious trouble. According to Edward Grant, a prominent historian of science,

> *Thus were the seeds of a science-theology confrontation planted*, the bitter fruits of which would grow to maturity in the thirteenth century following upon the introduction of Aristotle's scientific works . . . .[14] (Emphasis added.)

The teachings of Thomas Aquinas (1224-1274) became part of this confrontation. Aquinas attempted a synthesis of Aristotelian natural philosophy and Christian theology. "Aquinas . . . regarded Aristotle as the greatest of philosophers, one who had achieved the highest level of human thought without the aid of revelation."[15] For Aquinas, Aristotle's principles found in nature were put there by God; God, in his providence, respected the integrity of those principles and *cooperated* with them. Even though Aristotle held to a universe that is eternal and does not need God, Aquinas evidently maintained that insights derived from the study of Aristotle and the Bible are complementary. This was the beginning of a two-domain, or *dualistic*, approach to knowledge—an approach that ultimately will fail.

An important event of the thirteenth century was when the Bishop of Paris proclaimed the Condemnation of 1277. It reflected a sharp division within the church. The thrust of the Condemnation was to repudiate Aristotelianism, which did not teach a need for God, and to preserve the absolute power of God. The Condemnation spoke to 219 errors, some of which were related to science. For example, the Condemnation maintained that God could create more than one world and that he could create a vacuum.[16] Nevertheless, even after the thirteenth century, Aristotle's ideas were respected for several centuries. The Condemnation did not reverse the trend toward the acceptance of Aquinas's claim that the thought of believers and the highest level

Background 9

of thought of unbelievers can exist side by side in agreement.

Modern Period up to Darwin. At the beginning of the modern or the scientific period, key scientific ideas developed in a culture in which belief in God was generally assumed. But the theistic beliefs associated with the new developments were not necessarily orthodox. For example, Nicolaus Copernicus's (1473-1543) heliocentrism (the idea that the planets move around the sun) seems to have been partly due to his acceptance of Neoplatonism, a strange third century A.D. mixture of Platonism, Christianity, and Oriental mysticism. Johannes Kepler (1571-1630), who developed the laws of planetary motion still used, depended strongly on Plato's ideas concerning the mathematical ordering of the universe. Kepler, a Christian, believed in the Trinity and also saw triads throughout Creation.[17]

Philosophers usually consider Sir Francis Bacon (1561-1626) to be the father of modern science. He, too, was a Christian. He spoke of two books. Bacon's statement concerning these two books is crucial in the development of the scientific enterprise:

> Let no man . . . think or maintain, that a man can search too far, or be too well studied in the book of God's word, or in the book of God's works . . . let men endeavor an endless progress or proficience in both; only let men beware . . . that they do not unwisely mingle or confound these learnings together.
>
> Our saviour saith, "You err, not knowing the scriptures, nor the power of God"; laying before us two books or volumes to study, if we will be secured from error; first the scriptures, revealing the will of God, and then the creatures expressing his power; *whereof the latter is a key unto the former: not only opening our understanding to conceive the true sense of the scriptures, by the general notions of reason and rules of speech; but chiefly opening our belief, in drawing us into a due meditation of the omnipotency of God, which is chiefly signed and engraven upon his works.*[18] (Emphasis added.)

Bacon's claim that the two books may not be mingled is surely not supported by his citation of Christ's reference to the Scriptures and the power of God (Matt. 22:29). It is difficult to see that Christ was saying anything about the two books.

Furthermore, the way Bacon described the two books was fundamentally flawed. His denunciation of mingling the two books supported the two-domain theory of knowledge. The Baconian approach was a political compromise. Even though Bacon eloquently praised the study of God's word, he maintained that the book of God's works is a key to understanding the book of his word—in spite of his claim that the two kinds of learning were not to be mingled. Earlier philosophers had claimed that both nature and the Bible contain signs to be discovered; these signs taken together constitute a single vast text. For these philosophers, the two kinds of signs were equivalent sources of truth; they were on the same plane. But Bacon would not consider putting the two kinds of signs on the same plane. He would not allow "things in nature [to] conform to words in the Scriptures."[19]

The two-domain theory of knowledge led to an emphasis on the importance of one of those domains, the "book of God's works," the book that was allowed to aid in interpretation of the other book. It began to seem that the book of God's word did not make a significant contribution to knowledge. Therefore, the spirit that prevailed among many thinkers at the beginning of the modern period is represented by Rene Descartes (1596-1650) who said that he would never accept anything as true that he did not clearly know to be true. He emphasized the importance of the human ability to reason:

> Those long chains of reasoning, simple and easy as they are, of which geometricians make use in order to arrive at the most difficult demonstrations . . . [convinced me that] *there can be nothing so remote that we cannot reach to it, nor so recondite that we cannot discover it.* (Emphasis added.)

Descartes said that a person could start out with those things that are simplest and therefore the most easily understood. But who could find such truth? According to Descartes, only mathematicians had produced reasons in the sciences which were "evident and certain."[20] This was another way of claiming that the two books could not intermingle: "truth" in studying the world could be obtained only by *human* effort. Investigators are to use mathematics, the ultimate achievement of the *human* ability to reason. Descartes did not suggest that God's word could provide "evident and certain" knowledge about the world. Descartes was not far from the position taken by Ahmes, the Egyptian scribe, in 1800 B.C.

Thomas Kuhn, an American science historian, summarized how Descartes and his successors thought about the universe:

> After about 1630 . . . and particularly after the appearance of

Background

Descartes' immensely influential scientific writings, most physical scientists assumed that the universe was composed of microscopic corpuscles and that all natural phenomena could be explained in terms of corpuscular shape, size, motion, and interaction.[21]

The universe contained nothing but matter in motion.

In other words, in natural scientific work Descartes believed the universe to be closed: one need not consider anything outside the universe. Aquinas's highest form of unbelieving thought and Bacon's book of God's works are enough. Of course, both Aquinas and Bacon accepted a Creator-creature distinction between God and the universe; God was not part of the universe. But natural scientific work could proceed as if the universe was closed. The closed-universe concept was included in the *definition* of natural science. As we shall see, eventually it was easy to slip into the belief that the scope of natural science defined reality. Therefore, the definition of natural science given in the sixteenth and seventeenth centuries eventually led to the denial of the reality of anything outside the universe.

With the growth of science, interest in the study of living things increased. The first systematic attempt to classify organisms was made by John Ray (1628-1705). Carolus Linnaeus (1707-1778) elaborated this system, and his system is still used. At first Linnaeus held that one species could not come from the seed of another and that the species were fixed, with no new species appearing after creation. But in his later work Linnaeus had trouble defining species and so decided that genera, not species (for example, the oak tree, not the white oak) were separately created.[22]

Biologists did have an explanation for the structure in the world of living organisms before evolutionary thinking took hold. They postulated a "Great Chain of Being." The Chain was static: each organism was put into a certain place by God and stayed there. This hierarchy was eternal.[23] The doctrine of the fixity of species and the Great Chain of Being rested on a foundation not easily discarded. Certain aspects of this doctrine could be traced back to Plato, whose unchangeable "ideas" ("ideas" are reality while the various parts of the world are reflections of that reality) were said to underlie fixed discontinuities in the world of living things.[24] In this discontinuous, typological view of nature, fixed boundaries limit biological variation.[25] For those who accepted the Great Chain of Being, catastrophes, such as the Noahic Flood, were important. Evidence for the Flood that they produced included sea shells on mountain tops, the sudden extinction of and freezing of mammoths, and massive heaps of bones in caves.[26]

Adherence to the Bible was not the reason the founders of modern biology and geology held that life is discontinuous. Even some Christians held that the universe is in effect closed. For example, Baron George Cuvier (1769-1832), a French zoologist, said that the Scriptures are instructions for moral behavior, not for natural history. In Richard Owen's (1804-1892) early and highly critical review of Darwin's *The Origin of Species* (1859), Owen did not defend special creation, the teaching that there were many separate—"special"—creations of living things.[27] For many nineteenth-century scientists, natural law was enough: after the beginning, God did not miraculously interfere with the history of the earth.[28]

Even though the Great Chain of Being was widely accepted, evolution was "in the air" before the work of Charles Darwin. One manifestation of this tendency was the frequent blurring of the distinction between human beings and other living things. For example, unusual creatures were rumored to have been found in the Americas during the eighteenth century. A book published in Constantinople contained a picture of the American wakwak tree, a tree that bore women rather than fruit.[29] In the mid-nineteenth century the poets Tennyson and Whitman had ideas that fit well with evolutionary thought. For example, Tennyson anticipated the postulated mechanism of evolution when he said that many species are now gone because nature is red in tooth and claw. Because of human progress, Whitman claimed he could "launch to . . . superior universes."[30] Edgar Allan Poe, who died ten years before the publication of Darwin's *Origin*, wrote of an animal who acted like a man in "Murders in the Rue Morgue."[31]

Not only was evolution in the air, but scientists also speculated concerning biological change. Pierre Maupertuis (1698-1759) observed inherited modifications among human beings. He generalized from this observation and may have been the first to propose general evolution, including descent with possible modification. Erasmus Darwin (1731-1802), grandfather of Charles Darwin, used the term "evolution." (Interestingly, Charles Darwin did not use that term in *Origin*.) Erasmus Darwin defined evolution as change in a species; it could continue for an indefinite number of generations. Chevalier de Lamarck (1744-1829) speculated that change in the environment brought about change in successive generations. He postulated evolution from inert matter to man. George de Buffon (1707-1788), however, suggested separate creations by God, with only limited evolution. He also considered the driving force for limited evolution to be environmental change, such as change in nutrition or climate.[32] De Buffon's emphasis was similar to that of other scientists of the time who wanted to correlate scientific results with the Bible.

Thomas Malthus (1776-1834) presented an idea critical to the eventual

Background

development of evolutionary theory. In his *Essay on Population*, Malthus said that while the food supply of the world increases arithmetically with time, the population increases geometrically. Therefore, as time passes, the struggle for food intensifies. Before Darwin applied this concept to his theory of biological change, Herbert Spencer (1820-1903) said the Malthusian pressure on human society puts a premium on skill, intelligence, self-control, and the power to adapt. To describe the resulting struggle Spencer coined the phrase *survival of the fittest*.[33] Chapters 12 to 14 discuss the immense social effect of Spencer's ideas.

Charles Darwin. Therefore, at the time the Darwinian revolution began, people saw a structure in the natural world. They held to a hierarchy of being, a Great Chain of Being. Many Christians saw that the parts of the natural world fit together, that this fitting together is just what one would expect. After all, God made it. In fact, this structure constituted evidence that God designed Creation. Christians knew that their God was unerring, and so the design they perceived in the nineteenth century could not be better than or even different from the original design of Creation. *Natural theology*—seeing God in Creation—became important in the discussions of evolution in the nineteenth century.

For Darwin, however, design was illusory. Darwin said something else had happened. Occasionally organisms have progeny (offspring) that are different from their parents. Sometimes the progeny that are different will fit better in the environment. The better fitted progeny will, just because they are better fitted, produce more progeny than those who are less fitted. Eventually, after many generations, the less fitted ones will vanish and a new species will replace the original one. As this process, dubbed "natural selection," continues, the fit between organism and environment will improve. An observer should therefore expect to find a good fit between the organism and the environment.

Darwin's understanding of why some progeny are different is not the one held today, since he did not know about genetic mutation. Descent with modification, where the organisms with more progeny are better suited to the environment, accounted for what some people called design. Darwin said that what was observed was not true design, which would imply a designer, but only apparent design. Natural laws could account for everything including human life itself. God was not needed. Miracles certainly were not needed.

Some of Darwin's ideas, especially his reasons for the variability in progeny, are no longer accepted in any part of the scientific community. The evolutionary theory widely accepted today can be summarized by these statements:

(1) [L]iving organisms tend to produce more offspring than can survive; (2) there is always heritable variability within populations with regard to any given characteristic; (3) there is a competition for resources that results in a survival of the fittest; and (4) the resulting adaptation is gradual and occurs over a long period of time.[34]

Michael Denton, a critic of evolutionary theory, suggested four reasons, most of which relate to the historical context, for the acceptance of Darwin's theories in the nineteenth century.[35]

First, the conservative political and social hierarchy of Victorian England was fertile ground for Darwin's ideas: he claimed that "natural forces" were responsible for the hierarchy in the plant and animal world. These forces, just because they were natural, were also inevitable. Because of this inevitability, the existing world of living organisms is the best of all possible worlds. Those who occupied preferred positions in the political and social hierarchy could easily see the rightness of the social evolutionary process which brought that hierarchy into existence.

Second, the Victorian belief in the inevitability of progress matched the Darwinian hypothesis that the natural world continually improved with time, implying that according to a universal law things would get better.

Third, Victorians also affirmed a competitive spirit. Again, those who had preferred positions in the existing structure could comfortably claim that they or their families gained their positions through competitive struggle. The strongest had won. The most outstanding example of such a competitive process was nineteenth-century capitalism.

The fourth reason is not only the most important, but also the basic reason for the acceptance of Darwin. Without this reason, the others suggested would not have been enough. Darwin's theory brought the study of life into the sphere of science. No longer need one postulate miracles. This fourth reason is the key to the entire creation-evolution controversy of both the nineteenth and twentieth centuries.

Since Darwin. Extensive controversy concerning evolution has characterized the period since the publication of *Origin* in 1859. But those who uncritically adopted Darwin's ideas exhibited scientific pride. For most of the time since Darwin, and certainly today, that uncritical group of scientists has been by far the majority of the scientific community.

The expressions of this scientific pride usually demoted religion. The spirit of many modern scientists, almost all evolutionists, was typified in 1874 by John Tyndall (1820-1893), a physicist, when he said that scientists would

Background

". . . wrest from theology, the entire domain of cosmological theory." All schemes must submit to science.[36] In the twentieth century, Julian Huxley (1887-1975) held that *everything* can be reduced to matter or to a genetic formula.[37] His evolutionary vision dismissed the need for anything "spiritual."[38] In spite of the many important questions concerning evolutionary theory, Vincent Sarich, a frequently quoted biologist of our own day, said that today there is nothing to consider: for him, evolutionary theory is established and the "battle" ended a century ago.[39]

Thomas Huxley (1825-1895) and others, all ardent evolutionists, even wanted science to imitate the established church. In the 1870s Huxley proposed lay sermons and a new Reformation, the "church scientific," with himself as bishop of that church. At some scientific lectures the congregation sang a hymn to Creation. The Sunday School was imitated by Sunday Lecture Societies and the Natural History Museum in London was called "Nature's Cathedral."[40]

Modern Christian scholars have studied the nineteenth-century Christian reaction to Darwin. Some assert that the scholarly, courteous debates of the nineteenth century between Darwin and evangelicals, many of whom accepted most of Darwin's claims, constitute a model for modern discussion.[41] It has also been stated that many nineteenth- and early twentieth-century Christians separated theistic evolution from evolutionism: they did not make all other aspects of life subservient to evolution.[42] In adopting a "Christian" kind of evolution, they combatted Darwin by claiming that everything occurred according to God's design. They spoke frequently of providence. By continuing to describe the design of which so many were enamored before Darwin, they thought they were successfully refuting any atheistic component present in Darwinism. They were wrong. I shall return to their reliance on providence at the end of this chapter.

In analyzing nineteenth-century American religious developments, James Ward Smith maintained that the evangelical accommodation, the desire to establish common ground between Christian theology and evolutionary science, was not true accommodation. He asked what this attempted accommodation achieved:

> What, after all, was accomplished by the peacemakers? So long as one was not too literalistic in his reading of the Bible, so long as one concentrated on the general metaphysical concepts of the Christian tradition, he was bound sooner or later to discover that these are general enough to adjust to anything contained in evolutionary science.

Smith explained what he means by "adjust to anything":

> Sporadic variation could be discussed in the terminology of Divine intervention and miracle; the origin of species could be discussed in the terminology of God's purposes; the concept of creation could itself be adjusted to the facts of continuous development through time . . . . *Literalism might be embarrassed by the new discoveries, but the subtle metaphysical temperament need have no fear.* (Emphasis added.)
>
> The only thing to be feared was that somebody would wake up to the fact that this kind of metaphysical or purely terminological accommodation *was* superficial.[43]

In other words, Smith believed that it was not possible to establish common ground between Christian theology and evolutionary science.

There are many strands in the nineteenth- and twentieth-century debates concerning evolution. Tracing the argument is complicated, and it is not made easier by those who are difficult to classify. William Jennings Bryan (1860-1925) has been pictured as a buffoon because of his opposition to the evolutionary concept in the 1925 Scopes trial in Tennessee. But that picture is only a caricature; the actual situation was much more complicated. His opposition to evolutionary theory arose mostly because of its doctrine of the survival of the fittest which was, from Bryan's standpoint, the cause of senseless militarism. For Bryan this militarism was epitomized by the immense carnage of World War I, which had ended only a few years before the trial. Bryan believed that evolution subverted Christian morality.[44] Bryan and others perceived that evolutionary thinking impacted society, and they did not like what they saw. Another example is Benjamin Warfield (1851-1921), an important conservative theologian, who said that evolution could have been the method whereby God created. At the same time, Warfield refused to rule out miracle in the creation process.[45]

The intense feelings of common people in the modern period mirrored those of the nineteenth and early twentieth centuries.[46] Thus, the American South saw strong anti-evolutionary sentiment after the Civil War. Southern Christians thought that secularization was overtaking them; but here was one place that they, who had lost the War, could at last take a "no compromise" stand.[47] Seventh Day Adventists, Dispensationalists, and Jehovah's Witnesses also opposed the evolutionary idea. In the first decades of the twentieth century George McReady Price (1870-1963), a Seventh

Day Adventist, became a leader in a movement similar to the creation-science movement (usually characterized by holding to six 24-hour creation days and a large number of separate creations) of our own day. Missouri Synod Lutherans also actively opposed evolutionary thinking in the early years.[48]

In any case, Darwin provided new glasses, a new paradigm. Those who looked at the data after Darwin saw the same data as those who preceded him. But after Darwin they saw things in a different light.[49] However, not all accepted the new paradigm, so two groups of people who saw the same evidence could differ sharply. Not surprisingly, this division could exist within one person; first the facts suggested one model, then another.

One incident in the history of paleoanthropology exhibits the problem of the paradigm. Included in the paleoanthropological paradigm is the assumption that human beings descended from animals. But only a limited number of very old fossils have been available to support this assumption. Therefore, it was easy to accept the claim that the so-called Piltdown fossil was in the line from animals to human beings. But 40 years after the discovery of this fossil, it was shown to be a hoax.[50] Thus, because the paradigm was accepted and because of one false piece of evidence, a large number of scientists were off track for almost half a century.

The reason some progeny vary is an important component of evolutionary theory. The cause of variability that is accepted today is quite different from Darwin's reason. Darwin proposed gradual change, postulating that change is Lamarckian, that is, species change as the environment changes. But late in the nineteenth century the work of Mendel became well-known, leading to the founding of genetics. The environment could not alter inherited characteristics. With the advent of genetics, the criticism of Darwinism, which depended so much on the relationship between an organism and its environment, greatly increased.

Not until the 1930s, when the *synthetic theory* was proposed, did a strong reversal occur. The synthetic theory, presented in T. Dobzhansky's *Genetics and the Origin of Species* in 1937, held that gradual change occurs because of occasional gene mutation. The characteristics which an organism's progeny will inherit do not depend on environment; instead, those characteristics will be different from those of its parents if an abrupt (albeit small) change in one or more genes—a mutation—occurs. While the environment is not the cause for the change, the new organism will produce more progeny than the unchanged progeny if it is better suited to that environment.[51]

The introduction of the synthetic theory is not the end of the story of the development of evolutionary theory. A recent potentially radical idea replaces Darwinian evolution by natural selection with evolution by purely random changes.[52]

Another recent suggestion is important for this historical survey. This suggestion is based on a growing realization in the scientific community that the synthetic theory does not account for the gaps in the fossil record, such as the lack of fossils to account for the hypothesized jump from invertebrates to vertebrates. For this reason, in 1972 Niles Eldredge and Stephen Jay Gould developed the theory of *punctuated equilibrium*. In their theory, they account for the observed stability in a population over very long periods of time (a stability seen in the fossil record) by postulating an occasional very rapid jump across a gap, leaving so few fossils in the gap that none is found. For Eldredge and Gould, *microevolution*, a series of small changes explained by the synthetic theory, can account for the changes actually exhibited by the fossil record. But *macroevolution*, the jump across the gap, requires a new mechanism. Nevertheless, many evolutionists still maintain that the synthetic theory is sufficient.[53]

At present, evolutionists are confident that they will eventually solve the major problems, and they look forward to much greater achievements. If it is indeed true that life has evolved and can be explained by chemical and physical laws and that those laws are in turn explainable by mathematics, then perhaps natural scientists can use natural laws to synthesize life. The creation of artificial life has indeed been an articulated goal.

Recapitulation

Working Back from the Present. It is instructive to examine the present state of affairs and then determine how we got to where we are.

Scientific pride characterizes the present time. This pride is based on demonstrated scientific results *and on the scientific method used to obtain those results*. According to prevailing opinion, by using that scientific method it is possible to obtain answers concerning the entire world and even that which seems to be "spiritual"—the existence of which is denied by those who are most confident.

This attitude is not new. It also motivated many scientists of the nineteenth century. Darwin depended on natural laws to explain all phenomena. The world of living things in principle contained no mysteries. For him, design was a red herring, a "non-fact"; design is only apparent.

Why did Charles Darwin think as he did? He knew of the Great Chain of Being; he knew that at least some people thought they saw motion within that chain. Others had already suggested that organisms could acquire

Background

heritable characteristics, so changes in the environment could conceivably cause species to change.

Notice that his teaching concerning natural selection could probably have been made even if he had not personally observed small differences within certain groups of animals. His theory could have been the result of a "thought experiment." All that is needed are a few general ideas concerning the possibility of small changes in some descendants, the large number of progeny, and the relatively small amount of food. Then the conclusion that, given enough time, this species will change is not difficult to accept.

But could one then be convinced that all life had a common ancestor? That would take some imagination, a willingness to extrapolate from the small changes already accepted in the thought experiment—a willingness to accept macroevolution. Darwin did have such an imagination and did make such an extrapolation. One wonders if the actual observations he made played a large role in this extrapolation. I suggest that scientific endeavor had already been assumed capable of all explanation, and that such endeavor was always to be based exclusively on natural law, a body of laws formulated by human beings.

The nature of scientific activity had been established ever since the work of Bacon and Descartes in the sixteenth and seventeenth centuries. True, the world was considered to be the work of God. But what could be learned by investigating that world and using human reason seemed to have no limit. The world was one thing; the Bible, another. Surely Bacon and Descartes's separation between the two ultimately led to the rigid exclusion of design by so many who accepted the ideas of Darwin.

But let us go back further than Bacon and Descartes. The idea that whatever goes on in the world must somehow be considered apart from God derives from Thomas Aquinas and his use of Aristotle's ideas. According to Aquinas, one could correctly contemplate ultimate matters, as Aristotle did, without invoking the true God. As a result, the idea of separating "natural" and "spiritual" things, dualism, has characterized the scientific period since its inception in the sixteenth and seventeenth centuries.

The separation between God and the world, or the separation between "spiritual" and "natural" things, found in Aristotle and Plato, seems to have had greater effect on Aquinas than the teachings of Augustine, who held to a unified world. The dualism of Aristotle and Plato was also found in their predecessors. That at least one god existed was usually admitted, but such a god was certainly not sovereign. Also, such dualism was implied in the attempts of Pythagoras and the Ionian philosophers to find all cause within the world.

If causes were to be found within the world, then going back in time one would expect things to be derived from other things. Many did indeed attempt to reduce higher orders to lower. Some ancient Greeks postulated an eternal flux of matter from which all objects eventually appeared. Pythagoras and Ahmes the Egyptian reduced everything to number.

Thus, the scientific climate of the nineteenth and twentieth centuries derives from the ancient desire to separate any god or gods from the world and to explain all phenomena by means of causes within the world.

But the world did not begin with the Egyptian and Greek civilizations. What, then, is the source of the idea that things and phenomena can be explained by other things and phenomena that are within the world? What is the source of the desire to keep causes within the world? To put it simply: when and where did human beings begin excluding God from the world?

This question takes us back to Adam and Eve in the Garden of Eden. The essence of their first sin was their claim that they could live apart from God. They certainly did not deny his existence. But when they ate the fruit that God had told them not to eat, they were in effect saying that they and their world did not need him.

It is no surprise, then, that many descendants of Adam and Eve thought that even though a god might exist, the world could get along without him. The tragedy is that the Christian contribution to the discussion of the nature of Creation was eventually characterized by compromise: Christians said that an altered form of Aristotle's teaching would not be so bad. Science was defined so that not only were all scientific studies restricted to "natural" causes, but it was also permissible to use the idea that there are no other causes. Finally, it would be sufficient for Christians to use the evolutionary model for life, based on the idea that all causes are within the world. All that Christians needed to add to the picture is the idea that God had designed it. Even though Darwin vigorously opposed the introduction of design, the Christian introduction of this outside cause actually affected the model very little.

Providence. I previously mentioned that nineteenth-century Christians who wanted to make peace with Darwin emphasized God's providence. Darwin could be accepted if only he would admit that God had designed Creation. Darwin himself would have none of that.

But could nineteenth-century Christians have done better? Could they have done anything to rescue society from the blight of dualism and its natural offspring, all the modern problems that spring from an almost universal acceptance of evolution from nonlife to life to human beings? I cannot avoid wondering what would have happened in the nineteenth century if Christians would have insisted that Christ, the God-man, was active in creation and would have maintained, along with the Apostle Paul, that everything comes together in Christ:

> For by [Christ] all things were created: things in heaven and on earth, visible and invisible, whether thrones or powers or rulers or authorities; all things were created for him and by him. He is before all things, and in him all things hold together. (Col. 1: 16-17)

The Spirit did not teach Paul that the world is divided so that one cannot use God's word to investigate God's works. Nor did the Spirit teach Deism, the belief that God created at one time and then could be seen only from afar.

Nineteenth-century Christians could have done better than insist on either a God-designed static universe created long ago or a God-designed evolutionary universe. They should have staked out their position on the basis that Christ, their Savior and the Redeemer of Creation, was active when the world was created and holds all things together now. Then they could have insisted that it was never right to divorce scientific work from Christ's upholding of all Creation. *It has never been correct to maintain that scientific activity must exclude consideration of acts of the Triune God.* All human activity, including scientific activity, must be related to the work of the Father, the Son, and the Holy Spirit in history to save the world. But nineteenth-century Christians were willing to opt for a general kind of "providence," perhaps thinking they could bring everyone but outright atheists into their camp. As a result, the history of the impact of evolutionary theory is dreary.

In subsequent chapters we shall see that while many good things can be said about the modern growth of the scientific enterprise, people who debate about its foundation and direction often use wrong assumptions. The scientific community does not take the Lordship of Christ as the starting point. Consequently, the influence of the scientific enterprise on modern society is flawed in the worst possible way.

Chapter Three
Design

To complement the historical sketch of the previous chapter, this chapter and Chapter 4 examine more closely the spirit of thought, the worldview, of the Western world prior to and at the time of Darwin's work. The present chapter describes the background of Darwin's work, including the general attitude toward "reason" and the new science of geology, both of which contributed to the understanding of "design." Chapter 4 considers three objections to the concept of design in the natural world.

During the last two centuries natural scientists have given a great amount of attention to some important problems. But in their discussion of evolution, creation, design, the nature of things, and even miracles, they have generally not faced the central questions. How does God reveal himself in Creation? What does he reveal in the Bible? How do these two kinds of revelation relate? How does God reveal himself through his Son? In what way should our natural scientific work recognize that in Christ everything in Creation holds together (Col. 1:17)?

Therefore, the argument concerning design in the nineteenth century and the almost universally accepted conclusion of the present century is frustrating. It misses the point. But we do need to see why the modern form of dualism, evolutionism, bears such bitter fruit. We do need to see why evolutionary thought continues to have such a great impact.

Reason and Rationalism
From Plato to Agnosticism. Plato held to the existence of unchangeable "ideas." The natural world is the image of those ideas. Human beings are part of that natural world and because of the relation between ideas and the natural world human beings are, according to this position, rational. Reasoning human beings can therefore understand the world.[1] Reason is then the final authority for truth. Deductive reasoning becomes particularly important; inductive reasoning, which is based upon observation, is then secondary. Later, to the extent that the medieval church adhered to Greek philosophy, it emphasized reasoning. This dependence upon reasoning as a final authority is *rationalism*. Further, since the church had extensive influence in the West, the emphasis on deductive reasoning hindered research

Design

in the natural sciences, which requires observation and inductive reasoning.
But in the late sixteenth and the seventeenth centuries both reason and observation were respected. The natural sciences were born. For almost all natural scientists reason never lost its place of preeminence, and therefore many of them were rationalists. Thus, in Britain and America the eighteenth century was the Age of Reason or the Age of Enlightenment. Many supposed that human beings were becoming better equipped to understand the nature of the universe and to reason correctly. Human beings were now mature, they said, whereas once they had been primitive.

Eighteenth century Americans emphasized the practical results of correct reasoning. Leading American scientists were Botanist Cadwallader Colden (1688-1776), Chemist and Medical Doctor Benjamin Rush (1745-1813), and, above all, the quintessential Enlightenment man, Benjamin Franklin (1706-1790). Franklin's scientific efforts rested on the successful use of reason to obtain useful, practical results. For example, his reasoning about the nature of electricity enabled him to invent the lightning rod. The American faith in practical results was made possible because of the human ability to reason; but, as James Ward Smith pointed out, this faith actually rested on an unexamined speculative base.[2] It was a naive faith that did not ask *why* "reason," interacting with Creation, should produce something useful and presumably "good."

This period did, however, see some opposition to the Enlightenment. Romantic literature in particular expressed that sentiment. Peter Bowler stated that while there was some Romantic reaction in English-speaking countries (Samuel Coleridge Taylor in Britain is an example), the true home of Romanticism was Germany, where Goethe and his followers turned away from the materialism of the Enlightenment.[3]

The growing interest in natural science in the nineteenth century contributed to a continued emphasis on the finality of human reason. Thomas Huxley, an agnostic who greatly advanced Darwinism, presented his principle of agnosticism in terms of reason:

> Agnosticism, in fact, is not a creed, but a method, the essence of which lies in the rigorous application of a single principle.

What was that principle? It had two parts, a positive and a negative:

> Positively, the principle may be expressed: In matters of the intellect, follow your reason as far as it will take you, without regard to any other consideration.

And negatively: In matters of the intellect, do not pretend that conclusions are certain which are not demonstrated and demonstrable.

This ultimate dependence on human reason added up to a faith, actually a religious faith:

> That I take to be the agnostic faith, which if a man keep whole and undefiled, he shall not be ashamed to look the universe in the face, whatever the future may have in store for him.[4]

Christian Answers. If Christians were to learn about the nature of reason only from those who uncritically accept the principles of the Enlightenment, reason would surely have a bad name with them. Yet it is incumbent upon human beings, who bear the image of God, to honor God by investigating Creation. Such investigation calls for a highly trained reasoning ability. Human beings are certainly tempted to deify such a highly cultivated ability. The ability to reason often makes it seem as if dependence on God is unnecessary.

The Christian philosopher Alvin Plantinga of the University of Notre Dame stated that because human beings bear God's image they also possess reasoning ability. However, this ability is tainted because of our first parents' fall into sin. But sin has not completely destroyed that ability. Plantinga described levels of reliability, ranging from the most reliable, such as those that pertain to everyday conclusions, to the least reliable, such as those in the branches of natural science where conclusions are contrary to ordinary intuition, as in certain areas of physics.[5]

Attempts to use human reason to construct a consistent world picture have often been associated with positions taken on the origins questions. An example is Smith's claim that in the centuries prior to the twentieth century American Christians' attempts to make peace with Darwinism accomplished nothing. Smith described an American desire for a "cosmic sense," a sense that said one's position—no matter what position one took—had to account for everything: it had to be reasonable. But this cosmic sense was achieved, he said, always by superficial examination of the claims of natural science, including the claims of Darwinism. Such superficial use of science had not worked earlier and did not work when the claims of Darwinism were examined late in the nineteenth century. Therefore, by World War I American Christians no longer possessed that cosmic sense.[6]

To show how the rationalistic spirit was present at the very beginning

Design 25

of the formulation of evolutionary theory, I now turn to events in the world of natural science during the first part of the nineteenth century.

Reason and the New Science of Geology

What led to the loss of cosmic sense by the beginning of World War I? We must first see how the new science of geology was accepted in the first part of the nineteenth century.

Beginning of Geology. The systematization of the study of the crust of the earth and eventually the entire earth actually began late in the eighteenth century. Certain interesting phenomena, such as patterns in the crust of the earth and the apparent isolation of large rocks from other rocks, pointed to a new understanding of what had happened to the earth. The data suggested that slow changes were occurring on the surface of the earth and that, in fact, changes had been occurring for a very long time. The earth had a history.

To understand what is meant by "history," consider your reaction when you examine two houses that you have not seen before. The first house sparkles. You can smell paint. The house contains no furniture. You cannot find scratches on the walls, floors, counter tops—anywhere. Outside the house, a cement walk connects the front door to the road. But there is no lawn, tree, or bush. Surely you would be correct to conclude that the house is new; it has virtually no history. Examination of the second house quickly reveals scratches. A few of the ceilings have water marks. The basement has a musty odor. On the outside of the house, red streaks that look like rust are near the down spouts of the gutters. There are trees, bushes, and a lawn. But the lawn has uneven quality. Some of the branches of the trees look dead; the bushes crowd each other. No doubt you would say that this house has a history. In fact, you might deduce details of this history after carefully examining the rooms, the roof, the trees, and so forth. Thus, if the roof looks newer than the rest of the house, you would assume that the house had had at least one previous roof. By estimating the ages of the different trees, you might deduce that they were not all planted the same year.

In making these deductions, you would probably assume that the processes you already know about—how fast a pine tree grows, how water in a steel gutter tends to cause the formation of rust, and so forth—operated in aging this house. In the same way, the first geologists assumed that they could account for the differences in the various parts of the earth's surface by the kind of changes presently occurring, provided one could extrapolate back over a long time. James Hutton (1726-1797), often referred to as the father of geology, used this approach. Others had different ideas. For example, Georges Cuvier (1768-1832) and William Buckland (1784-1856) assumed that catastrophes played a major role in the history of the crust of the earth. But by 1830 many geologists were using Hutton's approach, which came to be called uniformitarianism. This was the assumption "that the past history of the Earth could be adequately explained in terms of causes that can presently be observed. . . ."[7] With long periods of time available there was no need to invoke one-time catastrophes.

The uniformitarian approach to geology has been generally successful; it represents one more triumph of human reason. Of course, ever since James Hutton some people have instead invoked the Noahic Flood to explain some geological phenomena. But geologists generally hold to the sufficiency of the uniformitarian method, especially if it includes one-time events that can be explained using natural laws, such as the near-collision of planets.

Other Sciences. Whatever the merit of the uniformitarian approach for geology, its implication for understanding biology is obvious. If no geological phenomenon requires an "unnatural" explanation, why should one need to invoke events such as miracles to explain biology? It is evident that many scientific problems can be solved by giving no attention to the fact that God created or that a miracle took place. When Charles Darwin did his work in the middle of the nineteenth century, he had before him the example of the new science of geology. Geology provided him with two things he needed. First, here was one more natural science, along with astronomy, chemistry, physics, and the others, that one could explain through human reasoning without invoking catastrophes. At least as important was the second contribution of geology: phenomena could be accounted for by slow changes over long periods of time.

Developments in other sciences, such as astronomy, helped to lay philosophical groundwork for Darwin. Pierre Laplace's (1749-1827) hypothesis concerning the formation of the solar system, a hypothesis that used only natural law, may have helped prepare the way for the naturalistic explanations Darwin gave for the observed phenomena in the world of living things.[8]

Consider this situation with reference to the dualistic trend described in the historical sketch of Chapter 2. Geology, astronomy, and biology qualified as sciences, *natural* sciences, because they conformed to the definition of science that had been assumed for centuries. According to this definition, scientific investigation can in principle explain phenomena by natural, explainable laws; in addition, many people add that *no other "real" phenomena exist.* But it is fallacious to assume that because some phenomena can be explained by natural law, all phenomena can be explained by natural

Design 27

law. As we proceed, we shall see that this fallacy is part of the reason for the present problem in the discussion of origins and, ultimately, for the impact of evolution on modern thought.

This fallacy is not the kind of error that, once it is called to the attention of those who make the error, is quickly corrected. This error is not an inconsequential mistake. Those guilty of this error need it lest their concept of science collapses. Putting human reason on a pedestal gives rise to this fallacy. If one cannot use the accepted scientific method to investigate *all* the phenomena of the natural sciences, then human reason loses its place of preeminence.

Design and Natural Theology
Christians have also been guilty of putting human reason on a pedestal. Because of that mistake, Christians can err concerning design in Creation. We shall see that there is design in Creation, that misunderstanding this design can lead to wrong theology, and that discussion of design has played a prominent role in the debate with Darwin and his followers.

Christians Assess Design. For a long time Christians have pointed out the wonderful coherence of the various parts of Creation. God himself indicates that Creation is not chaotic, but ordered, just *because* he made it:

> For thus says the Lord, who created the heavens . . . who formed the earth and made it . . . *he did not create it a chaos* . . . "I am the Lord, and there is no other. I did not speak in secret, in a land of darkness; I did not say to the offspring of Jacob, '*Seek me in chaos.*'" (Is. 45:18-19, RSV) (Emphasis added.)

Before Darwin, it was common for natural scientists to assume order in Creation because God was the Creator. Thus, the great naturalist Carolus Linnaeus said in the eighteenth century:

> By the [economy] of Nature we understand the all-wise disposition of the Creator in relation to natural things, by which they are fitted to produce general ends . . . All things contained in the compass of the universe declare . . . with one accord the infinite wisdom of the Creator. For whatever strikes our senses . . . are so contrived, that they concur to make manifest the divine glory, i.e., the ultimate end which God proposed in all his works.[9]

The *Zoological Journal of London*, founded in 1824, referred to the order in Creation in its first issue.[10] In 1857, Louis Agassiz (1807-1873), a Harvard naturalist, summed up his discussion of the fundamental relations of animals:

> The combination in time and space of all these thoughtful conceptions [i.e., relations] exhibits not only thought, it shows also premeditation, power, wisdom, greatness, prescience, omniscience, providence. In one word, all these facts in their natural connection proclaim aloud the One God, whom man may know, adore, and love; and Natural History must in good time become the analysis of the thoughts of the Creator of the Universe, as manifested in the animal and vegetable kingdoms, as well as in the inorganic world.[11]

Christians often claim that the existence of a food chain is evidence of design: breaks in the chain would mean that some organisms would have no food and therefore would not exist. If the earth were a slightly different distance from the sun, the earth temperature would be different and life as we know it could not exist. If the energy levels in the nuclei of the carbon and oxygen atoms were not just what they are, the carbon atom, as well as many others, would not exist, and once again life could not exist. One could make a very long list of such "ifs" and conclude that Creation exhibits an extremely complicated design. As we have already seen, some Christians have extended this claim to maintain that the existence of design implies the existence of a Designer. They have used design to try to prove the existence of God.

Natural Theology. Accepting the marvelous design of the world as proof that a Designer, a Creator, exists is *natural theology*. Some advocates of natural theology claim that examination of Creation reveals not only that God created, but also more about his nature.

In addition, some Christians of Darwin's day held that natural theology teaches not only about God, but also about Creation. This is the argument: God is perfect and therefore fashioned a perfect Creation; the Creation we observe must be—except for the effects of sin—the same as it was in the beginning. Any change from a perfect Creation would have been a change toward imperfection. This reasoning has obvious implications for any kind of evolution.

The most prominent theologian to argue that the existence of design in Creation proves the existence of a designer was William Paley (1743-1805).[12] But he was not the first; the idea of deducing a purpose behind observed phenomena goes back to Aristotle.[13] Paley claimed, for example, that the

Design

existence of wings of birds and fins of fish proved those organs were designed:

> Can it be doubted, whether the *wings of birds* bear a relation to air, and the *fins of fish* to water? They are instruments of motion, severally suited to the properties of the medium in which the motion is to be performed: which properties are different. Was not this difference contemplated, when the instruments were differently constituted?[14]

In the 1830s the *Bridgewater Treatises* appeared. They made Paley's case for design and thus taught natural theology. David Livingstone described the two principal activities of natural theologians in the early nineteenth century:

> By focusing on the perfect adaptation of organisms to environments, they first of all cemented the organic and inorganic worlds together in a single explanatory system. Because God had created each species in and for its own geographical province, there was a direct correspondence between the characteristics of the animals and their surrounding environments.

In their second activity, they utilized this explanatory system:

> Second, they devoted themselves to enumerating examples of these wonderful adaptations to nature. Often imaginatively and always extensively, they spelled out in the minutest detail how particular organs perfectly suited particular regions. They perceived the history of life and the history of the earth to be welded together . . .[15]

Darwin had an initial interest in design and natural theology, although he eventually rejected Paley's argument.[16] Natural theology rested on *common sense philosophy*: belief that facts are objective, that absolute truth can be known, and that inductive reasoning is valid. Instead, Darwin taught speculation, relativism, evolution, and rationalism.[17] Eventually, some of those who opposed Darwin did so because, in their view, Darwinism opposed creation with a purpose; they thought that he did accept a "creation," provided the Creator had no purpose.

Charles Hodge (1797-1878), a prominent American Presbyterian theologian, strongly opposed Darwinism.[18] He felt extremely uneasy about a theory that did not hold to unchanging species.[19] However, Hodge and Benjamin Warfield (1851-1921), another leading American Presbyterian, both argued that *assuming* the God of the Scriptures, we should expect to find design. They refused to argue *from* design to God and thus disagreed with natural theologians in that respect.[20]

Boundaries or Discontinuities in Creation. Agreeing with Paley and other natural theologians, many Christians see the hand of God in Creation in very specific ways. However, some Christians who do not accept natural theology do claim that God put boundaries in Creation, boundaries we can see. The existence of such boundaries constitutes one reason they reject Darwinism. Herman Bavinck (1854-1921), a Dutch theologian, referred to God as the boundary-maker. Herman Dooyeweerd (1894-1977), a Dutch philosopher, maintained that the boundaries between four realms—physical, plant, animal, and human—are uncrossable. Those who hold these ideas usually hold them for two reasons. First, in our observations of Creation we see boundaries. Second, the Bible states that some boundaries exist. God says in Genesis 1 that he separated light from darkness, the waters above from the waters below, the land from the water, and so forth. In addition, passages like the following depict God as the one who sets boundaries:

> Who shut up the sea behind doors when it burst forth from the womb, when I made the clouds its garment and wrapped it in thick darkness, when I fixed limits for it and set its doors and bars in place, when I said, "This far you may come and no farther; here is where your proud waves halt"? (Job 38:8-10)

> You set a boundary [the waters] cannot cross; never again will they cover the earth. (Psalm 104:9)

> He gave the sea its boundary so the waters would not overstep his command, and . . . he marked out the foundations of the earth. (Prov. 8:29)

With the idea of discontinuity suggested by the Bible itself, it has been no problem for Christians to discover discontinuities in the realm of living things. The principal discontinuities related to biology are between nonliving and living matter; between various groups of fossils, as indicated by gaps in the fossil record; and between animal and human life. Discontinuties are also suggested by specific parts of organisms (such as the feather, the avian lung, and the wing of the bat) that cannot be found in any hypothesized evolutionary precursor.[21]

Design

In the present-day discussion relating discontinuity to design, Philosopher Gary Colwell asked the following question: Suppose one encounters in a museum a series of bicycles arranged according to age. Would one then deduce from the obvious progressive change, ranging from the oldest models to the newest, that each bicycle had evolved from the previous one in the sequence? Would not discontinuity be an acceptable, perhaps even a preferred, interpretation of the data?[22] Michael Denton used a geometric analogy: by changing the lengths of sides and changing angles, one can change any triangle into any other triangle; also, any rectangle can be changed into any other rectangle by changing the lengths of sides. But one cannot transform a triangle into a rectangle by changing angles and the lengths of sides. An impenetrable barrier exists between triangles and rectangles, even though variability within each class is possible.[23] Denton, who does not claim to present a Christian position, asserted that pre-Darwin typology, which assumed an hierarchical Great Chain of Being, constitutes an interpretation of biological phenomena superior to Darwin's.[24]

Darwin's Objections. After Darwin rejected the argument of the natural theologians, he fought it with all his strength. His most vigorous debates were with people who wanted to accept evolution while clinging to design and a God who guided events providentially. Many analysts have erred concerning Darwin's position on this matter. He considered his opposition to design the essence of his entire evolutionary thesis. Thus, when he encountered an amazing, complex structure such as the eye, which apparently could never have been a one-tenth evolved eye, later a one-half evolved eye, and so forth, he was frustrated.[25]

Darwin's critics thought it was all very obvious. Were not the evidences of design everywhere? How could anyone not see both design and a Designer? In essence Darwin gave two answers.

Poor Design. First, Darwin and others claimed to see evidences of *poor* design. Trees produced far more seeds than needed. For most animals that lay eggs, almost all the eggs perish. This "fecundity problem" occurs throughout the animal and plant kingdoms. Also, no reason was apparent for the slight differences between some organisms. For example, Darwin claimed that little meaningful difference exists between the many kinds of orchids. Another evidence of poor design is that many variations that existed at one time have vanished.[26] Also, are there not many species— some insects, for example—that seemingly do no good? What about the diseases caused by pathogenic organisms; are those "good" species?[27] Darwin also claimed that organs—for example, the eye—are only as "perfect" as they need to be in competition with other organisms whose corresponding organs are less "perfect." For him the eye was not perfect.[28]

Some people still use these criticisms of design. In recent years questions like these have arisen: Why do flowers depend upon only one insect for pollination, when dependence upon several is "safer"? Why do some bees die after one sting? Why are some birds, such as ostriches, built so they cannot fly? Richard Dawkins maintained that the photocells of the human eye are "wired backwards" and that a good engineer could make a better design.[29]

My answer to these arguments has two parts. First, consider the nature of *positivism* and Darwin's attitude toward this philosophical idea. Positivists claim that at one time human beings had to invoke the existence of gods to account for unexplained phenomena; such explanations are now unnecessary. Thus, people explained lightning and thunder by a god who threw a thunderbolt. But now, by means of natural science, scientists can explain lightning and thunder: an electric charge on a cloud discharges; the discharge consists of a very large electric current; the current lights the sky and heats the air very rapidly, causing it to expand; this rapid expansion—actually an explosion—and the subsequent implosion are the source of the loud sound. According to positivists, our knowledge need not have gaps, gaps that force us to say that God did it. To the extent that Darwin attempted to remove all "unnatural" explanation from biology, he made it a positivistic science. Positivism is widely accepted among natural scientists, although by no means universally accepted among other scholars.

Now, to the second part of my argument. There is a serious inconsistency in those who see "poor design" in nature as evidence there is no design. On the one hand, they use the human inability to discern purpose in certain cases (e.g., the seeds of the tree and the pathogenic organisms) as proof that God does not guide affairs. On the other hand, as positivists they maintain that Christians rest their case on the gaps in human knowledge, that is, on the supposed human inability to explain certain phenomena. Positivists accuse Christians of using an argument ("God is in the gaps") which positivistic Darwinists use themselves when they suggest that a gap in their ability to find reasons for phenomena is evidence of the lack of design. They use *their* gap in knowledge to prove there was no Designer.

Besides claiming poor design, Darwin had a second reason for rejecting design.

Counterfeit Design—Observing the Process. Darwin's other answer to those who claimed that evidence of design could be found everywhere was that design was only apparent. In Neal Gillespie's analysis of Darwin's philosophical position, he claimed that Darwin held to *counterfeit* design.

Design

Blind, undirected evolutionary processes could counterfeit design that seemed to have a purpose.[30] Darwin claimed that a phenomenon which seemed to be an example of design could always be explained in another way. In biology, organisms best suited to their environment, that is, those producing the most progeny, would eventually, after many generations, seem to be very well adjusted to their environment. It would look like design.

Apparent or counterfeit design could be very subtle. I shall explain the idea by means of a hypothetical, nonbiological example. You will realize that the apparent design of this example is no more than counterfeit design. You will make this conclusion because you will observe the process, not merely the result which seems to exhibit design. Because you are not limited by seeing only the result of the process, you need not play detective and attempt to deduce the process from the result.

Consider the way cities of Western countries are often laid out and the attitudes of people in those cities. Actual cities are much more complicated than those of this example, but such complications merely mean that principles in addition to the one I shall describe are also at work.

Suppose cities are made up of homes that are each on a lot 75 feet wide and 150 feet deep; these dimensions amount to almost 2,500 homes per square mile. Consider the cases of three cities: A, B, and C. All three are square (other shapes, such as circular, yield the same general conclusion) but differ only in the size of the square. In each case, the land *next* to the city, just outside its perimeter, is vacant.

City A is one mile square and therefore its perimeter is four miles. Suppose, because of expanding families and immigration from other areas, the number of families that would like to buy those perimeter lots is 10% of the number of homes already in the city; that is, 10% of 2,500, or 250 families, want to buy lots. Can they all buy perimeter lots? A simple calculation shows this square has 282 vacant perimeter lots, each 75 feet wide. There would be 0.88 potential buyer per lot. Expansion of the city is no problem because there are enough available lots.

But such is not the case with City B, which is five miles square. With lots of the same size as City A, City B consists of almost 62,000 lots. Its perimeter of 20 miles would provide only 1,400 lots 75 feet wide. If, due to family expansion and immigration, the number of families seeking perimeter lots was again 10% of the population, that is, 6,200 families, the number of available lots would not be enough. Of course, it would be possible to move farther out. But it is very likely, because of the availability of city services and other such factors, that the first ring of lots would be the most desirable. A situation in which 6,200 families each try to buy one of 1,400 lots—4.4 potential buyers per lot—is a seller's market. The price per lot would rise and only the wealthier families would be able to buy.

In City C, ten miles square, the demand for perimeter lots would be even greater. Here the city contains about 250,000 lots; along the 40-mile perimeter 25,000 families seek 2,800 lots. This amounts to 8.8 potential buyers per lot. Such a situation is even more of a seller's market than in City B, assuming once again that the first ring of lots is the most desirable.

To summarize: For the three cities, A, B, and C, where A is the smallest and C the largest, the number of potential buyers per perimeter lot is, respectively, 0.88, 4.4, and 8.8. As a result, the price per lot increases in the same order. Several things then occur:

(1) In Cities B and C those who buy perimeter lots are the wealthier families. The effect is greatest in the largest city, City C, but is nonexistent in the smallest city, City A.

(2) If in Cities B and C the wealthier families occupy homes within the city before they move to the perimeter, they most likely will move from a less expensive home to a more expensive one. Their former, less-expensive homes will be occupied by those who would have moved to the perimeter had the cost been lower; that is, they will be occupied by the poorer families. After this process continues for a while, the average income of those living in the inner city is lower than the average of those living on its perimeter. Poor people moving into the area or children of poor families already living in the city who eventually form their own families will be forced to live in the city. This tendency might result in two or three families living in one house.

Since the perimeter effect will eventually extend well beyond the first "ring" of lots, we can refer to the area outside the original city as the suburban area; thus, suburban families will generally have a greater income than those in the city.

(3) The uneven geographical distribution of income will be greatest in the largest city-suburban areas and will be nonexistent in and around the smallest cities.

(4) As the wealthier families move out of Cities B and C, they tend to bring more resources to the suburbs. For right or wrong reasons, the suburbs will tend to have better streets, water supply, drainage, libraries, schools, and so forth, than the cities. This kind of superiority of the suburbs will increase the flow of wealth from the city to the suburbs. Eventually, a very great difference between the two areas develops, with the greatest difference being found in the largest city.

(5) The increase of the number of poor people in the city—because of

Design 35

the breaking up of 75-foot lots, the conversion of single-family to multi-family dwellings, and so forth—means the population density increases. Such an increase causes an increase in personal interaction. A sense of frustration accompanies this proximity; the use of drugs and the crime rate both increase. A significant difference in income between the city and suburban areas is the cause of many effects not yet mentioned. One is the tendency for nonwhites, unable to earn higher incomes because of racial discrimination, to be forced to live in the city rather than in a more expensive suburb.

The process whereby cities expand is related to apparent or counterfeit design. We can see why this is so if we consider what a person might think if he or she could look only at the product, not at the process.

Counterfeit Design—After Completion of the Process. Suppose that the proverbial visitor from another planet observes the situation in and around cities of Western countries. Such a visitor would have no knowledge of what has gone on earlier. But this visitor could make some interesting assumptions, such as the following:

(1) The average income in the suburbs of a very large city is much larger than that of those living in the inner city. This difference in income decreases with decreasing size of city and does not exist in small cities.

(2) The wealthiest people in the United States and other Western nations are entertainers, athletes, and business people of large commercial and financial enterprises. The organizations with which these people are associated find it convenient to locate in large cities. It is fortunate that such people are brought to these large cities, for it is there where the available lots for homes seem to be the most expensive.

(3) Evidently poor people like each other. They live in the same area and often very close together. While wealthy people do live in the same area as other wealthy people, the fact that they live farther apart raises some question about their feelings for each other.

(4) Street crime, burglary, and so forth, is greatest in the poorer areas. It is fortunate that the amount of such crime is not as high in the wealthy suburbs, for it is there where the most can be stolen.

(5) One extra cost of living in the suburbs is the cost of traveling to the city for work or recreation. Fortunately, this extra cost can be borne by these wealthier people, who can afford two or three cars per family.

The visitor from another planet might say: "These cities along with their suburbs are smoothly functioning units; the parts fit together. Why, the entire structure of these cities and their suburbs must have been *designed*! There must have been a city planner, a *designer*!"

The inference that a designer exists would not have been warranted. It would be incorrect to assume that a master hand had decreed that only those with better incomes may live in the suburbs, that the poorest families must share houses, that the very wealthy must live near large cities because they can purchase the expensive homes there, and that the highest crime rate be reserved for the area where it can do the least damage.

Those who had observed the process would say, "No, these effects can be traced to geometry. A big city has far fewer lots along the perimeter than can satisfy the demands of those wishing to buy lots. The bigger the city, the more extreme the effect. That's it. No master hand or city planner; just geometry."

Is this example of apparent or counterfeit design, one which provides false evidence that a city planner exists, comparable to design in Creation? Is the observed design in Creation no more than apparent design, false evidence that a "Creation-planner" exists?

It is a mistake to maintain that the false evidence for the existence of a city planner is comparable to design in Creation, and that the supposed design in Creation is false evidence for the existence of a Designer of Creation. Yet it is likely that those who take design in Creation to be no more than counterfeit design do indeed treat the two cases in the same way.

Here is the reason that false evidence for the existence of a city planner is not analogous to false evidence for a Designer of Creation. With the city, we ask a low-level question, namely, did a human being use the already-existing laws of Creation to plan the city so that poor people live near the center and so forth? A little knowledge of how the city grew immediately shows us that we do not have evidence for such a human planner.

But with respect to design in Creation, we must ask an entirely different question; there are no already-existing laws of Creation. We ask high-level questions, namely, do birds, because of God's creational laws, possess organs which allow them to find and digest food? Do birds—again because of creational laws—know when to fly to a warmer climate and when to return? Because of creational laws, do fish know when and where to lay eggs? For the Christian, to ask such questions is to answer them. Of course God designed Creation. Such an answer does not imply that we know all God's laws. For example, we cannot fit miracles into the natural laws that we have formulated. Nor do we imply that we will be able to discern design wherever it exists. If, however, we look at Creation understanding that God created all things, then we will never make the mistake of expecting the Designer of Creation to resemble a city planner who works with the already-existing laws of Creation.

Chapter Four
Objections to Design

Following are three objections to design in Creation and an evaluation of each objection. Many Christians raise the first objection; non-Christians often make the others.

Objection: Accepting Design Leads to Natural Theology
   Christians universally accept the sovereignty of God. Different Christian groups express that belief in different ways, but they all hold that God created and that he controls Creation. He purposely causes things to happen, and so in that sense, design is certainly inherent in his acts of creating and upholding Creation. But the problem many Christians raise is not with design itself. They are uncomfortable with using design to develop natural theology, the doctrine that the existence of God and perhaps even something about his nature can be derived from Creation.

Many nineteenth century Christians objected to natural theology because it reveals very little concerning God's ultimate purpose and because it attempts to explain away all the objectionable phenomena—the insects that seem to have no purpose, pathogenic bacteria, and so forth.[1] Therefore, Richard Owen (1804-1892) developed an alternate form of natural theology. He said that God has a divine purpose in the *general* plan of nature. God's plan is not piecemeal. Rather, an archetypal pattern exists. Biologist Richard Wright rejected natural theology partially because the design actually assumed in the early nineteenth century by William Paley and others was static. Today even anti-evolutionists generally reject static design. Wright also claimed that the idea of purpose built into Creation resembles deism.[2] The nineteenth century defenders of natural theology took a fatal step when they were finally reduced to claiming that the design was in God's mind, not in the world directly.[3]

No doubt some aspects of natural theology are good—for Christians. For those who love the Lord, an understanding of Creation—its beauty, its orderedness, and, in fact, its design—can give Christians reasons to praise him. Yet some of the most effective scientific opponents of evolutionary theory, which certainly denies design, are not Christians. Those non-Christian scientists reject natural theology even though they do see a structure in Creation. It takes more than the claims of natural theologians to convince an unbeliever. If natural theology was supposed to convert unbelievers, it has not succeeded.

Christians who use observations of the physical world to prove that God exists take a fatal step: they have suspended for the sake of the argument their belief that the world is not closed. Both unbelievers and Christians should see the power of the Lord in Creation; the heavens do declare the glory of God (Ps. 19:1). God says through Paul:

> For since the creation of the world God's invisible qualities—his eternal power and divine nature—have been clearly seen, being understood from what has been made, so that all men are without excuse. (Rom. 1:20)

But in the context of saying this, Paul also said that God punishes "men who suppress the truth" (Rom. 1:18). The implication is that while everyone should be able to see God in the world he created, those who are not God's people do not see him in the world.

Almost no one sees God in Creation if he or she is not first brought to God in another way. Just as Paul said, unbelievers *do* suppress the truth. No doubt God occasionally uses his witness in the natural world as the means whereby people are led to the Cross; and when they are at the Cross, they can look back on the path they took and say, "So that's how it is!" But those Christians who want to debate unbelievers on unbelievers' ground are like playgoers. They know that the acting is not "real" and for that reason deliberately engage in a willing suspension of disbelief, thereby temporarily neglecting what they know to be true. In order to debate unbelievers, some natural theologians engage in a willing suspension of *belief* in God, thereby temporarily neglecting what they know to be true.

Thus, Christians who object to the apologetic use of design are on firm ground. They know that God reveals himself in Creation and that everyone ought to understand this revelation. But they also know from God's revelation in the Bible and from their observations of what usually occurs that unbelievers remain unbelievers when they are confronted with no more than God's witness in Creation.[4]

However, often in their zeal to condemn the use of Creation to bring people to the Triune God, Christians *themselves* neglect to praise God for his works in Creation. God *did* design Creation. The parts do fit together unbelievably well. The fine tuning of the energy levels in the carbon atom and the fine tuning seen in countless other phenomena are the works of

Objections to Design 39

the omnipotent and omniscient God. The Bible teaches that the people of God are to praise him for the things he has done. We must praise God for his creation of the strange quasars and black holes. We must praise him for the creation of the fantastically intricate living cell that, with its many thousands of cooperating parts, resembles a large, very well-run factory. We must praise him for the creation of human minds capable of producing sophisticated theories that unravel physical phenomena, ranging from quantum mechanics to the explanation of the code of life in the DNA molecule.

What is the *fundamental* reason natural theology has not succeeded? To answer that question, I shall anticipate some of the discussion in Chapter 9 on how and why it is fitting for Christians to engage in scientific activity.

To consider the reason for failure, I want to speculate. Suppose Adam, when he was still in his sinless state, daily discovered more of what God had created. With each new discovery, he praised and thanked God. At the same time, he realized that what he could still discover was almost endless. But that was no problem. Discovering was wonderful work and each discovery provided him with a new reason to praise God.

After Adam fell, discovering became difficult. In addition, with each new discovery a question arose: Would he give God praise and thanks for what he found? Sometimes he did; sometimes he did not. He was not sure about the future. Would there be endless new discovery and endless reason to praise God?

In our world human beings behave the way Adam did after he fell. They stumble in their investigations. Sometimes they praise God and give him thanks; sometimes they do not. But the potential for unlimited unfolding and joyful praise to God for each new discovery is still present. People still discover what God created. They have every reason to praise joyfully as they eagerly rush forward for more. Here is the reason natural theology fails: Those who promote natural theology often assume that human beings can function today the way Adam did before he sinned. But to maintain that natural theology is completely in error is to deny that human beings can make new discoveries about Creation and, even in their stumbling, praise God for what they find.

Objection: It Is Blind Chance, Not Design

Many since Darwin have objected to design by challenging an example presented by Paley in the early nineteenth century. Paley said that a person who found a watch and examined it closely would conclude that it is a marvelous thing. In fact, wouldn't that person be forced to conclude that the existence of such an intricate watch meant that a watchmaker existed?[5]

Evolutionists have generally claimed that Darwin undermined Paley's watchmaker. Thus, George Gaylord Simpson, an American evolutionist who influenced much of the scientific community during the middle of the twentieth century, said that the human race is the result of a purposeless process that did not have the human race in mind.[6] Carl Sagan, well-known for his *Cosmos* television series, denied design and claimed that the fossil record indicates that nothing more than trial and error occurred.

Richard Dawkins, an Oxford zoologist and widely read author, challenged Paley much more specifically. In Dawkins's book, *The Blind Watchmaker*, he used modern scientific arguments as he contended that the complicated structures observed actually evolved by blind chance. In Paley's terms, a blind watchmaker could make a watch.[7] This concept harks back to Empedocles (fifth century B.C.) and others of the ancient world. Later David Hume (1711-1776) explained that with a never-ending flux of matter, sooner or later everything conceivable will appear, with only the viable surviving.[8] (A prominent physicist stated it this way: "I just saw in the parking lot a car with the license number QM7341. What are the odds against my finding just *that* number?") Dawkins even constructed a computer program to mimic natural selection in the evolution of the bat with its sonar navigational system.[9]

Dawkins also observed an extremely important philosophical truth. Before Darwin, both theists and atheists observed design. Theists claimed that the existence of design proved the existence of a designer. Atheists denied this claim, but they had no place to go. Dawkins stated that Darwin made it possible for a person to be an intellectually fulfilled atheist. The atheistic position was no longer irrational. Alvin Plantinga made an additional observation: since Dawkins' evolution-by-pure-chance is the only alternative to design usually offered, atheists are *forced* to be evolutionists. They do not have freedom of choice.[10]

Analysis of apparent imperfections or "poor design " is often associated with the blind chance objection to design. As I showed in Chapter 2, anyone who accepts imperfection and also positivism is inconsistent. But a modern variation on the idea of imperfection is that imperfections *must* exist; or, at least, the world must be less than optimum.

R.J. Herrnstein, a Harvard psychologist, recently developed this idea.[11] Although his interest was in behavioral evolution, his theory also applies to biological evolution. Herrnstein claimed that evolution does not necessarily produce the best result. This is the key to his reasoning: *The behavior of a single organism, as well as a group of organisms, such as a species, is such that it tends to focus on immediate goals at the cost of goals not*

Objections to Design 41

so immediate. Behavioral examples illustrating this idea are easy to find. Suppose football fans sit and watch a game in a stadium. To get a better view, one fan stands up without considering the long-range consequences of this action. Because one fan stands up, others behind this fan must also rise. Soon everyone, even those in front of the first fan, stands. As a result, no one has a better view than when all were seated. The first fan had a momentary advantage at the cost of discomfort for the rest of the game.

Again, consider the example of a company that competes more effectively and increases profits by deciding to spend less cleaning up waste water. When one company acts this way, the effect on the water supply might be minimal. But, to compete, other companies do the same thing, and eventually no one has increased profits. By this time the water supply is significantly polluted. The immediate advantage is lost, and in the long term the situation is worse.

In evolutionary theory, such behavior can be significant in determining the fate of various mutant forms of a species. Herrnstein discussed a hypothetical example (originally from John Maynard Smith) of two mutants of the same species. One is hawk-like: it always fights other members of the species until one wins and the other loses. The other form is dove-like: it always flees whenever it encounters one that is hawk-like. The two tendencies, being hawk-like or dove-like, are inherited. These two kinds of behavior are not necessarily best for the species as a whole, even though each brings an immediate advantage.

Herrnstein proceeded by assigning "reproductive fitness points" to each mutant and considered what happens, as time passes, in populations of various initial ratios of hawk-like to dove-like. It is crucial for the argument that the assignment of reproductive fitness points depends directly on the inherited hawk-like or dove-like tendency: reproduction, and therefore evolutionary survival, is linked to the two kinds of behavior.

I can give only the results of his calculations here. He showed, given his assignment of reproductive fitness points, that for *any* starting ratio of dove-like to hawk-like, the ratio will change in succeeding generations until the over-all makeup of the species will be 42% dove-like and 58% hawk-like, the equilibrium mixture. If the ratio were altered slightly by adding either hawk-like or dove-like mutants to the population, the new population would change until the 42%-58% percentages are once again achieved. Evolutionary biologists refer to the achievement of this equilibrium mixture as the *evolutionarily stable strategy.*

Here, however, is the surprising point: Herrnstein showed that *if the population were to have the highest possible over-all fitness, 83% would be dove-like and 17% hawk-like.* But an 83%-17% population would not be the most stable; it would evolve into a 42%-58% population. The population that continues to exist is not the most fit. Because of calculations like this one, Herrnstein rejected design or teleology:

> The failure of natural selection to produce the true optimum for the species [with the dove-like and hawk-like mutants] shows concretely why teleology, if it existed, would work better than higgledy-piggledy [i.e., a random process]. An external, benevolent hand should, given the variables, guide this species toward 83% doves and 17% hawks. *The "invisible hand" of evolution by natural selection will fail to do so well.*[12] (Emphasis added.)

Herrnstein presented an over-all view of his theory as follows:

> What looks to the untrained eye like a purposive unfolding of ever-more-adaptive forms seems, in the light of evolutionary theory, to be just mechanistic selection. *Evolutionary theory thus naturalizes purpose.* Purpose becomes part of the biological world, rather than being outside it as divine will or a mystical life force.[13] (Emphasis added.)

Herrnstein's theory is an attempt to explain imperfection in the evolution of behavior. For Herrnstein, imperfection is to be expected. This is not the best of all possible worlds.

His theory has an obvious extension to biological evolutionary theory. The appearance and survival of "imperfect" species is accounted for. Design has no place. Evolution leads to compromise, not perfection. Without doubt, the underlying thinking here is not healthy. Evolutionary thought expressed in this way—compromise instead of perfection—characterizes modern attitudes and significantly impacts our society.

Is that which is taken to be design no more than apparent or counterfeit design, as in the example of the growth of cities? Can everything be accounted for by the theory postulating blind chance, provided this theory includes the theory showing that on the basis of chance imperfections will arise? Chapter 6 will take up the matter of probability and will show that the probability of life arising from nonliving matter is vanishingly small. But the question of counterfeit design, with imperfections accounted for mathematically, requires examination on a more fundamental level than that of probability calculations.

Objections to Design

Behind the idea that one can make calculations or predictions about "blind" probability is the assumption that this universe, with its matter, radiation, and so forth, is all that exists. It is as if one can take the universe, put it in a beaker in a laboratory, and make calculations about what is in the beaker—what its contents are like now and what they will be like in the future.[14] Some Christians hasten to add that occasionally God, who is not part of the universe, intervenes for his special purpose: he performs a miracle. To put it another way, some persons maintain that everything is "natural," while certain Christians add that *some* phenomena are "supernatural."

Recall the historical sketch presented in Chapter 2. Throughout history, one particular trend in human thought has gained strength. Natural scientific activity, which has defined human investigative activity the last few hundred years, excludes consideration of any god; the universe is closed. Any investigation which assumes that the universe is not closed is not scientific. Of course, Christians have not accepted this premise; but unfortunately many have felt it is sufficient to *add on* to this atheistic idea one more concept: occasionally God intervenes and performs miracles.

But this is not how the Bible presents the works of God. For the purposes of this discussion, one can put God's works into three categories: "ordinary," everyday works; works that seem to be miraculous but that the Bible does not label as such; and works of God that the Bible does label miraculous. Typical of ordinary events that are nevertheless ascribed to God are the making of snow, hail, rain, ice, and lightning (Job 38:22-35) and the growth of crops (Acts 14:17). An example of a work of God that seems to be miraculous but that the Bible does not specifically label a miracle is the gift of manna to the Israelites in the desert (Ex. 16).[15] Manna appeared on the ground each morning except the Sabbath morning; but twice as much fell the day before the Sabbath, and the night before the Sabbath was the only night it did not spoil. Certainly one cannot explain these phenomena by either present or future natural laws. Another example of this kind of God's work is given in Matthew 17:27, where Christ tells Peter to pick a coin out of the mouth of the first fish he will catch. Finally, some phenomena, such as the many healings recorded in the Bible, are labeled by words that identify them as miracles.

What the Bible presents, then, is a continuum of God's works. Some we see as ordinary; they are the kind that we investigate in natural scientific activity. Others are works that we cannot possibly explain, while the biblical authors simply assume that God can do these things. Still other works that we cannot possibly explain the Bible labels as miracles. In other words, the classification of works of God is arbitrary. We decide what is "natural," that is, explainable. If we are not careful, we will label all the others "supernatural." But the Bible ascribes them all to God.

If God controls all events, then there is no fundamental distinction between those we can explain (or anticipate we will be able to explain) and those we cannot. All events taken together are like a seamless garment. Furthermore, when we make probability calculations or discuss chance, we merely find out what God has done. "Blind chance" is blind to us, not to God. The biblical authors make this assumption in several places. Here is an example:

> So they proposed two men: Joseph called Barsabas (also known as Justus) and Matthias. Then they prayed, "Lord, you know everyone's heart. Show us which of these two you have chosen to take over this apostolic ministry, which Judas left to go where he belongs." Then they drew lots, and the lot fell to Matthias; so he was added to the eleven apostles. (Acts 1:23-26)

Matthias, chosen by lot, was God's choice, the one "you have chosen." Just as God determined the outcome of the casting of this lot, so does he also determine every other event we would term chance or "something we cannot know." For example, some physicists claim that we cannot know simultaneously the path and velocity of a single electron in an atom, and so in the description of the atom the words "probability" and "chance" are often used. But with God there is no chance.

Consider calculations made on the basis of chance. For example, we can calculate the equilibrium percentages of the hawk-like and dove-like members of the same species. Furthermore, our calculation might be a correct prediction of what happens. But does this result prove the absence of design? Do we know that the best fitness-for-survival (the 83%-17% split) would be the best *design*? Are we certain that the equilibrium value (the 42%-58% split), even though it has less survival value, is less desirable in God's plan? It is simply not true that we know what perfection is in such cases, so we cannot maintain that the 42%-58% split is imperfect. We cannot disprove design if we do not know what design looks like in a universal, creational sense. We can know that design exists if God tells us he has put things together; then, when we look about, we will certainly find design. *Then* design is seen by the eye of faith.

Objection: Design Is Only in the Eyes of the Beholder
In *Dialogues Concerning Natural Religion* (1779) David Hume criticized

Objections to Design

the argument used to show design. He claimed that the design argument contains an anthropocentric bias. This bias means that human beings forget that they are unable to compare the "design" they see with whatever exists in another universe; they have only one universe to examine. Also, he objected, the reasoning used is too subjective; people tend to neglect negative evidence. In fact, he said, one could concentrate on the *disorderly* aspects of the universe and argue for a *disorderly* cause.[16] Hume also pointed out that human beings can learn only a very little about an immense system in the short time available during our lives. Our imperfect discoveries should not be the basis of conclusions concerning the origin of the entire universe.[17]

After initially admiring the design argument, Immanuel Kant (1724-1804) was later impressed with Hume's criticism of it. In 1787 Kant said in his *Critique of Pure Reason* that the categories of our minds determine what we find when we examine the world. We impose structure and order on what we observe:

> When [Galileo] experimented with balls of a definite weight on the inclined plane, when Torrecelli caused the air to sustain a weight which he had calculated beforehand to be equal to that of a definite column of water,...a light broke upon all natural philosophers.

What, according to Kant, was that light?

> *They learned that reason only perceives that which it produces after its own design*; that [reason must] compel nature to reply to its questions.[18] (Emphasis added.)

Most natural scientists did not accept Kant's claim that human minds create order. However, recent developments in the philosophy of science have changed the minds of some natural scientists.

To explain these recent developments, it is necessary to digress. Since the time of Kant physical scientists have greatly elucidated structures and processes in matter and in the entire universe. A description of a structure or a process either includes or assumes the existence of certain *fundamental constants*.

One such fundamental constant is the *speed of light in a vacuum*, 300,000 kilometers (186,000 miles) per second. The speed of light in a vacuum is a *fundamental* constant because it is everywhere the same. A detailed description of an atom, an aggregate of atoms, or of a process in the atom or the aggregate always requires knowledge of the speed of light. There are several fundamental constants.

It can be shown that if the value of even one of the fundamental constants were slightly different, this universe would be entirely different. The nature of structures and processes, which depend upon the values of these constants, would be different—so different, in fact, that human beings could not exist.

For example, with a slightly different "tuning" of the values of the fundamental constants, a certain sequence of events that occurred billions of years ago could not have occurred, the sequence now thought to account for the existence and amounts of the chemical elements. With slightly different values of the fundamental constants, atomic "energy levels" would be different; the atoms would not be the same.

Such an alteration in energy levels is important because the postulated sequence of element formation in stars long ago involves the combination of helium atoms to make carbon atoms and the combination of carbon atoms and helium atoms to make oxygen atoms. But if a certain nuclear energy level in carbon had been 4 percent lower, essentially no carbon would now exist; or, if a nuclear energy level in the oxygen atom were but 0.5 percent higher, almost no carbon would now exist. However, life depends upon carbon. Only because of these "fortuitous" energy levels does carbon exist and it is possible for life to exist.[19]

Fred Hoyle, an atheist (in spite of the quotation below) and one of the world's leading astronomers today, reacted to the situation concerning the energy levels in carbon in this way:

> Would you not say to yourself, "Some supercalculating intellect must have designed the properties of the carbon atom, otherwise the chance of my finding such an atom through the blind forces of nature would be utterly miniscule!"

Hoyle's answer was yes—and the case for yes is overwhelming:

> Of course you would. . . . A common sense interpretation of the facts suggests that a superintellect has monkeyed with physics, as well as with chemistry and biology, and that there are no blind forces worth speaking about in nature. The numbers one calculates from the facts seem to me so overwhelming as to put this conclusion almost beyond question.[20]

But not everyone is convinced. James Ward Smith said earlier:

> Is there anything empirical about the claim from the observed order

Objections to Design

and design of the world one can justly conclude that there must be a divine designer?. . . . Only if the chance existence of order (of *any* kind) is less probable than the chance existence of disorder is there any force to the demand that we must posit a cause of the existence of order.[21]

However, many natural scientists are convinced that the chance existence of order is indeed much less likely than the chance existence of disorder. The kind of design discovered in physics and other natural sciences in the twentieth century constitutes a challenge to those who want to reject design, purpose, teleology, and natural theology—to those who want to follow Hume and Kant. The *anthropic principle* arises out of this situation.

According to the anthropic principle, the universe is the way it is just because we are here. As we have seen, we would not be here if the universe were even slightly different, if the value of even one fundamental constant were slightly different. That claim was made by John Wheeler (of the Center for Theoretical Physics at the University of Texas) in his foreword to *The Anthropic Cosmological Principle* by John Barrow and Frank Tipler. This book, which presents an extensive analysis of the anthropic principle, is an extremely important contribution to the modern discussion of the design argument. Wheeler stated:

> It is not only that man is adapted to the universe. The universe is adapted to man. Imagine a universe in which one or another of the fundamental dimensionless constants [a special combination of some of the fundamental constants] of physics is altered by a few percent one way or the other?

What is the consequence of that slight variation?

> Man could never come into being in such a universe. That is the central point of the anthropic principle. According to this principle, a life-giving factor lies at the centre of the whole machinery and design of the world.[22]

There are two versions of the anthropic principle, the *weak* and the *strong*. The weak, more basic version says that human beings make the observations of which they are capable. The optical telescope, which collects visible light, provides an analogy. Not until other kinds of measuring devices were available could astronomers analyze other kinds of stellar radiation, such as radio waves. The kind of observation made could not go beyond the kind of instrument used. In the same way, human capability limits what can be observed. Barrow and Tipler showed that the Copernican revolution, after which it was no longer necessary to assume that the earth is the center of the universe, began the thinking that eventually led to the weak anthropic principle.[23] Furthermore, if the earth is not the only planet with inhabitants, perhaps the natural science that earth's inhabitants develop is not the only natural science.

The strong version of the principle calls attention to a point made earlier, namely, that this is the kind of universe in which human beings can exist. In fact, as usually stated, this version says that in this universe human beings—or, at least, some observers—*must* exist. The fundamental physical constants do not merely permit the existence of human life, but, given the inevitability of evolution, after a large number of evolutionary steps observers *will* certainly appear.

This version of the principle also contemplates the possibility of other kinds of universes. Several kinds of "ensembles of universes" could exist besides the kind already mentioned, universes where the fundamental constants would have different values. Barrow and Tipler give examples. Given the big bang or its equivalent, the starting conditions need not have been those of "our" big bang. Many possibilities exist, with each having the same effect as changing the values of the fundamental constants. Or, the universe might be infinitely large, with an infinite number of regions, of which our "universe" is but one; the fundamental constants in the other regions are different.[24]

Although Christians need not deny that God created other worlds, the motivation for the anthropic principle is unquestionably the desire to account for everything—in a group of universes, if necessary—without reference to a transcendent Creator. The universe or group of universes is closed.

What about the validity of the claim that design exists because our minds construct it? Is a modern version of this claim, either the weak or the strong version of the anthropic principle, valid?

We should not reject out of hand the idea that our observations, our minds, and design are intimately related. For example, no matter what natural scientists investigate, it is always correct to say that in some way they investigate that which is physical. Even living matter is ultimately composed of the same particles that make up everything else that natural scientists investigate. On one level, these most fundamental particles are atoms; on a more fundamental level they are electrons, protons, and neutrons; on a still more

Objections to Design

fundamental level, these particles are quarks and leptons. In addition to these particles, natural scientists investigate many kinds of *fields*, physical entities associated with radiation. A somewhat simplistic way of putting it is to say that natural scientists investigate matter and radiation. This conclusion has an interesting consequence. It arises because of the quantum mechanical understanding of the study of matter and radiation, which began in the first part of the twentieth century. One insight of quantum mechanics is that the observer is inevitably part of the system observed.

For the present purpose, consider what happens when one observes the behavior of a particle, for example, an electron. The involvement of the observer with the system means (this is not proved here) that one cannot know simultaneously the exact position and the exact velocity of a particular electron. In fact, the more precisely one knows the value of either its position or its velocity, the less precisely one knows the other value. If the error in one value is zero, the other error would be infinitely large. (In this context, "error" does not arise because of human mistake. Rather, it refers to the amount of theoretical uncertainty in a measurement. However, some physicists do not agree that uncertainty is wholly a matter of the observer being a part of the system observed. As a result, they would not agree with all the statements made in the following argument.)

Let us make a tentative assumption: *A certain electron is at rest*, so its velocity is exactly zero. Therefore, the *error* in our knowledge of its velocity is zero; after all, we have taken the *exact* value of its velocity as a given. But because of the inherent uncertainty described in the previous paragraph, as far as we know, its position could be anywhere. This conclusion arises because an error of zero in our knowledge of its velocity leads to an infinitely large error in our knowledge of its position. Let the electron we are discussing belong to one atom among other atoms in a certain beaker. We now know that that electron is in the beaker. That electron is not just anywhere. We have a contradiction: On the one hand, we say that our error in knowing where the electron is will be infinitely large; on the other hand, we know that its position is somewhere in the beaker. It follows that our tentative assumption is impossible: we cannot postulate the velocity of an electron to be zero. *We cannot say that any electron is at rest.*[25]

From our point of view each electron in the beaker must be in motion. But nothing can move without traversing space; also, nothing can move with infinite velocity (not proven here), and so the movement of an electron consumes time. What has just been said about the electron can be said about any particle. The same things about space and time must be said about radiation, since radiation always involves movement at a finite velocity.

We therefore arrive at this conclusion: Everything that is physical, that is, that which is composed of either matter or radiation or both, presupposes both space and time. The very existence of anything physical demands that both space and time exist. We cannot claim either that anything is absolutely at rest or that we can describe anything without taking into account the properties of space and time.

But notice how these three—physical things, space, and time—are united; they are bound together in *our* perception. It is in *our* scientific work that *we* tie the three together. In fact, as *we* tie them together in *our* observations, *we* conclude that *we* can never conceive of the existence of physical things without also involving space and time.[26]

Thus, the binding together of the three is but one reason that we cannot reject out of hand the idea that our observations, our minds, and design are intimately related.

In spite of that intimate relation, we ought not to accept either version of the anthropic principle or the older idea that perceived design is based on our mental constructions. I shall attempt to analyze this situation using Christian assumptions.

There is one God and he is sovereign. He was free either to create or not create. He chose to create. It seems that he could have created in any one of four ways: he could have created either an ordered or a disordered world, and in each case he might or might not have included beings capable of comprehending its order or disorder.

It is possible to decide which of the four ways corresponds to what he actually did. God has revealed to his people that he is one God and that he is sovereign; he created and by his providence he cares for Creation. Therefore, we know not only that he controls everything but also that there is no power that can successfully oppose him. Polytheists, who teach that there is more than one god and that none is sovereign, are in error. Because the one God has absolute control and no equivalent contrary power exists, everything will "hang together." Investigation of the world only partially reveals this hanging together. Yet even without investigation we know in principle that things do fit together; God has created and does govern. Therefore, because of what God has revealed to us, we know which of the four ways he created: he made an orderly world in which he placed beings that could comprehend its orderliness. In fact, he says that the earth is not a chaos and that we are not to seek him in chaos. (Is. 45:18-19, RSV)

Those who advocate either a version of the anthropic principle or design created by our minds claim that the universe is (or, is perceived to be) the way it is *only* because human beings are what they are. The implication is that even though human beings are not actually so very important, they cannot avoid putting themselves on a pedestal. But this implication neglects the biblical view of human beings.

First of all, human beings bear God's image (Gen. 1:26). God tells us of no other beings that bear his image. Of the beings we know, we are unique. God has put us on a pedestal; we are not on a pedestal because of an inherent relation (as expressed by the anthropic principle) we have with the rest of the universe.

Do other universes exist? If they do, we need not worry: we are in this universe and we bear God's image. Although the human family has fallen from its initial perfect state, we still can claim that God considers us unique. For the Son of God became one of us:

> [Christ Jesus], being in the very nature God, did not consider equality with God something to be grasped, but made himself nothing, taking the very nature of a servant, being made in human likeness. (Phil. 2:6-7)

But Christ Jesus, a human being, came to earth to redeem all things, the very things he created. By his coming and his work on earth he reconciled all things to himself (Col. 1:15-20). Thus, because Christ Jesus was a man, the Bible teaches an anthropic principle: all things have been reconciled to one man and all human beings bear the image of God. This is not the anthropic principle claimed by some modern scientists. It is not the principle a person accepts when he or she allows biblical teaching to be carried away by the tide of evolutionary thought. The biblical anthropic principle says that human beings *are* indeed at the center of Creation: God put them there. It is because of God, not human beings, that the design perceived by human beings is real.

Chapter 5
Scientific Consensus: The Scenario

The Status of the Argument
Consider the argument developed in the previous chapters. It is an argument concerning how evolutionary theory came to be fixed in the mind of Western society. The consequences of how evolutionary theory affects the way we think are yet to be discussed. But let us review what has been said.

From the earliest times some leading thinkers said they could investigate the world without considering any god or his acts. When Christians entered the scholarly conversation, some were not willing to easily cast aside the sovereignty of God in all things. Eventually, the momentum was against them. As the modern scientific period began in the late sixteenth century, the working definition of natural science assumed that the universe is closed. Many Christians developed a dualistic worldview: God is sovereign in "supernatural" matters, but "natural" things are neutral. The so-called neutral approach was tempting because it seemed so successful in the day-to-day problems natural scientists faced. When, however, scientists and philosophers of the modern period began to think more intensively about the larger picture, including the nature of things, the place of people in the universe, and the very origin of the universe, the predominant approach was to take as much as possible to be "natural." Non-Christians were quite satisfied to consider the universe closed; many Christians, in their dualistic approach, wanted to allow some divine "intervention" in the larger matters, while they attempted to put as much as possible into the neutral area.

Christians saw design in the world. Dualistic Christians contended that here was evidence that God had intervened—in this case, in the act of creating. But the scientific community had already defined natural science in terms of a closed universe. Investigation of the world, including living things, was part of the scientific enterprise. Since investigation of the world was part of that enterprise, the ground rules of the enterprise had to be obeyed: it was not possible to discover intervention from outside the universe. Everything had to be consistent with natural law. Dualistic Christians were no match for non-Christians who insisted that all phenomena, including the phenomena grouped under the rubric "creation," could be put under one umbrella. Dualistic Christians had already admitted the effective autonomy of natural law in much of life; now it was only a matter of extending this sphere of influence to include whatever scientists—or, at least, natural scientists—investigated.

The principal obstacle to the extension of this sphere of influence was observed design. Could this obstacle be overcome? Yes, it could: evolutionists had to make a case showing that observed design is nothing more than what Neal C. Gillespie called counterfeit design (see Chapter 3). It was not really difficult to make such a case, given the fact that scientific investigation dealt only with natural law. If it was *a priori* assumed that phenomena were explainable, sufficient ingenuity could produce explanations. Thus, what had at first seemed a formidable problem, observed design, could be denied in several ways: its assumed corollary, proof that a god existed, is not a valid proof; random processes can produce that which seems to be design; or, the very existence of human beings means order will be observed, and so the observation of order does no more than prove that human beings exist.

These different ways of counteracting Christian claims about origins have been very successful because, in a dualistic system, they move phenomena from the spiritual sphere to the natural sphere. In the natural sphere, they are amenable to treatment. In the natural sphere, the correlation of phenomena can lead to the formulation of natural law; and if part of that body of natural law is evolutionary theory, so be it. In fact, some people will take a theory that purports to explain in principle all natural phenomena, as does evolutionary theory, and extend it to cover phenomena heretofore supposed by dualists to be nonnatural, that is, supernatural. In other words, the tendency to absolutize evolution, thus adopting evolutionism, is almost inevitable.[1]

But rejecting dualism, recognizing that long ago those who investigated Creation made a wrong turn, is simply not enough. The natural scientific enterprise has gone far; what we have today is a mountain of results. With respect to origins, these results have largely been interpreted in terms of a closed-universe model. In the remainder of this book, I want to carry the argument beyond merely rejecting dualism. Christians themselves must present their perceptions of truth, truth gained from studying Creation in the light of God's Word.

This chapter, along with subsequent chapters through Chapter 11, describes and analyzes the evolutionary scenario, *taking into account both general and special revelation*. Following is a summary of my argument: I have no problem with a great age for the earth and the rest of Creation, but I cannot agree with those who attempt to explain ''the beginning'' naturalistically. I do believe that some kind of evolutionary development of energy, matter, stars, galaxies, and planets is not only possible, but also seems reasonable. However, I am virtually certain that life did not evolve from nonliving matter. Although many changes in living things have no doubt occurred, the general evolutionary scenario that calls for the evolution of the simplest life into complex life is almost certainly wrong. I am certain that human beings did not evolve from other living creatures. Because I am certain that human beings cannot be included in the evolutionary scenario, I am also certain that an evolutionary unification of the universe is impossible. As we shall see in the last part of this book, the attempt to force evolutionary unification has resulted in a disastrous impact of evolutionary theory on modern life.

In this chapter, I discuss the age of various parts of Creation (necessary as a background for the main part of the chapter) and the evolutionary scenario developed in the last century and a half. Chapters 6 and 7 constitute an analysis of this scenario, with Chapter 6 taking up the postulated evolution from nonlife to life and Chapter 7 the rest of evolutionary theory. As the analysis will show, many conclusions described in the present chapter are consistent with a nondualistic Christian worldview, but others ought to be questioned.

Ages

Cosmologically relevant ages—hundreds of thousands, millions, or even billions of years—are very great when compared to familiar time spans. But in a scientific discussion we ought to become accustomed to large numbers. The body of a 150-lb. (about 68-kg.) person consists of about a billion billion billion atoms. The nearest star (besides the sun) is more than twenty thousand billion miles (about thirty-two thousand billion kilometers) distant, and the farthest stars known are from three to five *billion* times farther.

Perhaps secularism, which has affected even Christians, has contributed to the difficulty of comprehending time spans of billions of years. An atheist thinks of a personal future of only a few years: death ends everything. But Christians, who have a sure hope, know better. The future is endless. Furthermore, the Christian belief in the resurrection of the *body* takes future life out of the realm of the vague, the ethereal. Possessing bodies in heaven means that we will also know time. To think of a billion years in the *future* is then not an impossibility. Such a consideration does not prove that God first created billions of years ago, but it puts such a great age into real, possible terms. God made us so that the immense age of his Creation is not unfathomable.

Scientific Consesus: The Scenario

The ages of various parts of Creation determined by natural scientists are usually valid.[2] The discussion of Chapter 10 shows that great age is not inconsistent with the biblical witness. Questions about evolution need not rest on questions about age. Of course, many Christians have doubted that great ages are possible, and some have presented counter-arguments. My rejection of their claims of a young earth is not a rejection of the validity of their Christian faith. I align myself with those brothers and sisters in the Lord, who also struggle against false witness in the natural sciences and other scholarly disciplines.

Geological Methods. In what follows, I present some of the geological evidence that the earth is very old.

The basis of some of these methods is the difference in the ability of water to dissolve different substances. Before considering geological examples, let us examine the ability of water to dissolve two common substances, ordinary table salt and limestone. If one puts a few crystals of salt into a cup of water, the salt dissolves instantly. Even so, that amount of water dissolves only a limited amount of this substance: a cup of water would dissolve about three ounces (eighty-three grams), but no more. Any amount over the three ounces that one adds remains a solid and settles at the bottom of the cup. But a cup of water dissolves only two ten-thousandths of an ounce of limestone. Any additional amount settles at the bottom. Suppose you have a cup of water in which one ten-thousandth of an ounce of salt and an equal amount of limestone are dissolved. These amounts are so small that neither substance settles to the bottom. Now let the water evaporate. When half the water is gone, the slightly-soluble limestone will begin to settle to the bottom. But water can dissolve salt much more easily, and so the salt will not settle to the bottom until almost all the water is gone. At the bottom of the cup there will then be two solid layers; a limestone layer covered by a salt layer. Suppose we have a way of refilling the cup with water so that the layers persist and that the added water once again contains salt and limestone. With another evaporation, a second pair of layers, first limestone then salt, appears. This process could continue for a long time, producing many double layers.

When substances dissolve in large bodies of water, such as a lake or an ocean, and eventually the body of water disappears, only to reappear, successive double layers will once again be expected. In fact, the body of water need not disappear; all that is needed is an appropriate change in environmental conditions (not described here) for settling out to occur, producing a double layer. With many changes in conditions, many double layers will appear. An example is provided by the Great Bahama Bank off the coast of

Florida, over 14,500 feet thick. The Bank consists of a very large number of alternating layers of two minerals, limestone and dolomite. These two compounds settle out under different conditions. Because environmental changes are slow, the conditions for settling out change slowly. Yet each pair of layers represents one such change. Therefore, this immense bank must have formed over a very long period of time.

Coral reefs provide another indication of great age. A reef builds as successive generations of coral die. The most rapid growth rate found is about one-third of an inch per year; the deepest modern coral reef, one in the Eniwetok atoll in the Pacific Ocean, is 4,610 feet. Thus, use of the most rapid growth rate indicates the age of this reef is over 150,000 years; more realistic slower rates yield even greater ages.

Corals provide another interesting means of estimating great age. Corals exhibit annual growth bands like tree rings. Very careful examination indicates that they also possess two other bands: one monthly (according to the lunar month) and the other daily. Obviously, the number of daily bands within an annual band is the number of days in a year. Some corals found in deep strata in New York and Ontario show that when the corals lived, the year consisted of about 400 days; or, to put it differently, the day was not 24 hours long, but about 22 hours. How is this possible? The length of a day is getting longer because the rotation of the earth is decreasing by 0.000015-0.000020 second each year; thus, one million years ago the day was between fifteen and twenty seconds (that is, one million times 0.000015 and one million times 0.000020) shorter. If the earth's rotation decreased twenty seconds each million years, the day was about 22 hours long approximately 400 million years ago, and therefore this is the age of the deepest part of the coral bed.

Analysis of sea-floor spreading provides another indication of a great age for the earth. For example, a vast ridge in the Mid-Atlantic "unfolds" so that South America and Africa are moving farther apart. Examination of a world map reveals that the eastern coast of South America roughly "fits" into the western coast of Africa near the Equator. Furthermore, many of the geological features of the two coasts are similar. The two continents were once together. The rate at which the ridge unfolds is about an inch a year. Daniel E. Wonderly, an American geologist, discussed the constancy of this rate:

> The fact that the sediments are thin near the center line of the ridge, and become gradually thicker farther away from the ridge, on each side, is an indication that the spreading has been practically continuous and gradual for a long period of time.[3]

Scientific Consensus: The Scenario 57

A movement of only an inch a year, leading to a continental separation of thousands of miles, takes an extremely long time. This movement of *tectonic plates* also occurs in other parts of the world and always indicates that processes occurred over vast reaches of time.

The behavior of certain magnetic compounds also indicates great age. The earth is magnetic. Therefore, if a magnetic particle is free to move, it will align itself with the magnetic field of the earth, much as the needle of a compass aligns itself with the magnetic field of the earth. Suppose a lava flow contains material that is magnetic when the lava cools and hardens. The magnetic particles will align themselves with the magnetic field of the earth and will freeze in that position. If the rock itself does not move, those particles will point in a direction determined by the magnetic field of the earth at the time of cooling. These indicators of direction will not move even though the magnetic field of the earth does move. What geologists have actually found is interesting: the sequence of magnetic reversals deduced from a series of rocks in one place is the same sequence deduced from various series of rocks in other places. But magnetic reversal consumes a long time. Therefore, the series of magnetic reversals consumed a very long time.

Several of the geological methods of determining age are *radiometric*, that is, they are related to the radioactive properties of certain atoms. Perhaps the following analogy will help in understanding the principles involved.

Visualize a land area that at the beginning consisted of lots for 10,000 homes. You did not see the land before any homes were built. But when you do see it, you are told three things: first, the land can hold 10,000 homes; second, the land now has 1,000 homes; third, the present building rate is 100 homes per year, with the rate decreasing in proportion to the number of available lots. You are not told when the building project started. But can you figure it out?

Your approximate answer would be ten years, that is, 1000 homes divided by 100 homes per year. (Since the number of available lots decreases each year, the more accurate answer—calculations not given here—is 9.5 years.)

The calculation is similar to determining age by means of the radioactive properties of atoms. Thus, because the nucleus of Atom A emits a particle, Atom A becomes Atom B, a different kind of atom. Suppose that by the time we can analyze a sample that initially consisted only of A atoms, many B atoms are present. Evidently the emission of a particle from A to make B occurred many times. Although we did not see the first transformation of A into B, we can (perhaps by chemical means) count the number of A and the number of B atoms. We can also—using a counter found in any physics laboratory—count the number of particles emitted per minute—or day or year; we therefore know how fast B (analogous to the homes) is "built." These might be our observations: we have 9 billion A atoms and 1 billion B atoms; A changes into B at the rate of 100 million per year. When did the process start? The approximate answer is again ten years ago, that is, 1 billion B atoms divided by 100 million B atoms appearing per year. (Since the number of A atoms changing into B atoms per year decreases as the number of A atoms decreases, the more accurate answer is 9.5 years.)

Before proceeding to real atoms and real results, one additional point is important. Slight variations in atoms of a given element are possible. Thus, both "argon-36" and "argon-40" exist; both are argon, but one contains 36 particles in its nucleus and the other 40. Each kind of argon atom is an *isotope* of argon.

For the present purpose, one of the more important atom-to-atom changes is the *decay* of potassium-40 to produce argon-40. Suppose we have a sample of potassium-40. How long does it take for half those potassium-40 atoms to become argon-40 atoms? It would take more than one billion years. How, one might ask, is it possible to measure such a slow rate? The reason accurate measurements are possible is that atoms are so small or, alternately, a very small sample of potassium-40 contains a very large number of atoms. Thus, for only 0.001 gram (1 ounce is about 28 grams) of potassium-40, about 250 atoms decay to argon-40 each second. Measuring a number that large is not difficult.

Some people object to radiometric dating because, they claim, one does not know what the sample, usually a rock, was like when it formed. Or, in the analogy given earlier, how could one know that the present rate of building homes accounts for all the homes seen? Is it safe to assume that the land was initially empty?

Such questions concerning the analogy might be pertinent. But in the potassium-argon case we know the answer: for a certain kind of rock, no argon was present when the rock formed.

Think of the molten lava poured out by a volcano. The rock formed by the cooled lava contains several compounds of potassium. But the molten lava can contain no argon: because argon is unreactive, it cannot become a part of any chemical compound in the rock; and because it is a gas with a very low boiling point, -186° Celsius (about -302° Fahrenheit), none can dissolve in the hot lava. At the beginning, then, no argon is present. When the rock cools, argon-40 begins to build up because of the decay of potassium-40. Later, by measuring the amounts of potassium-40 and argon-40 present, a geologist can determine the age of the rock, that is, the time elapsed since its cooling. The more argon-40 present, the older the rock.[4]

Scientific Consensus: The Scenario 59

The potassium-argon method yields great ages for many rocks. Thus, in northern New Jersey several Beemerville igneous rocks (the material in an igneous rock was once molten) yield ages between 425 and 450 million years. Rocks of the Palisades Sill, also in New Jersey, are about 190 million years old. Other places and ages (in millions of years) of rocks according to the potassium-argon method are the following: Portland, Connecticut, 265; Spruce Pine, North Carolina, 349; Parrysound, Ontario, 970; Keystone, South Dakota, 1520; Viking Lake, Saskatchewan, 1850; Bikita, Zimbabwe, 2550.[5]

Geologists use several other radiometric methods to determine the ages of rocks. These methods also require information about the initial state of a rock, that is, what it was like when it first cooled. By now, geologists have developed several ingenious ways to ascertain this initial state. In many cases, they make a tentative assumption about the initial state of a rock or a rock formation; subsequent independent methods produce similar ages and therefore add support to the determination of age.[6]

Decay of potassium to argon occurs in one step. Several multi-step processes also provide the basis of radiometric dating of rocks. In each of the following four processes, one atom decays to another, the second decays to a third, and so forth, until a nonradioactive atom forms. Thus, in 14 steps uranium-238 decays to lead-206; in ten steps, thorium-232 to lead-208; in 11 steps, uranium-235 to lead-207; and in 11 steps, neptunium-237 to bismuth-209. Just as the decay of potassium-40 to argon-40 can be shown by laboratory measurements to be very slow, measurements show each of these processes to be very slow, consuming from several hundred million up to a few billion years for a significant amount of change. None of the four processes depends upon any of the others; they constitute independent methods of determining age. For a given rock or rock formation, these independent methods have in many cases yielded the same age, several hundred million or even a few billion years.

Investigators have applied the radiometric method to meteorites as well as rocks that were always on the earth. Analysis of the one-step decay of palladium-107 to silver-107 in the massive Allende meteorite that fell in northern Mexico in 1969 yielded an age of 4.6 billion years, the greatest age found radiometrically.[7,8]

Astronomical Methods. Astronomical distances can also lead to conclusions about the age of Creation. For example, the sun is about 93 million miles from the earth and the speed of light is 300,000 kilometers (186,000 miles) per second. The time taken for sunlight to reach the earth is 93 million miles divided by 186,000 miles per second, or 500 seconds, about eight minutes. The sunlight that we observe at the present moment proves to us that God created the sun at least eight minutes ago. Similarly, light from the nearest star (besides the sun) takes about four years to reach the earth; we conclude that God created that star at least four years ago. For stars farther away, we deduce that the latest possible time of creation was even earlier. Some stars are so far away that their light takes several billion years to reach us, and so we conclude that they were created at least several billion years ago.

Evidently each of these calculations depends upon two measurements. We need to know the speed of light and the distance from us of the object of interest. That the speed of light is and always has been 300,000 kilometers (186,000 miles) per second is not in doubt. What is of interest here are the ways astronomers determine distances.

They use a stepwise procedure. First, they ascertain the distances of some of the heavenly objects closest to us, the sun and the planets of the solar system. For the next step, determination of the distance to the nearest star after the sun, one must know the distances determined for the solar system. In a similar way, later steps utilize the results of previous steps. The entire process includes several steps and the error could tend to accumulate going from step to step. Therefore, one might think that the calculations of the greatest distances contain considerable error, and that claims of great age determined by astronomical methods would be highly questionable. But one of the strengths of astronomical methods is that cross-checks are possible. After the first few very reliable steps, the path branches; parallel steps lead to the end of the path.

The first step depends upon observing the object of interest in a cloudless night sky from two different places. Instead of concentrating at first on distant objects such as the moon and the other planets, think of an object very close to the earth. Suppose the object is a lighted balloon some distance above the earth. How can you determine how high it is?

You can observe the position of the light of the balloon against the background pattern of stars; in fact, you could imagine a line extending from your position to a certain star. Suppose the balloon is on that line. Then you could move a known distance—say, 0.1 mile—and make the observation again. The stars, far away, would not seem to move. Imagine a line from you to the same star again. Because of the great distance of the stars, the two lines would be essentially parallel. But while the balloon lies on the first line, it does not lie on the second. Imagine a third line, this one from your eyes—after you have moved—to the balloon. Knowing the distance you moved, 0.1 mile, and the angle between the third line and the two parallel lines, you can determine the distance to the balloon.[9]

Scientific Consensus: The Scenario   61

In a similar way, two observers at points on the earth that are several thousand miles apart, making simultaneous observations, can use the star background to determine the distance of a planet several hundred million miles away. Astronomers determine distances to the planets and the sun in this way. One result is the earth-sun distance, 93 million miles.

This information makes it possible to proceed to the second step and determine distances of some stars beyond the solar system. Since the earth completes its circular orbit in one year, in six months it moves from one point in its orbit to the opposite side of the circular orbit whose diameter is 186 million miles (that is, 2 X 93 million miles). With a base line of 186 million miles instead of 0.1 mile (for the balloon) or several thousand miles (for distances of the sun and the planets), astronomers can determine the distances of many nearby stars. For the distances obtained in the three examples just given, the base of the triangle is 0.1 mile in the first, several thousand miles in the second, and 186 million miles in the third. The distances of more distant stars are too great to use triangles.

To proceed to other methods of determining star distances, consider the difference between *apparent brightness* and *absolute brightness*. What we observe is the apparent brightness of an object, whether it is a light bulb or a star. We might observe Star A and Star B to have the same brightness, but suppose Star B is actually much farther away than Star A. Since apparent brightness diminishes with distance, evidently Star B is actually much brighter than Star A. If those two stars were instead at the same distance from us, the apparent brightness of Star B would be much greater than that of Star A. Obviously, to compare brightnesses, we want to imagine the stars all at the same distance. Therefore, astronomers have chosen a standard distance, 32.6 light years. (A light year is the distance light travels in one year.) Thus, the apparent brightness of a star that is 32.6 light years away is its absolute brightness. (Astronomers could have chosen any value to be standard. Astronomical results do not depend upon the choice of standard any more than the boiling of water depends upon which thermometer, Fahrenheit or Celsius, one uses to measure the temperature of boiling water.)

Using a simple law of physics, we know the relation between apparent brightness and distance. Thus, if the distance of one star is 32.6 light years and second star of equal absolute brightness is twice as far away, that is, 65.2 light years away, the apparent brightness of the second will be one-fourth that of the first. If the distance of the second star is three times that of the first, that is, 97.8 light years away, its apparent brightness will be one-ninth of the apparent brightness of the first star, and so forth.

Because astronomers know this relation between apparent brightness, absolute brightness, and distance, they need to know only two of those three quantities to determine the third. This rule is the key that unlocks for us vast reaches of the physical universe. This rule enables us to possess an enormous amount of information about distant stars and galaxies. Let us see how this rule makes possible the determination of distances.

First, we return to the large number of stars whose distances astronomers can determine using the triangle whose base is 186 million miles. Astronomers observe many differences between the stars of this group. For example, the apparent brightness of one class of stars varies periodically; perhaps in one such variable star a given level of apparent brightness returns weekly; in another, every two weeks, and so forth. But the distances of these stars is known and so, using the rule connecting apparent brightnesses, absolute brightnesses, and distances, astronomers can calculate the absolute brightnesses of these stars.

Now, comparing the absolute brightnesses and the period of variability (one week, two weeks, or whatever), astronomers made one of the most important discoveries of the twentieth century: *The period of variability is related to absolute brightness.* For this particular kind of variable star, determination of the period of variability is enough to determine absolute brightness.

But this kind of variable star exists at greater distances as well, distances too great to determine using the triangle whose base is 186 million miles. Measurement of the period of variability of such a star will, however, enable one to know its absolute brightness. Obviously, its apparent brightness, the observed brightness, will be known. Using the rule relating the three quantities once again, astronomers can therefore calculate the distance of such a star, because they know the apparent brightness and can calculate the absolute brightness using the period of variability. This procedure constitutes the third step in determining astronomical distances, whereas the first two steps utilize triangles whose bases are several thousand and 186 million miles, respectively.

Astronomers relate other properties of stars to their absolute brightness and, step by step, determine distances farther away. Finally, the properties of entire clusters of stars and even whole galaxies play a role in ascertaining very great distances. Some stars are several billion light years distant, indicating creation of those stars at least several billion years ago. It is important, however, that the later steps are not simply sequential; through parallel paths, astronomers have determined great ages.

Scientific Consensus: The Scenario

The Evolutionary Scenario

The brief outline of the evolutionary scenario presented here is generally accepted by the natural scientific community. The scenario begins with the so-called big bang and carries through to life as we know it. There is no "one" accepted scenario, and so I shall occasionally note a few points of difference.

But the entire matter is, of course, extremely controversial from the point of view of a minority of the natural scientific community and a large number of people outside that community. I attempt a critical analysis of some parts of the scenario in Chapters 6 and 7.

The Big Bang. Big bang theory says that expansion of the universe began between ten and twenty billion years ago. What the term "big bang" means is that the universe began extremely small, much smaller than an atom. We do not know what it would mean to say that it began at a "point."[10] In any case, space and time for such a universe do not mean the same as the space and time we know. In some way, space and time were bound together. The universe was very hot and compressed. According to the general relativity theory of Einstein, such a universe would expand. This expansion is called the big bang. Cosmologists held to this comparatively simple picture of the big bang for several decades.[11]

Some recent suggestions concerning the big bang are not necessarily part of the "scientific consensus"; too many scientists disagree. These ideas are, however, part of the present discussion; they give us a sense of how the scientific community functions with respect to questions about origins. Thus, in recent years some cosmologists have intensified efforts to elucidate the "beginning." They have asked what caused the big bang and even what occurred before the big bang. A digression to explain a few ideas developed by physicists is necessary.

Physicists often discuss a phenomenon in terms of a *field*. The *magnetic field* is a familiar example. A magnet can attract a piece of iron even though the two are not in contact. The *field* of the magnet thus affects the piece of iron. Similarly, the *gravitational field* is responsible for gravity; here, too, attraction exists even though the objects are not in contact. Physicists think that ultimately the various fields are but manifestations of a single unified field.

Physicists also say that the different fields, as well as the unified field, are *quantized*. This term refers to the *energy levels* of the field; it says that the differences between those levels are finite. A staircase provides an analogy. Suppose one drops an object from the level of the top step, Step 1, that stops (in this case) on the only step it hits, Step 4. The dropped object, which had energy while falling, will, as it stops moving, impart its energy to Step 4. Now drop the same object from Step 1 to Step 5. Because Step 5 is farther from Step 1, it will receive more energy than did Step 4. The point to note is that the amount of energy Step 5 receives is a finite, not an infinitesimal, amount greater than that which Step 4 receives. This is so because the difference in the two energies is proportional to the difference in the height of the two steps, and this difference in height is finite, not infinitesimal. As a result, one can say that the energy levels of the staircase are *quantized*. (To put it another way: as you climb the staircase, you can climb one step, two steps, three steps, and so forth; but you cannot climb 2.3 steps. The energy you then use must be enough to climb one step, two steps, three steps, and so forth; but you will not use the amount of energy corresponding to 2.3 steps.)

Fields are quantized in that their strengths can increase or decrease finite, but not infinitesimally small, amounts. One particular consequence of the quantization of the strength of a field is of importance here. *The time that the strength of a field increases or decreases is uncertain.* The staircase analogy is not very good here, but it is as if the following were true: we know that the object that imparts energy can move not only from Step 1 to Step 4 or Step 5, but it can also move between other steps—say, from Step 4 to Step 5, or from Step 5 to Step 7, and so forth. Furthermore, the uncertainty of time in this case would mean that *we cannot tell when the object is going to move down one or more steps*.

Some physicists apply these ideas to the beginning of the big bang. Nothing but a quantized field existed. Then this field changed: the compressed, hot universe began to expand. But such a fluctuation could not have been infinitesimally small. Also—and this is a relatively new big bang idea—at some uncertain time before this "beginning," a fluctuation in the field led to the "beginning."[12]

The uncertainty in quantum fluctuation is fundamental. Stephen Hawking, well-known theoretical physicist and professor of mathematics at Cambridge University, combined this idea with certain ideas from Einstein's general relativity theory concerning space and time and suggests *the possibility of the nonexistence of a time zero* and that, in fact, space and time would form a "closed surface without boundary." In such a universe we could not speak of a boundary of either space or time. It would then be a closed universe. Hawking said:

> So long as the universe had a beginning, we could suppose it had a creator. But if the universe is really completely self-contained, having no boundary or edge, it would have neither beginning nor

Scientific Consensus: The Scenario 65

end: it would simply be. What place then, for a creator?[13]

Some physicists state this conclusion in another way: the laws of physics, especially those that relate time and space, can account for creation.

Certain cosmologists make another radical suggestion for the time immediately after the big bang. Here, too, no consensus yet exists. The suggestion is that very shortly after the beginning of the big bang, for a short period the universe expanded much more rapidly than previously imagined. This rapid expansion gave the theory its name: the *inflationary theory*. The theory answers some questions about the unusual distribution of galaxies determined by astronomers. Some cosmologists have made a few serious scientific objections to the theory. What is truly objectionable, however, are the statements some cosmologists have made concerning this theory. Since inflationary theory solves previous problems, some claim that divine intervention is no longer needed to explain the structure of the universe. It permits the existence of any number—trillions, or any desired number—of other "universes," presumably giving advocates of the anthropic cosmological principle (discussed in Chapter 4) whatever they need. Sounding like Stephen Hawking in the above quotation, cosmologist Henry Tye of Cornell University said that inflationary theory changed the philosophical question, "Why did God do what he did?" into a scientific question; if scientists have the correct model, they can calculate the results.[14]

Later big bang events are less controversial. At the beginning nothing existed but quantum fields, that is, nothing but energy. Expansion and cooling followed; matter began to appear. One millionth of one millionth of a second after the beginning (the postulated period of inflation was already over), cooling produced many particles familiar to us, such as electrons and photons. A photon is a "particle" of light; more properly, a particle of light energy. Particles called *quarks* appeared. Within one millionth of a second after the beginning, groups of three quarks (not all the same) began binding together to make up either protons or neutrons, particles familiar to us. Very soon all the free quarks were gone.

At about three minutes after the beginning, the temperature was still extremely high, but cool enough to permit protons and neutrons to combine. This joining together of protons and neutrons, an example of nuclear fusion, actually requires a very high temperature. Today nuclear fusion occurs only in the interior of a star, in a hydrogen bomb, and more recently, in controlled fusion devices. The first fusion consisted of the combination of two protons and two neutrons. This cluster of four particles is the nucleus of the helium atom. Eventually, but not at this time, some helium nuclei fused to make the nuclei of heavier atoms.[15]

Within 700,000 years, expansion and cooling permitted electrons, negatively charged, to combine with both protons and helium nuclei, both positively charged. Thus atoms formed. The combination of one proton and one electron is the hydrogen atom and the combination of the cluster of two protons and two neutrons, the helium nucleus, with two electrons is the helium atom. Two hydrogen atoms combine to form the hydrogen molecule; hydrogen gas is made up of hydrogen molecules. Helium atoms do not combine with other atoms. (In fusion, helium *nuclei*, not atoms, combine with other nuclei.)

At this time, 700,000 years after the beginning, the universe consisted of radiation (that is, photons) and neutral particles, including hydrogen and helium. The radiation did not disappear. But as the universe expanded the radiation "cooled," that is, the wavelength of the radiation increased. Calculations show that by now the wavelength should be very long, in the microwave region, and correspond to a temperature about three degrees above absolute zero. Microwave measurements in the 1960s confirmed the existence of this radiation. In 1989 the Cosmic Background Explorer satellite launched by the U.S. National Aeronautics and Space Administration (NASA) very accurately measured this radiation, which corresponds to a temperature of 2.735 degrees Celsius. What is particularly interesting is that the radiation observed by means of the satellite is precisely the *kind* of radiation ("kind" is not explained further here) that is convertible to temperature, just as the model predicted.[16] On May 23, 1992, George F. Smoot, head of the NASA Explorer satellite team, made a sensational announcement: the Explorer had detected very small variations in the background radiation. In addition, in early 1993 the detection of variations was confirmed by extensive analysis of measurements made by a balloon in 1989.

Since matter is not distributed evenly throughout the universe—after all, there are void spaces between stars and galaxies—these variations had been predicted. When the variations were first announced by Smoot, they were generally taken to be confirmation of the prediction. A few physicists, however, are not so sure: they think the variations may be due to gravitational waves. If Smoot's analysis is correct, the results strongly support the big bang theory—in particular, the inflationary version of the big bang theory. Certain other versions of the big bang theory are thus ruled out.

The Formation of Stars and Galaxies. According to big bang theory, during the next four billion years (that is, up to six billion years ago if the beginning was ten billion years ago), gravitational attraction caused aggregates of hydrogen and helium to form. As objects drew together because of gravity they released energy. (Thus, a meteor falling to the earth or the moon can release enough gravitational energy to form a large crater.) Therefore, the temperature of the hydrogen and the helium increased. These very hot aggregates are stars. Aggregates of aggregates, galaxies, also formed. Two kinds of nuclear processes occurred in the hot hydrogen and helium. One is nuclear fusion: hydrogen nuclei, which are protons, and helium nuclei (clusters of two protons and two neutrons) fuse in various ways to form the nuclei of heavier elements. Fusion causes the release of energy. Eventually, fusion produces the nuclei of many elements, such as carbon, oxygen, fluorine, chlorine, calcium, and, the heaviest of this group, iron. But the fusion process does not proceed beyond iron because instead of releasing energy, fusion beyond iron requires energy input; in other words, such fusion is an energetically unfavorable process.

For the production of nuclei heavier than iron, the second nuclear process is important. Neutrons collided with nuclei, electrons were emitted, and heavier atoms were the result. Later, some stars collapsed and then exploded. The nuclei became cool enough to pick up electrons, neutralizing the electric charge on the nucleus, thus forming atoms. In this way, the heavier elements became "available" outside of stars and added to the hydrogen and helium already present.

Around five billion years ago, another process occurred that is of particular interest here. Before this time, stars had formed from the original material of the big bang; subsequently some had collapsed and exploded. Those "original" stars are called first generation stars. But the heavy elements, along with the hydrogen and helium already outside of the stars, drew together by gravitational attraction and formed new stars, second generation stars. Our sun is such a star.

The Formation of Planets. The theory of planet formation is generally the same in the big bang theory as in other cosmological theories (not described here).

Some of the aggregates that formed from the elements dispersed in space were not large enough to become stars. The energy released as the elements came together by gravitational attraction was not nearly enough to cause nuclear fusion. These "cold" aggregates near the sun are the planets. The inner planets (Mercury, Venus, the earth, and Mars) as well as the asteroids (a belt of debris between Mars and Jupiter) contain enough heavy elements so that they eventually became solid. (Much of the earth's interior is, of course, molten, but the molten matter would become solid if it were at the crust's temperature.) The outer planets are rich in the lighter elements. By about 4.6 billion years ago, the solar system reached its present form.

Early Earth History. Let us use this time, 4.6 billion years ago, as a new starting point. At that time the earth had no atmosphere, no water, and, of course, no life. At this "starting point" it was similar to the present-day moon except, of course, that the earth was much larger than the moon. For the first 200 million years, radioactive decay of some elements produced considerable heat. (Even today, some of the energy from radioactive decay in the earth's crust keeps the earth at its present temperature.) But by the end of this 200-million-year period, the crust had cooled significantly.

For the next 400 million years, that is, until the earth was about 600 million years old, molten material from the interior rose to form volcanoes. These volcanoes delivered some gases to the surface of the earth, including carbon dioxide, nitrogen, and water vapor; and so for the first time the earth had an atmosphere. As we shall see, the question of whether oxygen was present is very important but has not been answered to the satisfaction of everyone.

Chemicals Necessary for Life. The next 500 million years, bringing us up to 3.5 billion years ago, are extremely critical in the evolutionary scenario. Evolutionists maintain that during this period complex molecules and then the simplest living cells formed. The starting materials were carbon dioxide, nitrogen, water vapor, hydrogen, methane, carbon monoxide, and ammonia.[17] Meteorites may have carried to the earth other simple molecules from interstellar space. Many of the molecules assumed to be in the sequence between the first molecules and the desired products would, however, react with—in other words, be destroyed by—oxygen if it were present. If any significant amount of oxygen were present in this "primitive earth atmosphere," the evolution of life from nonlife as presently perceived could not have occurred.

During this 500-million-year period, according to the evolutionary model, the simple molecules reacted, perhaps with the aid of large electrical discharges, lightning, and sometimes at high temperatures, to form more complex molecules. In addition, certain substances not in the atmosphere but on the surface of the earth could take part in the process of forming complex molecules.

Among the molecules necessary for the functioning of the living cell, eight classes are of particular interest. Most of these biologically-interesting molecules are large and complicated. Since the evolutionary scenario calls for the spontaneous formation of these molecules, it is necessary to describe them. The remainder of this section consists of a description of the properties and functions of the eight classes—amino acids, polypeptides, proteins,

Scientific Consensus: The Scenario

sugars, DNA (deoxyribonucleic acid) and RNA (ribonucleic acid), base-modified riboses, phosphate, and fatty acids. (Except where indicated in the following discussion, RNA refers to the form of RNA that carries the message, mRNA.)

(1) According to evolutionary theory, *amino acids* appeared early when some of the simple molecules of the primitive atmosphere reacted. An amino acid is an organic compound that contains the following: (a) an acidic group, that is, a group of atoms in which a carbon atom has a certain group of four bonds to other atoms—one to another carbon, two to one oxygen, and one to another oxygen, with the latter oxygen also bonded to a hydrogen atom; and (b) an amino group, which is basic (the chemical opposite of acidic), consisting of a nitrogen atom bonded to a carbon atom and to two hydrogen atoms.

(2) *Polypeptides* appeared when amino acids reacted with each other. In this reaction, the acid group of one molecule reacts with the basic amino group of another molecule. One of the hydrogen atoms attached to the nitrogen of the basic group leaves to react with the singly bonded oxygen of the acidic group, along with its hydrogen. Water, a combination of the three released hydrogen and oxygen atoms, H_2O, is a by-product of the reaction.

Therefore, the main product is a molecule that contains the two original amino acids, less the water molecule. Notice, however, that this larger molecule still has one unreacted amino group and one unreacted acid group; in other words, it is still an amino acid. Therefore, this new molecule can react with another amino acid and make a still larger amino acid, and so forth. A polypeptide is the product of several such reactions.

These first polypeptides would have been similar to, but much simpler than, proteins. According to evolutionary theory, the first polypeptides may have functioned as proteins and even as enzymes, which are biological catalysts. (Catalysts are substances that cause certain reactions to take place rapidly.) Actual enzymes are much more complicated; evolutionists assume that they developed later.

(3) *Proteins* consist of many amino acids—ranging from as few as eight to as many as 500—and form according to the kind of reaction described above, with the amino group of one amino acid reacting with the acid group of another, and so forth. Only twenty different amino acids combine to form almost all known proteins, even though a large number of amino acids exist. Obviously, since a protein consists of up to 500 amino acids, some amino acids appear repeatedly in a given protein.

The backbone of a protein is a chain of atoms. The sequence in this chain is the same in all proteins: a repeating -C-C-N- unit; three such units are ...C-C-N-C-C-N-C-C-N.... The hyphens designate bonds, the C's represent carbon atoms, and the N's represent nitrogen atoms. Of course, the chains vary greatly in length from protein to protein. The component amino acids differ from each other. The difference arises because chain carbon atoms form two bonds in addition to bonds to two other atoms of the chain. We are interested in the central atom of the -C-C-N- group. As that carbon atom forms two additional bonds, one might be to a hydrogen atom and one to a group consisting of one carbon atom and three hydrogen atoms; in another -C-C-N- group, that central carbon atom might form one bond to a hydrogen atom and another bond to a group consisting of three carbon and seven hydrogen atoms. The difference in the twenty constituent amino acids of proteins lies in these attached groups or "side chains."

Thus, each -C-C-N- with side chains constitutes a unit, a unit with an identifiable amino acid origin. Since a given protein requires no more than twenty different amino acids, this unit appears several times in the sequence of hundreds of amino acids. Each protein has a purpose for existence, so the sequence of units in the protein is very much like the sequence of letters in a sentence, communicating a message. It is possible to "read" the sequence of units (the -C-C-N- groups with their side chains) in a protein, much as it is possible to read the sequence of units (letters) in a sentence.[18] This sequence of units enables the protein to fulfill its purpose.

The theoretical problem of accounting for the existence of proteins is formidable. This difficulty arises partially because they are made in cells. However, functioning cells have many requirements, including the presence of certain chemicals. Chapter 6 discusses some of the problems.

(4) The functioning cell requires *sugars*, another class of large molecules. Sugars are complicated combinations of carbon, hydrogen, and oxygen. Evolutionists assume that sugars, too, were products of reactions between some of the molecules available on the primitive earth.

(5) *DNA* and *RNA*, the famous molecules related to the "code of life," also had to appear for the first time. The DNA molecules contain the code for their own replication, carrying information from generation to generation. They also carry the information necessary to manufacture needed proteins.

The RNA molecule consists of a chain of alternate phosphate (one phosphorus atom plus four oxygen atoms) and modified *ribose* groups. A modified ribose group consists of five carbon atoms, seven hydrogen atoms, and two oxygen atoms, along with the modification, an attached base. The attached base varies from ribose group to ribose group along the chain.

Scientific Consensus: The Scenario   71

If it were not for the attached base, RNA would be simply a chain of alternate phosphate and ribose groups. But each *modified* ribose group is like a letter of a word in a sentence. The sequencing of the different ribose groups is important because it carries a message.

In this case, only four "letters" are possible; the symbols used and the bases attached to the ribose group are, respectively: C, cytosine; U, uracil; A, adenine; and G, guanine. Each of those four molecules is made up of carbon, nitrogen, hydrogen, and (except for adenine) oxygen atoms; the largest (guanine) contains fifteen atoms. The arrangement and number of atoms vary from base to base.

The DNA molecule differs from the RNA molecule in three ways: first, the ribose group contains one less oxygen atom (hence the name *deoxy-*ribonucleic acid). Second, one of the bases in RNA (U, uracil) is slightly modified to form thymine, symbolized by T. Thus, RNA carries the code by means of various combinations of C, U, A, and G; in DNA, by C, T, A, and G. Each of these letters represents a *nucleotide*. Third, the DNA molecule is much longer than the RNA molecule.

Suppose two DNA chains lie next to each other. An A base of one molecule might be near a T of the next; or, a G base near a T; and so forth. It is one thing to be relatively near; it is another thing to bond together. If a G base and a C base are sufficiently close, three weak bonds form between the two bases; similarly, two weak bonds form between an A and a T. The two bases bonded together are *base pairs*. (Bonding between the other conceivable pairs, A-C, A-G, T-G, and C-T, as well as the like-like, such as A-A, does not occur.) We can now imagine two *complementary* DNA molecules: If the sequence of nucleotides in the first is A, G, T, C,..., the sequence in the second is T, C, A, G,...; then A in the first bonds with T in the second, G with C, T with A, and so forth. The complementary chains bond at every base position.

To consider the shape of this double chain, consider another important property of molecules. Very few molecules consisting of more than two atoms form straight chains. No large molecules form straight chains. In the DNA case, each of the two complementary, antiparallel chains is a spiral. The two chains fit together and constitute the famous "double helix" discovered in 1953 by James Watson and Francis Crick, molecular biologists at Cambridge University.

Also, some DNA molecules can be extremely long, containing several million units or "letters." DNA molecules are the information-carrying component of the *chromosome*. In the human cell there are 23 chromosomes. The entire information content of the cell, that is, all the genetic information of all the chromosomes of the cell—for the human cell, about 6 billion base pairs—is the *genome* of the organism.

DNA and RNA molecules are combinations of base-modified riboses and phosphate. According to evolutionary theory, these substances had to be present for the first DNA and RNA molecules to form.

(6) *Base-modified riboses* form by reaction between one of several bases and a certain sugar. These bases were in turn the products of earlier reactions involving simple molecules, some of which were components of the primitive atmosphere.

(7) *Phosphate* is postulated to have come from the phosphate occurring in many rocks of the crust of the earth. The base-modified riboses and phosphate then formed the appropriate alternating chains in DNA and RNA.

(8) *Fatty acids* are also needed for a cell. According to evolutionary theory, the same primitive substances—water, hydrogen, and so forth—reacted to make fatty acids, that is, long-chain organic acids. The formation of lipids required these acids; the synthesis of cell membranes then became possible.

So much for the eight classes of substances needed for the living cell. Finally, of course, the components of the cell—DNA, RNA, proteins, and a cell membrane—had to get together. Evolutionists claim that many of the reactions already described and the assimilation of the components of the cell occurred in a "hot dilute soup," a reference to bodies of water containing the components that were warm enough for reactions to occur. The hot dilute soup is more properly referred to as the pre-biotic or primordial liquid medium.

Because of the difficulties of visualizing the spontaneous formation of the cell, some evolutionists have postulated an intermediate stage between the components of the cell and the cell as we know it; they claim that a *protocell* formed in this intermediate stage.[19]

Protein Formation. An important function of living cells is to make proteins. Outlining that process demonstrates its complexity and the magnitude of evolutionists' claims:

(1) One of the two strands of DNA, which never leaves the nucleus, forms a complementary copy of part of its chain; this copy is an RNA molecule.

(2) This RNA molecule carries a coded message from part of the DNA molecule; therefore, it is called messenger RNA, or mRNA. The code it carries is the *genetic code*.

(3) The message that the DNA molecule sends contains instructions for the sequencing of amino acids in a protein that is to be synthesized. A given DNA molecule can send messages for a large number of proteins; which

protein is synthesized depends upon which part of the DNA strand is copied. The code for a protein takes about one thousand nucleotides, and so the mRNA molecule is about that length. This group of about one thousand sequential nucleotides in the DNA molecule is the *gene*.

(4) Three successive code letters carried by mRNA constitute the *codon*, the instruction for putting one of the twenty amino acids in its proper place in the sequence. For example, the sequence of the nucleotides U, U, and G carry the code to place in the protein sequence the amino acid leucine, in which the side chain consists of a group of four carbon and nine hydrogen atoms; likewise, UCA is the codon for serine; and so forth.

(5) Consider the number of possible messages. Four code letters—U, C, A, and G—exist. A single instruction requires three of the letters. How many different instructions can DNA send? The first letter can be one of four; for each of those four, the second letter can be one of four, each leading to four possibilities for the third letter. Therefore, a three-letter code allows 4 X 4 X 4, or 64, different messages or codons.

(6) These 64 codons perform several functions. Sixty-one code for the placing of the 20 amino acids. Two codons of the 61 do double duty: besides coding for the placing of amino acids, they also initiate the formation of chains, that is, the reaction of amino acids to make longer chains, eventually making the desired protein. The other three of the 64 codons perform other functions, such as terminating the incorporation of amino acids in the growing chain.

Of the several substances that the cell requires, one group of molecules is especially important. It is the transfer RNA (tRNA) family. Each member of this family recognizes a specific triplet (a group of three letters) in mRNA and decodes it. This tRNA molecule provides the instructions for putting a particular amino acid into the proper place in the sequence. Only one tRNA molecule codes for each of the 20 amino acids.

Now the process is complete: another protein has been made according to the prescription given by the appropriate part of the DNA chain. Molecular biologists frequently refer to the *central dogma of molecular biology*, which summarizes the synthesis: DNA to RNA to protein.

Evolution Beyond the First Cells. According to the generally-accepted evolutionary scenario, the earliest life on the earth, which appeared when the earth was about 1.1 billion years old, or 3.5 billion years ago, consisted of single cells. They could reproduce. Photosynthesis, that is, metabolic reactions that utilize sunlight, carbon dioxide, and water, occurred. Oxygen molecules are among the products of photosynthesis reactions. This process is common to all plants.

The process continued for about 1.3 billion years until the earth was about 2.4 billion years old, or 2.2 billion years ago. During the next period of about 800 million years, until about 1.4 billion years ago, many kinds of single-celled marine organisms appeared. Subsequently the single cells that appeared were more complex.

According to the evolutionary scenario, the accompanying table summarizes the appearance of life forms after the complex single cells had already appeared.

Appearance of Life Forms

Approx. Earth Age (bill)	Beginning of Period (yrs ago)	Events During This Period
3.8	850 mill.	Multicellular life; e.g., jelly fish
3.9	675 mill.	Invertebrates
4.2	410 mill.	Land: ferns, club mosses, centipedes; water: fish
4.3	345 mill.	Land: insects; land and water: amphibians
4.3	280 mill.	Reptiles; coniferous forests
4.4	195 mill.	Mammals; dinosaurs
4.5	136 mill.	Flowering plants; birds
4.5	67 mill.	Dinosaurs disappear
4.6	3.5 mill.	Footprints similar to human left in volcanic ash
4.6	2 mill.	Primate that makes tools
4.6	1.6 mill.-500 thous.	*Homo erectus* appears, spreads widely
4.6	100 thous.	*Homo sapiens*; Neanderthal; fire is used
4.6	30 thous.	Modern *Homo sapiens* everywhere but Americas; art
4.6	12 thous.	*Homo sapiens* in Americas

Concerning the history of life as summarized in the table, two additional matters are important.

First, before about 600 million years ago, a relatively small number of organisms existed. Rather suddenly large numbers of species, many quite complex, appeared in the fossil record. This appearance is "the Cambrian explosion." ("Cambrian" is the name of a geological period.)

Second, the disappearance of dinosaurs about 67 million years ago was actually accompanied by the disappearance of most other life as well. The widely accepted reason for this disappearance was a collision of a meteor with the earth. This collision was the cause of dust, darkness, and temperature change over a long period of time.

The next two chapters critically examine several parts of the evolutionary scenario.

Chapter Six
Analysis: From Inert Matter to Cells

The purpose of this chapter is to analyze the inert-matter-to-cells part of the scenario using natural scientific information. Chapter 7 analyzes the cell-to-human-beings part of the scenario. An analysis of the entire scenario from a biblical perspective is the subject of Chapters 8-11.

In this chapter we again encounter the confidence that evolutionary thinking generates. It is extremely difficult to accept the current evolutionary claim that, after many reactions, relatively simple chemicals became some of the most complicated molecules. But since chemists do understand individual chemical reactions, each of which is often a single step in a complicated chemical process, someone will always construct an ingenious model showing how a sequence of simple reactions can ultimately produce the complicated molecules necessary for life. If one assumes *a priori* that life did evolve from nonlife, then it is only a matter of choosing between clever models (or of claiming that the correct model is yet to come); it is not a matter of contending that life did not evolve from nonlife.

The First Reactions of Chemical Evolution

Search for Proof: Laboratory Simulations. Many scientists have reasoned this way: if the first living cells evolved from nonliving chemicals, then it should be possible to simulate in the laboratory some of the chemical steps in the postulated nonlife-to-life process. In the 1950s Stanley Miller and others subjected the postulated atmosphere of the primitive earth to the extreme conditions supposed to have existed: heat, ultraviolet radiation, electric discharge to simulate lightning, and so forth. In numerous experiments since the 1950s, chemists have synthesized in this way many compounds thought to have been prebiotic, including some amino acids.

For at least three reasons this procedure is questionable:

(1) This approach assumes more knowledge of the primitive atmosphere than we actually have. In particular, it assumes that the primitive atmosphere was a *reducing* atmosphere. The term "reduce" has a technical meaning of extreme importance in the present discussion.

To understand reduction, consider the fact that chemical reactions consist of the complete or partial transfer of electrons from one chemical species

Analysis: From Inert Matter to Cells

to another chemical species. If molecule A is capable of *reducing* molecule B in a reaction, then some of the electrons of molecule A (all molecules contain electrons) move at least part of the way toward molecule B when the two molecules react. In this example, molecule A is a *reducing agent* and the molecule toward which the electrons move, molecule B, is an *oxidizing agent*. Obviously, these two terms, oxidizing and reducing, are relative; in many cases, molecule B can transfer electrons to a molecule C; then molecule B would be the reducing agent and molecule C the oxidizing agent.

But the term "reducing atmosphere" is generally taken to mean that while some of the molecules in this presumed primitive earth atmosphere reacted with each other, none could receive electrons easily. Certainly none of those assumed to be present can receive electrons as easily as the oxygen molecule, an oxidizing agent.

Those who claim that the primitive earth atmosphere was a reducing atmosphere say two things: first, oxygen was not present; second, those molecules that were present could either yield electrons easily or at least did not receive them easily. Examples of such molecules postulated to be in the primitive atmosphere are water, carbon dioxide, and ammonia.

I doubt the assumption that oxygen molecules were not present in the primitive earth atmosphere. But the presence or absence of oxygen, an oxidizing agent, is an extremely important matter. If oxygen was present, it would have reacted with and therefore changed many other molecules either initially present or assumed to have formed later. For example, oxygen reacts with amino acids. Such a reaction would break an important link in the postulated sequence of steps between nonlife and life, which calls for the reaction of amino acids to form proteins.

A more familiar example of the destructive power of oxygen is its reaction with natural gas. The chief component of natural gas is methane, a small molecule consisting of one carbon atom and four hydrogen atoms. The reaction between oxygen and methane (if they are initially heated) is a vigorous burning reaction: if enough oxygen is present, all the methane is destroyed. The products are carbon dioxide and water. This burning reaction, as well as all other familiar forms of burning, such as the burning of gasoline or coal, are alike in that oxygen acts as an oxidizing agent: as oxygen receives electrons it reacts with and therefore changes the substances with which it reacts.

How high would the oxygen concentration in the primitive earth atmosphere have to be to break the chain in the postulated sequence of events that led from inorganic chemicals to life? Even a low concentration, such as one or two per cent (not nearly as high as the present level, 21 per cent) would have been enough; after all, reaction with and destruction of the critical molecules could occur any time during a period of several hundred million years.

The question of whether oxygen was present in the primitive earth atmosphere is important for another reason related to the postulated sequence of reactions leading from nonlife to life. In this sequence the radiation from the sun which reaches the earth plays a role. The sun's radiation covers a wide range of energies. Some is ultraviolet radiation. While all ultraviolet radiation is highly energetic, at present the atmosphere filters out most of the more energetic ultraviolet radiation. In the laboratory simulations referred to above, the presence of the more energetic ultraviolet radiation was considered a necessary condition. If all that ultraviolet radiation arrived at the surface of the earth today, life could not exist. But why does the atmosphere now filter out most of that radiation? The key is oxygen in the atmosphere.

At present, some of the more energetic ultraviolet radiation available in the upper atmosphere causes oxygen molecules, which consist of two oxygen atoms, to react to form ozone molecules, which consist of three oxygen atoms. The ozone formed acts as a screen for the more energetic ultraviolet radiation, severely limiting the amount that reaches the surface of the earth. (For this reason, widespread anxiety exists concerning the partial destruction of the ozone layer, a phenomenon probably due to ozone reaction with certain industrial substances that reach the upper atmosphere, such as chlorofluorocarbons.)

But evolutionary theory postulates that this lethal radiation was needed at the surface of the early earth. The theory states that certain small molecules of the primitive atmosphere could react with each other only if this radiation was available. If *some* oxygen was present, was it enough to form sufficient ozone to filter out the ultraviolet radiation necessary for the first nonlife-to-life reactions? According to several reports, the ozone screen exists even if the concentration of oxygen is only one thousandth of its present concentration, that is, even if its concentration is only a few hundredths of a per cent.

Note that nonlife-to-life evolution could not occur along the postulated lines if the oxygen concentration in the primitive atmosphere exceeded either of two concentrations: the concentration necessary to interfere with the postulated sequence, perhaps by destroying amino acids; or the concentration needed to produce enough ozone to filter out needed radiation.

What, then, was the actual concentration of oxygen? Reviewing this ques-

Analysis: From Inert Matter to Cells 79

tion, Charles Thaxton, Walter Bradley, and Roger Olsen listed three possible sources of oxygen in the atmosphere: volcanic exhalations; dissociation of water under the influence of radiation, that is, photodissociation of water; and photosynthesis, the metabolic process whereby plants, with the aid of radiation, cause carbon dioxide and water to react, with oxygen being one of the products.[1]

It is not necessary to consider photosynthesis here, because the present discussion focuses on the pre-biotic atmosphere, before photosynthesis could have occurred. Also, volcanoes cannot be the source of oxygen. Volcanic exhalations are at a very high temperature and any free oxygen present reacts with other substances, leaving no free oxygen. Volcanoes today do not produce free oxygen.

But it is necessary to consider the photodissociation of water. The photodissociation of water is the breakdown of water under the influence of ultraviolet radiation into hydrogen and oxygen molecules. The hydrogen molecule is much lighter than the oxygen molecule and therefore possesses a significantly greater tendency to escape the atmosphere of the earth, leaving a net balance of oxygen. Since 1960 some chemists and geologists have extensively studied this means of producing oxygen on the primitive earth. But investigators do not agree: depending upon the assumptions made, estimates of the concentration of oxygen for the early earth atmosphere range from less than one hundred-billionth of the present level up to one-fourth of the present level.[2] In any case, as oxygen formed, an ozone layer formed and reduced the amount of radiation that could cause the photodissociation of water; even if the process of photodissociation was once important, it eventually decreased in importance. On balance, it seems that the oxygen concentration in the pre-biotic atmosphere was between one-hundredth and one-tenth the present concentration, that is, at least a few tenths of one per cent and perhaps as high as two per cent.[3] It was probably high enough to cause a pre-biotic oxidation problem and almost certainly high enough to interfere with the need for ultraviolet radiation at the earth's surface in postulated early evolutionary processes.

Geological evidence also suggests the presence of oxygen in the early earth's atmosphere. Thus, many minerals are the oxides of metals, that is, they are compounds formed by combining oxygen with metal, such as iron oxide and uranium oxide. Detailed analysis of this situation lends credibility to the claim that the early earth's atmosphere may have contained free oxygen. Geologists have found iron and uranium oxide minerals at least 3.5 billion years old. Since a considerable amount of such material exists, the concentration of oxygen could not have been low. This argument does not prove that the *pre-biotic* atmosphere contained oxygen; after all, the oldest microfossils are older than 3.5 billion years. But the existence of these very old oxides does suggest either (a) that the concentration of oxygen arose to a high level at an unaccountably rapid rate after the first life appeared or (b) that oxygen was present before life existed, with no unaccountable rapid increase.[4] A scientist who desires to remove the unaccountable from the model he or she adopts is thus faced with a problem: the first possibility does not remove the unaccountable, but the second removes one kind of unaccountability while leaving the origin of life unaccountable.

Therefore, attempted laboratory simulations of reactions occurring before life existed seem to be flawed. The critical assumption that the primitive earth atmosphere was a reducing atmosphere, or at least one that contained too little oxygen to form an ozone screen, is almost certainly not justified.

(2) Another problem with these simulations is not so much with the simulations themselves, but with the difficulty of resolving *this* scientific question in the usual give-and-take manner, the procedure usually assumed to be a necessary part of natural scientific progress. In this procedure, scientists openly debate the validity of a scientific claim, taking into account all the available evidence. One can always understand why a proponent of a theory clings to that theory when it is challenged. But when the subject is evolution—especially the chemical evolution of life—the give-and-take procedure is often not used. Consider this statement concerning the origin of life by chemists James P. Ferris of the Rensselaer Polytechnic Institute and David A. Usher of Cornell University:

> The primitive atmosphere *must* have contained reducing equivalents [reducing agents] in some form to yield amino acids, since no biomolecules or their precursors are formed when a mixture of carbon dioxide, water, and nitrogen is sparked. Amino acids are formed when hydrogen [a reducing agent] is added to the mixture of carbon dioxide, water, and nitrogen, or when a mixture of carbon monoxide, water, nitrogen, and hydrogen [a reducing agent] is sparked.[5] (Emphasis added.)

The critical word here is *must*. If no reducing agent was present, or alternately, if a significant amount of oxygen was present, amino acids could not have formed. But Ferris and Usher assumed that amino acids and later other biomolecules did form. They place their formation within a sequence of events that led to the appearance of life. Therefore, *must*. Such a procedure, assuming the evolution of life and concluding that therefore the

Analysis: From Inert Matter to Cells

primitive atmosphere *must* have been reducing, is simply not the procedure used in ordinary scientific work. This type of assumption is but one of the ways, then, that evolutionary thinking has made an impact *within* the natural sciences.

In the 1920s A.I. Oparin, a Russian biochemist, led the way in developing some of the modern ideas on the evolution of life from nonliving chemicals. Compare the statement of Ferris and Usher above, made in 1988, with the following statement made by Oparin in the 1938 English edition of his book, *Origin of Life*. Oparin's remark refers to the entire sequence from nonlife to life, not just the question of nature of the primitive atmosphere.

> Life has neither arisen spontaneously nor has it existed eternally. It *must* have, therefore, resulted from a long evolution of matter, its origin being merely one step in the course of its historical development.[6] (Emphasis added.)

Here, too, *must* is critical. Reasoning that chemical evolution *must* have occurred just because life exists is not legitimate science. Perhaps the fact that Oparin is often considered the father of chemical evolutionary theory says something about the entire program of determining the sequence of chemical events that evolutionists assume produced life from nonlife.

The nature of the primitive atmosphere is a major subject of the book, *The Mystery of Life's Origin* (1984), by Thaxton, Bradley, and Olsen[7]; some of their conclusions are given in the above discussion. The authors treated each component of this question with the scientific caution one expects in a scientific book. But how did the chemical community receive this chemistry book?

Richard C. Lemmon, a prominent figure in the literature of chemical evolution, reviewed *Mystery* in the widely-circulated weekly chemical news publication of the American Chemical Society, *Chemical and Engineering News*. Lemmon did not discuss either the questions raised about the primitive atmosphere or any of the other major points of the book. But Lemmon did attack the book vigorously because the authors stated (only in their epilogue) that they believe in the creation of life by a Creator. It is a good thing that the following is not characteristic of scientific writing:

> The authors claim to have "presented a case that chemical evolution is highly implausible" in developing a scenario leading to life.

What, then, was Lemmon's objection?

> So what other explanation is there? Aha! If it's implausible, the authors think that we should turn from scientific inquiry and consider creationism. Knowing that their fellow scientists regard creationism as nonscientific, the authors try hard to put some sugar around their nonscientific pill.[8]

Here was an opportunity for fruitful dialogue about an *extremely* important chemical problem in the appropriate arena, a publication read by a very large number of chemists in many countries. It is almost impossible to discuss the details of chemical questions in most popular journals, but it is possible in this publication. Yet the issue was not debated. It is as if the question does not exist. It is reminiscent of the use of *must* in the quotations above, another proof that evolutionary theory has made a significant impact on activity within the natural sciences.

(3) The next problem with the laboratory simulation of the postulated evolution of life from nonlife arises with the latter steps of the process. In laboratory simulations of supposed reactions in the primitive earth's atmosphere, the experimenter inevitably guides the chemicals that are to react. While any process in an early earth situation would be random, laboratory experiments are not random, but planned. When the experiments do not produce the desired results, that is, molecules that are important biologically, the experimenters modify the conditions until the desired results are obtained.

Thaxton, Bradley, and Olsen listed some conditions imposed in laboratory simulations of pre-biotic reactions that do not represent the "unplanned" actual pre-biotic events.[9] Following are only some of the ways in which the investigator guides the reacting chemicals as he or she carries out a simulation experiment: (a) In simulation experiments, investigators used only some of the radiation presumed to have come from the sun. Using the rest of the radiation would cause other reactions to occur. (b) The investigators used much higher temperatures in the simulation experiments than can reasonably be expected to have existed for the necessary extended period on the early earth. (c) The electrical discharge used is an unrealistic substitute for actual lightning. (d) Simulated experiments do not include all the large number of chemicals—some of which would interfere with the "desired" reaction—that were actually present billions of years ago. It is not just oxygen that would interfere.

As we shall see later, the matter of guiding the chemicals supposed to have produced life is of incalculable importance. Consider the construc-

Analysis: From Inert Matter to Cells 83

tion of a computer program. A computer program guides by a series of instructions. These instructions consist of tiny "bits" of information. It is these bits that the computer sees and that enable it to carry out the program instructions. In the same way, the products of a laboratory simulation of early earth conditions contain a few bits of information, the very information the experimenter put into the reacting system when the experiment was planned. By contrast, the ultimate product, the cell, an extremely complicated entity, contains billions (maybe trillions) of information bits. If the laboratory experiments truly simulate the synthesis of a few simple molecules in the primitive atmosphere, then the primitive atmospheric conditions are the source of the few bits of information in those molecules. But it takes considerable imagination to imagine that the early earth was also the source of the virtually infinite amount of information in the simplest cell.

Other Searches for Proof. One reason some natural scientists attempt to show that life exists in other parts of the universe is their belief that such a demonstration would prove that evolution from nonlife to life occurs. Those who look for such evidence usually assume that if life does exist in other places, it evolved wherever the conditions were favorable—the right primitive atmosphere and so forth.

Thus, a principal reason for the U.S. NASA *Viking* mission to Mars in 1976 was to determine if traces of life exist on that planet. Of all the planets in the solar system besides the earth, Mars is the most likely to have had at some time in its history conditions capable of supporting life. On the surface of Mars *Viking* deposited equipment that executed several exotic chemical experiments, each of which could have produced results that prove the existence of life or, at least, of substances associated with life. No such evidence was found.[10]

In other research, investigators assume that if life can evolve from nonlife, then the appropriate conditions for such evolution existed in millions of places in the universe. They also assume that life did evolve in those places. Further evolution, finally producing civilizations, occurred on millions of planets. Some of those civilizations ultimately were able, much as we are able, to send out radio signals that can reach other galaxies. Finally, they assume that such radio signals were sent. Therefore, we should be able to detect such radio signals. Up until now, all attempts to find such signals have failed.[11]

Neither the attempt to find life on Mars or to detect meaningful radio signals from outer space would, if successful, prove that life evolved from nonlife. Success would only show that life can exist, but we already know that. After all, God could have created life in many places. Even so, the search for extra-terrestrial life may have another consequence: as the search becomes increasingly sophisticated, what conclusions should one make if the search continues to turn up nothing? There are two possible answers.

(a) The conditions for the evolution of life from nonlife are surprisingly rare; favorable conditions existed in at most a few places, perhaps only one place, the earth. This might be the answer of one who subscribes to some version of the anthropic principle. But those who accept this principle opt out of the discussion; they define their position so that one can neither prove nor disprove it. Their position is unfalsifiable.

(b) Life did not evolve; God created it. The random processes envisioned by those who attempt laboratory simulations of the first steps of the postulated evolutionary sequence are not relevant. The committed evolutionist obviously finds this answer entirely unacceptable.

Another part of the search for proof that life evolved from nonlife is the attempt to formulate a theory that can explain some of the difficult parts of the postulated sequence. One aspect of that search for appropriate theory concerns *thermodynamics*, which technically is the science of heat flow. Usually, however, it is applied more generally and includes the flow of any form of energy.

The following question summarizes the fundamental problem with chemical evolution: starting with disorder, how did energy flow through chemical systems to produce very great order? Can thermodynamics explain order?

"Ordinary" thermodynamics focuses on systems at equilibrium, systems that do not undergo net change as time passes. Living systems are far from equilibrium; the processes that occur within cells and all living organisms are far from the no-net-change criterion. When an organism dies, life processes stop as it disintegrates; then the matter that was formerly alive moves toward and eventually achieves the state of equilibrium.

Nonequilibrium processes are common; for example, the water flowing in a river is not at equilibrium. For the purpose of investigating such processes, Ilya Prigogine developed *nonequilibrium thermodynamics* and received the 1977 Nobel Prize in Chemistry. Some evolutionists have suggested that this new theoretical tool can solve the energy flow problem and that disorder can lead to the order of the cell.[12] But others have given reasons why this claim is not justified.[13] Prigogine and co-workers were much more cautious than those who thought the new theory would solve the energy flow problem; notice carefully their choice of words in discussing biological—as distinguished from pre-biological, that is, nonlife to life—evolution. They said, "One is tempted to hope" that the theory could indicate how higher organisms develop. If the theory *would* work, it "would

Analysis: From Inert Matter to Cells

provide a . . . unifying principle" for evolutionary processes.[14] Obviously, the problems are at least as great for the evolution of life from nonlife. Since these words were written in 1972, many articles and books by Prigogine and others on the nonequilibrium approach have appeared. The cautious words were justified: evolutionists are far from a consensus that the nonequilibrium approach will solve the problem of energy flow. Evidently enthusiasm concerning the possibility that the new theory will solve any of the immense problems inherent in chemical evolution is not warranted.

The Problem of Complexity

As we have seen, it is difficult to show that even the simplest molecules needed to begin the evolutionary process did in fact form. But the problem is much greater. The cell is perhaps the most complex structure known. It is made up of extremely complex molecules, including DNA and the various forms of RNA. How do those who accept chemical evolution account for the existence of the cell? They provide ample evidence of the impact of evolutionary theory on their thinking: they usually start out with the proposition that evolution *must* have occurred, so then the problem is not *if*, but *how*. Even some Christians take this approach. Thus, the late A. Van Der Ziel of the department of electrical engineering, University of Minnesota, said:

> . . . the transition from non-living to living matter must have been a *unique elementary event* that cannot be further described scientifically.
>
> The objection is often made that such an event had an extremely small probability.

He continued by responding to that objection:

> But that is no valid objection, for all *unique* events share this extremely small probability. For example, if I have to figure out what the probability is that I am what I am, and take into account all the events that produced me and all the ancestors that preceded me, I come to an extremely small probability. Nevertheless, I *do* exist.[15]

Surely one may compare the probabilities of the occurrence of different events and determine that some events are much more likely to occur than others. Such a calculation is, in effect, what many people have carried out with respect to the formation of the components of the living cell. The probability that atoms and molecules would combine to form those components is vanishingly small compared to the probability that those atoms and molecules would have reacted to form nonbiological substances.[16,17]

The General Mathematical Problem. In 1966 a landmark conference of mathematicians and biologists focused on the mathematical probability of the occurrence of the various postulated events in the evolutionary process.[18] Although their emphasis was on evolutionary steps beyond the appearance of the first life, their conclusions have relevance for the more difficult nonlife-to-life process.

Because of the availability of high-speed computers by 1966, it was possible to consider seriously the mathematical formulation of the various processes of evolution. Summarizing the conference, John McIntyre (of the department of physics of Texas A&M University) doubted that even a billion years available for evolution enables one to formulate an acceptable mathematical model of evolution:

> While the one billion years assumed to be available for evolution may appear to be a long time, the number of generations is finite and the changes occurring between all generations in evolutionary history can be simulated on a computer in a few days (10 days using one of the mathematical formulations presented at the conference) . . . . *The results of such analyses of the theory of evolution were, without exception, spectacularly unsuccessful.*[19] (Emphasis added.)

Evidently probability calculations constitute a stumbling block for anyone who contemplates accepting evolutionary theory.

The Mathematical Problem for the First Cells. The evolutionary scenario for the formation of the first life postulates organic molecule intermediates between the simplest molecules of the primitive earth atmosphere and the highly complex molecules that eventually appeared in the cell. *Prebiotic soup* is the term evolutionists use for bodies of water that contained these complex molecules. But certain sedimentary rocks, some found in Western Greenland, which are between 3.8 and 3.9 billion years old, do not contain such organic molecules. The rocks would contain those molecules if they had been present during the sedimentation process.

Let us consider how much time was available for the evolution of nonlife to the first cells. In Chapter 5, I indicated that the age of the earth is about 4.6 billion years. For 200 million years radioactive decay caused the earth

Analysis: From Inert Matter to Cells

to be very hot, and for the next 400 million years, up to about 4 billion years ago, volcanic gases produced the atmosphere. The evolutionary process could not have begun until the earth was cool enough. I also indicated in Chapter 5 that the oldest known cells were formed 3.5 billion years ago. Therefore, even assuming that the earth cooled more rapidly than usually thought, evolution of nonliving chemicals to the first cells could have taken no more than 500 or 600 million years. This is a forbiddingly short time for the necessary random events to take place. Yet, with respect to the entire nonlife-to-life probability, Jacques Monod, a well-known evolutionist, said that before life appeared, the probability that it would appear "was virtually zero."[20] The opinion of G.C. Mills (a biochemist and geneticist at the University of Texas Medical Branch at Galveston), echoed the opinion of many other biochemists. After analyzing the formation of proteins in a pre-existing cell, he said:

> It is concluded that protein function is a consequence of a unique arrangement of the individual amino acids, and that this arrangement could not be achieved by chance. . . . The data strongly favor the view that "design" or "intelligence" must be involved in the beginning of life.[21,22]

If life evolved from nonlife, consider two alternate means whereby the first cell appeared. First, over a long period of time the components could form and then get together in one place to constitute a cell. But the components are unstable and in any case would be very rare. In advancing this mechanism, evolutionists have suggested that something preceded the cell; they have given it the name *protocell*. No evidence suggests that a protocell ever existed, and even many evolutionists are unconvinced.

The other possibility for the spontaneous appearance of the first cell is that the components arose in the same place over a short period of time, a period short enough to minimize the breakdown of inherently unstable substances. This second model calls for calculation of the probability that cell molecules formed. Before giving the results of these calculations, I must make two points.

(1) As amino acids react with each other randomly, only an extremely small fraction of proteins made are useful proteins. (See Chapter 5 for a description of the reaction of amino acids to form proteins.) The fraction is small for two reasons. First, many amino acids that could conceivably form from simpler molecules and therefore could become parts of proteins are not among the twenty amino acids in useful proteins. Second, the number

of ways of placing a given group of amino acids in a sequence is unbelievably great, although only one of those ways would be "correct," that is, functional.

(2) *Enzymes*, a class of proteins, are particularly critical in the functioning of the cell. Enzymes are biological catalysts: they facilitate certain biological reactions. Cells contain a large number of enzymes. But the probability that a functional protein, one with amino acids in the correct order, will form by means of random reactions is about one in 10^{20} (1 followed by 20 zeroes). Suppose that a cell requires *two* functional proteins; then the probability for *each* is one part in 10^{20}; it then follows that the probability that *both* will appear is one part in 10^{20} times 10^{20}, that is, one part in 10^{40} (1 followed by 40 zeroes). Cells require many more than two proteins, and so the actual probability is much smaller. F. Hoyle and C. Wickramasinghe (in a procedure not given here) applied the probability of one part in 10^{20} to enzymes:

> By itself, this small probability could be faced, because one must contemplate not just a single shot at obtaining the enzyme, but a very large number of trials such as are supposed to have occurred in an organic soup early in the history of the Earth.

However, according to Hoyle and Wickramasinghe, there is a big problem:

> The trouble is that there are about two thousand enzymes, and the chance of obtaining them all in a random trial is only one part in $(10^{20})^{2000} = 10^{40,000}$ [1 followed by 40,000 zeroes], an outrageously small probability that could not be faced even if the whole universe consisted of organic soup.[23]

Hoyle and Wickramasinghe stated that only by invoking unproved postulates can one still maintain that life evolved from nonlife. This kind of calculation convinced Hoyle and Wickramasinghe to turn away from the conventional evolutionary picture to a radical view (more of that below). Note that their calculation is only for the enzymes of the cell; it does not take care of the DNA and RNA molecules and the other components.

Why, in the face of these daunting, unfavorable odds, do so many people accept the idea that life evolved from nonlife? One answer is that many, including scientists, do not truly understand the consequences of postulating a *random* process. Two examples illustrate this point.

The first example focuses on comments often made concerning evolu-

Analysis: From Inert Matter to Cells

tionary theory during its early years. That theory, as promulgated in the nineteenth and early twentieth centuries, denied the existence of design in Creation. That which exists is the product of nothing more than random change and natural selection.[24] Evolutionists applied this doctrine first of all to explain evolution from species to species; later, as biochemistry developed, they used it to explain the origin of life from nonlife.

In those early years, especially before evolutionists seriously attacked the nonlife-to-life problem, it was fashionable to say that given enough time, one could imagine anything occurring randomly. In fact, Julian Huxley said that a large number of monkeys would, typing randomly, eventually produce all the works of Shakespeare and also *The Encyclopedia Britannica*. Anyone who thinks along these lines would probably have no difficulty imagining how amino acids combined to produce the needed proteins. But Charles Townes, winner of the Nobel Prize in Physics in 1964, contradicted this kind of thinking. He pointed out that

> . . . a simple calculation shows that one billion monkeys typing randomly as fast as they can 24 hours a day on one billion typewriters for the entire lifetime of the universe as we know it [Townes assumed 15 billion years] would probably not yet have typed out the correct sequence of letters in the title *The Encyclopedia Britannica*.[25]

The idea that random events will produce some desired result persists in the face of sober calculation. The idea that randomness is not truly *random* will not go away.

The popularity of lotteries provides a second example. In one state-operated lottery, the lottery ticket contains six separate numbers, ranging from one to forty. At the "drawing," colored balls, numbered from one to 40, are in a large vessel. A machine chooses six balls at random. The object is to match the numbers on the lottery ticket with the numbers on the six balls. At first glance, it seems that this might not be so difficult, especially because the *order* of numbers on the ticket need not match the *order* in which the numbers are chosen.

Here, too, intuition is not correct. What is the probability that *one* of the numbers on the ticket will match one of the numbers on the six balls? The probability is one in 40/6, or one in 6.7. Beyond that, the calculation is a little more complicated. The chances that two of the six ticket numbers will match two of the six balls is one in 53; three, one in 494; four, one in 6,093; five, one in 110,000; all six, one in 3.8 million. Thus, a person who purchased 3.8 million tickets would have a reasonable chance to have a six-number winner, the grand winner. If the potential buyer of a ticket could *see* 3.8 million tickets and understand that he or she must pay money to pick out the grand winner, very likely a much smaller number of lottery tickets would be sold. Hoped-for groups of numbers arise no more in lotteries than hoped-for sequences of letters arise with monkeys typing or hoped-for sequences of amino acids occur in random reactions to make proteins.

In Darwin's day evolutionists avoided this objection by using ideas no longer tenable. They thought one could justifiably postulate very tiny, almost infinitesimal changes; the increments were nothing like adding a letter of the alphabet to an existing string of letters, thereby making a different English word. Their theory of biological change is *gradualism*. Peter Vorzimmer likened this theory to mixing paints: one can begin with one color, add extremely small portions of another color, until finally the result is a different color. Thus, two populations could blend to form a new population.[26]

But with the eventual development of genetic theory, evolutionists came to claim that the process does not work that way. It is not blending; a mutation occurs and descendants either do or do not possess the mutation. It is either yes or no; there is no partial change. This situation has obvious implications for the formation of biochemical molecules, such as proteins, where one can identify discrete steps and identify changes in structure.

One could have expected the response to calculations which show that random events simply cannot account for the existence of the cell. Evolutionists re-examined the situation and declared that the events were not *quite* random. To put it simplistically: If segments A-B-C were to form in that order, once A-B formed, some evolutionists claimed that the conditions were favorable for A-B to add C and form the desired A-B-C, and so forth.[27]

No one has shown that this argument can come even close to accounting for the amazingly complicated and highly specific protein structure. Furthermore, the cell consists of much more than proteins. Concerning the entire process of building up the cell, Denton made a useful observation: The evolution of the horse, from *Eohippus* to the modern horse, took about 60 million years.[28] Basically, this was evolution from a small animal to a large one—not a tremendous change. By contrast, only eight to ten times as much time is available for the evolution of the cell, perhaps the most complicated structure ever known, developing from disorganized, nonliving materials.

But what about the existence of cells smaller than those we know? Could such cells be steps from nonlife to the cells of present-day living things?

Analysis: From Inert Matter to Cells

The average cell contains about 100 billion atoms, weighing about one-trillionth of a gram. H.J. Morowitz (a molecular biologist at Yale University) attempted to calculate the smallest possible size of a cell.[29] A cell cannot exist without the ability to perform certain functions. For example, it must be able to replicate itself and also make at least a minimum number of proteins. To construct his hypothetical small cell, Morowitz removed many important functions, so many that the cell was probably vulnerable and might not have been able to exist. It is a bit like imagining how small one can make a certain kind of factory, stripping away functions until finally the factory cannot continue to exist. Morowitz calculated the size of his hypothetical cell. He arrived at a cell diameter of over 1000 Angstroms (100 million Angstroms = 1.00 centimeter = 0.39 inch) compared to a diameter of a little less than 3000 Angstroms for the smallest known cells. The important result of such a calculation is that this hypothetical 1000-Angstrom-diameter smallest cell is an indescribably great distance from disorganized nonliving molecules, and essentially all the problems inherent in synthesizing actual cells by random processes are also problems for such a hypothetical cell. No feasible set of steps between nonlife and life seems likely.

The Problem of Replication. Cells must be able to replicate themselves. According to evolutionary theory, the cell obtained the ability to replicate itself by random events. It may be impossible to make calculations for replication of an entity as complex as the living cell. Suppose, however, one hypothesizes the existence of a structure simple enough to make possible the necessary calculation. Presumably replication of the simpler structure would, on the average, take less time than the more complex. Then, if one obtains a vanishingly small probability of replication for the simpler structure during the life of the universe, it is even more unlikely that the more complex structure could have replicated during that time.

Such a calculation could serve another purpose as well. Some evolutionists realize the improbability of the evolution of the actual cell; they agree with much of the argumentation presented above. But suppose, they say, a much simpler cell, a "protocell"—perhaps similar to the hypothetical smallest cell discussed above—evolved and became the forerunner of the modern cell. A calculation could determine the probability of the replication of such a simpler cell.

Robert Newman[30] made a calculation for a very simple, nonbiological structure, based on earlier work.[31,32] John Byl[33] criticized Newman's calculations; later, Newman responded.[34] (Newman is a physicist at the Interdisciplinary Biblical Research Institute of the Biblical Theological

Seminary in Hatfield, Pennsylvania; John Byl is a physicist at Trinity Western University in Langley, British Columbia.)

The simple structure for which Newman made calculations consists of a "cell" that is a pattern of digits on the screen of a computer monitor. As the computer makes random "moves," the cell expands step by step. Five questions summarize the steps of the problem. First, what rules does one need to replicate a pattern? Second, given these rules, what is the smallest pattern that obeys these rules? Third, assuming random moves, what is the probability that the computer will make the correct moves to achieve replication? Fourth, given what we know of the physical makeup of the universe, how can we link these moves or steps to the replication of an aggregate of atoms as simple as the pattern on the computer screen? Fifth, given what we know of rates of chemical reaction, how long, on the average, would it take for one cell to duplicate?

This is a summary of the discussion: In Newman's first article, he concluded that on the average such a replicating event would occur once in 10^{129} (1 followed by 129 zeroes) years. But Byl disagreed with some of the assumptions and arrived at a very much greater probability: replication would, said Byl, take place almost instantaneously using Newman's assumptions. On the basis of Byl's suggestions, Newman then re-calculated and arrived at 3×10^{79} (3 followed by 79 zeroes) years, with the possibility that this time span might actually be much larger. Newman's modified argument, although he allowed for a very large margin of error, seems valid. In any event, both Newman and Byl concluded that the probability of the evolution of a replicating *biological* cell during the life of the universe (presumably their conclusions apply for any cell large enough to be a protocell) is vanishingly small.

The various considerations of this chapter have shown that the cell is immensely complex. While many scientists cling to the idea that the cell evolved from nonliving matter, they do not doubt its complexity. Denton demonstrated its complexity by presenting the modern picture of a functioning cell For the purpose of discussion, he visualized a scaled-up model of the cell, about a dozen miles across. Denton's very striking description of the cell, though long, is worth considering carefully. He said that this large structure

> . . . would be an object of unparalleled complexity and adaptive design. On the surface of the cell we would see millions of openings, like the port holes of a vast space ship, opening and closing to allow a continual stream of materials to flow in and out. If we were to enter

Analysis: From Inert Matter to Cells

one of these openings we would find ourselves in a world of supreme technology and bewildering complexity. We would see endless highly organized corridors and conduits branching in every direction away from the perimeter of the cell, some leading to the central memory bank in the nucleus and others to assembly plants and processing units. The nucleus itself would be a vast spherical chamber [almost a mile] in diameter, resembling a geodesic dome inside of which we would see, all neatly stacked together in ordered arrays, the miles of coiled chains of the DNA molecules. A huge range of products and raw materials would shuttle along all the manifold conduits in a highly ordered fashion to and from all the various assembly plants in the outer regions of the cell.

We would wonder at the level of control implicit in the movement of so many objects down so many seemingly endless conduits, all in perfect unison. We would see all around us . . . all sorts of robot-like machines. We would notice that the simplest of the functional components of the cell, the protein molecules, were astonishingly complex pieces of molecular machinery, each one consisting of about three thousand atoms arranged in highly organized 3-D conformation.

We cannot design even one functional protein, but

> . . . the life of the cell depends on the integrated activities of thousands, certainly tens, and probably hundreds of thousands of different protein molecules.[35]

Other Explanations for the Origin of Life. What is the alternative to random evolution of life from nonlife by means of physical and chemical processes? I shall discuss the Christian doctrine of creation in Chapters 8-11. But what of those who do not accept the Christian position?

The answer to that question usually resembles one of the following three options:

(1) Perhaps we need new natural laws to account for the process of nonlife to life. In particular, since the problem is that the cell is so very complex, the new "law" would explain how highly organized structures could appear.

Michael Polanyi, a British physical chemist and philosopher, claimed that in principle the laws of physics and chemistry cannot include all the laws applying to living systems. In other words, neither present laws nor new laws of physics and chemistry will suffice.[36]

Why did Polanyi claim that such reductionism, using the laws of physics and chemistry to explain living things, is not possible? He pointed out that chemical and physical systems can be described mathematically by a certain kind of equation. To solve such equations, one must provide the *boundary conditions*. But, as we shall see, the situation is different for living systems.

I must digress to explain this statement concerning boundary conditions. Consider the following example. You are a detective in a room on the fifth floor of a building. You are searching for a gold bar that someone stole. You look out the window and see the gold bar descending! But you are very alert and use your stopwatch to determine the time it takes the bar to fall from the top of the window to the bottom. After you measure the height of the window, you can calculate the bar's velocity from the height of the window and the time of fall. Now, this building actually has fifteen stories. By knowing the velocity of the bar and the laws of physics, can you determine on which story that you will probably find the thief?

You cannot make such a determination because you lack one piece of information: one of the boundary conditions. In this case, you could not solve the problem unless you knew the *initial* velocity of the gold bar; its initial velocity is one of the boundary conditions. Thus, the thief could, using considerable force, have thrown the bar straight down out of a sixth-floor window, one floor above you, giving the bar a large initial velocity; or, the thief could have merely dropped it from the fifteenth floor, in which case its initial velocity is zero. Alternately, if you knew the initial position (which floor) of the gold bar, then you could calculate, given its velocity at the fifth-story window, its initial velocity. Therefore, this example has two boundary conditions: the initial velocity and the initial position.

But, said Polanyi, the boundary conditions in living systems are fixed. For example, the boundaries (shape and size) of a single-cell bacterium are set. Those boundaries are not arbitrary. So it is with any organism: it is a separate entity. In the example of the descending gold bar, different boundary conditions are possible: the bar could have started from any of the floors above the fifth and different initial velocities were possible. Because boundary conditions are not arbitrary in the biotic world, said Polanyi, one cannot devise physical and chemical laws to describe organisms because those laws do involve arbitrary boundary conditions.

However, in spite of this argument natural scientists committed to evolution will probably continue to insist that chemical and physical laws will eventually solve nonlife-to-life problems.

(2) Since the nineteenth century natural scientists who are not satisfied

Analysis: From Inert Matter to Cells

that Darwinian evolution can account for the origin of life have turned to another possibility: *panspermia*, the idea that the seeds of life came from outer space. The concept does not explain how such seeds came into existence; presumably, the thought is that some place provided more hospitable conditions for the evolution of life from nonlife than the earth did. Up until recently, natural scientists almost universally discarded this idea. Besides the problem of merely putting the problem in another place, the theory had to face the problem of seed survival in outer space, where radiation would surely kill anything alive.

Recently, however, claims of the discovery of amino acids in some meteorites have revived interest in this theory. The claims are disputable and, of course, the presence of amino acids does not indicate that amino acids combined to make proteins. Such a synthesis is infinitely more difficult than any ever accomplished in the most advanced laboratories on earth.

The acceptance of panspermia by a very prominent scientist is another reason for the revival of interest in panspermia. For decades Fred Hoyle, a well-known astronomer, has produced stimulating ideas, some very radical. Recently he proposed a panspermia model. In *Evolution from Space* (1981), Hoyle and N.C. Wickramasinghe suggested some startling ideas. Following is a summary of their model: (a) Genes, not necessarily whole cells, with a protective layer to prevent destruction by radiation, arrived from some other place in the universe. (b) Such material is still arriving. (c) An intelligence higher than the human intelligence, but not a god, created this material. (d) One proof of the existence of an intelligence higher than the human intelligence is that we have not exterminated even one insect species. (e) Insects might be the higher intelligence.[37]

Evidently blasphemy is alive and well.

A similar approach is taken by Francis Crick, co-discoverer with James Watson of the double helix structure of DNA. Because of his research, Crick knows that the cell is tremendously complex and how improbable it is that a cell could form by random processes. Crick is one of those who suggest "directed panspermia."[38] This is the idea that an extraterrestrial intelligence deliberately sent living cells to earth in a space ship. In spite of the criticism of his fellow scientists, Crick still maintains the panspermia suggestion.

(3) In some cases, the suggested alternative to random evolution invokes nonphysical forces. Nonphysical options are usually intended to remove randomness wherever it occurs in evolutionary theory, not just to remove randomness in the formation of life from nonlife. Following is a description of two theories that postulate nonphysical forces:

The first is *vitalism*, the idea that physical substances possess properties that make possible processes not explained by chemical and physical laws. Pierre Teilhard de Chardin (1881-1955), a Roman Catholic zoologist whose radical ideas were published posthumously in *The Phenomenon of Man* (1955),[39] was a vitalist.[40] Teilhard held to the consciousness and "Christification" of matter. No longer are material events random: creatures now direct evolution.[41] Teilhard reduced "the development of life to a purely immanent operation within [an operation inherent in] nature."[42]

H. James Birx, author of *Theories of Evolution* and professor of anthropology at Canisius College, Buffalo, New York, summarized what is often called Teilhard's "synthesis":

> Teilhard's ingenious synthesis argues for a personal god, free will, immortality of the human soul, and a divine destiny for our species.

But, said Birx, this synthesis hasn't convinced modern scientists or "enlightened" theologians:

> Yet it has failed to convince modern scientists that organic evolution is teleological, to persuade natural philosophers that this universe is spiritualistic, or to demonstrate for enlightened theologians that those basic religious beliefs of traditional Christianity are defensible in terms of scientific evidence.

Birx claimed that in spite of this failure Teilhard accomplished something:

> Even so, in the last analysis, Teilhard does ground his unique vision of human evolution in a cosmic mysticism far removed from the mechanism and materialism of Neo-Darwinism as well as scientific naturalism and rational humanism.[43]

Teilhard's mystical vision of matter led to the following vision. Three leaps forward and upward occurred: sudden emergence of matter, of life, and of thought. These leaps—geogenesis, biogenesis, and noogenesis—cause a geosphere, a biosphere, and a noosphere to come into existence. Finally, a creative synthesis will create the theosphere.[44] Thus, for Teilhard the "barriers" along the evolutionary route from matter to human beings are not real barriers. The nature of Creation itself—this includes human recognition of the "fact" of human evolution—drives the development process. Not only has evolutionary thought made an impact on our society, but, according to Teilhard, that thought is also responsible for even more evolution.

Analysis: From Inert Matter to Cells

William Fix postulated a different kind of nonphysical force. It removes randomness from the process which has ultimately produced human beings. In *The Bone Peddlers: Selling Evolution* (1984), Fix claimed that the evolutionistic and the young-earth models are both wrong. He very effectively attacked these two models. Fix proposed a different theory, a "psychogenesis" or an "apparition" theory. He said:

> Many serious investigators have now moved to a view of nature that brings them full circle with the ancient proposition that everything from the most humble plants to stars have some kind of spirit or intelligence.[45]

Evidently Fix's attempts to solve origin problems leads him to espouse a pagan idea, an ancient form of pantheism.

My thesis is that from the very beginning of human life some people have depended on God and that others either qualified that dependence or did not depend upon him at all. Those who at most qualified that dependence carried the day when it eventually came to defining science: the world was to be understood "naturally." Yet at the same time we encounter an approach that at first seems to be a third way. What of the ancient thinkers whose ideas Fix and others claim have now come full circle? Many people maintain that such a view is truly different. But the key is not so much whether the boundary of natural science lies at the edge of things that are "physical"; the question is whether we see Creation as the product of the sovereign Triune God. Maintaining that matter has spirit is essentially a means of holding to a closed universe and of believing that the operation of some heretofore undiscovered laws (forces? for plants and animals, vitalistic forces?) account for phenomena that conventional natural science has not explained.

The basic questions remain. Are we willing to confess that Christ was active in creation and that all things exist to serve him? Does not such a confession include a belief that a division between "natural" and "supernatural" is impossible? As a result, are we then willing to confess that naturalistic explanations, even when they invoke as-yet-undiscovered laws, might not exist for some phenomena? I want to defer my opinion on what ought to be our attitude toward the formidable problems evolutionary theory has encountered. By now we ought to be able to see that the natural scientific enterprise cannot solve all the problems of evolutionary theory.

Chapter Seven
Analysis: From Cells to Humans

The previous chapter describes some scientific problems that arise when one attempts to construct a model of the evolution of the simplest cells from nonliving matter. It seems that no such model exists. The purpose of this chapter is to examine some of the scientific problems encountered if one accepts evolution beyond these simplest cells to all other life, including human life. In the first part of the discussion, I analyze nonhuman evolution; in the second, questions related to the postulated evolution of human beings. I call attention to several discontinuities in the postulated evolution of life, that is, gaps in the supposed smooth path from the first cells to human beings. Each discontinuity constitutes a problem for evolutionists.

Before 1980, many people who found fault with biological evolutionary theory did not, however, criticize physical evolutionary theory. They did not quarrel with most of the features of the "big bang" theory, which called for evolution from energy to matter to stars and galaxies and eventually to planets. I generally agree with the big bang theory, except, of course, the part that attempts to explain the beginning. Is this a consistent position for those who find fault with biological evolutionary theory? If evolutionary theory is wrong in one place, is it not wrong in every other explanation of origins?

Before 1980, physical evolutionary theory differed from biological evolutionary theory in several ways. First, physical evolution had nothing corresponding to biological discontinuities. Second, for physical evolution, investigators had proposed models utilizing known physical laws. Many scientists attempt to account for biological diversity using known physical laws, but, as we shall see in this chapter, they have encountered significant problems. Third, physical evolutionary theory did not depend upon unorthodox views of chance or random events, the kind needed in a biological evolutionary model. Fourth, most of the conclusions that physical evolutionists proposed can be consistent with a faithful reading of Scripture; however, some aspects of biological evolution strain such a reading. In fact, an evolutionary origin of the human family is inconsistent with Scriptural revelation.

But I showed in Chapter 5 that recent developments in physical evolutionary theory are unacceptable for those who believe that Creation had

Analysis: From Cells to Humans

a beginning. While no consensus exists, the suggestion by some physicists that a "beginning" has a physical cause and that, in fact, there never was a true beginning, is not consistent with biblical teaching. Obviously, Christians cannot deny the possibility that God's first act of creation occurred before, and not at the same time as, the beginning of the big bang. There was a first act of creation. That some physicists deny that there was an unexplainable beginning seems to proceed from the same mindset that insists that everything in biological history is in principle explainable by natural law. This constitutes another example of how evolutionary thought has made a significant impact *within* the natural sciences.

Evolution of Animals and Plants

Use of the Fossil Record. Biological evolutionary theory postulates that all living things descended from a common ancestor. If one knew enough, one could diagrammatically arrange in a tree-like order all the species that have ever lived. The common ancestor would be the trunk of the tree, its first descendants the principal branches, with later descendants the secondary branches, and so forth, with the outermost twigs representing species alive today. When an organism dies, some parts of its body fossilize. If paleontologists found representative fossils of all extinct species, then they could arrange these fossils in the same tree-like order. But if, in spite of the discovery of a large number of fossils, they cannot make these connections, then the fossil record contains gaps.

Evolutionists base their theory on what they perceive to be structural similarities among living organisms; they then attempt to reinforce the theory with evidence from the fossil record. Thus, they do not depend completely on the fossil record, but, as we shall see, their theory makes certain predictions about what that record will eventually reveal.

I perceive two general reasons for skepticism concerning the fossil record. The first is *convergence*, the concept that some species have similar characteristics, even though evolutionists do not claim the species are biologically related. Michael Denton discussed this matter:

> Nature abounds in examples of convergence: the similarity in overall shapes of whales, ichthyosaurs and fishes . . . the similarity of the forelimbs of a mole and those of the insect, the molecricket; the great similarity in the design of the eye in vertebrates and cephalopods . . .

But note Denton's summarizing statement:

In all the above cases, the similarities, although very striking, *do not imply any close biological relationship.*[1]

Denton discussed an incredible similarity in appearance of the skeletons of the Tasmanian wolf, a marsupial, and the placental dog, even though no one claims evolutionary relation. In other words, evolutionists conveniently choose when similarities in the fossil record show biological relationship and when they don't.

The second reason for general skepticism arises from the fact that fossil evidence reveals information only about the part of the organism which has been preserved. Preservation depends both upon the environment and what part of the organism is capable of preservation. The remains of a dead plant or animal are subject to erosion. The "soft" part tends to disappear. For example, the part of a marine skeleton that does not dissolve in water might lie undisturbed for a very long time at the bottom of the sea. Thus, the term "fossil" always refers to what is left after a long time. (In some special cases, the environment might be favorable for preservation of much of the organism; examples are animals caught in amber or a tar pit.)

Consider, then, what happens when evolutionists use the fossil record as an aid in constructing a hypothetical evolutionary sequence. This procedure can produce surprises. For example, in 1938 a fisherman caught a living coelacanth, a fish thought to have been extinct for about one hundred million years. This discovery was important because it provided an opportunity to examine the "soft" part of an animal, the part that does not fossilize. This examination raised serious questions about the evolutionary connection between the coelacanth and other fishes. The discovery suggests that perhaps evolutionists have assumed too much about the nature of the unfossilized part of extinct species and that those assumptions may be biased by the presumption of the evolutionary model.[2]

Microevolution and Macroevolution. What kind of biological diversity do anti-evolutionists usually accept? What kind do they reject? To answer these questions, we must see what evolutionists claim. They usually maintain that by small changes called mutations, new species appear, that is, *speciation* occurs. They also claim that over the long span of time available these small changes accumulate; plants, animals, and human beings appear. Anti-evolutionists usually do not deny that speciation occurs. But they also claim that there is no evidence to show that change from some starting point continues indefinitely until, say, both the elephant and the mouse appear. A small change is *microevolution;* the accumulation of small changes, including jumping across a gap in the present fossil record, is *macroevolution.*

Analysis: From Cells to Humans 101

Evolutionists present ample evidence of speciation. Denton, not an evolutionist, presented several examples.[3] Thus, in England wherever surfaces are dark because of industrial smoke, the peppered moth is dark. Where surfaces are light, such as in modern rural areas and in rural areas and cities before industrialization, the peppered moth is light. In this way the peppered moth maximizes avoidance of predators. Evidently the dark moth species is newer than the light. By natural selection, the dark moth predominates just where survival is most likely.

Two species of gull provide another example of speciation. The herring gull and the black backed gull, both European, do not interbreed and so they are separate species. Imagine going east from Europe. You would not find the herring gull. The gulls you find first differ slightly from the black backed gull; this difference increases with increasing distance from Europe. Now visualize going west from Europe. You find the herring gull, but not the black backed gull. The farther from Europe, the greater the difference from the herring gull. In Eastern Siberia, the two forms of gull meet and interbreed. Thus, starting in Eastern Siberia, no matter which direction you go, east or west, by small changes you find a new species of gull by the time you reach Europe.

All such examples of speciation are no more than examples of microevolution, which I accept. They are similar to the appearance of new breeds seen by animal breeders and new varieties seen by horticulturalists. They are not examples of macroevolution.

As we shall see, the case against macroevolution is very strong. But if one allows microevolution, is it not possible for changes to accumulate, eventually bringing about a very great change? Are great changes *in principle* impossible?

Perhaps one cannot prove that such large changes are *in principle* impossible. But the inability of small changes to accomplish large changes in other matters, unrelated to biological history, may suggest the possibility of natural barriers within biology. Two nonbiological examples illustrate the point.

Imagine a common metal (or plastic) puzzle, consisting of a square of four rows and four columns, with sliders numbered from 1 to 15 situated in 15 of the 16 positions; one position is vacant. You can move a slider vertically or horizontally to an adjacent position, providing that position is vacant. Suppose someone arranges the sliders in your puzzle randomly, for example, starting from the upper left, 12, 3, 7, and so forth. Your goal is to move the sliders to attain some desired order—let us say from 1 to 15—starting from the upper left. Usually this takes a few minutes. But suppose that after you have arranged the sliders in order you violate rules; you make an illegal move by prying out Number 14. Then, again using force, you place Number 14 in the empty space *after* Number 15, so that the last three are 13, 15, and 14 instead of 13, 14, and 15. Now move the sliders around (using only legal moves) so that once again the order is random. Then challenge someone to arrange the sliders in numerical order. The person challenged will become frustrated. For, by small moves, analogous to microevolutionary changes, the 1-to-15 order cannot be achieved. The gap from . . . 13, 15, 14 to . . . 13, 14, 15 cannot be crossed; *this* "macroevolution" is not possible.

Some people have called attention to other kinds of uncrossable non-biological gaps, suggesting at least the possibility of uncrossable biological gaps. Consider the following word game. The player is given a pair of English words of equal length, for example, *the* and *new*. The player must begin with the first given word, substitute a single letter, obtain another English word, and by a series of such changes obtain the second given word. One solution is *the, tee, ten, men, met, net, new*. Changing the game from single English words to English sentences makes it more difficult to get to a target sentence, providing that each intermediate sentence must make sense.[4] In fact, some target sentences are inaccessible. The small changes are analogous to microevolution, particularly because genetic theory calls for evolutionary change by a finite jump, a change involving a group of atoms in the DNA code. Using "microevolutionary" steps, one can produce a family of closely related sentences. But we may encounter an uncrossable barrier if we attempt to go from the initial sentence to a predetermined target sentence; no macroevolutionary path may exist.

Gaps in the Record. The earliest cells arose 3.5 - 3.6 billion years ago. Very simple multi-celled animals appear in the fossil record about 700 million years ago. The jump from single-celled to multi-celled species is one gap. Suddenly, between 570 and 500 million years ago, a large number of marine animals appear in the fossil record. This was an explosion of life.[5] The difference between life before the explosion and life at the beginning of the explosion constitutes another gap.

Anti-evolutionists claim and evolutionists admit that the fossil record is incomplete. In 1959 the prominent evolutionist George Gaylord Simpson said that the imperceptible changes supposed to lead to new organisms, changes anticipated by Darwin, were seldom found.[6] G.A. Kerkut, a biologist at Southampton University, England, was not an anti-evolutionist. But in *Implications of Evolution* (1960) he maintained that evolutionists claim too much. He said that serious problems existed in attempts to establish

Analysis: From Cells to Humans

the connections that evolutionists claim in spite of the confidence they exhibit. Some of the problematical connections are within the following groups: viruses, bacteria, and *Protozoa*; *Protozoa* and *Metazoa*; various invertebrate phyla; and vertebrates and invertebrates.[7] In 1982 Pattle P.T. Pun maintained that the situation had changed but little.[8] Denton listed several sudden appearances in the fossil record, including the following: among the invertebrates, molluscs; among plants, the angiosperms; among vertebrates, various fishes; among modern amphibia, frogs and toads.[9]

Darwin knew the fossil record was not complete. But he predicted with confidence that eventually, with the discovery of more fossils, that the gaps would disappear.[10] The gaps are still there, even though scientists have discovered a large number of fossils since Darwin's time; about 99.9% of the fossils we have today were not known to Darwin.[11] In fact, instead of contributing to the verification of the supposed evolutionary sequence, the discovery of a fossil has occasionally made the problem more difficult. Thus, in 1900 the phylum *Poganophora* was discovered. Far from being a missing link, *Poganophora* required new missing links to account for its existence.[12]

In 1966 A.S. Romer, a Harvard zoologist, approached the adequacy of the fossil record in a different way. Fossilization usually requires a long period of time. Therefore, organisms that recently died would ordinarily not be found as fossils. Suppose that living orders and families have existed for a time long enough for fossils to form. Are those orders and families represented well in the fossil record as presently constituted? If so, then the search for fossils has been fairly successful; it would be incorrect to conclude that only a small fraction of the orders and families have been found.

Here is the present situation. Of the number of living orders of terrestrial vertebrates, 42 of 43, or 98%, are in the fossil record. Of the number of living families of terrestrial vertebrates, 261 of 329, or 79%, are in the fossil record. But bird skeletons, which are often very fragile, do not become fossils easily. If one excludes bird families from terrestrial vertebrates, then the percentage rises from 79 to 88%.[13] (The results are similar for other fossil counts.)

In other words, the fossil record with respect to living terrestrial vertebrates is reasonably complete. If those who look for fossils of terrestrial vertebrates have missed a large number of orders and families, the fossil record would be incomplete with respect to orders and families which we know should be in the record, namely, the living orders and families. By this criterion, those who look for fossils have done well. We have no reason to suspect that they have done poorly with respect to those fossils called for by evolutionary theory but that are not represented by living orders and families. These data provide small comfort for one who claims that new fossil discoveries will fill in the gaps.

Gaps Between Organs. The existence of certain fully formed organs suggests another biological discontinuity.

A somewhat simplified evolutionary theory accounting for the appearance of new organs says that an organ does not appear fully formed, but appears gradually. By mutation a species changes very slightly; another change builds on the previous one, another builds on this change, and so forth. Finally, through a gradual process a new organ appears. For each step along the route the mutation must have some survival value. The incomplete organ is *pre-adapted*: while it cannot yet perform its ultimate purpose, its partial adaptation allows it to function usefully in some other way. Perhaps the species fits into its environment better because of this pre-adaptation, says the theory.

However, for a number of organs no evidence suggests that intermediate forms ever existed. Furthermore, the hypothesized intermediates seem to have had no conceivable advantage over their predecessors.

The classic example is the eye. The eye consists of many interacting parts; how could a partial "eye" function as an eye? Some evolutionists invoke gradual change and pre-adaptation: the partial "eye" performs some useful function other than seeing; it has survival value. The appearance of the mammalian kidney presents a similar problem for the gradualist.[14] Richard Goldschmidt (1878-1958), a geneticist at the University of California, was an evolutionist. But for many organs he claimed that this gradual process is untenable. After briefly outlining the problem in his book, *The Material Basis of Evolution* (1940), he challenged evolutionists who hold to gradualism to explain the evolution of the following:

> . . . hair in mammals, feathers in birds, segmentation of arthropods and vertebrates, the transformation of the gill arches in phylogeny including the aortic arches, muscles, nerves, etc.; further, teeth, shells of mollusks, ectoskeletons [exoskeletons], compound eyes, blood circulation, alternation of generation, statocysts, ambulacral system of echinoderms, pedicellaria of the same, cnidocysts, poison apparatus of snakes, whalebone, and finally, primary chemical differences like hemoglobin vs. hemocyanin, etc. Corresponding examples from plants could be given.[15]

Without doubt, these problems constitute truly great roadblocks for one who

Analysis: From Cells to Humans

considers accepting a gradualistic version of evolutionary theory.
Organs found in one species but nowhere else constitute another kind of gap. Denton provided several examples, such as the male dragonfly's use of its reproductive organ in its mating flight:

> The male flies ahead of the female and grips her head with terminal claspers. The female then bends her abdomen forward and receives the sperm from a special copulatory organ which is situated toward the front on the undersurface of the abdomen of the male dragonfly and which he fills with semen from the true reproductive aperture before the start of the mating flight.

Denton concluded:

> This strange manoevre, which seems a curiously roundabout way to bring sperm to egg, depends on the unique and complex machinery which forms the male copulatory organ . . . . No other insect possesses anything like [this organ], nor is it led up to gradually by a sequence of simpler transitional structures.[16]

Thus, the copulatory organ of the male dragonfly provides another example of a gap. Taken together, these gaps provide a formidable problem for evolutionary theory.

Molecular Methods. A comparison of the rate of evolution determined two different ways leads to another difficulty with evolutionary theory. In one way, biochemists use one of several *molecular clock* methods; the other approach depends upon the rate at which structure evolves. The pictures derived from the two different approaches should be similar, but they are not.

One molecular clock method depends upon the rate of change of the order of amino acids in a protein related to a certain structure. According to evolutionary theory, this rate has been constant over several hundred million years. However, some biochemists do not agree that the rate has been constant. For those who do maintain the rate has been constant, there are problems.

For example, evolutionists assume that human beings and chimpanzees descended from a common ancestor; at one time, then, two lines of descent diverged—one from the common ancestor to modern chimpanzees, the other to modern human beings. With respect to the order of amino acids in a protein, the molecular difference between chimpanzees and that hypothetical ancestor is about the same as the difference between human beings and that ancestor. This result conflicts with results obtained comparing the difference between the organs of the chimpanzee and the hypothetical ancestor, with the corresponding difference for human beings and that ancestor. The time at which structural differences appeared is determined by examination of the fossil record. While the *molecular* chimpanzee-ancestor and human being-ancestor differences are about the same, the *organismal* difference between human beings and that hypothetical ancestor is at least five times that of chimpanzees. According to evolutionary theory, if it is five-to-one using one method, it should also be five-to-one in any other method; if it is one-to-one using one method, it should also be one-to-one in any other method, and so forth.

This example is not an isolated result. In general, if one assumes the validity of the evolutionary model, the rate of molecular evolution appears to be smooth, while structural evolution appears to be erratic.[17]

Another molecular method of determining the rate of evolution is *DNA hybridization*, developed in the 1980s. In this method, one compares the overall structures of the DNA molecules of a pair of living species. The rate of change of overall structure for the two DNA molecules must be known. It is assumed that the lines of descent of the two organisms meet at a common ancestor, and that the greater the measured difference in overall DNA structure, the longer the two species have existed independently. Using these assumptions and the measured difference in overall DNA structure, one can obtain the time of divergence from the common ancestor. Since DNA carries the genetic information, this method has the advantage of determining the total difference between two organisms.[18,19]

Still another molecular method is the determination of the *immunological distance* between two proteins of the same kind found in two different species. In an immunological reaction, organisms protects themselves against foreign substances. Suppose an experimenter works with four organisms, A1 and A2 from Species A, B1 from Species B, and C1 from Species C. If the experimenter introduces into A1 a foreign protein from B1, which is an antigen, then A1's immune system reacts to protect A1 by producing an antibody. The antibody, a lock, immobilizes the antigen, the key that fits into the lock. How much A1 reacts to this foreign substance can be measured. Then the experimenter introduces into A2 a protein from C1; once again, how much A2 reacts can be measured. If the amount of reaction is about the same for A1 and A2, then Species B and C are immunologically close to each other and presumably closely related. The greater the difference in the two reactions, the greater the immunological distance between Species B and C. According to evolutionary theory,

Analysis: From Cells to Humans

the greater the immunological distance between Species B and C, the earlier the lines that led to those two species diverged from a common ancestor.[20]

The problems here are similar to the problem already referred to. Thus, the times of various postulated evolutionary events obtained using one of these methods (DNA hybridization and immunological distance) might disagree with the times obtained using the fossils alone. Here, too, using molecular evidence for the ancestry of human beings leads to a branching time not confirmed by fossil evidence.[21] Concerning these problems, Elwyn Simons, a prominent paleoanthropologist at Yale University who did not accept any molecular method, said:

> If the immunological dates of divergence devised by [Vincent] Sarich [one of the inventors of the method] are correct, then paleontologists have not yet found a single fossil related to the ancestry of any living primate. . . I find this impossible to believe. It is not presently acceptable that *Australopithecus* sprang full-blown five million years ago, as Minerva did from Jupiter, from the head of a chimpanzee or gorilla.[22]

That a worker in the field does not accept a new method is not particularly remarkable. But his conclusion that acceptance of the new method destroys all the other work in the field certainly raises questions about the scientific status of research on human ancestry.

Response to Anti-Evolutionary Objections. Evolutionists have answered the objections to evolution—more specifically, to macroevolution. I shall now discuss four of those answers.

(1) Evolutionists call attention to a few species that they claim are transitional, that is, species in the gaps in the fossil record. Isn't it possible that these species point to an eventual filling of the gaps? I have already presented strong evidence that the gaps seem to be permanent. But let us look at transitional forms that evolutionists have proposed.

The *Archaeopteryx*, an ancient species possessing both bird and reptile characteristics, is the best known proposed transitional form. Did this bird have reptile ancestors? Close examination indicates that it was truly a bird. It could fly. There is only a slight suggestion of reptilian features. Furthermore, this "transitional" form was so far from reptiles that evolutionary theory requires additional, as-yet-unknown transitional forms between the *Archaeopteryx* and reptiles.[23]

With species at first thought transitional, one often finds that the individual organs of the species are not at all transitional. Thus, the lungfish has fins, gills, and other organs like any fish, but lungs and a heart like an amphibian. Yet evolutionary theory requires that *both organs and organisms* be transitional. The duck-billed platypus is another example. It is unusual. Even so, its organs are not transitional. While it lays eggs like reptiles, its hair and mammary glands are like those of mammals.[24]

(2) Evolutionists attack the design argument that anti-evolutionists present, discussed in Chapters 2-4. Those not accepting evolution claim that obvious design in the world of living things shows that random evolution has not occurred. Evolutionists have sometimes answered by calling attention to the existence of vestigial organs. These organs, so the evolutionary argument goes, were once useful. Because of evolution, organisms no longer need these organs, and in time they will disappear altogether. Therefore, says the argument, if there was design, it was not good design.

But the inability of scientists to demonstrate the usefulness of an organ, such as the human vermiform appendix as an example, is not proof that the organ does not have a function. Pun made the point well:

> At one point, there were thought to be up to 180 vestigial organs in humans alone; however, the number has been dwindling as the functions of these organs are slowly being discovered.
>
> The most frequently cited vestigial organ in humans is the vermiform appendix. . . . It can be surgically removed without any apparent ill effect to the body. However, there are good indications from the studies of the appendix in rabbits that this organ functions as part of the immune system.[25]

Pun then described the evidence for this claim, and indicated further that the rabbit appendix may also be involved in the manufacture of certain lymphocytes.

(3) Some evolutionists have proposed a theory that builds on two facts about the history of life that heretofore anti-evolutionists thought proved their case. The one fact is the existence of gaps in the fossil record; the other is the amazing stability of life forms. I have already described the gaps. The tuberculosis bacillus provides an example of stability. Tuberculosis was known in ancient Greece; after perhaps 4 million generations various strains exist, and yet the bacillus is still the tuberculosis bacillus. Stability is a fact. Microevolution has not led to macroevolution.

Niles Eldredge and Stephen Jay Gould use gaps and stability as the basis of their evolutionary theory, *punctuated equilibrium*.[26] (Gould is a zoologist

Analysis: From Cells to Humans

at Harvard University and Eldredge is in the fossil invertebrates department at the American Museum of Natural History in New York City.) According to their theory, the fossil record has two outstanding characteristics: species appear suddenly, fully formed, and they remain almost exactly the same for their entire existence, spanning a very long period of time. How, then, does macroevolution occur? Eldredge and Gould postulated that macroevolution cannot occur in a large population because it has built-in defenses against great change. It can, however, occur over a short period of time in a small part of the population of a species that is geographically isolated from the main part of the population. The main part of the population is in *equilibrium*; because the period of isolation is short, the equilibrium is *punctuated*. The evolution that occurs rapidly in a small population in a short period leaves so few fossils that the probability of finding any of them is vanishingly small. All these things taken together, they say, mean that we *should* observe stability in past or present species and that the fossil record *should* contain gaps. Gould claimed that the gaps in the fossil record are real; evolutionary change is episodic, not continuous. He claimed that the gaps in the fossil record are not discussed enough:

> The extreme rarity of transitional forms in the fossil record persists as the trade secret of paleontology. The evolutionary trees that adorn our textbooks have data only at the tips and nodes of their branches; the rest is inference, however reasonable, not the evidence of fossils.[27]

Those who hold to evolution by punctuated equilibrium thus maintain that evidence for their model is the absence of transitional fossils.

What fossil evidence refutes evolutionary theory? Any new fossils that bridge the gaps would add credence to general evolutionary theory but tend to refute punctuated equilibrium theory. Failure to find such fossils would confirm the punctuated equilibrium model of evolution. In other words, no matter what happens in the search for fossils, some form of evolutionary theory will be confirmed. This is but one more illustration of the impact evolutionary theory has had on the scientific establishment. Many natural scientists do not ask if new evidence confirms or disproves evolutionary theory; rather, they ask if the new evidence modifies or adds to our understanding of evolutionary theory.

(4) To avoid problems with evolutionary theory, many evolutionists have made bizarre suggestions. Chapter 6 indicates that many natural scientists admit the extreme difficulty, even impossibility, of constructing a model

of the evolution of the simplest life from nonlife. The wall between life and nonlife is too high. But some of them are unwilling to admit that God created. I described a few extremely radical suggestions made to avoid accepting the creation of life: perhaps the seeds of life came from another part of the universe or perhaps some beings we think of as creatures actually did the planning. In a similar way, some scientists have suggested radical scenarios explaining the jumps across the gaps. (Punctuated equilibrium theory may fall into that category.)

An extremely unlikely suggestion arose in response to a 1966 conference of mathematicians called to examine the claims of evolutionists who maintain that evolution has occurred by random mutations. (This is the same mathematical conference mentioned in Chapter 6.) Mathematicians at the conference concluded that evolution by random processes is highly improbable. But evolutionary biologists answered that the model the mathematicians used was too simple. Specifically, they claimed that mutation did not need to occur by alteration of a single base within a gene; it is possible for a piece of a gene to shift. Also, large segments of a DNA molecule, representing many genes, can move from the DNA of one chromosome to DNA in another chromosome. According to this suggestion, thousands of genetic changes could occur in one generation.[28,29]

Goldschmidt had earlier made a proposal concerning the shift of genes. He postulated a large-scale genetic change, thus producing an individual radically different from its forebears. In Pun's words:

> Goldschmidt therefore advocated a wholesale chromosomal rearrangement that he called "the systemic mutation" as the novel genetic process to account for speciation. Such a drastic chromosomal rearrangement is supported by observations of *Drosophila* chromosomes. While natural selection usually eliminates such individuals who arise from systemic mutation, occasionally it may allow them to propagate as "hopeful monsters" under special circumstances.[30]

The phrase "hopeful monsters" is from Goldschmidt. Pun indicated a lack of empirical evidence for the theory.

Perhaps the idea that random mutation occasionally leads to an improvement is comparable to a "mutation" in an entirely different context. Consider this question: how often is a printed text improved by a typographical error?

The Question of Human Evolution

The Basic Question. In the present discussion I intentionally separate human evolution from other biological evolution. The question of the evolution of the human body—not even considering the total person—is different for six reasons.

First, many people consider this question the most important part of evolution. The heart of most controversies over evolution centers on whether the human family descended from animals.

Second, much of the evidence presented for the evolution of the human body is not like that supposed to show animal evolution. For example, concerning human evolution, much attention is given to the behavior of fossilized animals that are supposed to have preceded human beings.

Third, to the extent that we limit the discussion to the evolution of human beings from primate animals, the question of microevolution versus macroevolution is not so prominent. If we limit our attention to the evolution of the *body* of the human being, it *might* be possible to postulate a reasonably short series of microevolutionary steps between the body of a nonhuman primate and the body of a human being.

Fourth, many of the arguments advanced to refute general evolutionary theory, such as the vanishingly small probability for the occurrence of some of the postulated evolutionary steps, do not have much relevance in a discussion of human evolution.

The fifth and sixth reasons for discussing human evolution separately are the most important.

The fifth reason is the attitude modern society takes toward the question. It assumes that modern human beings are the culmination of the evolutionary process; that human evolution determines the nature of society's institutions; and that human evolution will continue indefinitely into the future, transforming the human family as it moves to the planets of distant stars.

The sixth reason for a separate treatment of human origins is the presentation and description of human beings in the Bible. It is imperative that any discussion of human origins include biblical teachings. I discuss this issue along with other questions concerning the relation between biblical teaching and evolutionary theory in Chapters 8-11. Ultimately, consideration of the nature and origin of the human family leads to a different approach to origins, one that counters the impact of evolutionary thought on modern society.

For Christians who do entertain the possibility that human beings descended from animals, the question of human origins breaks down into two questions. Have all human beings descended from Adam and Eve? If they did, did Adam and Eve descend from animals? But the scientific evidence concerning the origin of the human family does not distinguish between the two questions. Rather, scientists who work in this field condense these two questions into one: "Did humankind descend from animals?"

Some announcements by scientists reported in the popular press might make it seem that such scientists do consider whether Adam and Eve existed. A 1988 *Newsweek* article describing an analysis of mitochondrial DNA in different persons bore the title, "The Search for Adam and Eve." The article concluded that the entire human family descended from one woman who lived in Africa about 200,000 years ago.[31] But scientists who make the one-woman claim do not maintain that she was the first woman, and so this "Eve" has no necessary relation to the biblical Eve.

Dating. During the last few decades, fossils discovered in East Africa have stirred up considerable interest because evolutionists believe they play a significant role in the ancestry of human beings. Popular accounts have focused on the Leakey expeditions in that area.[32] Of particular interest to most people are the very great ages assigned to many fossils claimed to be in the human ancestry. Radiometric methods are particularly important.[33] (See Chapter 5 for a general description of radiometric methods used to determine ages of rocks.)

In one radiometric method, the analyst determines both the total amount of carbon and the amount of carbon-14 in a sample taken from the fossil of interest. The method rests on the fact that a radiation reaction in the upper atmosphere produces carbon-14. Therefore, a small part of carbon dioxide in the atmosphere becomes carbon-14 dioxide; virtually all the rest is carbon-12 dioxide. Because both kinds of atmospheric carbon dioxide are part of the food chain, a small, known fraction of the carbon in all living organisms is carbon-14. But carbon-14 is radioactive; each time a carbon-14 atom emits a particle, there is one less carbon-14 atom present. (Because this process is very slow, no significant amount of carbon-14 breaks down during the lifetime of the organism.) Carbon-12 is not radioactive. At death, the organism can no longer take in carbon dioxide. At that time, the carbon-14/carbon-12 ratio in the corpse is essentially the same as the ratio in the atmosphere. In 5,770 years, the *half-life* of carbon-14, half of it will have decayed, and so the carbon-14/carbon-12 ratio will be half its value when the organism died. It will be one-fourth its initial value in 11,540 years (2 X 5,770 years); one-eighth in 17,310 years (3 X 5,770 years), and so forth. In ten half-lives, that is, in 57,700 years, the ratio will be less than 0.1% of its initial value. Measurement of this ratio in the fossil thus yields the age of the fossil. Because of the difficulty of measuring very small ratios, the upper limit of ages that can be determined by this method is between 50,000 and 100,000 years.

Analysis: From Cells to Humans 113

Another radiometric method depends upon the association of some fossils with volcanic deposits. Thus, the decay of potassium-40 to argon-40 in those deposits, described in Chapter 5, is another radiometric tool for the determination of the ages of associated fossils. To correct for the problem of losing argon gas over the long periods of time involved, special techniques are required.[34] Still another radiometric method used to date fossils utilizes the decay of uranium-238 in rocks associated with the fossils. Both of these last two decays—of potassium-40 to argon-40 and of uranium-238—are extremely slow; therefore, each of these methods is used for fossils whose ages may be many millions of years.

These radiometric methods provide reasonably accurate ages for fossils claimed to be either pre-human or human and for material found with those fossils.

The Fossil Evidence. The names of some creatures in the fossil record that are of interest in the present discussion (not all from East Africa) and the estimated periods of their existence (in years before the present), respectively, are: *Australopithecus afarensis,* 3.8 million-3.1 million; *Australopithecus africanus,* 2.5 million-1.1 million; *Australopithecus robustus,* 2.1 million-1.1 million; *Homo habilis,* 2.0 million-1.4 million; *Homo erectus,* 1.8 million-400,000; *Homo neanderthalensis,* 150,000-30,000; and *Homo sapiens,* 40,000-present. The modern human being is *Homo sapiens.* Paleoanthropologists have attempted construction of the human lineage using these fossils and others not listed here.[35]

Paleoanthropologists generally agree on the ages of the fossils given above. They also agree that certain items, discovered along with *Homo erectus* and *Homo neanderthalensis* fossils, are useful for classifying fossils. Stone tools, found in many places, constitute one example. Often a tool kit is found with a fossil. But some investigators maintain that tools are an unreliable guide.[36] The association of one fossil with charred deer meat suggests that a hunter was buried at that place. Fireplaces have been found. One fossil was found on a bed of flowers, suggesting belief in a life after death. Examination of another fossil indicated that complicated arm surgery had been carried out.[37]

Paleoanthropologists are not sure what constitutes "human." What must one look for in a fossil or in its grave, they ask, to lead us to accept it as the fossil of a human being or a creature similar to human beings? At one time several criteria were available, but with a better understanding of animal behavior, some of those criteria are now in question. It was once thought that only human beings could fashion and use tools. Yet some modern animals make tools. Likewise, ability to learn, to plan ahead, to conceptualize, and to count are debatable criteria.[38]

Problems. Many of the fossils and hypotheses concerning human origins are due to the East African discoveries of the Leakeys—Louis (1903-1972), his wife Mary, and their son Richard. In Roger Lewin's account of the Leakey work he showed repeatedly that the Leakeys and others in the field are prima donnas. Discoveries are kept from competitor paleoanthropologists to prevent them from making their own analyses.[39] Some paleoanthropologists complain that Richard Leakey determines who may work at the East African sites.[40,41] Lewin quoted one paleoanthropologist who maintained that Louis Leakey said in effect:

> The fossils I find are the important ones and are on the direct line to man, preferably bearing names I have coined, whereas the fossils you find are of lesser importance and are all on side branches of the tree.[42]

Donald Johanson, another well-known paleoanthropologist, made a telling comment concerning controversies among paleoanthropologists: "Anthropologists who deal with human fossils tend to get very emotionally involved with their bones."[43]

In paleoanthropology it is difficult to obtain enough data for the older creatures in the list at the beginning of this section. Therefore, it is not easy to formulate a scientific theory. Furthermore, the fossil record contains several gaps in time. These two problems—paucity of evidence and gaps in time—are the principal problems of paleoanthropologists who insist that ultimately they will be able to show that human beings have animal forebears. At present, however, most critics focus attention on the paucity of evidence. David Pilbeam, another prominent paleoanthropologist, said, "If you brought in a smart scientist from another discipline and showed him the meager evidence we've got, he'd surely say, 'Forget it, there isn't enough to go on.'"[44] In addition, paleoanthropologists do not agree on how the fossils they do have relate to the human lineage. Some insist that fossils which are undoubtedly animal fossils are, however, also in the human lineage. Others construct a sequence leading to modern human beings that includes only fossils of creatures that seem to have had human characteristics.

Thus, it is not surprising that Roger Lewin, who was close to Richard Leakey, wrote an entire book, *Bones of Contention: Controversies in the Search for Human Origins* (1987), on the debates among paleoanthropologists.[45] Since the debate that Lewin described is very important in the present discussion, I devote much of the remainder of this chapter to parts of his book.

Analysis: From Cells to Humans

Lewin showed that paleoanthropology depends more than most branches of science on individual opinion and bias.[46] He quoted Sir Grafton Elliot Smith, a British anthropologist, who said, "Almost every new discovery has started afresh such disputes as followed the finding of the Neanderthal skull."[47] In the same vein, Lewin quoted Sir Wilfred Le Gros Clark, another British anthropologist, who said in 1958, "Every discovery of a fossil relic which appears to throw light on connecting links in man's ancestry always has [aroused] controversy."[48]

Lewin devoted two chapters to the long struggle concerning whether a certain skull, that of the so-called "Taung child," was legitimately in the human line. (It was named *Australopithecus africanus*, that is, a southern ape from Africa.) The debate began in the mid-1920s, and by the end of the 1940s certain prominent anthropologists changed their minds and accepted the skull as part of the human line. But even in the 1980s, said Lewin, the claim was not universally accepted. Lewin's account of the Taung skull is as important for the claim itself as for what it reveals about differences of opinion in the paleoanthropological community. Observing these differences, the outsider is likely to have a feeling of uncertainty.

David Pilbeam's dramatic change of opinion in 1978 contributed to this uncertainty. For about 15 years prior to that time, said Lewin,

> ... Pilbeam, with his Yale colleague Elwyn Simons, had embodied the science's virtually unanimous commitment to one particular view of human origins. Namely, that humans split away from ape ancestors at least fifteen million years ago; and that the first member of the line leading to us was a baboon-sized creature known as *Ramapithecus*.[49]

But in 1978 Pilbeam shocked his colleagues:

> I will never again cling so firmly to one evolutionary scheme. I have come to believe that many statements we make about the hows and whys of human evolution *say as much about us, the paleoanthropologist and the larger society in which we live*, as about anything that "really" happened.[50] (Emphasis added.)

Pilbeam also said,

> I try hard to detect [assumptions] in my own thinking, to isolate those assumptions that are not articulated because they are so "obvious," yet will seem so silly a few years from now. I am also

aware of the fact that, at least in my own subject of paleoanthropology, "theory"—heavily influenced by implicit ideas—almost always dominates "data" . . . . Ideas that are totally unrelated to actual fossils have dominated theory building, which in turn strongly influences the way fossils are interpreted.[51]

The *Ramapithecus* fossil had been discovered in 1932. For paleoanthropologists it was extremely important: it indicated that the hominid line split off from the ape line about fifteen million years ago. Lewin reflects on the effect of Pilbeam's "dramatic public recantation" (Lewin's phrase) concerning this fossil:

> Here, then, was a very complete picture of an animal—not just what it looked like, but also how it lived. And all based on a few fragments of upper and lower jaws and teeth. "Yes, what you see there is the complete Darwinian view of human origins, the complete package," Pilbeam now observes. "What we saw in the fossils was the small canines, and the rest followed, all linked together somehow. The Darwinian picture has a long tradition and it was very powerful."[52]

Part of the reason Pilbeam and others changed their minds was the new molecular clock evidence from biochemistry, discussed above. The debate reduced to this: if one did not use the biochemical evidence, apes and human beings separated about fifteen million years ago; if the biochemical evidence was admitted, they separated about five million years ago.

The outsider who is uncertain about paleoanthropological developments may not, however, use the events leading to this uncertainty as proof that human evolution did not take place. What these controversies and occasional recantations do indicate is that confident claims of human evolution have a weak basis.

The sizes of the brains of the various fossils supposed to be in the human line constitute another problem for evolutionary paleoanthropologists. Loren Eiseley (citing Tilly Edinger, a well-known paleoneurologist) noted that human evolution must have been very fast, for the size of the cerebral hemispheres increased 50% while the body size did not increase at all.[53,54] (Eiseley also stated that the trebling of the size of the human brain in the first year, "a peculiar leap," is unknown in the animal world.) In discussing the *Australopithecines*, Lewin claimed that certain supposed forebears of modern human beings, who already stood upright, had very small brains and therefore, according to one theory, intelligence could not have been an important factor in human evolution.[55]

Paleoanthropologists have also debated this question: Are human beings naturally aggressive? At first they said yes, but later some paleoanthropologists changed their minds.

The picture of the aggressive primitive human being arose when tools that could be used as weapons were found with hominid fossils. Lewin quoted Raymond Dart, the discoverer of the Taung skull in the 1920s, as saying in 1953 that human beings have always been extremely aggressive:

> The blood-bespattered, slaughter-gutted archives of human history from the earliest Egyptian and Sumerian records to the most recent atrocities of the Second World War accord with early universal cannibalism, with animal and human sacrificial practices, or their substitutes in formalized religions, and with world-wide scalping, head-hunting, body mutilating and necrophiliac practices of mankind proclaiming this common bloodlust differentiator, this predacious habit, this mark of Cain that separates man dietetically from his anthropoid relatives and allies him rather with the deadliest of carnivores![56]

But after 1953, said Lewin, paleoanthropologists became convinced that the creatures thought to be human were in fact not human, and that a branch in the line eventually led to human beings. In this new view, the earliest human beings were not believed to be bloodthirsty. Lewin suggested that the newer idea is more palatable: the image of a peaceable early human is simply more desirable than a warlike image.[57] So, said Lewin, paleoanthropologists have both scientific and nonscientific reasons for assuming what people were like:

> These peaceable theories of human origins, like the beast-in-man idea, become "a mirror which reflected back only those aspects of human experience which its authors wanted to see."[58]

Lewin continued by introducing "four dimensions":

> The Truth about man's place in nature is therefore to be sought in four quite separate dimensions. In the first three levels—of time, form, and behavior—there is scientific evidence, from fossils, stone tools, comparative anatomy and behavior, and molecular biology.

Using this evidence, it may one day be possible accurately to draw lines back through time, connecting ourselves with our forebears, their forebears with theirs, and so on until a detailed evolutionary tree traces the link between humanity and brute nature.

But the fourth dimension, one that does not often enter discussions, is the one that gave Lewin a problem:

> Exactly where brute nature ends, however, and humanity begins is not a question for molecular or comparative biology. It is a question of the fourth dimension: a question of self-image. Here there are no lines accurately to be drawn, no hypotheses to be tested, *for humanity's view of itself is constantly shifting, depending on the experience of the moment.*[59] (Emphasis added.)

Lewin maintained that paleoanthropology shares some of the limitations of other sciences, corresponding to the limitations inherent in any human activity. But, he said, only paleoanthropology must work with that fourth dimension, with humanity's ever-changing self-image.

Here Lewin is wrong. After all his discussion, Lewin is quite willing to welcome the impact of evolutionary theory not only on paleoanthropology, but also on other sciences. Human beings may not decide how to define what is human. It is not necessary to take into account current human self-image to make a fundamental decision about the fossil record. What is important is an absolute standard, not what we decide. The answer to Lewin's question is not subjective. The Bible provides the correct answer: human beings are those creatures which have been created in the image of God.

Conclusion

What can we say about the scientific evidence for the evolutionary scenario? The evidence for some parts of the scenario is reasonably good. Examples are the great age of Creation and the general picture of the formation of elements, stars, galaxies, and planets.

But in my opinion, the evidence for most of the scenario is either very weak or nonexistent. For example, efforts to prove there was no beginning are obviously improper. It also strains credulity to accept any hypothesis so far presented that explains evolution from nonlife to life.

I do not doubt that microevolution has occurred and continues to take place. But evolutionists have not successfully met the challenges to explain gaps in the fossil record. Nor have they shown why there are gaps between

Analysis: From Cells to Humans

the organs of different species presumed to bear evolutionary relationship. Furthermore, molecular clock and structural evidence disagree concerning times of divergence.

The evidence *might* indicate that the first human beings lived a few hundred thousand years ago. Some Christian scientists who do not accept general evolutionary theory think that the first human beings may have been *Homo erectus*. Other Christian scientists think they were *Homo neanderthalensis*. In my view, either group might be correct. The scientific evidence presents a picture of creatures who lived a very long time ago and behaved like human beings: they hunted, they buried their dead with flowers, they performed surgical operations, and so forth. The evidence does not prove that these creatures, even if they were human, descended from animals.

Another possibility exists for these ancient creatures. A large number of species are extinct. It could be that God created now extinct animal species which were unrelated to human beings and did not bear the image of God, but may have borne some of the characteristics of human beings. After all, it is bearing the image of God that makes creatures human, not the ability to use tools or to carefully bury their dead.

In the next four chapters I discuss the nature of scientific activity and the evolutionary scenario in the light of biblical teaching.

Chapter Eight
Revelation

In the face of the problem of dualism described in Chapter 2, what should Christians do? It is one thing to criticize the trend in natural science during the last few centuries, to show how its very definition depends on incorrect ideas that go deep into human history, and to claim that evolutionary theory has had and probably will have in the future a devastating effect on society. But we cannot stop there. This earth that human beings investigate is the Lord's. The purpose of this chapter and Chapter 9 is to discuss what Christians should think of natural science, what they should do with it, and how they should see that natural scientific activity is one more way of honoring the Lord.

Let us start by reversing the problem of dualism. Dualism disallows interaction between the realms of natural science and the Bible (or, if there is interaction, it is one-way—from natural science to the Bible). By reversing the problem I mean that I shall emphasize that we would not have natural science were it not for *general revelation* and that the Bible is *special revelation*. The nature of those two kinds of revelation determines how this discussion should proceed in examining the nature of Christian natural science.[1]

In this chapter I shall discuss the two kinds of revelation. In the first section, I take up the origin of general and special revelation, how they are related, Christ's work of redemption, and the extent and purpose of general revelation. The subject of the second section is the phrase, "the Bible and science." As usually understood, the phrase is inadequate. I conclude this section with a closer look at Christ's redemption of all Creation. This background makes it possible to consider a Christian approach to the sciences in Chapter 9.

General and Special Revelation

Origin. Before God created Adam and Eve, he created all other forms of life, the earth, the planets, and the stars. But Creation was not complete until he created the human family. Without human beings, Creation was "good" (Gen. 1:25). With human beings, God pronounced Creation "very good" (1:31). Those human beings were to subdue Creation and replenish it. Adam and Eve were at the head of the "very good" Creation.

Revelation

The assignment to be fruitful and subdue the earth (Gen. 1:28) meant that Adam and Eve had work to do. As they subdued the earth, they would investigate it. Their investigation—for example, as Adam saw and then named the animals—made them, as the days passed, more and more aware of the mighty works of God. Only because God *revealed* his works to them could they become aware of them. This is general revelation.

In their perfect state Adam and Eve did not, as they investigated, merely learn more about animals, trees, the sun, and so forth. They did not abstract their knowledge from its context. In no way was their investigation separated from the relation of Creation to God. Because they were obedient, all their work, including their investigative work, was a *conscious* response to the command to be fruitful and subdue the earth.

Human response to Creation is not equivalent to general revelation. God reveals; human beings respond. Part of this response is investigation of Creation, eventually called scientific activity. Some of this scientific activity is natural scientific activity, which is incomplete and flawed because human beings were always limited and also became sinful. But such a statement says nothing about what God did and does; his *revelation* is flawless and infallible.

In the beginning Adam and Eve had a perfect life with God. Because he spoke to them and because they continued to learn more of his works, they praised him. The relationship between God and human beings changed fundamentally when they rebelled against him. Furthermore, rebels were now at the head of Creation, a Creation that was therefore no longer "very good."

God acted to clean up the mess. By his word, he had created. Now there was an additional word, a new word. He promised Adam and Eve that he would reverse the situation. A long time after Adam and Eve lived God caused this new word, describing his works and plan of salvation, to be written down. God fulfilled his promise by sending his Son, the Word who became flesh. While God spoke to human beings in various ways in former times, the written word that we now have, the Bible, is God's special revelation. It is the word that reveals his Son to us and which supplements general revelation.

Relation Between General and Special Revelation. It is not enough to say merely that we have both general and special revelation. Those two ways in which God reveals his works are related. General revelation came first; special revelation was required as a corrective. Only because something went radically wrong in Creation, where God revealed himself generally, did he reveal himself in another way. In one sense special revelation is a re-publication, a second way in which God tells us that he is the Creator and, because of Adam's sin, the Redeemer. Because of human sin, general revelation was no longer enough.

God did not provide special revelation because of some deficiency in general revelation; rather, the deficiency lay in post-Fall human beings. Because God gave special revelation to human beings who no longer found general revelation sufficient for their needs, it "fits into" general revelation: special revelation is a supplement that opens up general revelation. Those who now believe have eyes to see. Naturally, it is impossible for general and special revelation to contradict each other.[2]

Because of this intimate relation between general and special revelation, we can in no part of our lives be "free" of either kind of revelation. God always asks human beings to respond to both kinds of revelation. We usually acknowledge that those who respond to special revelation, even when they do not respond correctly, are religious. However, God also reveals himself by means of general revelation and demands response to it. Every person does indeed respond, correctly or not, to general revelation. Just as the response to special revelation is religious, so must the response to general revelation be religious. No part of our lives is separate from the revelation of God. Therefore, nothing in life is neutral with respect to the response God requires. In other words, all life is religious. Not only scientific activity but also every other activity in life constitutes a religious response to the revelation of God. Even a response of rebellion against God is a response and is therefore religious.

Neglecting to recognize our inevitable response to general revelation as religious is the source of considerable difficulty. Some Christians err by assuming that only special revelation is important. They see this life as only transient and short at best; only our future life, which we can anticipate because we have special revelation, is important. As a result, their recognition of the relevance of special revelation to "this life" tends to fall short. Other Christians, even though they understand that both general and special revelation are important, err by not seeing that both reach into all life and that therefore nothing in life is religiously neutral. By drawing a line between general and special revelation they put scientific activity into a supposedly neutral area. These two kinds of incorrect response to revelation are the source of much of the difficulty among Christians as they struggle to solve questions concerning the Christian faith and scientific activity, including, of course, questions about evolution and its impact on society.

Redemption. If God is not only the Creator but also the Redeemer, what does he redeem? Rebellious human beings require redemption. But it was the creation of human beings that made Creation "very good." Therefore, the Creator-Redeemer redeems the flawed Creation as well.

I could not make these points were it not for special revelation. The relation between general and special revelation is so intimate that we would not otherwise know what God has planned for all Creation, including human beings. In what follows, I shall indicate some of what the Bible teaches about God's intentions.

What does it mean to say that "God" is the Redeemer? *It is the Triune God who is active in redemption.* The Father sent his Son, the head of the Church, to sacrifice himself; and the Holy Spirit teaches the Church. But the Bible also teaches that the Triune God—the Son and the Holy Spirit as well as the Father—created the world.

> . . . The Spirit of God was hovering over the waters. (Gen. 1:2)

> In the beginning was the Word, and the Word was with God, and the Word was God. He was with God in the beginning. Through him all things were made; without him nothing was made that has been made. (John 1:1-3)

If Christ is the Creator-Redeemer, then he will redeem the Creation that human beings spoiled. He is for all time the King of Creation. Paul brings it all—Christ, Creation, redemption—together:

> For by [Christ] all things were created: things in heaven and on earth, visible and invisible, whether thrones or powers or rulers or authorities; all things were created by him and for him. He is before all things, and in him all things hold together . . . . For God was pleased to have all his fullness dwell in him, and through him to reconcile to himself all things, whether things on earth or things in heaven, by making peace through his blood, shed on the cross. (Col. 1:16-17, 19)

The Extent of General Revelation. Before Adam and Eve sinned, the Creation that they could investigate was perfect. Is general revelation limited to that perfect Creation? In other words, as we investigate the world we know, can we claim that we interact with general revelation? Special revelation makes precisely that claim.

David told people in a fallen world that they could see the wonders of God's Creation with their own eyes:

> The heavens declare the glory of God; the skies proclaim the work of his hands. (Ps. 19:1)

In Lystra, Barnabas and Paul told people that they ought to see that God testifies of himself through rain and seasons:

> In the past, [God] let all nations go their own way. Yet he has not left himself without testimony: He has shown kindness by giving you rain from heaven and crops in their seasons; he provides you with plenty of food and fills your hearts with joy. (Acts 14:16-17)

Paul summed up the matter in one of the most powerful passages in the Bible. General revelation is for everyone; and it is their fault if they do not see God in his Creation:[3]

> For since the creation of the world God's invisible qualities—his eternal power and divine nature—have been clearly seen, being understood from what has been made, so that men are without excuse. (Rom. 1:20)

The Purpose of General Revelation. Thus, both general and special revelation are from God and are for the purpose of revealing God to us. We might think that our response to general revelation is sufficient if we merely stand amazed at his works. We marvel at the grandeur of Creation, at its unimaginable size, and at the fantastic complexity of the subatomic world. Is that not enough? There is more, and if we do not see that there is more, we actually miss the point.

After all, God created Adam and Eve for a purpose. He gave his reason:

> Then God said, "Let us make man in our image, in our likeness, and let them rule over the fish of the sea and the birds of the air, over the livestock, over all the earth, and over all the creatures that move along the ground." (Gen. 1:26)

God's command two verses later contains the same idea:

> God blessed them and said to them, "Be fruitful and increase in number; fill the earth and subdue it. Rule over the fish of the sea and the birds of the air and over every living creature that moves on the ground." (Gen. 1:28)

Revelation

These passages indicate that the interaction of human beings with Creation, that is, their understanding of general revelation, is intimately associated with their God-appointed tasks in life. Human beings could not carry out the command to subdue without understanding Creation. In modern terms, we cannot feed, clothe, and house the billions of people on the earth without having previously engaged in natural scientific activity—interaction with Creation and thus a response to general revelation.

The calling each of us has in his or her life is to serve the Lord. As we serve, we interact with Creation and thus respond to general revelation. Two examples show how this comes about for those who are not directly engaged in natural scientific activity.

Consider a farmer whom Isaiah describes:

> When a farmer plows for planting, does he plow continually? Does he keep on breaking up and harrowing the soil? When he has leveled the surface, does he not sow caraway and scatter cummin? Does he not plant wheat in its place, barley in its plot, and spelt in its field? His God instructs him and teaches him the right way. Caraway is not threshed with a sledge.... Grain must be ground to make bread; so one does not go on threshing it forever.... All this also comes from the Lord Almighty, wonderful in counsel and magnificent in wisdom. (Parts of Is. 28:24-29)

He describes "a farmer," that is, a typical farmer. God does not give the typical farmer a special revelation on how to farm. No, he learns how to farm in the way modern farmers learn—by farming, by listening to others, and so forth. Yet, says Isaiah, God teaches him. This kind of teaching—through experience and from other people—is therefore also part of general revelation. In this general revelation, as with all revelation, what God teaches is without error. But the learner is fallible.

Modern life provides another example showing how God teaches by means of general revelation. Consider social workers, who encounter a wide variety of problems in modern families. Social workers interact with Creation; they, too, have opportunity to respond to general revelation. For example, social workers attempt to sort out the difficulties in family situations where family members hate each other; where problems arise because of cocaine or alcohol abuse; or where trouble is the result of incest, fornication, or adultery. Even if a social worker knows absolutely nothing of special revelation, he or she will know by looking at families that life can be harmonious if love, not hate, is present; if drugs are not abused; if incest, fornication, and adultery are absent. How will a social worker know such things? This knowledge comes from observation of families where these problem situations do not exist, that is, where families live according to the ordinances that have existed since the beginning and are a part of Creation itself. As social workers interact with the present world, they interact with general revelation.

In special revelation God reveals his longsuffering love and ultimately his plan to redeem Creation. In other words, he reveals something of himself. But what does he reveal in general revelation? Once again, he reveals something of himself. To a social worker, he reveals what human life is like if people obey God's laws for families. A social worker might know nothing of special revelation and would therefore suppress the truth that God is the source of the laws for families. Yet that social worker realizes that if all families obeyed those laws, we would have "heaven on earth." The farmer whom God teaches knows that if all farmers obeyed the laws for farming, this earth would be a much more pleasant place than it presently is. God reveals something of himself in both examples because he is a God of harmony, not strife, a God whose Creation we are to enjoy, not destroy. Through these means we learn of the life we all seek—a life of harmony and enjoyment. He is just that kind of God, one who redeems and promises that kind of life.

Modern developments in the natural sciences are excellent examples of human responses to Creation and interaction with general revelation. One fact stands out above all others in modern natural sciences: those sciences are structured. It seems more certain as time passes that the diverse phenomena of chemistry and physics, along with sciences that depend upon the laws of chemistry and physics, such as astronomy, geology, and meteorology, are linked by means of a structure of related physical laws. Even natural scientists who know nothing of special revelation are impressed by the existence of this structure.[4] The nature of the structure in the biotic world is, of course, controversial. But all agree that structure exists.

This structure or orderliness in Creation is also a means whereby God reveals himself. Things fit together in Creation. Isaiah said that God did not create the earth a chaos and God did not tell his people to seek him in chaos (Is. 45:18-19). Natural scientists who become aware of the structure in Creation are without excuse.[5]

"The Bible and Science"

The Phrase. "The Bible and science" is a weak phrase. Yet this phrase is often used as a title or a springboard for a discussion of deep questions, such as the role scientific activity should play in the life of the Christian community. It is, of course, a phrase that immediately suggests controversy—about origins, the first chapters of Genesis, the validity of the scientific work of non-Christians, and so forth. The "and" in the phrase often suggests to Christians the existence of two separate entities: the Bible, the eternal Word of God; and "science," often vaguely defined but usually referring to an aggregate of natural sciences, such as astronomy, biology, chemistry, geology, meteorology, paleontology, physics, and applied sciences.

Several problems can arise when people use the phrase "the Bible and science" in a discussion of the role that scientific activity should play in the life of the Christian community. First, the Bible (to the extent the modern Bible is faithful to the original) *is* now one of the two kinds of revelation, while scientific activity is now part of the human *response* to one of the two kinds of revelation. Comparing our response to both kinds of revelation would be more to the point.

Second, too often the unspoken assumption is that "science" is "natural science." Of course, there is nothing wrong with using the term science as shorthand for natural science, assuming that the context so indicates and assuming that in the context it is proper to limit science to natural science. But the scientific aspect of the human response to general revelation includes all scientific activity, such as developing a new antibiotic, studying the relation between languages, or doing research on learning disorders. In this case, then, the context does not warrant limiting science to natural science.

Third, the emphasis on "the Bible and science" can lead us to skew our philosophy of science. Special revelation opens up general revelation. To the extent that our scientific activity, no matter which science, neglects that relation, we go along a path that leads to wrong conclusions.

For these reasons, discussion of "the Bible and science" ought to be discussion of various kinds of scholarship. All such scholarship, including the study of the Bible, is scientific activity. Therefore, analysis of the relation between the Bible and science should be an analysis between the relation of our understanding of the Bible and our understanding of the various parts of Creation. Such analysis is ultimately a study of the relation between the two ways God reveals himself, in a general way in Creation and in a special way through his Son, revealed to us in the Bible.

Often people who distinguish between God's revelation and our study of his revelation note that God does not contradict himself. Any conflict between the Bible and science is only apparent; the fault lies in our understanding of what God said in the Bible and in Creation. If we had perfect understanding, then all conflict would vanish. This distinction is reasonable as far as it goes. Obviously, the human error that arises from human limitation and human sin can cause conflict between the results of various kinds of study. Usually, however, people who emphasize this distinction do not emphasize the relation between the two kinds of revelation. They might remove conflict in one of the following three ways.

First, they might assume that only the Bible is important. Those who put all their emphasis on the Bible view scientific activity as merely something carried out in this life, soon to pass. Of course, some scientific results are useful. But certainly, they say, scientific results have nothing to do with the Bible, which has eternal significance.

Second, those who put all their emphasis on scientific activity and neglect the Bible (presumably non-Christians) might see the Bible as archaic. Even if it is from God, it is certainly not relevant to modern life, of which scientific activity is such an important part.

For both these approaches, conflict cannot characterize the relation between the Bible and science. Both approaches are obviously wrong—the first, because it does not take Creation seriously, and the second, because it is an open rejection of God's grace.

A third way of removing conflict is also incorrect. But the error is not so obvious and warrants more attention. Here, too, the relation between the two kinds of revelation is weakened; but the people who use this method do not, however, err by de-emphasizing the importance of either the Bible or scientific activity. They remove conflict by claiming that scientific activity reveals the nature of Creation while study of the Bible reveals something else and little, if anything, about the nature of Creation. Different people take "something else" to be different things. Some say it is "God's plan of salvation"; others, "the relation of God to Creation"; still others, "God's will for our spiritual life." The two subjects of study—Creation and the "something else"—are different. For those who take this view, conflict arises when these two subjects are one, or at least mixed. Because of its subtlety, this erroneous view, rather than the first two views, is more likely to lead us in the wrong direction as we work at developing a satisfactory approach to the question about "the Bible and science."[6]

I claimed earlier that special revelation came because human beings sinned; God decided to redeem that which human beings had spoiled. He would, in fact, redeem Creation. Understanding this relation between the two kinds of revelation can help us work out the relation between biblical studies and other kinds of scholarship.

"Intersections." Consider biblical passages supposed to have a direct bearing on science, that is, on scholarly studies of Creation. Perhaps the passage describes some part of Middle Eastern history, history that is a part of the larger historical picture that scholars construct. Or, a passage may contain botanical or geological information. Because of this situation, the idea that secular and sacred studies sometimes *intersect* has arisen. Those who claim that the Bible and Creation teach different things contend that those passages, the "intersections" of the two fields, are at most tangential to the biblical message. Some critics go even farther. They claim that the purpose of the Bible was not to provide scientific facts and therefore nothing in the Bible—history or anything else—is useful for scientific purposes.

Underlying all this criticism runs the idea that the Bible consists of two parts—the essential and the nonessential. The "tangential" is the nonessential; it may or may not be useful for scientists, but it certainly has no bearing on the purpose of the Bible. I shall contend that this division is untenable because of the relation between general and special revelation. Some examples illustrate the point.

(1) The first chapter of Numbers contains a census of the Israelites taken the second year after they left Egypt. The number of the men over 20 who were able to serve in the army was 603,550 (Num. 1:46). Including women and children, the exodus probably consisted of more than two million people. Such an exodus is a significant fact of ancient Middle Eastern history. The oft-repeated theory that Israel was only a small tribe is wrong.

Think of what the size of the number of people in the exodus means for both sacred and secular history or what it indicates about both special and general revelation. God sustained millions of people in a *desert* with food, water, and other necessities of life for a long period of time. Moses, in his farewell speech to the Israelites near the end of their 40-year trek in the wilderness, described God's sustaining care for them in this way:

> Because he loved your forefathers and chose their descendants after them, he brought you out of Egypt by his Presence and his great strength, to drive out before you nations greater and stronger than you and to bring you into their land to give it to you for your inheritance, as it is today. Acknowledge and take to heart this day that the Lord is God in heaven above and on the earth below. There is no other. (Deut. 4:37-39)

For the present discussion, the *size* of the Israelite nation in the wilderness is critical. One of the ways special revelation tells the world of God's love for his people is the biblical account of the provision God made for this *immense* number of people in the wilderness for many years. In the eyes of unbelievers, special "care" could well be illusory had Israel been only a small tribe: we could perhaps imagine a small group of people managing to leave Egypt and traverse the desert without, however, describing the event as miraculous. But God shows us that he can do that which we find impossible. He also does the "impossible" by removing his people from the slavery of sin.

Of what importance for general revelation is this large number in Numbers 1:46? It is a vital statistic in the Israelites' history. To instead use a comparatively small number, a few hundred or at most a few thousand, would seriously distort what actually occurred. The historian who assumes the smaller number would have an entirely wrong picture of what this nation looked like in its early years. If a historian's picture of the early years of a nation would be that far wrong, so the picture for later years would be wrong. Historians rightly abhor such errors, especially when correct information is available. So the large number in Numbers 1:46 is an integral part of both special and general revelation.

(2) The subsequent history of the Israelite nation, mostly in the land of Israel—the invasion of Canaan, the period of the judges, the period of the monarchy, the exile, and the return—is described in Joshua, Judges, Ruth, First and Second Samuel, First and Second Kings, First and Second Chronicles, Ezra, Nehemiah, Esther, and parts of Isaiah, Jeremiah, Ezekiel, and Daniel. This history is also simultaneously general and special revelation. It is general revelation because this history is part of the history of the Middle East. The wonderful works of God—drying up the flooding Jordan River and enabling the Israelites to cross, collapsing the walls of Jericho, withholding rain for more than two years and then giving rain in answer to Elijah's prayer, and many more miracles—are an integral part of the history of Israel. Miracles were but examples of God's care; day-to-day events, which at first do not appear to be the kind of special care associated with miracles, fit into the entire pattern of God's care for his chosen people. Just as with the history of the exodus, one cannot understand the history of the world and the Middle East in particular without incorporating the history of the people of Israel.

At the same time, the history of Israel as given in the Bible is special revelation. The Israelite nation was the chosen people of God, the Old Testament church. The family into which the baby Jesus was born was neither Roman, Egyptian, Syrian, Chinese, Native American, nor any other na-

Revelation 131

tion foreign to Israel. In God's plan of salvation, Jesus was to be born into the Old Testament church. The events of the history of Old Testament Israel pointed ahead to and prepared the way for Jesus Christ, who fulfilled the covenant promise God had made with his covenant people. Special revelation is a coherent unit: its various parts, some of which seem mundane, fit into God's plan to reverse the rebellion of Eden. Because the history of Israel cannot be separated from general revelation, I conclude that the parts of general revelation also fit together and that it, too, is a coherent unit.

That the history of Israel is simultaneously a part of both special and general revelation has certain consequences that may seem to be trivial, but which actually show that one cannot remove special from general revelation. Biblical history is not merely an account of events that took place in some never-never land, quite apart from this world.

I shall list a few of these seemingly trivial consequences.[7] Both Samson and David encountered lions in southwestern Asia, animals not found there today (Judges 14:5-6 and I Samuel 17:34-37). The ancient Hebrews were aware of the Pleiades star cluster and referred to what was probably the Ursa Major constellation as the Bear (Job 38:31-32), as did other ancient peoples. Eastern Mediterranean lands were in ancient times prone to earthquakes (Ex. 19:18, I Sam. 14:15, I Kings 19:11, Matt. 27:51 and 28:2, and Acts 16:26). The Valley of Siddim at the south end of the Dead Sea in Israel contained many tar pits, that is, petroleum seeps, in Abraham's time (Gen. 14:10).

The Old Testament in particular describes many customs of interest to cultural anthropologists. An example is the practice in early Israel of levirate marriage, where a relative of the deceased husband of a childless widow marries her; an example is the marriage of Boaz and Ruth. The Old Testament describes not only cultural practices in Israel, but also those of many other Middle Eastern nations.

Each of these examples, from lions to cultural practices, are useful in some branch of modern science. Each plays a role in both general and special revelation.

(3) A person who refuses to identify the parts of special revelation cited above with general revelation might base this refusal on the claim that the New Testament puts matters differently. One might claim that the accounts of the death and resurrection of Jesus, numerous instructions and models for holy living, and prophecies of the end time have no discernible connection to general revelation. Then, since the Old and New Testaments are related, does not the message of the New Testament remove the entire Bible from the realm of general revelation?

I contend that such a claim concerning the New Testament is not valid. The miraculous events of the New Testament are just as much a part of general revelation as are those of the Old Testament. They are part of the seamless garment of world history. To make such a claim, it is not necessary to prove that miraculous events, such as the resurrection of Christ, were so stupendous that the world would never be the same again. Of course, they were that stupendous, but the point is that they were events in world history and as such become a part of general revelation.

What about the nonhistorical parts of the New Testament—the instructions and models for holy living and the prophecies of the end times? What about similar passages in the Old Testament? To see that these parts of the Bible are also part of general revelation, it is instructive to inquire how they affect those non-Christians who have no knowledge of the Bible. Their only contact with any part of the Bible is by contact with God's people. Obviously, some believer-unbeliever contact is by way of the preaching of the Gospel, that is, by showing unbelievers that God has revealed himself in a special way. But much more believer-unbeliever contact is outside of the explicit communication of the Gospel. Thus, Christians exhibit Christian virtues, such as love, willingness to help the downtrodden, patience, and peacemaking. Christians have been strongly instrumental in great movements, such as freeing slaves, removing women from the near-slave status they once had, helping orphans, founding great hospitals, and introducing general education. In spite of fundamental mistakes outlined in Chapter 2, it was the Christian belief that Creation is neither mystical nor divine that was responsible for the blossoming of the sciences. Even today, in those parts of the world never significantly affected by Christians, the attitude toward slavery, women, orphans, medicine, general education, and scientific activity is often pre-Christian and wicked. But all these things— Christian virtues and the great movements in which Christians have been active—do not in themselves directly communicate the Gospel. They communicate something to unbelievers, but they do not constitute special revelation. From the point of view of the unbeliever, these things are part of general revelation. Therefore, *all* of the Bible is simultaneously special revelation and general revelation.

By means of this argument, I have attempted to show that claiming "intersections" between special and general revelation is inadequate. It is not enough to say that in a few places biblical phenomena are of interest to scientists of today, such as lions in southwest Asia and levirate marriages in ancient Israel.

In adopting a form of this argument, some people maintain that God

Revelation

revealed himself in a special way when he "entered into history." He made a covenant with Abraham, a historical person. Through Moses, he gave his law—in history. Finally, God himself broke into history as he became man at a specific time and place. Christ will come again for the purpose of ending history. The emphasis in this argument is that God's love, expressed through his plan of salvation, is not other-worldly; he came *here* to save his people.

This approach contains much that is good. But claiming that God "entered into history" may imply that not all the history of God's acts of salvation are integral to history as a whole. Those who use this approach usually admit that God is sovereign in all things, but they seem to suggest that his sovereignty is over two kinds of history, sacred and secular. It is better to say that God's revelation is of one piece and that every bit of his special revelation, which shows his love and give his plan of salvation, is part of general revelation.

Probably most people intuitively feel that all historical events must be of one piece. It does seem that events cannot be completely isolated from other events. Modern physical and mathematical theory has put that intuition on a better basis. "Chaos theory," a theory that has received considerable scientific and popular attention in recent years, builds upon an assumed nonisolation of events and makes predictions of resultant physical behavior. The theory shows that the effect of seemingly insignificant events can sometimes be very great, leading to startling consequences. For example, a disturbance of a small part of the air over Tokyo can ultimately affect the weather in New York. Patterns exist in systems that seem to be chaotic—in this case, the atmosphere in various parts of the world. An entire branch of science is developing on the assumption that ultimately all events are related and that a mathematical description of that which seems to be hopelessly chaotic is possible.[8]

An Obvious Question. Suppose it is conceded that special revelation is integrally related to general revelation, that biblical teaching—whether it is of historical fact, how to live the Christian life, or anything else in the Bible—is also general revelation. But I claimed earlier that *both* kinds of revelation reach into all life. Even assuming that general revelation always accompanies special revelation, does special revelation always accompany general revelation? For two reasons I claim that special revelation does indeed always accompany general revelation.

(1) A person cannot properly comprehend God's revelation in Creation without understanding that this revelation, general revelation, is a revelation of God himself. In passages already cited, God teaches that Creation

declares his glory (Ps. 19:1); by studying Creation, farmers learn from God how to farm (Is. 28:24-29); and the rain and seasons are his witnesses (Acts 14:16-17). Furthermore, the entire scientific enterprise, including both the natural sciences and the other sciences, exists because Creation is orderly. That enterprise, properly interpreted, tells us of a God who did not create a chaos or speak to us out of chaos (Is. 45:18-19, RSV). The Bible presents more examples, but the point is that God reveals himself in all his general revelation.

Yet all these examples may seem to only reiterate the point that God reveals himself in general revelation. After all, everyone who has ever lived has been able to see the eternal power and divine nature of God in Creation (Rom. 1:20). But without special revelation, people do not make correct conclusions concerning general revelation. Their sinfulness causes them to suppress that which they should know (Rom. 1:18). Without sin, we would not need special revelation, or at least, the kind of special revelation we do have. Only by means of special revelation in this sinful world can we see that God reveals himself in general revelation.

John Calvin (1509-1564) said that without special revelation, we are like persons whose eyes are dim and who therefore cannot appreciate even the most beautiful book. But with spectacles, they can read. For Calvin, the Bible provides those spectacles. The spectacles help to keep us from making mistakes about God's revelation of himself in Creation. Sinners must interact with general revelation by using spectacles, special revelation.[9,10]

Often when Calvin's remark concerning spectacles is cited, it seems to be little more than a platitude. Thus one might say, "Of course we need the Bible for us to understand that God created; of course only the Bible can tell us that the Triune God is sovereign." But there is more.

First, the Bible provides specifics concerning God's authority in Creation. It states that his authority extends to all parts of Creation—to the seas and the living creatures in the seas, to snow and hail, to mountains and mountain goats, to the cedars of Lebanon, to the stars of the heavens, to all peoples of the earth. Special revelation claims for God so many diverse parts of Creation that the message is clear: everything belongs to him. Special revelation is thereby linked to all general revelation.

Second, we can see what happens when people neither accept, nor is their work influenced by, special revelation. They might be experts in observing and analyzing the created world, but if their work does not exhibit any influence of special revelation, they develop a badly distorted picture of the world. In what follows, I consider only those ideas or systems that unbelievers have advanced either in the complete absence of the biblical message or after they have consciously rejected foundational ideas necessary for modern science, such as the de-deification of the world (rejection of the divinity of matter and the prohibition of experimentation) by Christians at the beginning of the modern scientific period.[11]

(a) Chapter 6 provides several of those distorted pictures of Creation. For example, insects might be the long-sought "higher intelligence." The universe had no beginning. Psychogenesis, where every object, such as a star, has a spirit, explains the history of the universe. Vitalism, a claim that matter is alive, explains evolution and will be the driving force for a future march to a perfect life. This kind of vision of the future is a consequence of the impact of evolutionary thought on modern society.

None of these ideas would be advanced if everyone allowed special revelation to take its rightful place, allowing it to permeate all of general revelation.

(b) Moslems, Hindus, Buddhists, animists, and other followers of ancient religions all receive general revelation. They either do not know about or do not accept special revelation. As a result, their picture of Creation is distorted. They might view events fatalistically, or they might have a circular view of history, where there is neither beginning nor end. They might fear or hope for reincarnation. Their lives might be lived out in fear of the gods that live in animals and trees. Were they to allow special revelation to penetrate general revelation, the fears and distortions would vanish.

(c) Certain scientists have related pagan worldviews, some of them ancient, to modern physical discoveries.

Taoist thought provides one example. It dates from the writings of Lao Tzu and Chuang Tzu in China some time between the third and sixth centuries B.C. One of its principal teachings is about mystical union with "the absolute." A person should follow "the Way," or *Tao*, that precedes and underlies everything. Its teachings are vague and open to various interpretations. In modern times, Fritjof Capra emphasized that part of Taoist thought which attempts to unite various aspects of the universe. He claimed the same property for the physical theory which attempts to unite the fundamental particles of physics and which might eventually unify all physical theory. Therefore, he said, we are forced to perceive the world the way Taoists do. Because of Capra's views, his book *The Tao of Physics* (1975) attracted considerable attention.[12] Capra has been rightly criticized for linking theological or philosophical ideas to a particular physical theory which can, of course, change.[13]

Another system dependent upon Eastern religion has been propounded by John Hagelin at Maharishi International University of Fairfield, Iowa.[14] Hagelin, a theoretical physicist—also the 1992 U.S. Presidential nominee of the Natural Law Party—related Vedic thought to modern field theory as he built on a suggestion made by Maharishi Mahesh Yogi. Hagelin claimed that the unified field of modern physics is identical to the field of "pure consciousness." (The Vedic system derives from the Vedas, the sacred books of Hinduism. Transcendental meditation, "TM," is part of the Vedic system.) Without doubt, Hagelin has responded well to part of general revelation: his discussion of several of the more difficult parts of modern physics is sophisticated. But he claimed that attempts to relate physics and metaphysics will fail because metaphysics does not exist; the science of consciousness explains everything.

The "Gaia hypothesis," advanced by James Lovelock, says that the earth is one great organism. ("Gaia" refers to the name of the earth goddess of ancient Greece.) This hypothesis is an example of New Age thinking in science.[15] According to Lovelock, the earth-organism manipulates the atmosphere of the earth. Even though the idea is based on a response to environmental and ecological problems—certainly a response to general revelation—it has pantheistic overtones, harking back to the time before Christians led the way in de-deifying the world. In response to scientific criticism, Lovelock himself no longer holds that the earth acts with a sense of purpose. Those natural scientists (in contrast to people who are part of the New Age movement) who now embrace at least part of his theory hold that the earth preserves its life-giving properties by a feedback mechanism.

(d) Computer age thinking has begun to contribute to non-Christian models of the universe. Ed Fredkin, a scientist at the Massachusetts Institute of Technology, made a bizarre suggestion.[16] Fredkin begins with the "cells" of a pattern on the screen of a computer monitor. (Chapter 6 discusses such cells in a different context.) Each cell is either lit or not lit, that is, "on" or "off." Consider a square cell and its four adjacent neighbors. One set of rules for the lighting of the cells could call for the lighting of a cell when an odd number—one or three—of its four neighbors are lit, and that, when this change takes place, the four neighbors reverse; those that were lit become dark, and those that were dark light up. Using the same rules, the process of changing dark to light and light to dark continues. Once such a process starts, that is, once initial conditions are established, the subsequent flickering might, depending upon the rules used, produce an interesting pattern.[17]

The set of rules is information; it is a certain kind of computer program. In Fredkin's theory, information is more fundamental than matter or energy:

> The prime mover of everything, the single principle that governs the universe, lies somewhere within a class of computer programs known as cellular automata. . . .

Computer programs? What about matter, energy, all sorts of other "things"? Fredkin has an answer:

> "You see, I don't believe that there are objects like electrons and photons, and things which are themselves and nothing else," Fredkin says. "What I believe is that there's an information process, and the bits, when they're in certain configurations, behave like the thing we call the electron, or the hydrogen atom, or whatever."[18]

Fredkin claimed that both space and time occur in very tiny bits, each a bit of information that, like either the computer bit or the square cell, is either on or off. From our point of view, the flickering of these bits is unpredictable; hence, the uncertainty principle. We do not observe these bits of time because our own clock ticks are the same as the clock ticks of time itself. To us, time seems continuous. The intelligence behind it all is the set of rules that determine on and off for each cell. The intelligent designer of the universe is a computer program, not God. Fredkin's analysis is another example of the consequence of not using special revelation to illuminate natural scientific investigation. Such investigators do not realize that what was analyzed is in fact God's general revelation.

(2) Another reason for claiming that special revelation always accompanies general revelation is that special revelation reveals redemption. I mentioned earlier that Christ redeems Creation; let us look into that matter further. Consider the following three points:

(a) Christ's redemptive work was a work of reconciliation. Paul states that Christ reconciles both Jew and Gentile to God:

> [Christ's] purpose was to create in himself one new man out of the two [Jew and Gentile], thus making peace, and in this one body to reconcile both of them to God through the cross, by which he put to death their hostility. (Eph. 2:15-16)

We tend to limit this reconciliation to personal salvation; after all, each of us is either a Jew or a Gentile and we ought to look to Christ for our salvation. For Paul, however, reconciliation involves more than people. In Colossians 1:16-20 he indicates that all things in Creation hold together in Christ and links this role of Christ to his reconciliation of all Creation. An important part of this argument is that he uses the same Greek word for "reconcile" in the Colossians and the Ephesians passages. Christ's work of reconciling sinful Jews and Gentiles to God is the same work whereby he reconciles *all* of Creation, things on earth or in heaven, to God.

(b) Even though John 3:16 may be the best-known verse of the New Testament, many people might miss its importance for the present argument. Consider "world" in this verse:

> For God so loved the world that he gave his one and only Son, that whoever believes in him shall not perish but have eternal life. (John 3:16)

In the original language, "world" is *kosmos*, obviously the source of the English word "cosmos."

What was the *kosmos* that God loved enough to give his own Son? My conclusion is that God loved the cosmos, the entire universe, and that therefore he will redeem the cosmos. But there is a contrary view, namely, that he rejects part of the cosmos and loves only his people. To analyze this situation, we must look at the two arguments.

To show that the world which God loves is the cosmos, it is helpful to observe how New Testament authors use *kosmos*. *Kosmos* appears over 75 times in the Gospel of John and more than one hundred times in the rest of the New Testament. It almost always designates a complete entity, usually the whole earth if not the entire cosmos. In fact, New Testament authors use it ten times in the phrase "creation [or beginning] of the world."[19] *Kosmos* often indicates everything on earth. Some examples where *kosmos* is translated "world" are the following: the devil shows Christ the kingdoms of the world (Matt. 4:8); Christ was the light of the world (John 9:5); God made the world and all things (Acts 17:24); and by one man sin entered into the world (Rom. 5:12).[20] Taken together, these uses of *kosmos* indicate that the word refers to everything related to the subject of the particular text, up to the entire cosmos.

But those who interpret John 3:16 in a way which denies that Christ came to earth to redeem the entire cosmos usually refer to the places in the New Testament in which *kosmos* has a negative connotation. Some examples with a negative connotation where *kosmos* is translated "world" are the following: the world can hate Christians, who are not of the world (John 15:18,19); to avoid associating with the immoral people of the world you would have to leave the world (I Cor. 5:10); the world in its present form is passing away (I Cor. 7:31); and when we were children, we were enslaved by the basic principles of the world (Gal. 4:3).[21]

Concerning the negative connotations of *kosmos* in the New Testament, probably the most important is the following, which is part of Christ's prayer to the Father in the Garden of Gethsemane just before his arrest, trial, and crucifixion:

> I pray for them. I am not praying for the world, but for those you have given me, for they are yours. (John 17:9)

This prayer and the other negative references to *kosmos* do not disprove my earlier claim about the redemption of the cosmos. One must consider the context of this prayer. Christ knew that some people would be saved, but others not: God chose those who were to be saved before the foundation of the world (Eph. 1:5). His disciples were with him. He prayed for those disciples who were to be saved, as well as others God had chosen, many as yet unborn. Christ's knowledge that some people were not chosen made it incongruous for him to pray for every person.[22]

This understanding of Christ's prayer may help us understand the negative connotations of *kosmos* in certain New Testament passages. Wickedness is a reality and God rejects it. Redemption of the world implies just such a rejection: without a cleansing, there is no redemption. To say that Christ redeems the world is not to say that God blesses the good and the bad; rather, he separates the good from the bad in the *whole* world.

Therefore, *kosmos* does not have two contradictory meanings in the New Testament. In some uses, it tells us of the cosmos that Christ will save; in others, of the purging of that cosmos. *Furthermore, its use never contradicts the context.* Thus, John 3:16 does *not* say, "Even though God hated the world, he gave his one and only Son, so that whoever believes in him shall not perish but have eternal life." John 3:16 teaches that God loves Creation.

(c) The New Testament does not describe in detail Christ's redemption of Creation. But it does provide some information relevant to the present discussion. In Revelation John says

> The seventh angel sounded his trumpet, and there were loud voices in heaven, which said: "The kingdom of the world [*kosmos*] has become the kingdom of our Lord and of his Christ, and he will reign for ever and ever." (Revelation 11:15)

Christ's now-completed work of redemption was therefore a transformation: he converted the cosmos into the eternal "kingdom of our Lord and of his Christ." He redeemed the cosmos. It is necessary, however, to look into John's use of words.

Even though John uses *kosmos* a large number of times in his other books, he uses it in Revelation in only two places besides the passage just cited. When John refers to "everything" in Revelation, he almost always uses the word for earth, *ge*. There may be a reason. Throughout Revelation, the emphasis is on change, on before-and-after. For the persecuted Christians of John's day—as well as all beleaguered Christians since that time—it was the *earth*, their home, that required redemption. It is against this background that John mentions transformation of the cosmos sparingly but teaches a large number of times that God will redeem the earth. Following are two examples:

> Then I saw a new heaven and a new earth, for the first heaven and the first earth had passed away, and there was no longer any sea. (Rev. 21:1)
>
> The city does not need the sun or the moon to shine on it, for the glory of the Lord gives it light, and the Lamb is its lamp. The nations will walk by its light, and the kings of the earth will bring their splendor into it. (Rev. 21:23-24)

(The "new heaven and a new earth" of 21:1 is also used by the Lord in a promise given in Isaiah 66:22.) When we have a perfect life with the Lord, there will still be an earth—a new earth, the result of Christ's redemption of the old earth. It will be cleansed and the kings of the earth will pay tribute.

At the heart of Christ's redemption is the redemption of those called out from the human family. Once again, perfect human beings will be at the head of Creation. Far from passing out of existence, Creation, with redeemed human beings at the head of it, will once again be "very good."

I conclude that special revelation may not be limited to God's plan of salvation of souls or of people. Special revelation must always accompany general revelation.

We then understand that special and general revelation both reach into all of our lives. All scientific activity is part of our response to general revelation. What follows from this understanding is the question addressed in the next chapter: What is Christian scientific activity?

The argument concerning revelation and scientific activity eventually leads into the main question posed by this book. What in the Christian position effectively counteracts the impact of evolutionary thought?

Revelation: A Summary

General revelation, in which God revealed himself through Creation, was sufficient until Adam and Eve sinned. God then revealed himself in a special way, through words written down and by sending his Son. At present, everyone responds to both general and special revelation. This response, which reaches into all of life, is religious. Neglecting either kind of revelation is a mistake. We must see that they are related and that therefore nothing in life is religiously neutral. Creation required redemption because the head of Creation sinned; Creation was no longer "very good."

General revelation includes not only Creation as it was before sin entered but also that which exists today. The purpose of general revelation is to reveal God's works to us and to enable us—Adam, the farmer, the social worker—to do our work. In both general and special revelation God reveals something of himself. In special revelation, he reveals his longsuffering love. In general revelation, he reveals his glory, an orderly Creation, and the role of human beings in Creation.

Using the phrase "Bible and science" can lead to difficulties. Attempting to remove apparent conflict between the Bible and science by considering only one of the two kinds of revelation to be important is obviously wrong. Attempting to remove apparent conflict by considering both to be important, while weakening the link between the two, is also a mistake.

Consideration of the "intersection" between the Bible and information ordinarily thought to be of scientific value leads to the conclusion that general revelation always accompanies special revelation.

Also, special revelation always accompanies general revelation. The Bible itself teaches that we need special revelation to interpret general revelation properly; we need Calvin's "spectacles." To show that special revelation must accompany general revelation, it is particularly helpful to consider what happens when people do indeed interact with general revelation but do not know, or at least do not accept, special revelation. Modern pseudo-sciences, sometimes based on Eastern religions, are examples of the resulting distortion of the understanding of general revelation. The biblical teaching that Christ redeemed the entire cosmos also indicates that special revelation must always accompany general revelation. It is not correct to limit special revelation by referring to it as no more than "God's plan for the salvation of our souls."

Chapter Nine
Science

To investigate the nature of science, let us build on the conclusions of the previous chapter. God revealed himself first in a general way through Creation.[1] Special revelation arose because of human sin. Both general and special revelation reach into all parts of our lives. Our interaction with—or response to—both kinds of revelation is inevitably religious: all life is religious. In special revelation God reveals that his Son is King of Creation. Christ redeems Creation, not just his people. As we analyze our response to Creation we may never forget the fact of human sin. Christ's redemption consists of a cleansing, a renewing.[2] After Christ returns, his people will live with him and they will be sinless. There will be a new heaven and a new earth. Our earth will be renewed, not destroyed.

If all life is religious, we should expect our scientific activity to reflect our faith. Such a conclusion is not surprising if we remember that Christ is the King of Creation. Theologian Helmuth Thielicke said, "*Faith* never retires from the scene in doing science. It continues to believe as it does science. It draws the *rational* enterprise into itself. *Faith* never bows out. It knows no boundaries."[3] (Emphasis added.) Thielicke thus refused to separate that which so many people put at opposite poles: faith and rational activities.

Thus, Christian faith, never separated from belief in Christ's Kingship, ought to be part of the *rational* scientific enterprise. That human rationality is required to work out the incredible design in God's Creation was also emphasized by Owen Gingerich, an astronomer at Harvard University. Gingerich also said that God has given us Christ's sacrificial love and this gift suggests a starting point in scientific work:

> Created in the image of God, we are called not to power or personal justice, but to *sacrificial love*. I confess that this is not the logical conclusion of my line of argument; *indeed, it is the beginning, the point of departure for a way of perceiving science and the universe*. But unless we can see the universe in those terms, I believe that we are headed with the rest of the fallen human race to nuclear suicide. (Emphasis added.)

Ever since the beginning of the natural scientific enterprise, it has been necessary to remind people that research can reveal more of God's wonderful works. Gingerich said:

> I [quote] from the seventeenth-century English virtuoso, Thomas Browne: "The wisdom of God receives small honor from those vulgar heads that rudely stare about, and with a gross rusticity admire his workes; those highly magnifie him whose *judicious enquiry into his acts*, and *deliberate research into his creatures*, returne the duty of a devout and learned admiration."[4] (Emphasis added.)

The foregoing discussion highlights four ideas. First, our starting point in scientific activity must be faith in God and love for him and his Creation, a desire to respond to him. Second, sin permeates all human activity. Therefore, we must carry out all those activities, including scientific activity, without neglecting the light of special revelation. Third, human beings must be able to reason to do scientific work. Human rationality is absolutely essential. Fourth, Christ will redeem the earth. Sin taints our present work, including our scientific activity; but Christ will redeem our work. In a way we do not fully understand, our present work is not temporary.

I shall discuss science using these four ideas. But first two other matters must be taken up.

Definition and Views on the Nature of Science

An examination of the nature of science, relating it to general and special revelation, requires a definition of science and a review of the views of others.

What is Science? Up to now in this book the context indicates what is meant by science. If "natural," then science refers to all or part of the group of sciences usually assumed to be natural, such as astronomy or biology. If not natural, then science refers to those sciences usually assumed to be outside of this group, such as psychology or sociology. This procedure, although conventional, tends to be circular: it is usually based on the assumption that the body of knowledge called "astronomy" is that body of knowledge developed by astronomers, "psychology" by psychologists, and so forth. Also, the boundaries of a discipline are often unarticulated and perhaps vague.

Until now, these deficiencies in the meaning of science should not be problematic in this book. But a discussion of science in the context of the human response to general and special revelation requires a more fundamental look at the meaning of the word.

Science, a body of knowledge, is always the result of human activity. It is seldom, if ever, proper to say, "Science says..." With a more complete understanding of the context, it *could* be proper. Thus, nobody errs by saying, "Newspapers say..." Everyone knows that newspapers do not represent an absolute body of knowledge. They know that what appears in a newspaper is not the infallible word of an oracle. The body of newspaper knowledge is the product of human activity and certainly does not stand alone. In the same way, the body of scientific knowledge is the product of human scientific activity. The tendency to absolutize or make a god of science, often implied in "Science says...," is entirely unwarranted.

Human scientific activity is part of men and women's response to revelation. The principal characteristic of this type of response is that it requires human analysis of aspects of Creation. In broad terms, the sum of such analyses is the body of scientific knowledge. More specifically, of course, the body of scientific knowledge has parts, as described by the separate disciplines. Thus, the human analysis of God's revelation in Creation has led to the formulation of the laws of thermodynamics, as well as the construction of interplanetary probes and terrorist bombs.

Such an approach does not necessarily clarify which knowledge is scientific and which is not; after all, it might not be possible to draw the line between analytical and nonanalytical. Nevertheless, defining science in this way puts the emphasis on two ideas: scientific knowledge is the result of a response to Creation that is both *human* and *analytical*. As we shall see, these two factors are critical.

Nor does this approach make it easier to distinguish between "natural" science and other science. It may make such a distinction more difficult. The conventional distinction is to draw a line between the science of matter and energy—whatever is "physical"—and the nonphysical sciences. Therefore, in this definition natural scientists work with rocks and stars. Do they work with birds, also composed of matter, also energetic? Yes—and consequently, this concept of natural science can subtly lead to the understanding that an animal is nothing more than a certain aggregation of matter. Those who hold to this view usually make the same claim concerning human beings.[5] I reject such a naturalistic assumption.

The definition of science proposed here, the human analytical response to revelation, does not provide a neat solution to the problem of distinguishing between the natural sciences and other sciences; this definition does not tell us what is natural. In fact, this definition suggests that it is dangerous to define "natural": to do so hints that something else is nonnatural or, perhaps, supernatural. But that division is precisely what the concept of two revelations does not allow: the dividing line is between general revelation, which once could stand alone, and special revelation. With this *caveat* in mind, a person may refer to astronomy, biology, chemistry, psychology, sociology, and so forth, in the usual way. But then one should never imply more than what was put into the definition of science: it is the result of the human analytical response to revelation.[6]

Defining science as the human analytical response to revelation leaves unanswered an important question. Which revelation? Understanding Creation requires analysis, but so does understanding the Bible. Because of this situation, many people refer to the study and analysis of the Bible as *theological science*. At least three problems arise:

First, theologians, presumably the theological scientists, study more than special revelation. Christian theologians study the art (or science) of preaching the Gospel, church history, church government, comparative religions, and much more. Another complication is that theologians need not be Christian; their religion can be Buddhist, Shinto, or any other non-Christian religion. Therefore, human analytical interaction with special revelation and general revelation cannot be divided into theological science and the other sciences unless we limit the meaning of theological science to analysis of special revelation.

Second, many Christians do not understand that all scientific work is human analytical response to God's revelation of himself, and so they tend to put theological science on a pedestal. For them, the other sciences are passing away and only of this present world. As a result, the synonym for theological science that has gained some favor is "the queen of the sciences." Such a phrase seems to ignore Christ's redemption of the cosmos. For us to think little of investigation of the cosmos is not right.

Third, drawing the line between devotional study of the Bible and scientific analysis of it is extremely difficult. Of course, both are necessary. But using the results of theological scientific activity while excluding the insights obtained from devotional study seems artificial and probably not possible.

For these reasons, I shall not use the term "theological science," but shall refer to the study of special revelation, that is, the Bible. Also I shall continue to refer to natural science and its components, such as astronomy, biology, and the other sciences, without accepting the naturalistic assumptions described above.

The other matter necessary to take up, before examining further the four essential characteristics of scientific activity, is a brief description of some other views of the nature of science.

Various Views of the Nature of Science. Views generally fall into two categories, non-Christian and Christian.

(1) Non-Christian views tend either to draw a line between the material and all else or to absolutize the "material" in Creation. The dualistic view described in Chapter 2 attempts to draw a line. Before the scientific era, many people held that the material world is evil, characterized by darkness, while the spiritual world is good, characterized by light; the line was between matter and spirit.

But when the scientific enterprise became important in modern life, with the accompanying positivistic attack on religion, many people said that the spiritual side of the line, "light," was actually darkness. Thus, *The Berkeley Physics Course* (1962) said, "Through experimental science we have been able to learn all these facts about the natural world, *triumphing over darkness* and ignorance. . ."[7] (Emphasis added.) In the same spirit, Richard Lemmon could state confidently that the emergence of life by an evolutionistic process was inevitable, given the chemical properties of certain molecules.[8] The frequency that statements like Lemmon's appear in the current literature is ample evidence that evolutionary theory, which arose out of the natural sciences, is making an impact on those sciences themselves.

These views differ from each other only superficially. Neither recognizes that God reveals himself in Creation. Special revelation plays no role. But Christians must face the fact that most modern work in the sciences (all the sciences, not just the natural sciences) rests on the modern non-Christian version of dualism: all science triumphs over darkness.

(2) Christian views of science are generally answers to some variation of this question: what is the relation between science and theology? Such a question could be biased: it might contain the hidden assumption that the link between "science" and "theology" is not inherent, that somehow the association needs to be established. Those who phrase the question this way might not perceive the integral relation between general and special revelation. In addition, imprecise definitions of the two terms are possible.

In Chapter 8 I claimed that the effort to remove a supposed conflict between the Bible and science is misguided; it is better to assume that God reveals himself through both general and special revelation. Unfortunately, something besides removal of conflict was achieved: regardless of intention, the removal efforts also led to models of how things are. Therefore, the models of the relation between science and theology described below have a rough correspondence to the various positions described in Chapter 8. As we shall see, some of the same problems arise here.

Several models of interaction between science and theology have been proposed. Glenn Remelts, a science historian at Kansas State University, discussed models that were current during the early decades of the twentieth century.[9]

Those who subscribed to the "parallel model" maintained that the methods used by theology and science are similar and therefore the two groups of investigators could help each other:

> Broadly speaking, theologians and churchmen who accepted the parallel model were theological liberals who saw no conflict between science and religion. They argued that while both were distinct fields of knowledge much of the methodology of science could be used by theology and theology could give to science enlightenment and values.[10]

Natural theology, discussed in Chapters 2-4, was the source of the "derivation model." The name calls attention to the possibility of deriving theological knowledge from scientific results.

The "contrast model" emphasized that science and theology have separate, contrasting spheres of influence; Remelts said:

> Unlike the liberals represented in the Parallel model, [German theologians who held to this model] chose to redefine Christianity in a way that ensured its complete isolation from science. Albrecht Ritschl (1822-1889) and Rudolf Otto (1869-1937), among others, fashioned an ethical and social Christianity that was based on human feelings and not knowledge. Ritschl's religion, for instance, severed humanity from the cosmos, focusing on relationships within humanity.[11]

Remelts claimed that Karl Barth (1886-1968) and other neo-orthodox theologians retained Ritschl's separation of humanity from the cosmos. However, they did lead the movement to reverse the liberal trend and restore the relationship between God and humanity. Unfortunately, they held that while the Bible contains theological truths, the events recorded in the Bible were often mythical.[12]

Remelts concluded that in all three models—parallel, derivation, and contrast—theology gave up something to maintain a relationship with science. He described a fourth model, the engagement model, which, he said, many leaders of the Christian Reformed Church accepted early in the twentieth century:

Engagement entails binding together, being active in and entering into conflict. Generally, in any engagement two parties come together for a purpose but maintain their identity. In the Christian Reformed Church, theology critically engaged science in order to ensure harmony between the two. . . . *Science, however, maintained considerable freedom of action, being allowed to examine and discover what it could even when these discoveries contradicted certain beliefs.*[13] (Emphasis added.)

Perhaps in recent years the engagement model led to the *categorical complementarity* model advanced by many evangelicals, including some in the Christian Reformed Church. Howard Van Till, physicist at Calvin College, presented this position in *The Fourth Day*.[14] Thomas Dozeman, of the Union Theological Seminary in Dayton, Ohio, discussed Van Till's categorical complementarity in a review essay of the book. Two different descriptions of something, even though they say different things, can be correct. Dozeman said (taking an example from *The Fourth Day*), "[A] piece of paper could be described simultaneously as being both square and green. Thus, [the descriptions] are categorically complementary." He continued:

When Van Till begins to work out the concept of categorical complementarity in order to interrelate and to unify Bible and science, a more or less Kantian dichotomy develops, in which the essential content of biblical literature is relegated to the noumenal (external/material) realm, while the proper domain of scientific investigation is limited to the phenomenal (internal/material) realm.[15]

All four (or five, if Van Till's is separate from the engagement model) models seem to give "science" a degree of autonomy not warranted by the integral relation between general and special revelation. It seems that these models, with the possible exception of the derivation model, arose because of the physical and theoretical consequences of the modern scientific enterprise. All the models seem to be forms of Christian defense, that is, apologetic. But in actuality, the correct model should be one that not only has held from the beginning but also has had meaning for human beings from the beginning. It should arise out of biblical criteria. Above all, it ought not to be a model which suggests that in some way one can by-pass the Bible.

Having given a definition of science and the views of others, I shall now return to the discussion of science using the four ideas given in the introduc-

Science

tion to this chapter: faith in God and love for God and his Creation, the effects of sin, the nature of and need for human reasoning ability, and the execution of scientific activity with an eye on eternity.

Science and Revelation

Faith in God and Love for God and His Creation. Scientists who love God exhibit love in their scientific activity. Such a statement might seem to be no more than a platitude. But if scientists generally showed a love for God by having respect for each other, ugly controversy in the scientific community would be at a minimum. Differences among Christians concerning scientific questions would virtually vanish.

Such an attitude of love for God extends to love for his Creation. Love for his Creation means that one respects scientific results that are, after all, the results of investigating Creation. Naturally, results are not infallible, but it does seem that many scientists have exhibited an unwillingness to exchange ideas in good faith and examine fairly the work of others.

Consider the widespread, categorical denial of the existence of natural barriers in the world of living things, against mounting scientific evidence to the contrary. Even Stephen Jay Gould and Niles Eldredge, who certainly do not present a theistic position, suggest something like barriers: their punctuated equilibrium theory challenges those who assume that fossils will be found to fill in the gaps in the fossil record. I do not deny the legitimacy of investigation to fill a gap—unless, of course, it can be shown that the Bible teaches that the gap exists. But it simply is not proper to assume the nature of future scientific results or that gaps will be filled. Such assumption exhibits a lack of respect for the scientific enterprise and ultimately for Creation itself.

Unfortunately, many Christians seem to be equally obstinate in the face of mounting scientific evidence. Many Christians seek to show scientifically that the first acts of creation took place only thousands, not billions, of years ago. Their motivation is the belief that the Bible teaches such a young age. (I shall discuss that aspect of the question in the next chapter.) As a result, their understanding of the biblical message warrants a search for scientific evidence to prove their point. But the difficulty often arises in their attitude toward many scientific results, such as those given in the first part of Chapter 5 suggesting great age. Those who examine such results should say something like this: "We know because of biblical teaching that the earth is young, probably only a few thousand years old. But the scientific results we have at present point to a great age. Such a great age is not possible.

If the Lord allows us, we will eventually be able to demonstrate scientifically that the present scientific conclusions are wrong."

However, it seems to me that some of these Christians say something like this: "We conclude from both the Bible and scientific results that the earth is young. Those who conclude that scientific results indicate a very old earth are wrong. The scientific claims for an old earth have been disproved." These Christians realize that evil influences surround Christians, who live in a sinful world, and that too many Christians have uncritically adopted worldly scientific conclusions. I sympathize with their deep concern. But it would be a testimony to their love for God and his Creation if they exhibited more of an openness toward the results of scientific investigation. That is one way of showing love for Creation.

Love for God and his Creation motivates scientific work. In Genesis 1:26-28 God said that human beings, created in the image of God, were to subdue and replenish the earth; they were to rule over every living thing. These verses are not a license to wreck the earth. Rather, they are commands to develop the potential of Creation. Human beings can obey these commands only by using their abilities, including the ability to do scientific work. These commands also tell us what kind of scientific work we will carry out. Some of our investigation will help find out what God did so that we can praise him for specific deeds. Perhaps most astronomical and much geological work is of this kind. The same may be true in investigating the intricacies of molecular, atomic, and sub-atomic phenomena, as well as discoveries providing an understanding of the magnificence of the biological world. We stand amazed before the scientific results. But other investigation will have practical results, which are numerous and well-known.

In any case, faithful scientists recognize that God calls them to be a part of the great task of *developing* Creation. This task of developing recognizes that God did not err when he created; Creation was very good. At the same time, it was possible to develop Creation even before sin entered. It does not follow that just because Creation had potential for development that it was therefore imperfect. While some of God's creative acts were clearly creation from nothing, others seem to have been developmental. But developmental scientific work is part of the assignment given to the entire human family. Therefore, carrying out the various parts of that assignment—subduing, replenishing, and ruling—continues God's creative acts.

What a Christian may legitimately investigate is virtually unlimited. Investigation always involves hypotheses. Are some hypotheses illegitimate?

Science

Yes, some are. They arise because of the existence of *control beliefs*, described by Nicholas Wolterstorff, a Yale University philosopher. They function first of all in the life of the scholar as a means of evaluating theories. Wolterstorff said: "My contention. . .is that the religious beliefs of the Christian scholar ought to function as *control* beliefs within his devising and weighing of theories."[16] Wolterstorff gave an example of a control belief that is not based on biblical revelation:

> The reasons why a medical researcher rejects the theory lying behind the Chinese practice of acupuncture as not even the sort of theory he will entertain will most likely have little if anything to do with his religion [that is, his formal religious beliefs]. Rather, it will have to do with his being imbued with a whole orientation to disease developed in the Western world within the last century.[17]

It follows that if a control belief rules out a theory, then the hypothesis that eventually led to the theory is also ruled out. Thus, it would be wrong to hypothesize, and then to attempt to prove the hypothesis and thereby formulate a theory, that only a small tribe, not a nation of millions, crossed a desert after leaving Egypt. It would be wrong because the hypothesis assumes the Bible is wrong. (See Chapter 8 for a discussion of this event.)

But it would not be wrong to look for a fish large enough to swallow a man who remained alive three days (cf. Jonah 1:17). It would not be wrong to look for wood that could—perhaps by ion exchange—remove the bitterness often due to alkalinity from the water of a desert well (cf. Ex. 15:23-25). It is one thing to investigate *how* God acted (the great fish and the sweetened water). It is quite another to assume he did not do what he says he did (free a nation of millions from Egypt). God is the author of miracles as well as "ordinary" events, and so we have as much warrant to investigate the one as the other. One control belief of Christians is the reliability of the Bible. Therefore, they believe that a large nation fled from Egypt.

In other natural scientific activity, it would be wrong to adopt a cosmology that takes the present universe to be eternal; the Bible teaches otherwise. Thus, Christian control beliefs rule out both the Hindu teaching that the universe will never end, because of the supposed circularity of time, and the claim of some modern cosmologists that time will not end because of a never-ending series of big bang-implosion cycles in which this universe fades away. The universe did have a beginning. While the universe will change, it will not fade away. But, if the Bible allows for the possibility that chemical reactions ultimately produced living cells from nonliving matter, then it is not wrong to investigate this possibility, no matter how improbable it now seems.

Some miracles, such as the swallowing of Jonah by the large fish or the sweetening of the bitter water, can conceivably fit into natural scientific theory. But assuming that all miracles fit into natural scientific theory is a violation of a Christian control belief. Some phenomena may well be beyond our ability to provide an explanation that falls within natural law. Thus, while it is permissible to investigate the possibility that nonliving material became living cells by means of physical and chemical processes that we can understand, it is wrong to assume that the appearance of life *must* have occurred by natural, that is, explainable, processes. Those who have faith in God and love God and his Creation will not insist that human scientific theory can even in principle explain every phenomenon.

The Effect of Sin. Creation is ordered. Its parts fit together. How do we know these things? We observe and we investigate. Much of the conclusion that Creation is ordered we derive from our scientific—especially natural scientific—investigation. We can confidently claim that creational laws do exist. We can see that God does reveal himself in his power over and care of Creation.

Yet we also know that we make mistakes, sometimes very big mistakes, in our scientific work. We do learn enough from general and special revelation to know that creational laws exist. But we also know that our scientific conclusions do not always coincide with what God reveals. He speaks, but we do not hear clearly.

Even without sin, we would be limited. But the chief source of the lack of correspondence between what God says and what we hear is our sin. Sin has reached into every one of our abilities; all are damaged. That is not to say that we can do nothing correctly. But it does mean that sin taints everything.

How does sin affect our scientific activity?[18] The most important effect is what it does to our motivation. Without doubt, scientific activity enables human beings to have power that they would not otherwise have. But because of sin, they desire power for the wrong reason. They desire power to become independent of God. The desire for autonomy was the essence of the first sin; Adam and Eve thought they could obtain power that God had not given them. Henri Blocher, in his careful analysis of the first chapters of Genesis, said:

> By definite suggestion, [the writer of Genesis] tells us that *at the*

heart of sin lies the claim to autonomy, that sin is rooted deep in our hearts by doubt and covetousness, that it overthrows the created order, that it is both weakness and arrogance, and that it brings alienation to the human race, to the advantage of that spirit of false wisdom which corrupts the religion of men.[19] (Emphasis added.)

The first sin is repeated every time a modern scientist exults in new discovery believing it provides human beings with more power and will make it easier for them to be independent from any god. This attitude characterizes the secularization of modern society.

Sin also affects specific projects. Some scientific projects have ultimately brought about great harm to various parts of our world. Sometimes discussions of those projects have not taken sin sufficiently into account. But the sinful nature of human beings, a nature they acquired when Adam and Eve first sinned, is the cause of those projects.

The scientific enterprise often reacts to the effects of sin. Crime, war, sickness, and death exist because of sin. Consider the scientific effort put into defense against crime. Forensic science exists because of sin. An almost endless number of safeguards, from electronic locks to hidden television cameras in stores, depends upon sophisticated scientific development but would not be necessary in a sinless world. The development of police and military equipment falls into the same category as does much medical research. Even though these inventions are not in themselves bad, the scientific enterprise surely bears little resemblance to what it would be in a sinless world.

Perhaps we are not sufficiently aware of still another effect of sin on scientific projects. Even if our motivation is proper and our scientific project is God-honoring, sin still affects how well we do our work. The results of research can be incorrect.

It may help to put incorrect results into context by considering what life was like for Adam and Eve before they sinned. Could Adam or Eve stumble in the Garden and break a leg? No; God cared for them. The Garden could have had places we would call dangerous. But God took care of Adam and Eve; they did not make harmful mistakes. When they sinned, God did not completely remove his care. If he had, they would have ceased to exist. But having sought autonomy, they learned what it was like to lose some of God's care and to live on their own. God then allowed them to stumble in the Garden.

God also allows stumbling on a modern scientific project. Answers can be wrong. Of course, those critical of scientific results cannot very effectively use the sinfulness of scientists as an excuse for rejecting scientific results; after all, the critics are also sinful.

In fact, nothing in the Bible teaches that non-Christians will be unable to carry out useful scientific work. Because all human beings bear God's image, sin did not completely destroy their ability to carry out the command to rule and fill and subdue the earth. Carrying out this command includes carrying out scientific activity. Both believers and unbelievers interact with infallible general revelation and can realize some of their potential. The scientific work of unbelievers does have value.

The reason for this mistake about the validity of scientific work of non-Christians lies in a misunderstanding concerning assumptions. Scientists must make assumptions in order to obtain results. Some Christians therefore ask, "Isn't the making of assumptions the first place unbelievers get off the track? Isn't their scientific structure built on a flawed foundation and therefore bound to collapse?"

I shall answer this kind of question by presenting two examples; in both, I consider only fundamental assumptions. For the first example, assume that the laws of thermodynamics are valid. One of those laws says that energy (technically, mass-energy) can be neither created nor destroyed. The laws of thermodynamics are fundamental because they are a necessary part of the foundation of several natural sciences. These laws are not contrary to special revelation. Using these laws, a meteorologist deduces that when a body of warm air leaves one region for another, perhaps from the earth's equatorial region to the northern latitudes, that the first region becomes cooler than it would be otherwise and the latter becomes warmer. The energy one region loses is equal to the energy another region gains, consistent with the law of thermodynamics that says energy cannot be either created or destroyed. Meteorologists continually make conclusions like this one, as well as those that are much more complicated. They do so by assuming the validity of the laws of thermodynamics.

In the second example, suppose that a certain anthropologist assumes human beings descended from animals. This "law" is fundamental because it underlies a large part of anthropological investigation. Starting with this fundamental assumption, the anthropologist thinks that observation of the behavior of various primates should be helpful in studying human behavior. Conclusions which this anthropologist makes, after completion of the study of primate behavior, rest on a widely held assumption that is contrary to special revelation. The conclusions *might* be correct, but they certainly rest on an untenable assumption.

These two examples show that we should not assume that the work of non-Christians rests on false fundamental assumptions and is therefore useless. In these two examples, we do not know that the scientists involved are Christians. But we can see that fundamental assumptions vary: some are reliable, other are not. The central idea here is that everyone involved interacts with Creation; everyone responds either consciously or unconsciously to general revelation. But all are sinful and tend to make mistakes. It simply is not enough to decide that Christians, and only Christians, use correct fundamental assumptions.

Some fundamental assumptions are certainly devastating. For example, a very large number of natural scientists assume that all physical phenomena are explainable; miracles are impossible. I have already discussed this naturalistic view. Of interest here is the impact that this wrong (fundamentally evolutionary) view has on natural scientific activity. In Chapter 4 I mentioned that Philosopher Alvin Plantinga showed that Christians have more freedom than non-Christians in scientific work. Plantinga said:

> The believer in God, unlike her naturalistic counterpart, is free to look at the evidence for the Grand Evolutionary Scheme, and follow where it leads, rejecting that scheme if the evidence is insufficient.

Plantinga contrasted this freedom with the position of the naturalist, who does make a fundamental assumption:

> She has a freedom not available to the naturalist. The latter accepts the Grand Evolutionary Scheme because from a naturalistic point of view this scheme is the only visible answer to the question *what is the explanation of the presence of all these marvelously multifarious forms of life?*[20]

As I shall show in Chapter 11, one control belief is that the Bible teaches that human beings did not descend from animals. But Plantinga's main point is well taken: the naturalist *must* hold that evolution is the only possible explanation of the life forms we know. Not even one break in the evolutionary chain is allowed. For example, if conclusive evidence shows that oxygen was present in the primitive atmosphere, the proposed mechanism for the evolution of life from nonlife collapses. Then the naturalist is lost: one link in the evolutionary chain is gone. Of course, many other links are also vulnerable.

Human Reason and Scientific Activity. Some Christian nonscientists tend to belittle scientific activity because such activity depends upon the ability of human beings to reason and, say the critics, the onset of sin severely damaged this ability. Perhaps if such critics had lived several hundred years ago they would have judged that this fallenness would prevent the growth of the scientific enterprise. But modern scientific developments provide us with marvelous evidence of the ability of the human mind to reason correctly; a few examples are the development of quantum mechanics, the working out of the structure of DNA, and the theory of fundamental particles. Furthermore, these critics fail to present biblical evidence that post-fall human beings do not have amazing minds that can capably reason or imagine. To fail to praise God for creating the human mind is a serious mistake.

If we are to praise God for his intricate Creation, in which all the parts fit together, we should expect that the human mind will also fit into that Creation. Human beings, created to be at the head of Creation even though sin has affected their minds, still have minds that are very much "in tune" with Creation. Were that not so, our ability to praise God would be far more limited than it actually is. It is just *because* we are able to praise God for his amazing Creation that we *must* praise him. Failure to do so is itself sin.

I want to justify the claim that the human mind is in tune with Creation.[21] Because the human mind has responded to Creation in a certain way, the disciplines of mathematics, physics, and chemistry exist. Mathematics is simultaneously a human response to Creation and a product of human reasoning. Physical scientists utilize mathematics in formulating physical and chemical laws. By use of mathematics, they attempt to unify physical science. Therefore, this unification process ultimately depends upon a product of human reason. Will the goal, complete unification, be achieved? At the present time we cannot be sure. But a test of the laws' validity and unity is their predictive power. Here is the crux of the matter: some predictions have been successful, others have not.

In other words, there is work to be done. But the numerous successful predictions indicate that scientists have achieved something. Consider the following six predictions of the outcome of experiments or search for elements, all on the basis of previously determined physical and chemical laws. The first five predictions are from A. D'Abro's monumental two-volume survey of physics written more than a half-century ago.[22]

(1) Physicists knew that crystals could diffract rays of light. Theoretical prediction said that therefore one kind of crystal, under certain conditions, should spread out light into a cone as it enters the crystal. Experiment later verified this prediction.

(2) According to theory, light has the properties of waves. With this basis,

additional physical theory predicted that the shadow of a small disk would have certain very peculiar properties. Experiment proved this to be the case.

(3) On the basis of a mathematical theory of the nature of gas molecules and their movement, it was predicted that gases would be as viscous at one pressure as another; this surprising prediction was correct.

(4) Theoretical predictions said that a magnetic field would split light of one wavelength into light of three different wavelengths. This phenomenon, the Zeeman effect, is now well known.

(5) Theoretical predictions said that passage through a small aperture should cause diffraction of a stream of electrons. This was verified.

(6) When chemists first realized that one could arrange elements periodically, thus making possible charts of periodic classification, some elements were as yet unknown. Therefore, their positions in the chart were empty. But the periodic law said that those elements could exist. They have all been found.[23]

These types of verified predictions are many. In each of the cited cases, the phenomenon predicted was otherwise unexpected. Some of them were absolutely astounding, such as the diffraction of a stream of electrons and the existence of hitherto unknown elements. Predictions of the existence of fundamental particles, again on the basis of mathematical-physical theory, has guided research in that area and yielded considerable success.

These verified predictions justify the claim that one of the characteristics of scientific activity is its dependence on human reasoning ability. But there is another view of the meaning of scientific laws, *instrumentalism*. Christian instrumentalists would probably not emphasize human reasoning ability as much as I do in describing the relation between general revelation and scientific activity. I shall digress to explain instrumentalism.

Instrumentalists claim that a scientific law is never more than an economic summary of observations. Many modern natural scientists follow physicist Ernst Mach (1838-1916) who wrote in *The Science of Mechanics* (1883):

> It is the object of science to replace, or *save*, experiences, by the reproduction and anticipation of facts in thought... This economical office of science, which fills its whole life, is apparent at first glance; and with its full recognition, all mysticism in science disappears.[24]

Leegwater noted that Mach's ideas became part of the debates during the nineteenth century concerning the nature of matter, especially whether atoms are "real." Many physicists and chemists performed and described their experiments *as if* atoms existed.[25] This view is utilitarian because it sees scientists summarizing their results and using them as tools. They even use these tools to make predictions. Because of the tool concept, this view is called *instrumentalism*.

Physicist John Byl said that the roots of instrumentalism lie in the philosophy of Plato, who said that astronomers should attempt to devise models that would "save the phenomena" (or, as in the Mach quotation above, "save experiences"); the model would account for the phenomena, regardless of what "really" exists. On the other hand, Aristotle held that theories should tell us how things actually are. For Byl, theories are "useful fictions." He referred to "apparent conflicts between science and Scripture." But by adopting instrumentalism, Christians can

> ... retain the epistemological supremacy of Scripture—thus leaving us with a solid basis with regards to the essentials of the Christian faith—while still making use of the practical results of secular science.[26]

We should not respond to special and general revelation in this way. Rather, it is better in our response to emphasize their integrity. For this reason, I reject instrumentalism as a general approach to the understanding of scientific laws.

Yet instrumentalism does seem to be a view that serves as a means of questioning whatever theories are current. After all, some models of systems may be only useful fictions. (For example, in quantum mechanics one school of thought holds that the quantum mechanical equations are as far as one can go. If those equations ascribe contradictory properties to a particle, such as an electron, so be it: use the equations, not the supposed properties, to make predictions.) At various times in the history of science people maintained that certain theories, which were, however, later verified, were only useful fictions. Examples of theories claimed at one time to be only useful fictions are those which called for the centrality of the sun in the solar system, the existence of atoms, the existence of gas molecules, and the existence of ions. If the instrumentalist approach is maintained only temporarily until more evidence is in, then this approach can be useful.

There is still another side to the story concerning models and predictions. Consider the six specific predictions referred to above. Every one of the six predictions, as well as many others, arose from a theory now known to be flawed or at least incomplete. Obviously, if a theory is poor enough, it will provide no successful predictions. Evidently we have poor theories, fairly good theories, and very good theories; but it would be presumptuous to claim perfect theories. The claim that the human mind is "in tune" with the rest of Creation—even just the physical aspect of Creation—needs modification: we are limited and sinful, and perfect tuning is out of the question.

No one maintains that our scientific theories are perfect. However, over time we develop better theories with more reliable predictability. *The scientific enterprise does not move backward.* Of course, sideways movement and a retreat of a small part of the enterprise is not precluded. The conclusion that the scientific enterprise does not move backward is extremely important in evaluating its role in history, especially with respect to the future. But first I want to examine more carefully why theories, at the heart of this enterprise, change at all.

Of course, new theories build on old theories because of new data and new insights. But to leave the matter there implies that scientists deal only in abstractions, evaluate new data objectively, apply logic rigorously, and then produce a finely cut jewel: a new theory. Up until recently, natural scientists believed that this ideal model provided a correct picture of natural scientific activity. But Thomas Kuhn and others have shown that this picture of the scientist at work is not correct.[27] What is relevant for the present discussion is Kuhn's documented claim that forming natural scientific theories does not depend wholly on phenomena and theories within the natural scientific enterprise. Thus, psychological and sociological factors usually play a role. Scientists are not the objective, abstract persons of the traditional picture.

Philosopher Del Ratzsch of Calvin College took account of these extra-scientific factors. For Ratzsch, the major components of the structure of science are *data, theories,* and *presuppositions*.[28] We tend to think that data and theories constitute the whole of natural science, but Ratzsch showed that presuppositions, from outside natural science, affect both data and theories.[29] In fact, all three mutually affect each other.

What are some of these presuppositions? They are usually unarticulated assumptions: the reliability of our senses and our minds; how much data we need to verify an hypothesis; the degree of accuracy required of our data, that is, how close an agreement with our hypothesis we will require; how and if we shall apply the principle that the simplest theory is the best; the belief that the physical aspect of Creation is ordered; and so forth.

All such assumptions arise from outside the body of scientific knowledge, although they may rest partly on conclusions of previous scientific work. These assumptions tend to change as time passes. Following are a few examples of changing assumptions, selected from the presuppositions given above. The modern understanding of how accurate data should be is not at all what it was early in the scientific period. Also, the meaning of simplicity is now different from its meaning several centuries ago. Another changing assumption relates to the unity in the physical aspect of Creation; the history of this idea shows that it was expected to be true before verification by new data and theories, and therefore the idea itself took on a new form.

Because people tend to change their perceptions of themselves and the world and granting natural science contains a subjective element, natural science is bound to the historical process. This binding to the historical process leads us to the fourth part of the discussion of science.

Scientific Activity and the Future. Our scientific work should reflect our faith in God and love for God and his Creation. It must take into account the effects of sin. We may not dishonor the minds God has given us, and we ought to realize that our scientific work, by its very nature, is an integral part of history. How then should we think of the present scientific enterprise and the future?

First, even though the present scientific enterprise is distorted because of sin, we are nevertheless carrying out the command God gave to human beings before sin entered. The impact of evolutionary theory and other rebellious theories is real, but they have not destroyed scientific activity. Our minds have produced very sophisticated theoretical results in some sciences—results amazingly in agreement with what exists. But our experience teaches that better theories, capable of better prediction, always seem to be over the horizon. Finally, we now realize much better than we did earlier that our science is historically conditioned.

Second, our experience with the scientific enterprise helps us understand what the future will be like. In God's plan, history has a purpose. Therefore, both the past history and the future history of this enterprise are meaningful. In the future, we will continue to use our ability to reason and the sciences will continue to develop. God will use all historical events, including scientific developments, to bring history to a close.

But eventually the scientific enterprise will not be distorted by sin. At the end God will remove sin and make a new heaven and a new earth. We have no reason to doubt that the command given to Adam and Eve before they sinned will continue to hold after Christ has renewed everything. When sin is gone and when everyone sees clearly that Christ is King, God's people will praise him by showing more fully their love for him and his Creation. Part of this praise will result from investigation of his Creation.

God has not revealed more about the relation between that investigation and the present scientific enterprise. We do know that in this new life sin will no longer affect human analytical abilities, so essential for work in the sciences. Above all, we know that our investigative work and all other work will be carried out because we love God and his Creation. The response of God's people to general revelation will finally be properly motivated and carried out in the right way.

Chapter Ten
Genesis

Given the integral relationship between special and general revelation, we may not separate the Bible from our response to general revelation, part of which is our scientific activity. In particular, we need to allow the Bible to speak to the evolutionary scenario, which is so fundamental to the modern scientific enterprise. Therefore, what the Bible teaches concerning origins is the burden of this and the next chapter.

The present chapter discusses control beliefs and the principles of biblical interpretation. Then it takes up the first part of the biblical account of origins, Genesis 1:1-2:3, the Creation Week account. This leaves the most important question, the origin of the human family and the entrance of sin, to Chapter 11.

If an integral relationship between general revelation and special revelation exists, then we must do more than pay lip service to the idea. It means we will respect both kinds of revelation, for, after all, they are both revelations from God. It means that we will truly understand the relationship to be *integral*: each revelation will help us with the other. Not only will we allow the Bible to help us in our scientific activity, but we will also allow our scientific activity to help us in understanding the Bible. We will certainly not look for, nor, if we are careful, will we ever find, conflict between the two kinds of revelation. Conflict will be absent because both revelations are of one God; with both, he reveals himself.

In 1899 Abraham Kuyper, Dutch theologian and statesman, summarized the correct attitude as we react to the two revelations. As he addressed a university community of scholars, Kuyper challenged them to integrate the two revelations in their scientific work:

> . . . [W]e cannot read the book of nature anymore without glasses, as Calvin expressed it, and . . . we, neither from nature nor from the light of our reason, are able to know if, and how, there is a way to escape the power and the guilt of sin.

God has two purposes in giving us more than nature:

Genesis

From that follows the necessity, that to the general revelation in nature is added a special further revelation, and that with a double purpose, namely to teach us again the understanding of the book of nature, and to disclose to us the way of reconciliation with God. Thus a word of God in two shapes: A word of God in the creation, and a word of God which is added to the created things . . .[1]

Control Beliefs

We can err in our interaction with each of the two revelations; we are limited and sinful. Yet we may not leave the matter there. We may not assume that we are as likely to make a mistake in our response to one kind of revelation as the other. We may not assume that what we learn from one revelation is always subject to falsification by what we learn from the other revelation. I make that claim because our relationship to the two revelations is not the same: special revelation provides us with control beliefs that might override contradictory scientific conclusions.

Control Beliefs, the Bible, and Subjectivity. Instead of attempting to "harmonize the Bible and science," we need to identify control beliefs consistent with what the Bible actually teaches.

"Consistent with what the Bible actually teaches" qualifies "control beliefs" because otherwise a control belief is purely a subjective matter. Thus, to return to the example given in Chapter 9, the Western physician usually rules out acupuncture because of his or her training and background; hence, a control belief exists. But a Chinese physician would have a different control belief. Too often discussions about biblical matters assume that control beliefs are not important just because different people have different control beliefs. The objective nature of special revelation then drowns in a flood of subjectivity.

I shall examine various control beliefs concerning origins in this chapter and the next. No doubt control beliefs are never free of a subjective element. But surely it is legitimate to use the Bible to examine a control belief and then decide if the belief is warranted. A belief that still stands after extensive examination of the Bible is more likely to be free of subjectivity than one derived from a minimum consideration of the biblical text.

The source of much of the controversy among Christians concerning origins lies in differences between control beliefs. Christians desperately need to agree on control beliefs. However, I want to show that there is latitude in some matters and control beliefs concerning origins and, further, that it is not wise to elevate some ideas not yet firmly established to the level of an unchangeable control belief. At the same time, I shall show that we must retain certain control beliefs concerning origins.

Although they agree with the concept of control belief, many people contend that only a very few proposed control beliefs can withstand rigorous biblical examination. But subtly demoting a control belief to the level of an opinion can in itself be the first step in forming a different control belief. Thus, the person who states, "No control belief about how God created can be derived from the Bible," might therefore form this control belief: "No scientific conclusion about the 'how' of creation can conflict with the Bible, and so all scientific hypotheses on how this world came to be are legitimate."

But, some people ask, is it not possible that there are only a small number of required control beliefs? Doesn't the Bible itself state that belief in Christ is all that is required? Whether any biblical statement is that straightforward concerning what is required is problematic. But, without going any further into the matter, we must put the following two ideas together: first, the special revelation that God gives us today is the Bible; second, the Bible consists of several hundred thousand words. It is simplifying matters too much to reduce all control beliefs to—for example—the first message of a missionary to persons who have never heard of Christ, a message that may consist of only a few hundred words. Surely the several hundred thousand other words of special revelation should play a role in forming control beliefs.

Two Kinds of Control Belief. A characteristic of one kind of biblically derived control belief is the great importance such a belief has for those who hold it. Examples of such beliefs are well-known. Thus, we *must* baptize infants. We *must not* baptize infants. Christ will reign in Jerusalem for one thousand years before history ends. Christ will not reign in Jerusalem before there is a new heaven and a new earth. Each of these beliefs is strongly held and each has implications for attitude and behavior, that is, each is a belief that controls something.

But there is another kind of biblically derived control belief. Even though this kind of control belief is firmly held, it does not seem to be so foundational that we may never relinquish it. Some control beliefs about Genesis can change; as a result, not everything one believes about the Genesis message has ultimate importance for the central argument. To illustrate the point that sometimes control beliefs are not *extremely* important for those who hold them and that therefore control beliefs can change, I intentionally choose an example not related to questions about origins.

Until a few decades ago, Christians generally believed that the Song of

Genesis 165

Solomon is allegorical; one interpretation said that it is an allegory of the bride-groom relationship between the church, the bride, and Christ, the groom. Thus, the King James Version (KJV) contains chapter headings such as these: "Mutual love of Christ and his church," "The church's victory and glory," and "Christ awakens the church with his calling." But in recent years, biblical scholars, including many who claim the Bible is infallible and inerrant, have changed their minds. The introduction to the Song of Songs (even the title of the book has changed) in the New International Version (NIV) put it this way:

> [The Song] is wisdom's description of an amorous relationship. The Bible speaks of both wisdom and love as gifts of God, to be received with gratitude and celebration.
>
> This understanding of the Song contrasts with the long-held view that the Song is an allegory of the love relationship between God and Israel, or between Christ and the church. . . .[2]

Consequently, the NIV section headings identify the speakers as follows: Lover, Beloved, and Friends.

One's understanding of the nature of this book of the Bible—whether it is an allegory involving Christ and the church or a description of amorous love—certainly qualifies as a *control belief*; after all, this understanding determines the interpretation of an entire book of the Bible. As a consequence of the older control belief, theologians used details of this book to describe the nature of the relationship between Christ and his people. But the newer control belief probably contributes to the different, possibly healthier attitude toward amorous love generally held by modern Christians.

This radical change in theological teaching concerning the Song of Songs during recent years has not been controversial. The control belief changed quietly. In the same way, theologians *who believe in the Bible's infallibility and inerrancy* changed some of their control beliefs concerning origins during recent years. As we shall see, this tendency does not make it easier to sort things out. But at the end of this chapter, I conclude that openness is the best present attitude concerning some control beliefs about origins; later, however, we shall see that other control beliefs are rooted so deep in the Christian faith that they may not change. Openness concerning control beliefs may never compromise the integrity of the relationship between general and special revelation.

Miracles and Origins

One way to maintain the integral relationship between general and special revelation is to be open to the possibility that miracles could explain phenomena in both special and general revelation. Thus, it is not correct to hold that a miracle taught by special revelation cannot have relevance in our interaction with general revelation, that is, in our scientific work. But some people have an incorrect control belief. They claim that one should not attempt to "solve" any of the origins problems by invoking miracle. For example, in a discussion of what the Bible says concerning origins, John Stek stated:

> Since the created realm is replete with its own economy that is neither incomplete (God is not a component within it) nor defective, *in our understanding of the economy of that realm so as to exercise our stewardship over it*—understanding based on both practical experience and scientific endeavors—*we must methodologically exclude all notions of immediate divine causality.*[3]

Stek noted that he accepts "biblically attested miracles." But evidently he ruled out the possibility of discovering, as we carry out our stewardly scientific activity, that other miracles have occurred.

While we certainly may not postulate miracles merely to fill in gaps in our knowledge and thus be guilty of the charge positivists have made against Christians, neither should we rule out miracles. Of course, every claim advocating a miraculous explanation of a modern event has been vigorously contested, and it may well be that no miracle has occurred since the era in which the New Testament was written. But we are not privy to God's schedule of miracles. We may see miracles during our lifetime. Nor can we rule out that we might conclude from scientific investigation that natural law does not account for, and probably never will account for, the appearance of the first cells. Perhaps it is proper to speak of miracle in a description of some of the events associated with God's creative activity.

We do indeed have control beliefs. Further, the miraculous can appear anywhere in general and special revelation. But prior to an examination of what the Bible says about origins, a discussion of interpretation of the Bible is appropriate.

Interpretation of the Bible

Principles of Biblical Interpretation. These are principles relevant to the present discussion:

(1) *The Bible is the infallible Word of God.* Often the word "inerrant" is used. While God's special revelation is certainly without error, we can make a mistake in connection with the use of the word "inerrant." Thus, "inerrant" does not convey enough: we can certainly conceive of human

Genesis 167

documents that would be technically without error. But claiming that the Bible is infallible means that on whatever it speaks, such as origins, it speaks not only without making a mistake, but also *authoritatively*.

(2) *The Bible is its own interpreter.* This rule has three applications. First, consideration of any passage of the Bible must take its context into account. The context might be a few verses or a few chapters, but it could also be the entire Bible. Taking a text out of context is one of the most serious interpretive errors. Second, a more complete understanding of a word, a phrase, or an idea can be obtained by comparing the use of the same word, phrase, or idea in other parts of the Bible. Third, the Bible contains a large number of references to other parts of the Bible, constituting an internal "commentary," the only authoritative biblical commentary.

Careful attention to the three aspects of this rule of interpretation can prevent serious error and probably could have prevented many quarrels among Christians in the past.

(3) *The Bible is an authentic historical document.* Thus, the Bible contains reliable history. Of course, questions arise because some parts of the Bible are poetic, some are allegorical, and so forth. But to claim that the Bible is an authentic historical document is to claim that where the Bible itself identifies a passage as historical, its claim is correct. The next question is "What constitutes such identification?" This question cannot be answered in the abstract; it needs to be taken up with regard to specific passages.

(4) *The results of scientific activity can be an aid in understanding the Bible.* One obvious example of such scientific activity is the study of ancient languages, the knowledge of which is necessary for understanding the Bible. But since the Bible is a historical document, ancient history and knowledge of ancient culture can also help. According to Stek,

> Today interpretation of the Old Testament (not least Genesis) is undertaken on a new basis. The world out of which God called the patriarchs and within which ancient Israel emerged and walked with God (in both obedience and disobedience) has to a great extent been brought into the light of history: its peoples, its languages, its literature, its cultures, its politics, its religions. . . .

In fact, whole *libraries* of ancient documents are now available:

> The discovery and decipherment of whole libraries of ancient documents allow us for the first time to appreciate the range,

sophistication, and subtlety of ancient literature: the variety, fluidity, and significance of its many genres (types); its creative and imaginative use of language; the protean forms of thought it embodies.[4]

Just as we can use modern scientific results to praise God, we can use these ancient libraries to praise him.

(5) *The Old and New Testaments are closely linked.* The New Testament fulfills the Old; the Old anticipates the New. For example, theological propositions, especially those concerning moral behavior, are generally more obvious in the New Testament, but we may not divorce them from the Old Testament. That the New Testament is the fulfillment of the Old means that the revelation of God by his Son in the New Testament is directly linked to the very beginning of the Old Testament.

Some Difficulties. Certain difficulties arise with respect to interpreting Genesis.

(1) Some scholars contend that the meaning of a biblical passage can be separated from the conveyor of the meaning, the passage itself. Many of these scholars derive some message from the first part of Genesis (usually the discussion focuses on Genesis 1-3) but claim that part of Genesis is nonhistorical. Their concern about historicity should not be dismissed lightly. After all, the incidents in Christ's parables were not historical, even though the parables carried a message. Perhaps the best approach to this question is to insist that if a passage is nonhistorical, this fact should be evident from the context.

(2) The assumption that the Bible is easy to understand, an assumption widely made, can lead to an incorrect understanding of a passage that is in fact difficult. Two ideas at first seem to be contradictory. First, a person who has learned only the first rudiments of the Gospel can be a child of God. Second, the depths of God's special revelation cannot be fully comprehended by any scholar during his or her lifetime. The solution to this apparent contradiction is, of course, that salvation comes not by study or any other human effort, but rather by God's grace. After the reception of God's grace, his people respond with service—in the case of the biblical scholar, by intensive study of the Bible. Unfortunately, the idea has gained some currency that a quick, superficial reading of the Bible is enough; indepth study adds nothing. While the insights of biblical scholars are not necessarily correct, they certainly warrant serious consideration.

(3) Another problem arises because almost all Christians must depend upon a modern translation of the Bible. But the desire on the part of

translators to conform to modern idiom and thought patterns can lead to an incorrect understanding of the biblical message. Two examples, both concerning origins, follow.

For Genesis 2:4, the KJV says that God made the earth and the heavens in—using the singular—a "day"; the NIV is vague, with "when the Lord God made the earth and the heavens." Thus, the KJV telescopes the six days of creation into a single day, with obvious implications for the position that requires six 24-hour days. The NIV translation does not suggest telescoping the six days into one. In this case, the KJV is a more nearly correct rendition of the original Hebrew.

For Genesis 2:7, which describes the creation of Adam, the KJV says that God made man a "living soul," while the NIV says he became a "living being." The difference is critical: "soul," a word that earlier had a meaning different from its modern meaning, now gives the verse a meaning that it does not in fact have. The NIV provides a better rendition. (Chapter 11 provides a more complete discussion of this verse.)

The Creation Week

The remaining sections of this chapter take up the passage describing the Creation Week, Genesis 1:1-2:3, ending with my own conclusions. These sections are the introduction to the discussion of the origin of the human family in Chapter 11.

Various Interpretations of Genesis 1:1-2:3. Over the years various control beliefs concerning this passage have arisen. Each control belief leads to a particular interpretation; seven are of interest here. With each control belief and resulting interpretation, the question centers on the seven-day structure of the passage. It is not merely a question of what the word "day" means; it is also a question about the thrust of the entire passage.

(1) Those who hold to the *literal* interpretation of this passage insist, "The words mean what they say." The claim that words mean what they say is a control belief that has implications for the reading of the entire Bible. It is a belief that usually implies that a person's first reading of a passage provides the correct interpretation. Therefore, concerning this passage, the days are 24-hour days and each of the first six days begins and ends with the kind of morning and evening we experience every day.

In favor of this interpretation is its widespread appeal among Christians who are "in the pew." One need not be a scholar to understand the Bible; just read it like any other book intelligible to the general public. In addition, this interpretation is the traditional one, held for centuries by large numbers of Christians, including most Christian theologians.

As I indicated earlier, when nonnegotiable theological truths are involved, control beliefs may not change; in other cases, however, it is permissible for control beliefs to change. Perhaps it is not essential to insist on the usual implications of "the words mean what they say." As a result, it might not be necessary to cling to 24-hour days for Creation Week. At least two problems with 24-hour days arise.

(a) Those who hold to this interpretation seem not sufficiently careful in comparing Scripture with Scripture. Two examples:

First, the Bible does not indicate a radical difference between the length of the six days of creation and the seventh day.[5] Yet the seventh day must be indefinitely long: not only does it lack in the text the "evening and morning," which would indicate it had an end, but the Bible also says that the seventh day is a rest that continues until now (Heb. 4:3-5, citing Ps. 95:11 and the institution of God's rest in Gen. 2:2). It seems to be a case of adding to the text to claim that the length of day changed an unimaginable amount between the sixth and seventh days.

Second, we should compare the use of words in the Creation Week account with their use in other parts of the Bible. The problem arises in connection with statements such as the following, where Theologian H.C. Leupold referred to the appearance of "day," "evening," and "morning" in Genesis 1:

> ... [T]o make this statement refer to two parts of a long geologic period: the first part a kind of evening; the second a kind of morning; both together a kind of long period, runs afoul of three things: first, that "evening" nowhere in the Scriptures bears this meaning; secondly, neither does "morning"; thirdly, "day" never means "period."[6]

But the Hebrew word for "day" in Genesis 1, *yom*, sometimes refers to a period of time other than 24 hours. I have already referred to Genesis 2:4, where "day" refers to the entire period of creation. Consider its meaning where the Lord describes a process that will consume a period of time much longer than a 24-hour day and is yet described as a "day":

> A day of the Lord is coming when your plunder will be divided among you. I will gather all the nations to Jerusalem to fight against it; the city will be captured, the houses ransacked, and the women raped. Half of the city will go into exile, but the rest of the people will not be taken from the city. (Zech. 14:1-2)

Genesis

There are several similar uses of "day" in Zechariah 14:4-9. In many other places "day" seems not to refer to 24 hours, but to either an indefinite period or a long period of time. Examples include Deuteronomy 31:18 and 34:6, Psalm 37:13 and 137:7, and Isaiah 61:2. Therefore, it seems that one is not justified in assuming that the appearance of *yom* in the Creation Week account *must* mean that the days were 24-hour days.

Furthermore, consider the remark made by Leupold concerning "morning" and "evening," a typical claim made by those who adhere to 24-hour days in Genesis 1. By comparing Scripture with Scripture, one can deduce that his conclusion for "evening" is not correct. Thus, the Hebrew word for "evening" in Genesis 1, *ereb*, can indicate a long period of time within a long-period day, as it does in Zechariah 14: "a day [*yom*] of the Lord" (14:1) "will be a unique day, without daytime or nighttime . . . . When evening [*ereb*] comes, there will be light" (14:7).[7]

(b) This interpretation might not adequately take into account the integral relationship between general and special revelation. If, as just indicated, the Bible does at least *allow for* the possibility that Creation is very old, then it certainly is the better part of wisdom to consider very seriously the evidence for great age presented in the first part of Chapter 5. We ought not to err either in failing to allow our interaction with special revelation to aid us in our interaction with general revelation—using Calvin's "spectacles"—or in using our interaction with general revelation to augment our understanding of the Bible.

Perhaps many people have feared allowing scientific conclusions to help them understand the Bible because so often this procedure has been misused. Critics of the Bible have frequently used scientific results in attempts to refute the Bible. As a result, while not refusing to use scientific results, those who hold to 24-hour days have sometimes selected or incorrectly used results that to them seem to confirm ideas already held.[8]

(2) The *allegorical* interpretation of the passage says that it is not a description of events; rather, the entire text has a single, grand meaning, one obtained by interpreting the *picture* the passage presents. The relevant control belief is that we may put very few restrictions on what scientific investigation can reveal about origins; the idea of separate domains for "Bible" and "science" is controlling.

In favor of this interpretation is its recognition of the grandeur of the first part of Genesis. Those who accept this interpretation do not fall into the trap of trivializing the text, a problem that exists for interpreting any part of the Bible. After all, some people have claimed that Isaiah 40:31 ("They will soar on wings like eagles") prophesies airplanes and that Nahum

2:4 ("The chariots storm through the streets, rushing back and forth through the squares") prophesies automobiles.

But those who accept the allegorical interpretation seem to say that *in principle* that the Bible cannot speak to certain questions concerning origins. In particular, those who accept this interpretation usually contend that the first part of Genesis tells us *that*, but not *how*, God created. They come close to denying one of the principles of interpretation, namely, that the Bible is an authentic historical document.

In addition, this interpretation seems not to give sufficient attention to the unity of the Old and New Testaments, thus violating another principle of interpretation. Because the allegorical interpretation is also used for Genesis 2 and 3 (beyond the passage presently being considered), I shall illustrate the point concerning the unity of the Testaments by citing a problem with the allegorical treatment of the creation and fall of the human family described in that passage. For those who accept the allegorical interpretation, Adam and Eve (Genesis 2) are not real persons; their sin and the resulting curse (Genesis 3) constitute a description of the universal human condition. But the unity of the Old and New Testaments is a fact; it is therefore relevant that the New Testament does not permit this interpretation of Genesis 2 and 3. In Romans 5:12-19, Paul claims that because the entrance of sin is due to "one man" (Adam), the work of "one man" (Christ) followed.

We should not accept the allegorical interpretation because it denies the integrality of special and general revelation. Accepting this interpretation also undermines the New Testament presentation of Christ's work.

(3) The *day-age* interpretation says that the passage does refer to events; the "days" of the account correspond to geological periods. Strictly speaking, this interpretation precludes overlapping of periods.[9] The control belief here is not far from that of the literalist: the belief claims the existence of a discernible, one-to-one relationship between biblical teaching concerning origins and scientific statements concerning origins.

In favor of this interpretation is the attention it gives simultaneously to both scientific results and biblical study. This interpretation neither forces literalism where it is difficult to defend, such as 24-hour days, nor does it do what the allegorical interpretation does, that is, put the Bible where it cannot say much about origins.

But this interpretation does make the mistake of finding a confirmation in the Bible of scientific conclusions that are, after all, only tentative. Obviously, this danger always exists if one is to insist that our interaction with the two revelations must be just as integrated as the revelations themselves.

Genesis 173

How can we avoid this danger? By vigilance; by evaluating each case as it arises. It is difficult to provide a general answer to that question.

Because of the nature of this approach, a weakness in the day-age interpretation appears. A careful look at the geological periods reveals that they do not follow the sequence of Genesis 1. Pattle P.T. Pun described one problem:

> However, [assigning days to geological periods] seems to ignore the inconsistency of the creation of land plants, including herbs that yield seeds and trees that yield fruit, in the third day that is usually treated as corresponding to the Silurian Age. In the geological record the first fossil of fruit-bearing Angiosperms was found in the Cretaceous period that is more than 220 million years *later* than the Silurian Age.[10]

Thus, if the third creation day is assumed to be the Silurian Age, then some plants were created later than the third day, contrary to the Genesis account. It is not that there is something wrong with either the Genesis account or the traditional assignment of geological periods and subdivisions of periods. It seems to me, however, that there is no biblical warrant for claiming a one-to-one linkage between the beginnings of the days of Creation Week and the arbitrarily-assigned beginnings of geological periods or subdivisions of periods. This weakness is inherent in the day-age interpretation.

(4) The *overlapping day-age* interpretation, like the day-age interpretation, says that the days were long periods of time, but it does not identify those periods of time with geological periods. Because the days overlapped, the activity of the second day was still going on when the third day started, and so forth. Likewise, each day ended before the next day ended.[11] Here the control belief is one step away from that of those who hold to the day-age interpretation. According to this belief, the Bible does address some matters that are the subject of scientific investigation; but, given the nature of the Bible and the nature of the scientific enterprise, it is unrealistic to expect that in every case the answers to a given question will be given in the same way in general and special revelation.

In favor of this interpretation, like the day-age interpretation, is its attention to the integrated human reaction to the two revelations. Also, since it does not insist on a one-to-one correspondence of the days of Genesis 1 with geological periods, it is not tied to the specifics of scientific conclusions. Because the days overlapped and because they need not correspond to geological periods, this interpretation does not have the scientific problem arising with the day-age interpretation. The overlapping day-age interpretation is consistent with many modern cosmological models.

Another point in favor of this interpretation is its assumption that the days of Genesis 1 not only began in the sequence given, but that the first six days also ended in that sequence; the sixth day ended with the creation of Adam and Eve. Insisting that the sixth day ended with the creation of human beings is consistent with two important biblical statements. First, God pronounced Creation very good after he created Adam and Eve (Gen. 1:31). Second, Genesis 2:2-3 (which defines God's rest as cessation of creation), Psalm 95:11, and Hebrews 4:3-5 taken together indicate that God rests now, and that this rest began when his works of creation were complete; the six days were over.

But the overlapping day-age interpretation of Genesis 1:1-2:3 also has weaknesses. While its flexibility can fit into all but a few modern cosmological models, we cannot be certain about the future. Will cosmological models appear that do not contradict the Bible but that do, however, contradict the overlapping day-age interpretation of the Genesis account of the Creation Week? Or, even if no one offers such a model, is it not possible that such a model is the correct model?

Another criticism, due to Richard Bube, a materials scientist at Stanford University, applies to several interpretations of Genesis 1:1-2:3. Because of the popularity of the overlapping day-age interpretation, a description of Bube's criticism is relevant here.

Bube claimed that there are only two basic views of origins and, by implication, of the first part of Genesis; any other position is but a way station on the road toward one of those two positions. The two positions on origins he described are close to those derived from the first two interpretations of Genesis 1:1-2:3 described above, the literal and the allegorical:

> Theories on the origin of the earth in the context of science and the biblical revelation fall into two general categories: (a) those involving instantaneous creation of a young earth and all that is in it, and (b) those involving natural process as the scientifically describable means by which God accomplished His purpose.

Bube said that attempts to hold an intermediate position, one that says God created at separate times and that the age of the earth is billions of years, is difficult to maintain:

Genesis

... [T]his position is difficult to defend, suffering the weaknesses of both positions (a) and (b) above with few of their strengths, and forming no more than a way station on the progression of thought from position (a) to position (b).[12]

While I do not claim that the various interpretations lie on a continuum with all but the two interpretations at the extreme ends no more than intermediate interpretations, Bube's analysis obviously constitutes a warning; it *is* easy to drift to Bube's position (b). Drifting is particularly easy for a person whose approach to "the Bible and science" is to minimize conflict, rather than an approach that assumes the integrality of the two kinds of revelation and ultimately challenges the impact of evolutionary thinking on modern society.

If a person accepts the integrality of the two kinds of revelation, then, in my opinion, the overlapping day-age interpretation is one of the better interpretations. But great care is required. It may be that even in this interpretation too much contemporary scientific detail is forced into the biblical text.

(5) The *fiat* interpretation says that whenever God gave a command, a *fiat* or a "let there be," whatever he decreed was as good as accomplished; it was inevitable. Each "day," the time of the *fiat*, was short. After each *fiat* history unfolded: what God had decreed would happen did happen. The time of unfolding could be a very long time. We work out the history of Creation, that is, the successive unfoldings; we do not observe the *fiat*'s. As a result, the history we work out consists of long periods.

Alan Hayward is the principal modern proponent of this interpretation.[13] Hayward explained the interpretation by "repunctuating" the creation account of Genesis 1:3-2:3. The following, which is part of his repunctuated account, illustrates his procedure. The fulfillment of a *fiat*, the events that took place as history unfolded, is an italicized parenthetical expression:

> And God said, 'Let there be light.' (*And there was light. And God saw that the light was good; and God separated the light from the darkness. God called the light Day, and the darkness he called Night.*) And there was evening and there was morning, one day.
> And God said, 'Let there be a firmament in the midst of the waters, and let it separate the waters from the waters.' (*And God made the firmament and separated the waters which were under the firmament from the waters which . . .*)[14]

The control belief here is similar to that held by proponents of the overlapping day-age model with, however, the added stipulation that one may derive new meaning from the text by deducing how it would appear if the biblical authors had modern grammatical tools at their disposal.

In favor of this interpretation is its obviously correct emphasis on the absolute sovereignty of God: he speaks, and whatever he commands comes into existence. This interpretation reminds us to take very seriously the biblical predictions about what is yet to come to pass. God has already spoken, and so fulfillment is inevitable. His people have a sure comfort for the future.

But punctuating a modern translation of the Bible by indicating that certain words were parenthetical (the original languages did not use this kind of punctuation) has obvious problems. Of course, modern translations do assume that certain words were parenthetical. Still, one might be guilty of adding to the Bible when an entire theory of the account of the Creation Week rests on the assumption that certain words were parenthetical.[15]

(6) The *modified intermittent-day* interpretation says that each day of Creation Week was short. It was the time for the beginning of the activity God decreed for that day. The activities of all six days still continue. The short days were far apart. The seventh day is in the future. This interpretation has been advanced principally by Robert C. Newman and Herman J. Eckelmann, Jr.[16] (Both are physicists; Newman is at the Biblical School of Theology in Hatfield, Pennsylvania and Eckelmann is now a pastor of a church.) Describing the operative control belief here is not easy. For the most part, it is the belief lying behind the overlapping day-age interpretation that the Bible addresses some matters that are the subject of scientific investigation. Even though Newman and Eckelmann are not literalists, their control belief probably includes some of the elements lying behind literalism; evidence is their adoption of the 24-hour day. Their ideas on the seventh day seem to derive from the eschatological position of some literalists.

In favor of this interpretation is the emphasis it puts on the continuing development of Creation (not the development of the general evolutionary scenario). It takes into account scientific results. There is a conscious effort to be faithful to the Bible.

Newman and Eckelmann have reasons for adopting the short day at the beginning of each period. Their principal reason:

> But what is the significance of these peculiar literal days in our proposed model of the Genesis account? After all, even though each day introduces a new creative period, only the seventh marks

Genesis

the complete cessation of creative activity in the previous periods.

Newman and Eckelmann explained "these peculiar literal days":

> [We suggest] that God highlights these seven days, among the many actually occurring during creation, in order to set up an ordinance by which man is to commemorate creation. The six days of work remind him that he was created by God, and the seventh day of rest looks forward to God's rest, when redeemed man will rejoice with all creation in the new heavens and the new earth (Rom. 8:18-25; Heb. 4:1-11).[17]

Since they do not adopt the literal interpretation, it seems that their adoption of the short day is speculative; perhaps it *could* be correct, but the biblical evidence for it is weak. Furthermore, I seriously question whether viewing the seventh day as still in the future is consistent with the entire biblical teaching on the nature of God's sabbath.

(7) The *framework* or *literary* interpretation has been favored by many theologians in one form or another ever since Augustine.[18] According to this view, the passage consists of an artistic framework of what happened to bring the world into being; what actually occurred fills out the framework and did not necessarily happen in the order given by the text. Henri Blocher described the approach in this way:

> The literary interpretation takes the form of the week attributed to the work of creation to be an artistic arrangement, a modest example of anthropomorphism that is not to be taken literally.

Blocher suggested why the author of Genesis used this approach:

> The author's intention is not to supply us with a chronology of origins. It is possible that the logical order he has chosen coincides broadly with the actual sequence of the facts of cosmogeny; but that does not interest him. He wishes to bring out certain themes and provide a theology of the sabbath. The text is composed as the author meditates on the finished work, so that we may understand how the creation is related to God and what is its significance for mankind.[19]

The control belief behind the framework approach includes a rejection of the literalist's control belief that the correct interpretation must of necessity be literal and that the text is not difficult to understand. The control belief for one who holds the framework interpretation says that one must give great attention to the text. Although on the surface this control belief may seem to be quantitatively, not qualitatively, different from that of the person who accepts the allegorical interpretation, such a conclusion is not correct. The person who adopts the allegorical interpretation rules out *a priori* the possibility of finding details about God's acts of creation in the text, whereas the person who follows the framework approach maintains that details could be there, but they are not expressed literally.

In favor of the framework interpretation is the structure of the text. Many authors have called attention to the grouping of the six days into two groups of three: what happened on the first day is related to the fourth; likewise, the second is related to the fifth and the third to the sixth. In addition, Blocher cited several other uses of 3, as well as of 7 and 10:

> The regular flow of thought conceals a careful construction which uses symbolic numbers: 10, 3, and particularly 7. Ten times we find '*God said*' . . . . Of those ten words, three concern mankind . . . and seven the rest of the creatures. The creative orders they include use the verb to be, 'let there be,' three times for the creatures in the heavens, and seven different verbs for the world below. The verb 'to make' also appears ten times, as does the formula 'according to its/their kind.' There are three benedictions, and the verb 'create' is used at three points in the narrative, the third time thrice. Above all we read seven times the completion formula 'and it was so,' . . . seven times also the approval 'and God saw that it was good,' and seven times a further statement is added (God names or blesses).[20]

And there is more. One example: after making a case for the centrality of the fourth day among the seven days and also the climax of the six days of work, Blocher emphasized the symmetry of the passage exhibited by the number of words: the total number of words for days 1-4 is 207; for days 5-6, 206.[21]

But a serious problem concerning the meaning of the text arises. Not only is the structure concealed (as Blocher stated, as quoted above), but so also is the actual history of God's works of creation. The framework conveys an idea—but it is not history. Obviously, God is free to speak in this way. If, however, we are convinced that he indeed spoke that way, we should

Genesis

not be surprised if different adherents of this interpretation have radically different ideas concerning origins.

Some adherents of this interpretation have rendered themselves unable to use biblical material necessary to defend their position on origins. Consider the following question. If the account of the Creation Week does not reveal historical events, where in Genesis is the transition from the nonhistorical to the historical? A good case can be made that the beginning of biblical history is Genesis 2:4. But many Christians who hold to the framework interpretation are not convinced of that case; for them, if Genesis 1:1-2:3 is nonhistorical, then so is much more in Genesis—perhaps all of Genesis 1-11. Biblical history then begins with the call of Abraham in Genesis 12:1-3. This position leads to a serious distortion of the biblical message. My criticism of the framework interpretation of Genesis 1:1-2:3 does not prove the interpretation is incorrect, but those who adopt it need to be aware of this very serious problem.

Masking the Meaning. When deciding on the interpretation of Genesis 1:1-2:3—or, for that matter, any other passage of the Bible—we need to be certain that we do not shut ourselves off from anything that God in fact does reveal to us. This situation arises as scholars study the Bible's message concerning origins. I take up only two such problems here, one related to boundaries in Creation and the other concerned with symbols in the biblical text. In both cases, there is a danger of masking the meaning of Genesis 1:1-2:3.

(1) Claiming that God did not create boundaries during Creation Week is equivalent to ignoring part of the text. As God created boundaries, he set limits. He reveals himself to us as one who separates and limits.[22] As God separated light from darkness, he limited where they could go. He separated the waters below the firmament from those above: not all the water of the atmosphere becomes a part of oceans and lakes, and so it rains only at his appointed times. On the surface of the earth, he separated land and water. Creatures made "according to its (their) kind(s)" are therefore separated from other creatures; each has its place. He created the sun, moon, and stars, all separate entities. He shut up the seas behind doors and fixed their limits, setting a boundary that the waters cannot cross. These are some of the boundaries and limitations that the Bible teaches. (See Job 38:8-10, Psalm 104:9, and Proverbs 8:29, all discussed in Chapter 3 regarding discontinuities in Creation.)

Regardless of which interpretation of the Creation Week account is adopted, one must always see God as the boundary-maker, one who sets limits, both at the time of Creation and later, such as after the Flood. The

Bible emphasizes this boundary making and limitation, and so every model of Creation should do the same. In fact, these passages may indicate—as some have said—that Creation consists of parts such that one part cannot be reduced to another. That God undoubtedly made boundaries and set limitations does not in itself provide us with a history of the creation process (he could conceivably have created everything simultaneously, boundaries and all), but it does reveal to us something of the nature of Creation.

Therefore, even if we adopt an interpretation that does not purport to reflect the history of events, such as the framework interpretation, we can still learn something of the nature of what God did.

(2) We must ask if the interpretation of the Creation Week account which we adopt masks that which God actually reveals. Assuming that we accept Blocher's claim in the above quotation that there are symbolic numbers in the Genesis 1-3 passage, must we conclude that the entire passage is symbolic?

Whether the Creation Week account of Genesis 1:1-2:3 contains other symbols is not the point here.[23] But does the presence of *any* symbol in this part of Genesis, even the symbolic numbers associated with the very words of the text itself, mean that the account of Creation Week is not historical? For three reasons the presence of symbols cannot constitute evidence that the account is itself nonhistorical.

(a) In many places in the Bible the authors use symbolic numbers in passages that are not symbolic. Some biblical symbolic numbers are 3, 7, and 40; note their use in some parts of the Bible:

For the number 3: Jonah was in the great fish three days and three nights. Job's three friends spoke with him. Christ arose on the third day. The Godhead exists in three persons.

For the number 7: Our week, based on God's week, consists of seven days. Jacob served seven years for each of his two wives. In Israel, after seven seven-year periods, the fiftieth year was to be the Jubilee Year. Some Old Testament feasts were kept for seven days. The office of deacon in the New Testament church began with the calling of seven deacons.

For the number 40: The Israelites were in the wilderness forty years. Moses was on Mount Sinai forty days and forty nights. David and Solomon each reigned forty years. Christ ascended to heaven forty days after his resurrection.

But nowhere does the Bible indicate that the use of these symbolic numbers means that a passage is symbolic. Christ did arise on the third day, there were seven deacons, and Christ did live on earth forty days after his resurrection.

Genesis

(b) The Bible contains another kind of artistic structure, an alphabetic structure, whose presence could conceivably lead a reader to take a passage to be nonhistorical. The use of an alphabetic structure is not directly related to interpreting Genesis 1-3. However, examination of the use of this structure in other parts of the Bible illustrates that the presence of artistic structural devices, which could conceivably put restraints on the text, is not a signal that a passage is nonhistorical.

Thus, some biblical passages have an artistic structure that is based on the sequence of the 22 letters of the Hebrew alphabet. As with the use of symbolic numbers, use of the alphabetical sequence requires a certain pattern of the text; it restricts the text. But does that mean that the alphabetical song of the virtuous wife in Proverbs 31:10-31 describes a husband who trusts her only symbolically (31:11), or that she engages in only symbolic commercial activity (31:16-19, 24)?

Again, the entire book of Lamentations has a complicated structure based on the 22-letter Hebrew alphabet. The book consists of five laments, with 22 verses in each of the laments, except the third; and 66 (3 x 22) in the third. The book contains even more structure. But does the existence of this structure mean that Zion's anguish is only symbolic (1:4)? Or that her king and princes experienced only a symbolic exile (2:9)? Or that Israel's inheritance was only symbolically turned over to aliens (5:2)?

Examination of the alphabetic structure, an artistic structure used in the Bible, shows that its use does not automatically imply symbolic language.

(c) Perhaps the most important reason that the presence of symbols in Genesis 1-3 does not render this passage nonhistorical is the Christian insistence that God does not hide his revelation; a "hidden" revelation is, of course, no revelation.

Contrast the symbols of Genesis 1-3 with other symbols. For example, when we see the flag of our own country, we see nothing but symbol; yet we know what lies behind the symbol: a certain part of the earth's surface, a nation, a history filled with ignominious defeats and heroic victories, and so forth. Now consider Genesis 1-3 and whatever other parts of the Bible aid in the description of God's works of creation, such as Psalm 104, Job 38-41, and Romans 5. Assume that in this body of biblical literature God tells us whatever he wants to reveal about his acts of creation. If, however, this body of biblical literature is *only* symbolic, the biblical authors told their readers nothing about what actually happened. Those readers cannot, as it were, go behind the flag and know what it stands for. Whatever stands behind this body of biblical literature is hidden. This body of biblical literature is then a flag of an unknown country.

Some people will immediately reply that finding out about origins is the task of the scientific community; they claim that finding out such things is not in the domain of the Bible. But Genesis 1-3 and the other parts of the Bible that speak of God's acts of creation *do* claim to speak of details concerning origins. Surely the Bible presents more than the message, "The gods of the pagans are no-gods, the One True God created everything, his Creation is good, and he is the King."[24] At the very least, the Bible teaches that God made boundaries and limitations. Surely one of the elements of a biblically based description of Creation must include that concept.

Conclusion

As Christians react to special revelation, they develop control beliefs concerning how to interpret various parts of the Bible. Since human beings can err, not all those control beliefs are necessarily correct, so sometimes a Christian will change his or her mind about a certain control belief. Yet some biblical ideas are nonnegotiable. Christians certainly do not agree on which ideas are nonnegotiable. In the present discussion concerning origins, what is negotiable and what is not? Which ideas does the Holy Spirit teach his people, and which do some people erroneously assume are Spirit-taught?

As much as possible I have separated the discussion of Genesis 1:1-2:3 from the remainder of the Genesis 1-3 passage, parts of which I consider in the next chapter. Very likely almost all Christians agree on the nonnegotiable matters of Genesis 1:1-2:3. For Christians, the truly significant disagreement on origins lies in their understanding of Genesis 2:4 through Genesis 3, the passage that describes the origin of the human family and the entrance of sin. In other words, the argument among Christians over control belief ought to center on the latter passage.

Why? Don't Christians spend large amounts of time debating the length of the days of creation? Don't many of them consider those who have adopted the framework interpretation to be theological liberals? Aren't those who adopt one of the day-age interpretations on a slippery slope, sliding toward the extreme of allegoricalism? Isn't this a trend we should deplore? These questions certainly do surface in a debate among many modern Christians. In all of this, Christians may have adopted a worldly agenda. They have spent too much energy defending control beliefs (and the ideas derived from them) that do not get at the heart of the origins question. Furthermore, they have generally been too confident of their interpretation of Genesis 1:1-2:3.

I shall now present my conclusions concerning the various interpretations.

The Literal Interpretation. It seems that theologians and other scholars *who, by any other test, exhibit belief in an infallible Bible* have been moving away from this interpretation for several decades. A century ago, a large part of the corresponding group of Christian theologians accepted the literal interpretation; no such claim could possibly be made today. Earlier in this chapter I described a small part of the biblical reasoning, such as the biblical teaching concerning the indefinite length of the seventh day, that has brought about this change. No doubt many have been influenced—whether rightly or wrongly—by the kind of scientific data on the age of Creation presented at the beginning of Chapter 5. In my opinion, however, adoption of the literal interpretation, even though it is increasingly difficult to defend, does not prevent one from arriving at suitable conclusions concerning the main issue, the origin of the human family.

The Allegorical Interpretation. This interpretation does prevent one from making a good decision concerning the main issue. This is the interpretation of theological liberals. It ultimately leads to many problems, not the least of which is perceiving human beings to be descendants of animals.

The Other Five Interpretations. The kind of differences between the other five control beliefs and the interpretations (day-age, overlapping day-age, *fiat*, modified intermittent-day, and framework) that flow from them are just the kind of differences that Christians who accept biblical infallibility and inerrancy tolerate quite satisfactorily on other biblical matters. The differences between the control beliefs involved are not the kind of differences that lead to different nonnegotiable conclusions. Of course, many who hold to the literal interpretation, not among the five, consider their control belief and its consequences to be nonnegotiable. But they should consider the example of the interpretation of the Song of Solomon. No great uproar arose when the scholarly community that accepts biblical infallibility and inerrancy came to a different conclusion; one could say the same of other parts of the Bible. So it should be concerning Genesis 1:1-2:3; many of these scholars have already moved from the literal interpretation to one of the last five interpretations. In my opinion, the adherents of all but the allegorical interpretation are in a position to focus their attention on the origin of the human family. These six groups can agree on many ideas taught in Genesis 1:1-2:3: there is only one God, he created everything, he is not part of his Creation, he set boundaries, and he created human beings male and female in his image. Each of these ideas is a control belief that will serve in understanding the biblical description of the creation of the human family and the entrance of sin.

But as I see it, these six groups cannot work with those who adhere to the allegorical interpretation. That group relies upon a radically different control belief, the belief that we may put very few restrictions on scientific investigation into origins because the domains of the Bible and "science" are completely separate. With this view, one's perception of the entire cosmos will ultimately depend far more upon scientific conclusions than biblical revelation.

Some people will object to my inclusion of the framework interpretation in the group of interpretations which are conceivably acceptable. But an adherent of the framework interpretation could hold to one of the cosmological models proposed by adherents of the other interpretations in this group. Such a person would object, however, to the claim that the *Bible* calls for this cosmological model. For example, a person who holds to the framework interpretation might say, "I agree with the description of the universe associated with the overlapping day-age model. That model is consistent with my understanding of the Creation Week account, but I maintain that it is not *in* that account." Thus, two Christians, one an adherent of, say, the overlapping day-age interpretation, and the other an adherent of the framework interpretation, could adopt the same cosmological model. The first Christian depends on both the biblical data and the scientific data to formulate the model; the second, except for a few fundamental concepts, on the scientific data.

What about Evolution? What of the claim, according to general evolutionary theory, that the simplest life evolved from nonlife and that all other life evolved from the simplest? Those who adhere to the literal interpretation will certainly deny this claim, while those who accept the allegorical interpretation will usually allow for it. But what of the other five? Are those interpretations evolution-neutral? No, they usually are not.

What often happens is that those who accept the day-age, overlapping day-age, fiat, or modified intermittent-day interpretations almost always deny macroevolution. They do so for two reasons. The first is that Genesis 1 describes separate creations and several times includes the phrase, "according to its (their) kind(s)". The second is the scientific objection to macroevolution, some of which is described in Chapters 6 and 7. But adherents of the framework interpretation, even though they find created boundaries and limitations in the text, often allow for macroevolution. However, if macroevolution is not part of their cosmological model, very likely their denial of macroevolution arises because of the scientific case against it.

In my opinion, it is difficult to make an ironclad case against plant and animal macroevolution *on the basis of Genesis 1:1-2:3*. The barriers and the phrase "according to its (their) kind(s)" are strong indications that

Genesis

macroevolution is not tenable. I think that the barriers and that phrase do not tell scientists where the fossil record contains gaps. In other words, Genesis 1:1-2:3 cannot be used to judge beforehand that certain kinds of fossil-hunting expeditions will be futile. The largest gap of all is between nonliving matter and living cells. I wonder if one is justified in concluding, *using only the biblical text*, that God did not make the simplest life by starting with inorganic materials.

It is one thing to claim that one part of the biblical account of origins probably does not contradict one part of evolutionary theory. It is quite another to insist, as do large numbers of natural scientists, that *because evolution occurred, no part of the Bible can teach anything against evolution*. This attitude exhibits the impact that evolutionary theory has had on all scientific thought. This attitude not only skews proposed scientific projects, but it also damages biblical study. The principles of biblical interpretation become subsidiary to the general evolutionary hypothesis. Of course, this is an intolerable situation.

My personal view of Creation Week is that two of the interpretations described, the overlapping day-age and the framework, are the best. The overlapping day-age interpretation is held by many who reject macroevolution. On the other hand, some people who advocate the framework interpretation also favor the general evolutionary hypothesis. But a person who believes the framework interpretation can consistently also hold to separate creations of various living things.

Chapter Eleven
Human Origin and the Evolutionary Paradigm

To say that it is permissible to change some control beliefs concerning Genesis 1:1-2:3 does not suggest that these first Bible verses are unimportant. They are of ultimate importance. From them we learn that the One True God created all things, that he made boundaries, and that he is sovereign. He is not part of Creation. There is no other God: neither the sun, the moon, nor anything on earth is divine. Finally, we learn from this passage that God created human beings, male and female. Human beings, created in the image of God, have a role to play: rule, be fruitful, and subdue the earth. Human beings are at the head of Creation. Although some beliefs concerning this passage may legitimately change, all Christians must hold what has just been reviewed. These conclusions are nonnegotiable.[1]

But extremely important differences among control beliefs do surface in connection with the next passage, Genesis 2:4 to the end of Genesis 3. They certainly are important for the passage that describes the creation of Adam and Eve and the entrance of sin.

This book is about evolution. In this context, the all-important question concerning Genesis 2:4-3:24 is whether Adam and Eve descended from animals. In this chapter I conclude from a consideration of biblical teaching that Adam and Eve did not descend from animals and that this conclusion is nonnegotiable; it is at the heart of the Christian position. Therefore, scientific evidence—partly described in the last part of Chapter 7—cannot change this conclusion. In fact, the conclusion that human beings did not descend from animals is itself a control belief, a belief that determines the attitude one should take toward all learning. For that reason the last section of this chapter discusses the evolutionary paradigm.

The Debate

Theistic evolutionists modify general evolutionary theory in this way: evolution did indeed occur, they say, but God caused it.[2] They thus avoid the improbabilities of evolutionary theory based on random chance. Theistic evolutionists usually extend one of the less-specific interpretations of Genesis 1:1-2:3 (Chapter 10) into the next part of Genesis. They cite scientific

Human Origin and the Evolutionary Paradigm 187

evidence to show the similarity between human beings and animals and conclude that human beings evolved from certain primates. Although theistic evolutionists do make claims concerning nonhuman evolution, it is not my interest in this section to review their ideas concerning that kind of evolution. In fact, Christians quite often link the term "theistic evolution" to *human* evolution.

A difficulty arises in analyzing the positions of Christians on theistic evolution. While many Christians maintain that the first human beings had animal ancestors, others only *allow for the possibility* of animal ancestry. Those in the latter group are technically not theistic evolutionists. Yet for them the denial of animal ancestry is not nonnegotiable, and so my argument is also against their position. In fact, it is difficult to see how evolutionary effects on modern life can be avoided when one accepts the possibility of human evolution.

Richard Wright, in presenting a Christian view of biology to college students, allowed for the possibility of human evolution:

> Did God create Adam . . . from nothing? Or did he use preexisting matter (dust?) in hominid form? Exactly when in history might this have happened? . . . . *These are questions for which there is far too little evidence to venture an answer.* They are what we shall have to leave as loose ends, even though there are many who would like to see them tied.

Wright described different positions people have held:

> . . . there are two classical views on the origin of humankind: Humans either evolved from preexisting hominids, or else they were created by God with many features that are similar to fossil and existing primates . . . Both of these views are held by different groups of Christians who believe in the reliability of the Bible. And there are some who believe that God in a miraculous way transformed preexisting hominids into the first humans . . . . *[T]he evidence simply is not capable of distinguishing clearly between these views.*[3] (Emphasis added)

In a debate among Christians on several issues related to origins, R.J. Berry, professor of genetics at University College, London, expressed a similar idea:

> There is clearly no difficulty in believing that God could have car-

ried out this special creation [of a human being] in a hominid ape . . . . it is quite possible that, at some time after God had created Adam, he then conferred his image on all members of the same biological species alive at the time.[4]

Berry took a similar position in his book *Adam and the Ape: A Christian Approach to the Theory of Evolution*.[5]

Philosopher Jesse De Boer, also a Christian, took a stronger position. He referred to those who ". . . profess the historicity of Adam and Eve. That view is ridiculous! The early chapters in Genesis are mythical and most of the Pentateuch consists of legendary material . . ."[6]

The debate among Christians concerning the origin of the human family depends on human interaction with both general and special revelation. In one sense, the roles of the two revelations are complementary. Some information from one of these sources cannot be obtained from the other, and so what we learn from the one can add to what we learn from the other. But if "complementary" implies that we can decide *a priori* that in one revelation God reveals that which he does not reveal in the other, then we fall into the error of categorical complementarity. Those who hold to categorical complementarity assume that we have information that we in fact do not have.

The question of the human family's origin actually contains two questions for those who consider biblical evidence: were two people, Adam and Eve, the parents of the human family? If they were, did they descend from animals? Non-Christians do not worry about this distinction. If they hold to an animal origin of human beings, it is enough to say, "Adam was a crowd." But, since I shall maintain that Adam and Eve are the parents of all human beings, I must consider the other question, the origin of Adam and Eve.

The claim that Adam and Eve were the parents of the entire human family does not preclude the possibility that microevolution occurred since Adam and Eve's creation. Microevolution within the human family explains different skin colors, hair types, body types, and so forth. In addition, Genesis 5:4-32 indicates that human beings once lived about ten times as long as they do now. Some scholars dispute that the great ages were actually in the original text; but if they were there, then those great ages could be one more indication of microevolution or, more properly, *devolution* from their early state.

The amount of microevolution observed in the human family may have required a long time. But an age of hundreds of thousands of years for the human family, suggested by some scholars, raises questions concerning the interpretation of Genesis 4:20-22. That passage may indicate that agriculture and metal-working began not long after the beginning of the human family itself. However, anthropologists claim there is evidence that the beginnings of agriculture and metal-working were only a few thousand years ago. Christian scholars have proposed answers to this question and it is evident that Bible-believers need not necessarily reject such a great age.[7] On the other hand, the Bible does not require a great age for the human family. If, however, we combine biblical information with observations that racial differences do exist, we might conclude that these changes took place in the human family over a very long period of time.

Some Christians claim that because the Bible was written during a prescientific or nonscientific era, the biblical text does not address the origin of the human family. But a Christian may allow study of special revelation to illuminate the results of our scientific work, which is part of our interaction with general revelation. One need not maintain, even given the limitations of the cultures of both the Old and the New Testament times, that the biblical authors were unable to provide answers to the two questions posed above concerning Adam and Eve. Obviously, much of the modern discussion concerning origins presupposes knowledge of modern science. But it was possible for the Bible, without going beyond either the culture of biblical times or the kind of questions asked during that period, to teach whether Adam and Eve were the parents of the entire human family and whether Adam and Eve had animal forebears.

The Nature of Human Beings

In discussions of origins many Christians maintain that what is important in the biblical testimony is *that* God created; when we ask *how*, so goes the claim, we ask a wrong question. But sometimes the biblical *how* is extremely important; the origin of the human family is one such case. Of course, sometimes asking *how* can be trivial. Thus, it is important to know *that* Jesus and his disciples traveled from Galilee to Jerusalem, but research into *how* (did they walk the entire way, or were other means available for part of the way?) would surely be pointless. But discussion of how God created human beings provides illumination on the nature of human beings. Ultimately we shall see that claiming the evolution of human beings from animals is the principal means whereby evolutionary theory, perhaps the chief modern expression of dualism, has an impact on contemporary life.

Even persons who do not claim a Christian basis for their understanding of the nature of human beings realize that in some important way human beings are different from animals. Paleoanthropologist Richard Leakey said:

> Humans are more than just intelligent. Our sense of justice, our need for aesthetic pleasure, our imaginative flights, and our penetrating self-awareness, all combine to create an indefinable spirit which I believe is the "soul."[8]

Consider the position that Roger Lewin adopted. Lewin, at the end of his long reflection on modern developments and controversies in paleoanthropology, *Bones of Contention*, concluded that the difference between animals and human beings cannot be clearly defined (Chapter 7). He showed that paleoanthropologists continually change the criteria used to determine which fossils were human. Lewin claimed that paleoanthropologists base decisions concerning criteria on extra-scientific ideas. For example, during one period of time paleoanthropologists assumed that human beings were killer-hunters, but later paleoanthropologists ascribed more peaceful attributes to primitive human beings. Lewin said that these attitudes reflected contemporary social experience. Therefore, ". . . Paleoanthropology alone among all the sciences operates . . . with humanity's self-image invisibly but constantly influencing the profession's ethos."[9] For Lewin, then, there can be no clear-cut set of criteria that determine which fossils were human. The human definition of what is human will forever be changing.

Leakey, Lewin, and others like them are vague. They do realize *something* is different about human beings. Most people live on two levels—the one seen by other people and the other, perhaps radically different from the first, involving self-perception and thoughts about the past and the future. Recognizing these levels makes one realize that human beings and animals are qualitatively different. Such a reflection is only one of the many reactions to general revelation that lead to the same conclusion.

Christians have a firmer understanding of the nature of human beings. Although they do not agree on whether the theistic evolutionary concept is correct, they do agree on the essence of the nature of the human being: each person is created in the image of God. That God created human beings in his image is established in the very first biblical statement concerning the human family, Genesis 1:26-28.

A typical Christian reference to God's image allowing for the theistic evolutionistic position is Berry's remark quoted above. Other Christians—some of whom hold to the theistic evolutionistic position—approach the question in various ways, but they all obviously have deep respect for the concept of the image of God. Thus, Henri Blocher found in "image of God" the definition of what it means to be human. At the same time, he said, the Bible contradicts other ideas:

> For the Bible, man is neither angel nor beast, nor even a little of both; the prologue of Genesis defines him as a creature made *as the image of God*. The perspective and vision are totally different [for those who take man to be a mixture of angel and beast].[10]

Wright stated that since God is a Spirit

> Imaging God is thus related to the spiritual attributes of God—not in any sense exactly, for we are only an image, but in some measure we demonstrate what God is like. We do this when we search for truth and beauty, when we are concerned about justice and other ethical issues, when we recognize the high importance of morality; these are God-like qualities.

Wright then suggested that our unique calling is the basis for human dignity:

> ... [T]hink of this possibility: Although God wants us to see his glory in the creation, he has specifically created humankind to reflect his glory, in ways that the rest of creation simply could not. This is the clearest basis for human dignity, for the high value we place on human life.

Placing a high value on human life has significant consequences, said Wright:

> For this reason, the severely impaired, the senile, the most degenerate human beings deserve to be treated with respect. All humankind bears God's image to some degree . . . although that image has been affected by the Fall . . . .[11]

Many suggestions have been made concerning what it means to possess the image of God. Some Christians claim that people will therefore be able to rule, be fruitful, and be able to subdue the earth (Gen. 1:26-28). The presence of the image of God confers the ability to reason, including the ability to formulate the laws of logic.[12] Ruling and subduing imply naming, consistent with the mandate that God gave Adam to name the animals.

In Semitic thought naming meant human beings had the ability to learn the inner secrets or essence of the thing named.[13]

These ideas concerning the image of God are helpful. But theistic evolutionists do not admit that any of these considerations in themselves prove that the first human beings did not descend from animals. That question requires a detailed look at the biblical testimony. The following section first takes up the biblical testimony concerning how Adam and Eve relate to the rest of the human family, then the question of whether they had animal ancestry.

The Biblical Testimony

Adam and Eve and the Human Family. The Bible clearly teaches that Adam and Eve were two persons and were the parents of the entire human family. The Bible places Adam and Eve at the beginning of human history. This is not only the general teaching of the Bible but also the teaching of several specific passages.

First, the Bible ends Creation Week and introduces the creation of Adam and Eve by the first *toledoth* ("account" in the NIV and "generations" in the KJV): "This is the account of the heavens and the earth when they were created" (Gen. 2:4, NIV). The *toledoth* passages, all taken together, provide the structure of the rest of Genesis after 2:4. Thus, the end of that section says, "This is the written account of Adam's line" (5:1). The main point of the present discussion is that the *toledoth* structure links Adam and Eve to historical persons. It links them to Noah in 6:9, the beginning of the next *toledoth* passage; to Shem, Ham, and Japheth in 10:1; to Shem in 11:10; to Terah in 11:27; to Ishmael in 25:12; to Isaac in 25:19; to Esau in 36:1; to Esau and all the Edomites in 36:9; and to Jacob in 37:2.

Also, among the descendants of Adam and Eve are some of civilization's "firsts," such as agriculturalists (Gen. 4:20) and musicians (4:21). The Bible also states that Eve was the mother of the entire human family (3:20).

The Bible mentions Adam in several places besides Genesis. The genealogies beginning in I Chronicles 1:1 and Luke 3:23 list Adam as the first man. Paul states in I Corinthians 15:45, "So it is written: 'The first man Adam became a living being.'" Without naming Adam, Paul told the Athenians at the meeting of the Areopagus, "From one man he made every nation of men, that they should inhabit the whole earth..." (Acts 17:26). In most of the Adam passages he appears with persons known to be historical. These passages and the others cited seem to be irrefutable evidence that Adam was the first man.

Finally, consider the reasoning that Paul uses as he links the work of Christ to the sin of Adam (Rom. 5:12-19 and I Cor. 15:22). Christ's work is sufficient to remove the sin of every person, sin that arose because Adam's

Human Origin and the Evolutionary Paradigm 193

sin polluted the entire human family. In that way Paul says that Adam is the father of the entire human family.

The Origin of Adam and Eve. I shall now show that Adam and Eve did not have animal forebears. The position of theistic evolutionists again warrants our attention.

The human being that theistic evolutionists claim has evolved from animals cannot be the same human being non-Christian evolutionists describe. Theistic evolutionists attempt to account for the origin of the human being that the Bible describes, the being that bears God's image. Therefore, general evolutionary theory will not suffice for the theistic evolutionist. Did God suddenly transform two animals into Adam and Eve, who were therefore qualitatively different from all animals? Or, did God guide a gradual process, ending with two individuals differing enough from their forebears so that it could be said of them that they bore the image of God and were morally responsible?

I shall present a biblical argument against each of these two kinds of theistic evolution, that is, against both sudden and gradual appearance of the first human beings from animal forebears. Genesis 2:7 describes the creation of the first human being:

> The Lord God formed the man from the dust of the ground and breathed into his nostrils the breath of life, and the man became a living being. (Gen. 2:7)

Consider the meaning of "dust." Could this "dust" have been alive? Thus, could human beings be descendants of other primates? Such an interpretation does not seem possible, since the word here translated as "dust," the Hebrew *aphar*, which appears over 100 times in the Old Testament, never seems to denote living matter *when it does not refer to human beings*. Following are typical uses of *aphar*; the relevant English word is emphasized.

> I will make your offspring like the *dust* of the earth. (Gen. 13:16)

> Then they are to take other stones to replace these and take new *clay* and plaster the house. (Lev. 14:42)

> For the unclean person, put some *ashes* from the burned purification offering into a jar . . . (Num. 19:17)

He ground it to *powder* and scattered the *dust* over the graves of the common people. (II Kings 23:6)

Can they bring the stones back to life from those heaps of *rubble*—burned as they are? (Neh. 4:2)

I know that my Redeemer lives, and that in the end he will stand upon the *earth*. (Job 19:25)

All go to the same place; all come from *dust* and to *dust* all return. (Eccl. 3:20)

The Ecclesiastes passage is, in fact, a biblical commentary on the creation of the first human being in Genesis 2:7 and the curse on human beings in 3:19:

By the sweat of your brow you will eat your food until you return to the ground [*adamah*], since from it you were taken; for dust [*aphar*] you are and to dust [*aphar*] you will return. (Gen. 3:19)

This passage warrants close examination. Here the first *aphar* is a person. Does this mean that in 2:7 (describing the creation of the first human being) *aphar* could refer to a living being and that therefore human beings could have had animal ancestors?

I do not think so. Genesis 3:19 uses *aphar* twice. It also calls our attention to its use in 2:7: the 3:19 phrase, "since from it you were taken," refers not only to *adamah*, ground, but also to its use in 2:7. Among those three uses, we have one reference point. We know what "to dust you will return" means: the body in the grave turns to "dead" dust. (It has been suggested that the grave, which often contains worms and insects, is actually alive. Surely this reasoning does not advance the argument that human beings descended from nonhuman primates.) If the grave dust is dead, so is the dust of "for dust you are." Then it follows that the dust of "from it you were taken," that is, the dust of 2:7, is also dead or, more appropriately in this case, nonliving. God seems to say in 3:19, "You were dead dust. I gave you life. By sinning, you signed your death warrant and so you are now as good as dead. You shall return to the dead dust from which you came."

Many theistic evolutionists quite freely admit that the dust of Genesis 2:7 was dead. But, they say, the description is only symbolic, in the sense

Human Origin and the Evolutionary Paradigm 195

described in Chapter 10. Symbolic elements are indeed present in Genesis—"God . . . breathed" in 2:7 must be one of them. Yet it is not correct to claim that part of Genesis consists of nothing but symbol. I made that general claim for Genesis 1-3 in Chapter 10; now I shall present a specific argument concerning 2:7.

The error of theistic evolutionists may be in part due to a modern misunderstanding of Genesis 2:7 as rendered by the KJV:

> And the Lord God formed man of the dust of the ground, and breathed into his nostrils the breath of life; and man became a living soul. (Gen. 2:7, KJV)

The problem is with "soul," a translation of *nephesh*. Many Christians maintain that a human being "has a soul," as if God added a soul to a body. Three views of the "body-soul problem" are of interest in the present discussion.

The first view states that God added a soul to a pre-existing body, a view that the KJV translation of Genesis 2:7 seems to suggest. This view implies one kind of dualism: what pertains to the body is lower, of this world, and not of ultimate importance, but what pertains to the soul is higher, eternal, and worthy of considerable attention. This undesirable result can be traced to the division of body and soul; it is not fair to accuse the KJV translators of maintaining this extreme dualistic position.

The second view concerning the relation between body and soul, advanced recently by John Cooper of Calvin Theological Seminary, is mildly dualistic. In this view, however, the human being is a whole.[14] For Cooper, the person is an irreducible whole consisting of two parts. Genesis 2:7 describes the creation of both: the body from dust, to which the soul, its life, is given. Evidently Cooper holds that the human body has no life without the soul. For Cooper this is "holistic dualism."

The third view, a holistic view, held by other Christians, is that the person is a body-soul. To see a person is to see all of that person, both body and soul. For example, those who saw Christ saw the whole person; in his case, there was no division between his body and his divine being: "For in Christ all the fullness of the Deity lives in bodily form . . ." (Col. 2:9)

While the second and third views are holistic, the first is not. Theistic evolutionists, to be consistent, must hold either the first view or something similar to it. They are body-soul dualists. But the first view is not correct. I shall now explain why I think the Bible does not allow for the first view.

What did God do in Genesis 2:7 when "the man became a living being"

(NIV) or "man became a living soul" (KJV)? In the KJV *nephesh* is indeed translated in many other places as "soul" (see, for example, Gen. 17:14, 27:4, 34:3, Ex. 12:15, and Lev. 4:2), but it is also translated as "beast" (Lev. 24:18), "body" (Lev. 21:11 and others), "breath" (Job 41:21), and so forth.[15] Of particular interest in the present discussion is that *nephesh* is translated "creature" in many places (Gen. 1:21, 1:24, 2:19, 9:10, 9:12, 9:15, and 9:16; Lev. 11:46) and as "life" in numerous others (Gen. 9:4, 9:5, and 19:17; Lev. 17:14; Deut. 12:23).

Genesis 2:7 can be translated as it is in the NIV: ". . . the man became a living being." Genesis 2:7 does not teach that God formed the first human being by adding a soul to something that existed previously. It does teach that God made the first human being *nephesh*, a living being. But he also made animals *nephesh* (see, for example, Gen. 9:4 and Lev. 17:14). Those who hold to either the instantaneous or the gradual addition of a soul to a body cannot appeal to Genesis 2:7.

The holistic view of the human being that Genesis 2:7 presents is also taught by the Old Testament in the many places it refers to the whole person as *nephesh*. Some examples (the KJV translation of *nephesh* is emphasized):

> These are the sons of Zilpah . . . even sixteen *souls*. (Gen. 46:18)

> No *soul* of you shall eat blood. (Lev. 17:12)

> And levy a tribute unto the Lord of the men of war which went out to battle: one *soul* of five hundred, both of the persons and of the beeves, and of the asses and of the sheep. (Num. 31:28)

> Joshua . . . utterly destroyed . . . all the *souls*. (Josh. 10:28)

In many other places *nephesh* probably refers to the whole person.[16]

Sometimes when *nephesh* is translated as "soul," it may seem to refer to a separate entity; examples are Genesis 34:3, Leviticus 4:2, Numbers 9:13 and 21:4, and Psalms 3:2. Typical of such passages is the following: "The *soul* of the people was much discouraged" (Num. 21:4). But in such a passage "soul" denotes the whole person: the people were hungry and physically tired. Their discouragement inevitably had a physical component that involved their bodies.

Although *nephesh* is used in many other places in the Old Testament, the citations above are typical. Summarizing concerning the biblical use of *nephesh*, I conclude that Genesis 2:7 does not indicate God added a soul to a previously existing being. Instead, 2:7 indicates that God created Adam's entire being at this time.

One more observation concerning Genesis 2:7 is relevant to the question of the origin of Adam. The *order* in that passage is just the reverse of what one would expect had God made the first man from an animal: the text says that man became a living being, *not* that a living being became man.

Theistic evolution is untenable for other reasons. Consider the details of the creation of the first human *pair*. After God created Adam, he told Adam he would make a helper suitable (NIV) or help meet (KJV) for him (Gen. 2:18). All the beasts of the field were then brought to Adam for him to name. No helper for Adam was among those beasts (2:19-20). Only then did God create his helper, Eve, from the body of man (2:21-3).[17]

The description in Genesis 2 of the creation of Eve provides two indications that the first human beings did not descend from animals. First, no animal could be a helper for Adam. Second, Eve came from the body of a male, not a female, as would have been the case if she had descended from animals. The priority of Adam in time indicated by this passage cannot be merely a symbolic priority. This priority was certainly not symbolic for Paul, who said, "For Adam was formed first, then Eve" (I Tim. 2:13).

Another indication that Adam and Eve did not have animal forebears is the fact that they died because of their sin. All animals are mortal. If, as theistic evolutionists claim, God transformed animals into Adam and Eve, then they, too, would have been mortal even before they sinned. But some theistic evolutionists object: they claim that the transformation from animals to human beings included the gift of bodily immortality. Many Roman Catholic theologians maintain this position.[18]

On the other hand, another group of theistic evolutionists holds that the transformation to Adam and Eve did not include the gift of immortality. According to this position, even if Adam and Eve would have remained sinless, they would have died in the biological sense. The curse of death mentioned in Genesis 3:3 and received in 3:19 would be a separation from God added to an already-existing bodily mortality.

I think that both views are incorrect. Concerning the first view, nothing in the Bible teaches that some animal bodies evolved to an *immortal* state, a state that would have been much higher than the state of modern human bodies. The idea is speculative and groundless.

The second view, that the death of Genesis 3:3 and 3:19 was a separation from God in addition to the mortality already inherent in the human body, does not stand up under close scrutiny. After all, part of the curse in 3:19 is that human beings will return to the dust, just as the death of animals, which Adam and Eve observed, means a return to dust.[19]

Consider also how Paul treats the Genesis curse of death. In Romans 5:12-19 Paul states that just as death entered because of the sin of one man, life comes because of the death of another man, Jesus Christ. Of course, this death and life include, respectively, separation from God and eternal life with God. But the life of which Paul speaks includes resurrection from *biological* death. The resurrection of Christ that Paul celebrated certainly included a bodily resurrection, so the sin of one man must have brought about *biological* death. Paul makes the same point in another place:

> For since death came through a man, the resurrection of the dead comes also through a man. For as in Adam all die, so in Christ all will be made alive. (I Cor. 15:21-2)

(See also I Corinthians 15:35-54, where Paul in several ways indicates that the resurrection gift of Christ includes *bodily* resurrection and immortality.)

Claiming that human biological death preceded the Fall is equivalent to claiming that human pain also preceded the Fall. Such a claim implies that good and evil existed side by side in human lives before the first human sin. This idea is unacceptable. Rather, Adam and Eve suffered pain and biological death because of their sin, not because their created bodies were mortal and inherently subject to pain.

To maintain that human beings descended from animals often implies that when sufficient biological and intellectual improvement appeared in a certain kind of animal, human beings ("higher" beings) appeared. This claim does injustice not only to the way the Bible presents the human family, but also to the rest of Creation. It suggests that the predecessors of the human family were not fully developed. Regardless of changes that took place in the world of living organisms, what did *not* happen is that inferior beings disappeared so that human beings could appear.

Perhaps the unique place that the Bible gives to human beings is the most important reason for rejecting animal ancestry. Only human beings bear God's image. Theistic evolutionists also claim that God created human beings in his image, but they will not admit this fact to be an argument against their position. Nevertheless, the defense of theistic evolutionists on this point is weak; their explanation of the origin of the human family does not seem to account for human dignity or humanity's unique and exalted place in Creation. Before God created human beings, he pronounced his Creation good; after, it was very good. Human beings are the only creatures who

Human Origin and the Evolutionary Paradigm 199

are free to choose to love God and his commandments. Finally, God bestowed on human beings the ultimate dignity when he became human.

Thus, because of specific passages and the general way the Bible presents human beings as whole persons, I conclude that the Bible teaches that Adam and Eve did not have animal forebears. This is a nonnegotiable conclusion.

Comments on the Scientific Evidence

The Role of Scientific Evidence. I have extensively discussed the relation between the human interaction with general revelation and the human interaction with special revelation. Given this relation, what role do the fossil finds, as well as the biochemical dating methods, mean for the origin and history of the human family? Let us recall two important points.

First, some ideas derived from the Bible are nonnegotiable. Neither new scientific results nor any other scholarship can legitimately change such ideas. For example, no conceivable scientific evidence can prove that water cannot be turned into wine or that adultery is permissible.

Second, it is one of the principles of biblical interpretation that scientific knowledge can help us understand the Bible. Thus, scientific results can contribute to a better appreciation of the works of God recorded in the Bible. Modern comprehension of the grandeur and complexity of Creation is infinitely greater than the comprehension of those who lived before the scientific era. As a result, we can give praise to God—praise that the Bible tells us to give—in ways not possible for people who lived several centuries ago. Scientific knowledge can also aid our understanding of the Bible when it elucidates the biblical account. Thus, modern archaeological discoveries help us understand why Belshazzar put Daniel third in command (Daniel 5:29), rather than second, as one would expect from the context.[20]

How do these two ideas—the nonnegotiability of certain biblical ideas and the use of scientific results as an aid to biblical study—relate to the biblical account of the origin of the human family and its place in Creation?

We must begin by assuming that the human family did not have animal forebears. Consequently, one need not ask whether scientific evidence contradicts this conclusion. If scientific results are correct, they cannot contradict nonnegotiable biblical teaching. The proper procedure is to ask the next question: given that Adam and Eve had no animal forebears, what do scientific results teach us about the origin of the human family? I suggested that scientific results could enable us to praise God even more for his works and elucidate the biblical record.

Both uses of scientific results are relevant for the present question. How is it, one might ask, that scientific results give us more reason to praise

God for the creation of the human family? Scientific investigation shows a human being to be infinitely more complex, with the parts marvelously fitted together, than people realized before the age of modern science. Scientists are also certain that there is much more to learn. Thus, Christian amazement at Genesis 2:7—dust to man—is better-informed now than it was a few centuries ago.

What about elucidation of the biblical record? For example, could the discovery of burial sites, including fossils, add to what the Bible says about Adam and Eve? Such discovery certainly could add to the rather small amount of information about early humans given in the Bible. Let us look at this matter.

Scientific Evidence and the Questions Posed. In Chapter 7 I stated that the scientific evidence offered in support of human evolution does not distinguish between the two basic questions that Christians ask, namely, whether the entire human family descended from the biblical Adam and Eve and, if it did, whether Adam and Eve had animal forebears. Evolutionary scientists discuss only descent from animals.

But the picture that paleoanthropologists present is blurred. Only a very small number of fossils of the extremely old hominids have been found. In addition, the evidence is such that paleoanthropologists do not agree on how those fossils relate to the human lineage. Some insist that fossils that are undoubtedly animal fossils are in the human lineage. Others construct a sequence leading to modern human beings that includes only younger fossils that seem to have had human characteristics.

No doubt we can trace much of the picture presented by paleoanthropologists to a bias in favor of animal ancestry of human beings. Very likely almost all those who have done the original work in the field do not believe that God reveals himself in a general way in Creation and in a special way in the Bible. As a result, as paleoanthropologists construct a model of human origins, they might not merely neglect biblical data; they might consciously oppose it.

Christians must not err at this point. Christians sometimes assume that the evolutionary bias of many investigators, the paucity of data, and the gaps mean that they need not look at scientific evidence; that, in fact, God did not reveal anything in general revelation concerning the early history of the human family. Claiming that the data are insufficient does not mean that all future data will also be insufficient.

In that context, I propose the following question concerning early human history: what if, in spite of the present bias and uncertainty, the scientific data stand the test of time? What if the paucity of data and the gaps, which now seem so important, eventually do not pose a problem? Surely the Christian position should be one that acknowledges that God speaks infallibly and without error in both his general and his special revelation. Naturally, investigators who are faithful Christians always understand that what God reveals in the Bible and in Creation might not be what human study concludes is in the Bible and in Creation. Yet none of this should stifle investigation of both general and special revelation. The Christian community needs to proceed, working with what it has.

This approach means accepting the biblical teaching that the first human being was unique, a special creation, and that he was, in fact, the Adam of the Bible. Investigators who are faithful Christians do not then proceed to ask if fossils and other scientific evidence contradict the Bible. But they do ask what fossils and other scientific evidence can add to the biblical picture.

The question concerning the early history of the human family then reduces to this: where are Adam and Eve, uniquely created in the image of God and the parents of the entire human family, in the fossil record? I suggested earlier that at least some microevolution has occurred since Adam and Eve and that they may have lived hundreds of thousands of years ago. In fact, some Christian scientists who are convinced general evolutionary theory is wrong are also convinced that Adam and Eve may have been *Homo erectus*; others think evidence indicates that they were *Homo neanderthalensis*.

If those who accept the biblical testimony are also willing to look at the evidence of human remains whose age is tens (or, in some cases, hundreds) of thousands of years, they may be able to add much to what they know from the Bible of early human beings. If the present evidence holds up, they will conclude that human beings lived in the Americas much more than ten thousand years ago, that very long ago they painted pictures on the walls of caves in Europe, that they lived a very long time ago in eastern Asia, and (if at least some of the Leakey discoveries hold up) that they lived a very long time ago in Africa. They left marks of their culture in these places.

Suppose paleoanthropologists generally said, "Because it is what the Bible teaches, we believe that God created human beings in his image and that they did not descend from animals. Here is the paleoanthropological data related to the history of the human family. With these givens, let's cooperate with biblical scholars and see what we can learn about human history." Putting together general and special revelation in that way would mean that we recognize that God speaks in both kinds of revelation. It is difficult to overestimate how much we would then learn about ourselves.

The Problem of the Paradigm

Let us see how the biblical revelation that God created human beings specially, so that they did not evolve from another part of Creation, affects the entire evolutionary picture.

The Evolutionary Paradigm. Scientists who carry on day-to-day work do so on the basis of unexamined assumptions. According to Thomas Kuhn, their scientific activity is then *normal* science within a *paradigm*.[21] It is difficult to imagine any scholar working any other way. But not examining assumptions can be the source of a problem, the problem of the paradigm.

Consider what the problem of the paradigm means in the present discussion. Evolutionary theory claims to be general: it applies to everything—stars, planets, and all life. Evolutionary scientists, who assume the validity of evolutionary theory in their day-to-day activity, work within this evolutionary paradigm. But if one part of Creation is shown not to have evolved, then evolutionary theory—the paradigm—collapses. The Bible does not permit us to believe that human beings evolved from animals. This knowledge is not proof that every part of the evolutionary scenario is wrong, but it is proof that evolutionary theory cannot be general. A new paradigm is needed.

Scientists may object, saying that biologists are constantly finding proof that evolution occurred. But closer examination reveals that many biologists merely fit new discoveries into an evolutionary framework without seriously asking if another framework—another paradigm—is more nearly correct. Many people who have examined paradigm theory have concluded that those working within a paradigm, carrying out normal science, have no good way of examining the paradigm itself. Evolutionists have difficulty in seeing their problem. Very seldom, if ever, do they test evolutionary theory itself. On the contrary, evolutionary scientists who attempt to trace the history of life make amazing leaps of faith. Some leaps are the assumption that life evolved from nonlife—in spite of the vanishingly small probability of each of the large number of steps required for the process—and the assumption of jumps across gaps in the fossil record, such as the jump from invertebrates to vertebrates.

The "proof that evolution occurred," resembles the defense other scientists offered for now-outmoded theories. Thus, by constantly modifying the nonlife-to-life scenario, evolutionary scientists are reminiscent of the astronomers who defended the Ptolemaic system (second century A.D.) for the motion of the planets. They modified the circular motion postulated by Aristotle by claiming that a planet also moves in a second circle built on Aristotle's circle. Its path then resembles a stretched-out metal spring, with the entire spring forming a circle: the entire spring is the first circle and the loops of the spring describe the motion in the second circle. If the addition of the second circle did not account for the observed motion of the planet, they further modified their theory. Eventually, astronomers needed many modifications. In a similar way, evolutionary biochemists continually add assumptions to the nonlife-to-life scenario when new discoveries in molecular biology make their hypothesis more difficult to defend.

The fact that human beings did not evolve from animals has serious consequences for much scientific work. It means that the evolutionary assumption can no longer remain unexamined. For each project investigating origins, workers need to ask if evolution applies in this particular case. Thus, it is not legitimate to assume that since nonlife-to-life evolution required the absence of oxygen in the primitive earth atmosphere, therefore no oxygen was present. It is not legitimate to assume that an organ for which no function can be found is therefore vestigial. In fact, it is not legitimate to assume that one may interpret the function or behavior of any living thing in relation to the function or behavior of a presumed evolutionary forebear. Perhaps the assumption of evolution is wrong.

Widespread Acceptance of the Evolutionary Paradigm. If there are serious problems with evolutionary theory and if neglecting these problems distorts scientific work, why do so many scientists accept evolution as a unifying theory? In explaining this phenomenon, Michael Denton said, "The fact that every journal, academic debate and popular discussion assumes the truth of Darwinian theory tends to reinforce its credibility enormously." Denton claimed that sociologists of knowledge know why this situation has arisen:

> This is bound to be so because, as sociologists of knowledge are at pains to point out, it is by conversation in the broadest sense of the word that our views and conceptions of reality are maintained and therefore the plausibility of any theory or world view is largely dependent upon the social support it receives rather than its empirical content or rational consistency.

What, then, has been the effect on Darwinism?

> Thus the all pervasive affirmation of the validity of Darwinian theory has had the inevitable effect of raising its status into an impregnable axiom which could not even conceivably be wrong.[22]

The way in which Richard Dawkins insisted on the validity of general evolutionary theory provides an example of the claims of the sociologists of knowledge. Dawkins writes lucidly and reinforces the credibility of the evolutionary paradigm. With approval he cited the eminent zoologist G.G. Simpson, who answered the question, "What is man?" by claiming that pre-1859 attempts to answer that question are worthless. Dawkins continued, "Today the theory of evolution is about as much open to doubt as the theory that the earth goes around the sun." Dawkins used a strategy so often used by those who advocate an idea already widely accepted: he assumed his position is much less popular than it actually is. He complained,

> Zoology is still a minority subject in universities, and even those who choose to study it often make their decision without appreciating its profound philosophical significance. Philosophy and the subjects known as 'humanities' are still taught almost as if Darwin had never lived. No doubt this will change in time.[23]

A Third Way. Why all this vigorous insistence that general evolutionary theory is true? Why the assumption that all the subjects in colleges and universities will be—if they are not already—taught with Darwinism as the basis? After all, even the *scientific* objections to evolution are extremely impressive. Haven't other paradigms, such as the Ptolemaic explanation for planetary motion, eventually been discarded?

Evidently the evolutionary paradigm is so widely accepted because non-Christians assume that the only other possibility, creation, is unacceptable.

But this is a very poor reason for accepting evolutionary theory, *even for a non-Christian.* Isn't there a third option—agnosticism? Sometimes scientists do admit that they cannot explain something they observe. When such a situation arises, they do not deny the observation. Why not admit the formidable difficulties in evolutionary theory, starting with the unbelievably great difficulty in determining how life arose from nonlife by chemical and physical laws we now have? I hope that even evolutionary scientists will admit that *in principle* scientific investigation can reveal that evolutionary theory is wrong, even if such investigation does not provide an alternative explanation of origins.

To see how important it is to keep one's mind open to this third way, consider a situation that recently arose in the physical sciences. In 1989 investigators at the University of Utah claimed that in some electrolysis experiments they produced energy and certain fundamental particles not previously produced under their experimental conditions. By giving the pro-

Human Origin and the Evolutionary Paradigm

cess the name "cold fusion" they *added* to their observations an explanation: they claimed they achieved fusion of atomic nuclei at ordinary temperatures, a nuclear reaction previously thought to occur only at millions of degrees. That tiny phrase, "cold fusion," caused a very great controversy. Many scientists said that the Utah group *could not* have observed what they claimed to observe. The reason? Cold fusion cannot occur. Almost certainly the latter statement is true, but some physical scientists called attention to another possibility, namely, that energy and particles appeared by a mechanism not presently understood.[24] Similarly, if one is unwilling to accept various acts of creation during Creation Week—in other words, accept that *creation* is the mechanism whereby the world appeared, it would be better to maintain that the answer is not yet in hand.

Perhaps the problem of the evolutionary paradigm is a little like the problem of tobacco addiction. If tobacco were discovered today, it surely would not receive governmental approval for human use: laboratory and clinical tests would prove it is a health hazard. It would be classified as a controlled substance along with various narcotics. Protests against such governmental action would be minimal. But in fact tobacco was introduced centuries ago; by now large numbers of people are addicted. Surely it is because of addiction that no government can succeed in prohibiting the use of tobacco. Likewise, it is highly questionable—assuming our present knowledge of the complexity of DNA, the gaping holes in the fossil record, and the many other problems with evolutionary theory—that anyone would seriously consider evolutionary theory if it were a new theory. But in fact evolutionary theory was introduced more than a century ago, long before natural scientists knew what problems accompanied this paradigm.

Paradigms and Ethics. While it is understandable that a scientist might not be able to think outside of the reigning paradigm, this inability may never be an excuse for unethical attitudes and behavior.

Questionable situations have arisen within the community of evolutionary scientists. For example, the objections to evolutionary theory have not been listened to. As a result, widely-used biology textbooks neglect the problems with evolutionary theory. Ethical scientific societies would condemn the practice of omitting these problems in the education of young people.

Furthermore, it is at least improper, perhaps unethical, for scientists to publicly claim that such-and-such will be discovered in the future, thereby verifying a presently-held theory. Darwin claimed that fossils would be found to fill the gaps in the fossil record. In the 1950s it was commonplace to claim that the laboratory synthesis of amino acids from inorganic materials meant that very soon chemists would manufacture life in a test tube. Many times evolutionary biologists have predicted that the human evolutionary story would be sorted out when more fossils were found. In all these cases, evolutionary scientists misled nonscientists. Instead of waiting for verification of a theory, they made public announcements and sometimes held press conferences. Such false prediction has been particularly harmful when opinion-formers who are not scientists have taken these pronouncements seriously. Too many people who are not scientists but who do give speeches and write articles have not grasped the immense difficulties with evolutionary theory. As a result, the public has not been well served.

Christians and the Evolutionary Paradigm. How is it that even some Christian scientists are influenced—perhaps even convinced—by, for example, Dawkins and Simpson's claim (as described above) that pre-1859 answers to the question "What is man?" are worthless? In my opinion, there are two reasons.

First, a large part of the Christian community has uncritically accepted the literal interpretation of the biblical passage describing Creation Week, the first interpretation described in Chapter 9. In doing so, they have invited trouble. Christians ought to realize that faithful biblical scholarship sees possibilities for other interpretations. Non-Christian scientists came to realize that here is the Achilles heel of the Christian position. Those scientists have been able to easily discredit this position by scientific means. *Non-Christian scientists have then linked the literal interpretation to all antievolutionary argumentation.* Because of the weakness of the young-earth position, Christians who study science tend to be influenced far more by those committed to an evolutionary unification of Creation, life included, than by those who maintain that creation by a sovereign God is the source of unity. In this way, a large part of the Christian community has failed to provide Christian students of science the kind of background they need to discern truth from error in the study of origins. Finally, Christian scientists who have become convinced of the evolutionary origin of all things— except for a creative act of God at the very beginning—have influenced many other Christians, students and others, of the validity of their position.

The other reason some Christian scientists have been influenced by those who accept the evolutionary paradigm is that Christians simply do not set the scientific agenda. Those who accept the reigning paradigm determine what Denton's "conversation in the broadest sense" will be like. In the over-all picture, Christians have very little to say about which research programs will be funded, which ideas will be acceptable ("politically correct") in universities, which articles will be published in professional journals, which subjects are acceptable for discussion at professional meetings, and

Human Origin and the Evolutionary Paradigm

which standards with respect to the teaching of evolution will be set by city and state boards of education. A Christian who becomes a professional in any one of the sciences must obtain approval from the scientific community in every one of the categories just mentioned—training, funding for research, publication, and so forth.

Christians who severely criticize other Christians who have adopted the evolutionary position often do not account for these two factors—their own contribution to the problem and the difficulty of avoiding the evolutionary stance in the professional world.

What has been the impact of the evolutionary paradigm on the other sciences, that is, on those outside the group of natural sciences? An examination of some of those sciences, such as those associated with psychology and sociology, reveals that the evolutionary assumption affects modern life. Evolutionary influence outside the natural sciences is the subject of the remainder of this book. The assumption of the evolutionary origin of the human family has broad consequences.

Chapter Twelve
Human Behavior

Accepting the evolutionary origin of human beings means more than ascribing the physical properties of the human body to animal forebears. Modern scientists—some in the natural sciences, some in other sciences—apply evolutionary theory in at least four areas besides biology. I shall describe each briefly before taking them up in more detail—the first two in this chapter, the others in the next chapter.

The first claim is that the evolutionary origin of human beings accounts for the behavior of individuals. Ever since Darwin, psychologists have debated just how human behavior is related to the behavior of animal forebears. Evolutionary psychologists have not doubted the existence of a behavioral continuum from animals to human beings; however, modern ideas on just how animal behavior eventually became human behavior are far different from those held a century ago.

Second, evolutionists use their theory to explain the behavior and nature of human societies. By nature, there is no clear line of demarcation between the study of the behavior of individuals and of groups of individuals, that is, between psychology and sociology. In the early years of Darwinian theory, the social Darwinism of Herbert Spencer (1820-1903) dominated the evolutionistic understanding of group behavior. Social Darwinism says that by natural selection the best and the strongest individuals rise to the top of a society. Likewise, the best and strongest societies also dominate. In modern times, sociologists realize that using this idea as a basis for social action is grossly unfair to weaker individuals and societies. As a result, modern sociologists do not accept social Darwinism in its original form.

Third, by means of evolutionary theory, it is said, we can understand progress in many human institutions and aspects of human culture. The principle of natural selection has been claimed to function, in religion for example, as people first accept polytheism and then monotheism, and in the marketplace as the most efficient businesses are successful.

Finally, according to evolutionists the picture we have of ourselves—the human self-image—ought to depend upon evolutionary theory. For example, literary critics have shown that many nineteenth and twentieth century authors deliberately depicted the "animal side" of human beings.

These four claims are not merely interesting theories. In Chapter 14 I shall contend that certain highly undesirable movements rest on the premise that human beings evolved from animals. The impact of evolutionary thinking on the societies of our time has been devastating.

These applications of evolutionary theory to the study of human life do not all depend upon the validity of biological evolutionary theory. Rather, biological evolutionary theory and all other evolutionary theories are based on a prior premise, namely, that there is a more general evolutionary principle, one that encompasses everything. Then biological evolution and other kinds of evolution are particular manifestations of the more general, universal principle. Therefore, one need not show that behavior is inherited genetically and that, consequently, individual, group, and institutional behavior change as the DNA code changes. An aspect of human life *might* be related to genetics, according to the theory, but the universal evolutionary principle itself is more fundamental. Of course, this absolutization of evolution is evolutionism; but, as explained in Chapter 1, evolutionists usually use the word "evolution" as if evolution is universal. They have little need for the word "evolutionism."

The Behavior of Individual Human Beings

If organisms inherit physical characteristics from their parents, it is conceivable that they also inherit behavior patterns. Furthermore, if a species descends from a long sequence of other species, one might think that not only physical characteristics, but also behavioral patterns have·an evolutionary history. Finally, if the human family had evolutionary forebears, then the behavior of an individual human being could be traced back to the animal world.

Many people find the inheritance of behavioral patterns from animals to be repugnant. But that is not the reason evolutionary psychologists have a problem. Their problem is first of all with inherited behavior—"instinct"—within a species. During the last century most psychologists have not accepted the existence of instinct. If parents do not pass along behavior patterns to their children, then, of course, human behavior is not inherited from animal ancestors. However, evolutionists claim to have solved that problem. Let us see how the discussion has progressed since Darwin's time.

Peter T. Hoffer, professor of German at the Philadelphia College of Pharmacy and Science and translator of some of the works of Sigmund Freud, claimed that evolutionistic teachings affected Freud.[1] Freud was Lamarckian: he held that acquired characteristics could be inherited. Primeval experiences of the human family were passed on through the generations.[2]

In 1912 Freud published *Totem and Taboo*, in which he attempted to account for the presence in the "collective unconscious" of the taboo of incest and the origin of guilt.[3] Very few modern psychologists accept Freud's basic scientific assumptions. Thus, at the end of Freud's life many doubted that acquired characteristics could be inherited. But he clung to the idea because "He had woven that view of evolution so thoroughly into his own thinking, that he needed it for the logical consistency of his own theories."[4] According to Hoffer, Freud might not have been as much in error with respect to inherited acquired characteristics as many have assumed. Hoffer cited recent research in molecular biology and genetics indicating the possibility that acquired characteristics would be inherited. Instinct would then be a genetic fact. But this is definitely a minority view among psychologists. Hoffer also noted that Jean Piaget—prominent psychologist, educator, and author—suggests that environmental adaptations are inherited.

Robert J. Richards, professor of behavioral science at the University of Chicago, surveyed the changing opinion in the psychological community since Darwin.[5] With the assumption of the animal origins of human beings, altruistic human behavior became particularly difficult to explain. After all, animals do not seem to behave selflessly. But Darwin did hold that altruism had an evolutionary origin.[6] In the following decades the psychological community did not always agree with Darwin on issues such as these.

By 1930, especially in the United States and England, *behaviorism* took over.[7] The rise of behaviorism coincided with the temporary decline of Darwinism. Behaviorism was due to John Watson, who worked at the University of Chicago with John Dewey, the promoter of pragmatic philosophy. Watson claimed that a teacher could train a healthy child to be any kind of specialist. Thus, the environment, not heredity, controlled behavior; behavior did not evolve.

B.F. Skinner, one of the best-known psychologists of the twentieth century, later carried behaviorism to its extreme.[8] For Skinner, the environment, the culture in which a person lives, is all-important. To by-pass the instinct problem, Skinner and others maintained that a culture evolves:

> The fact that a culture may survive or perish suggests a kind of evolution, and a parallel with the evolution of species has, of course, often been pointed out. It needs to be stated carefully. A culture corresponds to a species. We describe it by listing many of its practices, as we describe a species by listing many of its anatomical features.[9]

Human Behavior

The members of a culture carry its practices; the more members, the greater the chance the culture will survive. Skinner said that because biological and cultural evolution are both closely linked to the environment, the two kinds of evolution are closely interwoven. He did warn against carrying the analogy too far.[10]

At the conclusion of Skinner's argument, he contended that understanding the interaction of the human being with the environment has abolished "autonomous man"; the environment, not man, determines his behavior. He said, "To man [as autonomous] man we readily say good riddance."[11] He argued that while the autonomous human being has reached a dead end, human beings may be controlled by their environment—their culture—and, he said, it is this environment that human beings themselves control. Thus, back to the evolutionary concept: "The evolution of a culture is in fact a kind of gigantic exercise in self-control."[12]

There was another reason to doubt that behavior is inherited. Richards stated that opposition to racism early in the twentieth century contributed to opposition to belief in the evolutionary inheritance of behavior.[13] Thus, people opposed to racism wanted to reform the environment to improve the lot of blacks and other nonwhite races. But this reformation would have little power if the behavior of both racists and the oppressed races were inherited.

Dangerous ideas were abroad. Some people wanted to apply eugenics, the science of improving a species by breeding, to human beings. These eugenicists held that each trait could be ascribed to a specific gene.[14] The stock of "higher" races could be improved by not allowing its genes to be mixed with that of "lower" races. This belief was a factor in the passage of the U.S. Immigration Restriction Act of 1924, whereby southern Europeans, eastern Europeans, and others were to be kept out of the United States. Also, Nazi Germany adopted some of the eugenicists' ideas.[15] Largely because of the dangers associated with this view, said Richards, many modern social scientists in England and America reject the biological evolution of psychological traits, that is, Darwinian biopsychology.

During the period that behaviorism reigned in the United States, from the 1920s until the 1960s, another idea was gaining ground: individuals, as members of a group, behave in a way giving advantage to the group, not necessarily to the individual.[16] As early as 1931, Psychologist W.C. Allee traced social organization from animal aggregation to altruism in human groups; the key was the selective principle of cooperation.[17] Some examples (suggested by others later) of individuals acting for the good of the group were related to population dynamics. Thus, an organism such as a fish will not reproduce as much as it could, for if other fish did the same thing, the next generation would not have enough food. "Nature" supplied the regulatory mechanism accounting for this behavior and other behavior, such as the forming of hierarchies within a group of animals. But eventually the idea that the individual sacrifices for the group was modified: the individual's motivation is actually selfish. The individual acts to preserve the group in order to preserve its genetic heritage; genes are selfish.[18] With the appearance in 1975 of Edward O. Wilson's landmark book, *Sociobiology: The New Synthesis*, sociobiology became an important concept in the human sciences.[19] Wilson's ideas and fascinating style caught the fancy of his readers. Richard Wright said Wilson is a modern T.H. Huxley, the dynamic nineteenth-century advocate of evolutionary theory who attempted to describe religion naturalistically (see Chapter 2); Wilson made a similar attempt.[20] R.J. Herrnstein said that sociobiology is a modern form of social Darwinism.[21]

In summarizing Wilson's views, Richards said, "Our various cultural institutions—marriage, trade, religion, [aesthetics], habits of labor, and ethics—[all carry] an evolutionary legacy." Our religious aspirations are an artifact of "conformer genes"—like the genes that suggested that people obey Hitler. The desire for upward mobility arises from a gene. Ethics thus depends upon genetics.[22] Richards himself holds that morality has roots in our animal past, and that ". . . this conviction hardly demeans our humanity, rather it elevates our biology, our evolutionarily human and moral biology."[23] As explained earlier, many psychologists rejected instinct, which would depend upon genetic makeup. Yet we see that some modern theories of behavior do invoke genetics.

In Chapter 4 I described Herrnstein's argument against any kind of teleology, the teaching that there is design in the universe. Using both qualitative and quantitative arguments, he contended that individual behavior does not necessarily maximize the individual's options. Rather, behavior tends to achieve short-term, perhaps less-than-maximum, goals. Citing laboratory experiments with animals, Herrnstein said that behavior patterns are determined by a modified kind of natural selection, in which only short-term goals are maximized. Thus, a person might enjoy eating foods that are not the most healthful; such a person might maximize the short-term goal of eating tasty food, but not the long-term goal of maintaining good health. In this way Herrnstein claimed that this is not the best of all possible worlds and that these ideas must be taken into account in the explanation of behavior.

The basis of Herrnstein's argument is *reinforcement theory*: behavior is affected by local or short-term reinforcement. He addressed both ideas already discussed in this chapter—the more recent, that behavior is learned; the earlier (also associated recently with sociobiology), that behavior is biologically inherited. He said: "To critics of Darwinian thought who argue that behaviour is learned, rather than inherited, the answer from reinforcement theory is that experience and inheritance are inextricable."[24] The environment affects the organism and is therefore a behavioral shaping factor. At the same time, the behavioral consequences to the organism depend on its biologically inherited nature. For birds to build nests, the environment provides a place and material for the nest, but birds could not build nests if they did not have their particular biological makeup.

Herrnstein also has a message for those who invoke biological evolution to explain behavior: "On the other hand, to those whose trust in the selective powers of evolution is such as to lead to *laissez-faire* conservatism or more extreme brands of right-wing social Darwinism, the answer is that we now know that natural selection cannot be trusted to do the right thing."[25] Evolution does not always find the best solution to a problem that a species might face. Summarizing his reinforcement theory, Herrnstein addressed both groups. If we want to influence behavior, ". . . We must think small, in the local terms of the specific contingencies of reinforcement . . . ." It will not work to think ". . . in the global terms of general welfare or political philosophy."[26]

I shall now summarize evolutionary thought concerning behavior. Evolutionists once held that the behavior of individual human beings is inherited. But that belief has undesirable consequences—eugenics, racism, and so forth. As a result, behaviorists claimed that biological evolution played no role; environment—usually, culture—alone determined behavior. But, said Skinner, cultures evolve. It seems, therefore, that behaviorists claim that the evolutionary principle plays at least an indirect role in determining behavior. Early sociobiologists responded by claiming that individuals would sacrifice for the sake of the group to insure that the species would not die out. But later Wilson and other sociobiologists claimed the existence of a selfish component in the behavior of the individual with respect to preservation of the group: the gene is selfish. Furthermore, other behavioral patterns—such as the human desire to be upwardly mobile—also have a genetic origin. Herrnstein claimed his analysis shows that a god does not guide behavior— teleology does not exist—and that behavior will not necessarily optimize the future of either the individual or the species; rather, a modified type of natural selection determines behavior.

Has there been a significant impact of evolutionary theory on the understanding of human behavior since Darwin? Perhaps; the foregoing discussion shows that some students of behavior ascribe a direct effect: human behavior is inherited—ultimately from animals—in the same way physical characteristics are inherited. Others postulate a more indirect relation between evolution and behavior: the evolutionary *principle* operates on the group to affect individual human behavior and the behavior of animals. Still others are difficult to classify. Thus, evolutionary theory is not as firmly established in the study of human behavior as it is in biology. But notice that the various schools of thought utilize the basic assumption made in the natural sciences ever since the beginning of the modern scientific enterprise: *a natural explanation for any phenomenon is possible*. This assumption means that the universe is all there is.

Therefore, the Christian's problem in the study of the human psyche is the same as it is in the natural sciences. Thus, in both the natural sciences and the study of human behavior some Christians try to preserve belief in a god by postulating two realms: the explainable, the realm of the scientific; and the unexplainable, the realm of the nonscientific, the "spiritual." Just as with the natural sciences, this division is dualism. The problem of removing dualism is not simple. For example, studies of animal behavior have often been used to elucidate human behavior. Evolutionists justify this procedure because, they claim, human beings are animals. But are they wrong in assuming that studies of animal behavior can aid in understanding human behavior? Not necessarily; after all, God's different creatures are part of the same Creation, and he made both animals and human beings so that they could function in that Creation. At the same time, a nondualistic approach to the study of human behavior will begin with the assumption that human beings are unique.

In this discussion of individual human behavior, we have seen that often the behavior of the individual is linked to the group, as with sociobiologists. Even so, the study of the behavior of groups of human beings warrants separate study.

The Behavior of Groups of Human Beings

Cultural Evolution. Is cultural change analogous to biological evolution? Herbert Spencer said that it is: human society is supraorganic, an extension of the biological development of species.[27]

But David Livingstone warned of using metaphors in connection with evolution. Thus, said Livingstone, maintaining that society is an organism could be an improper biologization of culture. The claim might inhibit attempts to combat poverty, ignorance, and disease; lead to an approval of

Human Behavior 215

the late nineteenth-century cut-throat business ethics of Victorian England; or lead to eugenics.[28]

A.J. Cain, professor of zoology at Liverpool University, indicated several differences between cultural and biological evolution.[29] The factors causing cultural evolution come from all society, whereas genetic evolution is a parents-to-offspring phenomenon. Cultural evolution can occur—especially because of technology—much more rapidly than genetic evolution. It can take place by means of extremely small changes, that is, it is Lamarckian. Also, cultural evolution can be consciously directed; an example is the extermination by outsiders of the Tasmanian people and therefore their culture.

On the other hand, W.G. Runciman of Cambridge University emphasized the similarity between the evolution of societies and the evolution of species.[30] Runciman maintained that Darwin and Marx were partly correct; his goal was to build on their work. He proposed that because of competitive selection among the practices of classes of people, certain roles and institutions supersede others. He made a careful distinction between *practices* and *roles and institutions*: change takes place if the selection among *practices* leads to the strengthening of *roles and institutions*.

Evolutionists explain the evolution of species using natural forces. It is not surprising, then, that some people attempt to explain cultural evolution by invoking natural forces. In the hypothetical example of certain kinds of cities in Chapter 3 we saw that the distribution of wealth could be superficially explained using geometry, given several special conditions. Evolutionists would claim that the change that took place in those cities was one kind of cultural evolution.

More serious efforts to explain cultural processes have been made. One is related to the work of Ilya Prigogine, who developed a mathematical approach to "nonequilibrium" processes (that is, processes in which change is taking place, described in Chapter 6) in physical systems. But some nonequilibrium processes are social; examples are the functioning of transportation networks and the dynamics—the many inputs and outputs—of a city. For these reasons Prigogine and others used nonequilibrium methods to study these social processes. Some evolutionary scientists have suggested that Prigogine's approach will be successfully extended to a mathematical elucidation of how cultures evolve.

The physical concept of disorder has also been used in analyzing social situations. The disordering processes that seem to characterize many historical situations bear some similarity to the appearance of disorder in physical systems. In thermodynamics, *entropy* is the measure of the amount of disorder in a system. Loren Dow, a Christian sociologist at Emory and

Henry College in Virginia, claimed that some crisis events in history were atypical; the processes involved were nonsequential. These were times of disorder, times where cause-and-effect seemed not to operate. Dow suggested that until those times are explained that the term *social entropy* be applied to them.[31] On the other hand, Runciman, who does not present a Christian approach to culture, viewed social order and disorder differently. He claimed that social evolution, although random, produces order. Such progression does not violate thermodynamics; it does say, he said, that some social structures dominate over others.[32]

Animal Cultures. Because evolutionists assume that human beings descended from animals, questions about animal cultures arise. Cain claimed that there is no difference between human and animal cultures except that formal religions are part of human cultures.[33] John Tyler Bonner, a noted American microbiologist, included in *The Evolution of Culture in Animals* (1980) a discussion of the evolution of cultural behavior among bacteria.[34] Richard Dawkins contended that the social organization among animals evolves; however, he warned against considering an animal society to be a entity in itself, one that as an organization has a biological advantage.[35] Rather, he claimed that a society is maintained by the selfishness of individual genes. Dawkins stated that the evolutionarily stable strategy accounts for this group behavior and maintenance. (This strategy leads, for example, to an equilibrium distribution of the hawk-like and dove-like mutations different from the most-fit distribution as described in Chapter 4.)

Evolutionists have proposed various biological explanations for the derivation of the human concept of family from an animal culture. For example, Maurice Godelier, a prominent French social scientist, contended that human families formed when several biological developments had occurred. There had to be an enduring bond between a mother and her young; the mature male became bonded to his females; the human young matured late; and the female became sexually receptive all year because she had lost her oestrus.[36] As we shall see later in this chapter, Godelier invoked these biological factors to explain the concept of kinship and therefore of the existence of human families.

Social Darwinism. Adam Smith (1723-1790), a Scottish political economist, systematized classical English economics in his landmark *The Wealth of Nations*. Because of his analysis, many people claimed that a hands-off approach in business activity is best. Certainly this idea epitomized the approach of the Western world to economics. Perhaps social Darwinism rested on the principles enunciated by Smith. Thus, although Spencer coined the term *survival of the fittest*, this concept fit very well into Smith's

Human Behavior

economics.[37] Darwin used this term in his description of biological evolution. But Spencer's teaching applied to society: the strongest individuals and societies would survive.

Spencer also said that usually natural selection accounts for altruism and community spirit.[38] He thus invoked the result of a natural process (that which is) to account for a moral good (that which ought to be). Ordinarily people maintain that it is a mistake to confuse *is* and *ought*: what *is* is not necessarily that which *ought* to be. Yet in the early years Spencer's followers tended to view the progress they saw before World War I to be evidence that good things *could* come about because of the natural selection principle operating in society.[39]

Social Darwinism then fell into disrepute. But there is a modern revival of Spencer's thought.[40] Those who welcome this revival assume that evolutionary thinking cannot be confined to biology. They freely admit that excesses and wrong ideas flowed from the earlier form of social Darwinism; but, they say, Darwinian evolutionary thought does and should affect our understanding of disciplines outside the natural sciences.[41]

Other nineteenth and early twentieth century thinkers besides Spencer saw the human condition improving. Both Darwin and Karl Marx assumed—along with humanists in general—that humankind is on a long road toward perfectability. Darwin's principle of natural selection emphasized competition for existence. Marx taught the necessity of class struggle, and because Darwin provided a theoretical basis for this concept, Marx considered dedicating *Das Kapital* to Darwin.[42] Marx held that society is improving and that contradictions in society bring about improvement. Society is pushed toward a better state.[43] Marx, of course, was not willing to wait for natural processes; people had to act. Theodore Roosevelt, U.S. President during the first decade of the twentieth century (certainly not a Marxist), favored action for much the same reason:

> The twentieth century looms before us big with the fate of many nations. If we stand idly by, if we seek merely swollen, slothful ease and ignoble peace, if we shrink from the hard contests where men must win at hazard of their lives and at the risk of all they hold dear, then the bolder and stronger peoples will pass us by, and will win for themselves the domination of the world.[44]

The popular idea that the strongest in society would win out, along with the implication that they *should* win out, was either derived from or compatible with social Darwinism. Birth control for the "inferior" of society was advocated.

But the might-is-right philosophy of World War I, with the slaughter of millions, caused many to wonder. Realizing the devastating results of militarism, William Jennings Bryan, a three-time candidate for the U.S. Presidency, opposed evolution and testified in the famous Scopes "monkey" trial in Tennessee in 1925.[45] At about the same time, the Nazi concept of a super-race—another manifestation of the might-is-right philosophy—was gaining followers. The Nazis also favored the elimination of the weakest in society; hence, their practice of eugenics. The later recognition of Nazi cruelty supported arguments against social Darwinism. Also, many people ascribe the stark poverty and violence of U.S. inner cities, as compared to the affluence of other groups of people, to social Darwinism in action: the greedy take what they can and let others suffer.

Because of all these effects (militarism, eugenics, racism, and the Nazi legacy) social scientists have generally turned away from the early form of social Darwinism. Thus, as social workers react negatively to social Darwinism, they usually consider the *environment* as a given; they refuse to ascribe social problems to genetics. But in the general population the belief persists that the weakest in society are inferior. Consequently, those who attempt to help the underprivileged continually encounter opposition.

Perhaps racism is the worst form of modern social Darwinism. The existence of a hierarchy of races, with the Caucasian race at the pinnacle of the hierarchy, has been claimed for a long time. The advent of Darwinism reinforced the hierarchical idea. At the 1862 meeting of the British Association for the Advancement of Science, Robert Dunn stated that the Negro's brow, lower jaw, and limbs were like those of the Caucasian infant before birth. In America, the prominent zoologist Louis Agassiz compared the Negro brain to that of a seven-month white fetus. Roy Chapman Andrews of the American Museum contended that the progress of the races was unequal. He remarked that Tasmanians and Australian aborigines, for example, had not significantly advanced beyond the Neanderthals.[46]

Darwin himself accepted the concept of a hierarchy of races. In a discussion of the extinction of some races, he wrote of an extinct race which combined low, ape-like characteristics with advanced characteristics. He also explained race extinction by natural selection:

> Extinction follows chiefly from the competition of tribe with tribe, and race with race . . . . When civilised nations come into contact with barbarians the struggle is short, except where a deadly climate gives its aid to the native race.

He added, "The grade of their civilisation seems to be a most important element in the success of competing nations."[47]

In the twentieth century, Carleton S. Coon's study of differences between races became very controversial. Coon was an anthropologist at the University Museum of Philadelphia. Coon acknowledged that studying race is controversial; he said that fundamentalists of various religions oppose such study because they think it pertains to evolution. He then said:

> More serious are the activities of the academic debunkers and softpedalers who operate inside anthropology itself. Basing their ideas on the concept of the brotherhood of man, certain writers, who are mostly social anthropologists, consider it immoral to study race, and produce book after book exposing it as a "myth." Their argument is that because the study of race once gave ammunition to racial fascists, who misused it, we should pretend that races do not exist.[48]

Therefore, Coon was not afraid to present an outline of racial history.[49] He presented the ecological rules governing the size, shape, and behavior of human beings, claiming that racial characteristics fit into the various environments of the earth. Those rules apply to both animals and human beings.[50] Finally, because of these racial differences, race has a meaning. Thus:

> While Mongoloids and Negroids became adapted for living in physiologically trying environments, the Caucasoids or whites remained unadapted because they continued to live in parts of the world where climatic conditions were optimum in terms of heat and light . . . . The whites arose in the Old World's best land; it was they who carried the main line of civilization to the threshold of the ages of metal, and beyond.[51]

After admitting that some cultural changes and high civilizations were due to Mongoloids and American Indians, Coon said, "Our modern civilization would have been impossible without the pooled contributions of many races." However, to fairly understand Coon, one must be aware of his next remark:

> But during certain stages of cultural development, race served as a symbol of social and economic status, *useful in maintaining order* in a world in which many contrasts in wealth, technical skills, and levels of education had been preserved.[52] (Emphasis added.)

Thus, Coon correctly recognizes that races exist. No doubt his complaint about anthropologists who are soft-pedalers is justified. But surely the implication that the white race is most advanced is controversial. His claim that race has been "useful in maintaining order" cannot stand. In today's atmosphere, charged with racial tension, Coon sounds like a racist.[53]

Anthropologists have not easily avoided the stigma of racism. Whether it was the acknowledged racism of Darwin and his contemporaries or the rationalization of the existing condition by people like Coon, the result is the same: when human evolution is allowed, some parts of the human family can be thought to lag behind others. However, most of the anthropological community reject this conclusion.

Christians ought to accept the possibility that small changes in the human family—perhaps, microevolution—are possible. After all, races do exist; they are not mythical. But there is no hierarchy of races. Paul summarizes the biblical teaching of equality:

> There is neither Jew nor Greek, slave nor free, male nor female,
> for you are all one in Christ Jesus. (Gal. 3:28)

That race was not a factor in the New Testament church is reflected by the leadership of "Simeon called Niger" in the church at Syrian Antioch (Acts 13:1), where God's people were first called Christians (11:26). Simeon was undoubtedly a black person; his Latin surname, Niger, means "black."

Those who hold to the biblical view of the origin and unity of the human family do not need to account for a supposed slower evolution of some races or for supposed environmental factors that would cause some races to be inferior to others. Whatever changes took place, genetically or environmentally, occurred after Adam and Eve; and, according to the Bible, such changes did not introduce inequality. Finally, it is permissible to study the differences between races. Christian investigators ought to begin with the idea that the races are equal. Then their scientific results will not reveal any race is inferior to another.

Two examples illustrate the impact of evolutionary thinking on the scientific analysis of the behavior of human groups. The first is the explanation for the existence of human language; the second, the perceived origin of kinship and its relation to the incest taboo. In both cases, I shall suggest a Christian response to the evolutionary approach.

Human Language. Did human language evolve from noises made by animals?[54] Of course, languages change radically even within a few hun-

Human Behavior

dred years; this development is a kind of evolution. But the question is whether the starting point for human language was the noise that animals make. Philip Lieberman anticipated this problem in his important book, *On the Origins of Language: An Introduction to the Evolution of Human Speech*. Lieberman, of Brown University, defined language to take care of that problem: "A language is a communication system that is capable of transmitting new information."[55] Thus, communications of animals with each other qualify; the only problem left is to explain how those communications evolved into human communication. This definition, said Lieberman, does not require that all language systems have the properties of human language.

For Lieberman, the production and perception of human *speech*—not language—"appears to be uniquely human."[56] But Doreen Kimura, professor of psychology at the University of Western Ontario, uses the physical connection between the brain and speech to show that nonhuman language is possible. Summarizing Kimura's work, Marguerite Holloway said:

> By emphasizing the relationship between motor control and speech, Kimura argues that language is not uniquely human. The left hemisphere most probably controlled complex motor skills, including tool making, before speech. Evidence of primates' ability to learn gestural languages supports this idea, Kimura says.[57]

Godelier, who also accepts human evolution, stated the problem differently.[58] He said that a human peculiarity is the existence of *articulated* language. With this language, human beings can communicate abstract ideas, some not associated with the immediate physical environment of the communicator. But the existence of an articulated language presupposes the existence of thought. Godelier said that this language could not exist if human beings could not symbolically represent objects and relations perceived in past, present, and future contexts.

Human language assumes not only the ability to represent symbolically but also the ability to clarify. It is one thing to communicate; it is another to clarify. A noise—a bark, a grunt, a squeal—can certainly communicate an idea. But if the receiver of the noise needs clarification—an explanation—then immediately the concept of abstraction arises. The one who sends the message—the "speaker"—must be able to do more than bark, grunt, or squeal.

But people who claim an evolutionary origin of human language do not admit that human language has unique characteristics. Their position is strengthened by the significant number of linguists who insist that language and communication are identical and that all communication is mechanical. Thus, early in the twentieth century Leonard Bloomfield reduced language to its mechanics.[59] Bloomfield claimed that every communication can be broken down into stimulus-plus-response. He reduced language to the kind of sound a physicist can describe. The "Audio Lingual Method" depends primarily on the physical transmission of sound, not on meaning.

Do present-day languages give evidence of having evolved from the grunts, squeals, and barks of animals? If they do, then one might expect to find that languages were once simpler than they are now. But many people maintain that the history of languages indicates that they were once more complex, not simpler. Thus, although many nineteenth century linguists thought that ancient Chinese was much simpler than modern Chinese, later research showed that the ancient language was more complicated. For example, ancient Chinese was polysyllabic, unlike monosyllabic modern Chinese. Old English was more complex than modern English; the same is true of German, the Romance languages, and the Scandinavian languages. Claims of grammatical complexity exceeding that of modern Western languages have also been made for languages earlier thought to be "primitive." Examples are the languages of Native American tribes, African tribes, and Australian aborigines.

But some people hold that modern languages are not simpler. They maintain that increased vocabulary compensates for grammatical simplification. In any case, the evidence for a trend toward greater simplicity or toward greater complexity cannot pre-date the time languages became written: we have no way to analyze the languages of the pre-writing period. It may be, then, that the complexity-simplicity argument is based on too short a period of time to answer questions about human evolution, postulated to have occurred over several hundred thousand, or even a few million, years.

The real objection to the evolutionary hypothesis concerning human language is the complete absence of evidence that human language was ever simpler than at present. Evolutionists assume that human language *must* have evolved from that of animals, and so there *must* be "missing link" languages, with a continuum between animal noises and modern human languages. Lieberman implied *must* when he said, "Evolution proceeds in small steps, and the only reason that human language appears to be so disjoint from animal communication systems is that the hominids who possessed 'intermediate' languages are all dead."[60] Just as with other matters discussed earlier in this book (such as an oxygen-free primitive atmosphere, protocells, intermediate organs, and intermediate organisms), it is evidently acceptable to postulate that something once existed even if the only "evidence" is that evolutionary theory requires its existence.

According to evolutionists, what had to happen for language to appear? Some evolutionary linguists contend that language appeared as soon as the human anatomy allowed. Grammar is "in the brain," and language was possible as soon as the appropriate mutations occurred, speculates Allan C. Wilson of the University of California.[61] Richard Leakey and Roger Lewin said that the presence of a vocal channel in a hominid skull (in the famous Skull 1470) two million years ago does not prove speech existed at that time. Speech required such a channel, but speech had to evolve.[62] In addition, according to Lieberman, several anatomical features, such as special neural devices, a special supralaryngeal vocal tract construction, and the ability to form special pathways in the motor cortex, had to evolve before speech could exist.[63]

If biological evolution was critical for the appearance of language, then one might expect to find the rudiments of language in some present-day primates—animals that could eventually evolve, according to evolutionary theory, to the human level. Later speech could appear. Do animals give evidence of possessing the ability to communicate using a language? Experiments have been carried out using American Sign Language (ASL), the "gestural" language Holloway referred to (in the passage quoted above) in describing Kimura's work. Many workers claim that the ability of certain primates to communicate using ASL is proof that human language evolved from animal language. Thomas Overmire of Chicago State University discussed the question. One research team taught 30 ASL gestures to a chimpanzee, who could then read and transmit ASL messages. But experiments such as these, said Overmire, are flawed: the experimenters can misinterpret random movements; the experimenters might transmit unconscious clues; or the animals might be clever enough to "train their keepers," that is, to do what their keepers want them to do.[64]

Whether any animals can use ASL is not at all certain. Ultimately the test for animal language is not whether animals can use gestures—which, after all, could be communication on a par with grunts, squeals, and barks—but whether they can, when asked, clarify a previous communication. An animal's passing such a test does not constitute proof that human language evolved from animal language. But repeated failures to pass such a test constitute additional evidence that no such evolution occurred.

Consideration of the history of languages ought not to be left to non-Christians. Discussion of this history among Christians usually includes questions about the Tower of Babel incident, described in Genesis 11:1-9.

What role does the Tower of Babel play in the history of language? Neither of the following understandings of this passage calls for an evolutionary origin of human language.

First, there is the traditional understanding. Genesis 11:1 says, "Now the whole world had one language and a common speech." The end of the passage, part of Genesis 11:9, says, "[At Babel] the Lord confused the language of the whole world." It seems simple enough: up until this time human beings had but one language; to punish their disobedience God caused them to speak different languages, so he ". . . scattered them over the face of the whole earth" (11:9).

Because of problems with this interpretation, I shall describe a second possibility.[65] The "whole world" of Genesis 11:1 can also be translated "whole land." Since 11:2 places the Tower of Babel incident in the plain of Shinar, which the previous chapter (in 10:10) places in Babylon, the "whole land" is then Babylon, not literally the whole world. Furthermore, the table of nations given in Genesis 10 provides strong indication that language diversification occurred *before* the scattering of people of 11:9. Prior to the description of the Tower of Babel in Genesis 11, Genesis 10 associates the spreading of peoples with new languages, mentioned in 10:5, 10:20, and 10:31.

There is one more problem with associating the Tower of Babel with the first diversification of language. The Hebrew word translated as language, *saphah* (in 11:1, 6, 7, and 9), usually does not mean "language," as in "German language." Rather, *saphah* refers to "lip," as in the words of Moses, "...why would Pharaoh listen to me, since I speak with faltering *lips*?" (Ex. 6:12); or an attitude, as in the prophecy, "In that day five cities will speak the *language* of Canaan and swear allegiance to the Lord Almighty" (Is. 19:18). According to this understanding of the Tower of Babel incident, the Lord punished Babylonians by causing a breakdown of communication that was more profound than one caused by the appearance of different languages. The breakdown was, in fact, enough to cause a great empire to fall.

Even though Christians differ on the interpretation of the Tower of Babel account, they can agree on the nonevolutionary origin of language. The Bible provides significant information concerning its origin. When God breathed life into dust to make Adam a living being, he became a being who could speak. He was capable of thinking; he could receive and articulate complicated ideas. The Lord instructed him on what he could and could not do in the Garden (Gen. 2:15-17). The Lord brought the animals to Adam "to see what he would name them; and whatever the man called each living creature, that was its name" (2:19). Certainly naming is at the heart of the use of language. Adam articulated a short poem in his joyful response to the creation of Eve (2:23).

Bearing the image of God and carrying out the cultural mandate, the command to fill the earth and subdue it (Gen. 1:26-28), imply the ability to use the kind of human language we know. The Creator of the heavens and the earth communicates with his image-bearers using human language. He spoke to them both before and after they sinned. God speaks to us, we respond, and as a result our lives have meaning. Our response includes direct, spoken praise, and in a large number of ways we use language to describe his Creation. All literature is thus derivative—marred terribly by sin, but derived nevertheless—from God speaking to his creatures in love. To maintain that human language is nothing more than an extension of the grunts, squeals, and barks of the animal world is blasphemy. As with all of God's gifts to human beings, human language is to be holy, set apart for God.

Acceptance of kinship and the incest taboo are also aspects of human behavior. The analysis of these topics provides another example of the effect of evolutionary thinking on the modern investigation of human behavior.

Kinship and Incest Taboo. Many people do not realize that evolutionists cannot easily account for the existence of either the modern nuclear family or the more traditional extended family. Another way of stating the question is to ask why we have the incest taboo, the avoidance of sexual relations between primary kin. After all, it seems that without the incest taboo we would have neither the nuclear nor the extended family. As we shall see, the Bible explains the origin of the family. But let us first look at what evolutionists claim.

For the sake of discussion assume that human beings evolved from animals. Assume that human societies likewise evolved from animal societies. In 1967 Robin Fox, professor of anthropology at Rutgers University in New Jersey, made these assumptions. He then suggested that many people do not wonder why we have an incest taboo. In fact, he said, it is difficult to drive home to people that something needs explanation. But, he added, "There is *everything* to explain."[66]

Fox provided an evolutionary answer to the question he posed. In laying out his program, Fox stated:

> Man is an animal, but he puts the basic facts of life to work for himself in ways that no other animal does or can . . . . Many of the facts of life—including the all-important gregariousness that produces societies—he shares with the primates and other mam-

mals. But a feature he shares with the higher apes, and yet in which he excels even these, is his large brain.[67]

The key is the large evolved human brain and the long socialization period that then becomes possible:

> Thus, in primate society, we have some kind of ordered mating and a *protective function* exercised by the males over females and young. But the most successful primate adds to this the large brain and the consequences of this in a prolonged socialization period.[68] (Emphasis added.)

During this long socialization period, there must be an incest taboo. Fox brought these ideas together to show that kinship and evolution are related:

> The study of kinship is the study of what man does with [the] basic facts of life—mating, gestation, parenthood, socialization, siblingship etc. *Part of his enormous success in the evolutionary struggle lies in his ability to manipulate these relationships to his advantage* [Emphasis added] . . . . He utilizes [these relationships] in order to survive . . .[69]

Fox wrote a quarter of a century ago. Has the approach to kinship and the incest taboo changed? Godelier recently reviewed answers to the question of the origin of the incest taboo. He then suggested his own evolutionary answer.[70]

First, said Godelier, some people suggest the origin of the incest taboo is the result of behavior found in both human and other primate societies: mothers do not have sexual relations with their adult sons. Godelier's objection to this solution is twofold: because of the presence of hierarchies among primates, sons do not have sexual access to their mothers. But the incest taboo among human beings is broader—encompassing, for example, prohibitions against father-daughter and brother-sister sexual relations.

Second, others claim that human beings at one time acted to bring order to society by "inventing relations of kinship." One problem with this theory is the lack of evidence among primates—and, presumably, also among early human beings—that fathers can recognize their young once the young have left the family.

Godelier's own answer begins with four assumptions: the human female, in contrast to animal females, is sexually receptive the entire year; the period required for human maturation is long; sexual activity is important in family hierarchy and dominance; and with suitable brain development and other anatomical changes, it became possible for individuals to cooperate. The first three factors taken together would have resulted in sexual anarchy had it not been possible for human beings to cooperate and regulate the situation. Godelier said:

> There thus arose, *wherever this stage of biological and social development had been reached* [emphasis added] a situation that demanded the *conscious deliberate intervention* of men to *control and regulate sexuality* in such a way that it would once more be made *subordinate* to the reproduction of society.[71]

Godelier said that because of this control and regulation of sexuality, the sexual taboo, the concept of kinship developed. The prohibition of sex within the family made it necessary for sexual relations to occur only outside the family. All this could come about, however, only if "family" was defined. Godelier thus contended that the definition of family, or the establishment of kinship, and the incest taboo arose simultaneously.

For the present purpose, the chief point is that Godelier, just like Fox, accounted for the incest taboo by invoking the evolutionary biological development of human beings from animals. According to this view one of the most important characteristics of human society—kinship combined with incest taboo—rests on the assumption of biological evolution.

But what *is* the origin of the incest taboo? Why don't we have the anarchic situation that would be the consequence of mating father and daughter, mother and son, brother and sister—or other incestuous mating?

We cannot answer that question without consulting special revelation. The Bible teaches that God created the human family. After Adam rejoiced over the creation of Eve, his "suitable helper" (Gen. 2:20), God says through Moses,

> For this reason a man will leave his father and mother and be united
> to his wife, and they will become one flesh. (Gen. 2:24)

One man, one woman—his wife. This is the arrangement ordained by God. But sin entered the world and distortions entered the family. As a result, God gave his people laws. Some of these laws were codified in Leviticus. The passage begins:

> "No one is to approach any close relative to have sexual relations.

I am the Lord. Do not dishonor your father by having sexual relations with your mother. She is your mother; do not have relations with her." (Lev. 18:6-7)

In the rest of this passage (Lev. 18:8-23), God also prohibits sexual relations between a son and the wife of his father who is not his mother, a brother and his sister or half-sister, a nephew and his aunt (married or unmarried), a father and his daughter-in-law, a man with a man, a man with an animal, a woman with an animal, and many other named incestual relationships.[72] (Leviticus 20:11-21 repeats the incest law, this time with the punishment for violation.) That these practices existed is shown by what God says next:

"Do not defile yourselves in any of these ways, because this is how the nations that I am going to drive out before you became defiled." (Lev. 18:24)

Even though it was common in Old Testament times for a man to have more than one wife, God established a one-to-one relation before sin entered. The New Testament recognizes that this original arrangement is God's will. Jesus explained this to the Pharisees:

"Haven't you read," he replied, "that at the beginning the Creator 'made them male and female,' and said, 'For this reason a man will leave his father and mother and be united to his wife, and the two will become one flesh'? So they are no longer two, but one. Therefore what God has joined together, let not man separate." (Matt. 19:4-6)

The New Testament also presents God's ideal in another way:

An elder must be blameless, the husband of but one wife . . . (Titus 1:6)

How, then, should Christians respond to anthropologists who look for the origin of the incest taboo?

Christians ought to insist that God ordained the one-man-one-wife marriage when Adam and Eve were created. God prohibited sexual relations outside this marriage. If one of the spouses died, God permitted remarriage but it was wrong for the remaining spouse to marry a son, a daughter, and so forth: incest was taboo.

God will not be mocked: what he ordained at the beginning is still his will. He makes this clear in the New Testament. His Son, the King of the church, and the Holy Spirit, who teaches the church, have since the beginning of the New Testament church led God's people to bring God's Word concerning the family to many nations. Consequently, during the last two millenia the law against sexual relations outside of marriage and the incest taboo have been most effective wherever the Gospel has had its greatest impact. Therefore, even though evolutionists tend to naturalize every phenomenon, including the incest taboo, the universal human interaction with creational laws and the witness of the Christian church have ensured that incest is a foul word.

Conclusion

In this chapter we have observed a certain amount of acceptance of a general evolutionary principle that extends beyond biology. Different psychological schools of thought assume different kinds of evolution. If behavior is inherited, it could evolve in much the same way as the physical parts of organisms evolve. If it is not inherited, it could change as the environment evolves. Similarly, the evolution of natural forces could cause group behavior to change. In the minds of social Darwinists, dominance by the stronger groups in society is justified by the evolutionary principle. Other social phenomena, such as the existence of human language and the incest taboo, are explained by invoking the evolutionary principle.

These explanations of individual and group behavior generally imply that people are not responsible for their actions. Thus, evolutionary theory says that either human evolution or environmental evolution accounts for a person's behavior. Language is not a gift helping us to praise God with every part of our lives; rather, language is a tool we use in our struggle for survival. Incest is not to be avoided to honor God's law; rather, this taboo exists so that we can survive. An exception to the general application of the evolutionary principle is the widespread reaction of many people, including many non-Christians, to social Darwinism. Their interaction with Creation has shown them that the survival of the fittest cannot be the norm for human societies.

At the beginning of this chapter I listed two other important projections of evolutionary theory on human life. Both assume that evolution is a universal principle. One is the supposed reason for progress in human institutions; the other, the picture we have of ourselves, our self-image. They are both taken up in the next chapter.

Chapter Thirteen
Progress

It is commonplace to refer to social progress. Many people cite the collapse of Communistic governments as evidence of progress. The "end of history" is a phrase used in recent years to indicate that we have begun a new phase of historical development. The spirit is optimistic.

But the notion of progress is an elusive thing. In an analysis of the history of natural scientific ideas, Thomas Kuhn denied that progress in natural science implies motion toward a goal. For Kuhn, the reaction to Darwinism provides an analogy. Kuhn said most of Darwin's opposition came from those who insisted that if evolution occurred, it was evolution toward a goal; there was design. But, said Kuhn, Darwin successfully overcame this opposition. Kuhn maintained that just as belief in evolutionary progress toward a goal in biology was abandoned, so should any group of natural scientists abandon belief in progress toward a goal as they abandon one paradigm for a new paradigm.[1]

W.G. Runciman made a similar conclusion for social evolution. Runciman said that nineteenth century social evolutionists held that "evolution is something more than mere qualitative change . . . . It is change in some sense or other for the better and it is change in the direction of a goal." Examples are decreases in infant mortality and increases in real wages. But Runciman added that "progress" is in the eye of the beholder; that, in fact, the sum of all evolutionary trends in society is such that there is no progress.[2]

Even if some like Kuhn deny evolutionary progress toward a goal, the concept of forward movement has captured the imagination of scientists and nonscientists alike.

Progress in Human Institutions

This section considers human institutions in the broad sense. I shall discuss the human religious institution, various ideas about economics, and historical trends. In each of these areas, some scholars have proposed that the evolutionary principle is universal and that progress is inevitable. I will show that that opinion is by no means unanimous.

Religion. Scholars who hold to a naturalistic evolution of human institutions often contend that human beings always had a need for belief in an outside force. Either a single god or many gods could be the source of this outside force. Human understanding of the nature and source of this outside force changed as the physical and social environment changed. Many people have invoked environmental change to explain the development of religious ideas, including the Christian religion. (For this discussion, I use the popular definition of "religion," not the idea, which I defended earlier, that all life is religious.)

Studies in comparative religions often postulate an evolutionary origin of religion by hypothesizing that long ago an early human being, usually thought of as a "cave man," had a very simple first religious thought. This first thought was the beginning of the most primitive religion.

But what happened after this first religious thought? The Frenchman Auguste Comte (1798-1857), positivist and pioneer sociologist, suggested the mechanism whereby religious thinking evolved. Comte held that the human desire to unify ideas brought the human family through several religious stages. First was *fetishism*, the belief that material objects have their own wills; then, *polytheism*, where gods act through inanimate things; then, *monotheism*, where a single god or abstract force acts through things. In the modern, scientific phase, people abandon ideas about a god and other superstitions. Sometimes this sequence is summed up as follows: belief in supernatural beings, belief in abstract forces behind phenomena, and belief in the sufficiency of scientific study.[3]

Within the Judeo-Christian tradition there have been a wide variety of views regarding religious origins. In the nineteenth century, the documentary hypothesis, which supposedly explained the origin of the Pentateuch, reflected the belief that Israel's religion evolved. This supposed evolution began when Israel was a small tribe and ended around 400 B.C. Scholars who held to this hypothesis maintained that the Pentateuch was composed of several documents—named Jehovah or Jaweh (J), Elohim (E), Priestly (P), and Deuteronomic (D)—written over a long period of time. These scholars claimed they could link a given passage in the Pentateuch to its source—J, E, P, or D. But they often disagreed over which assignment to make. Some of them invoked many documents beyond these four. According to those who accepted the documentary hypothesis, Israel's religion slowly evolved before and during the long period in which the documents were written and the Pentateuch was compiled.

The Darwinian view of natural selection may have been a factor in some analyses of the history of Christian thinking. Thus, the nineteenth-century American theologian George Harris of Andover Theological School may have applied natural selection to Christianity when he said, "...the theology which gains currency at any time is that conception of Christianity which commends itself to the reason and experience of the most enlightened and spiritual Christians."[4]

Pierre Teilhard de Chardin, a mid-twentieth century Roman Catholic paleontologist and theologian, presented a radical view of human evolution and the Christian religion. According to de Chardin, God has been transforming people since the beginning. Christ's work gives direction to evolution. Christianity is a faith in the progressive unification of the world. He said that humankind is the spearhead of life, that Roman Catholicism is the central axis in human activity, and that Christ is at the center of Creation. His starting point has two parts: evolution and the Catholic faith.[5] Redemption is an evolutionary process. The "Adam" of Genesis is the entire human family. Adam's sin is the representation of every human sin. Thus, de Chardin denies the reality of the fall of the first man into sin, implicating the entire human family. His belief concerning sin is consistent with his teaching that the human family evolves out of the sinful state. Thus, many of the ideas that are part of his theology, such as the transformation of people by God and the centrality of Christ in Creation, have a meaning entirely different from their traditional meaning. Some of de Chardin's followers relate his ideas to the problems of their own societies. Thus, for Latin American Christian Marxist J.L. Segundo, Christ redeemed *society*.[6]

Evolutionary theory can contribute to the establishment of a new religion. In Chapter 2 I described a "science religion" envisioned by many nineteenth-century scholars, such as Thomas Huxley, who attempted to substitute scientific ritual for Christian ritual. In contrast, one twentieth-century religion that may be linked to evolution is very far from what Huxley and others envisioned. This religion is the New Age movement, a movement that is unscientific as well as anti-Christian. Irving Hexham and Karla Poewe-Hexham (in anthropology and religious studies, respectively, at the University of Calgary, Alberta) claimed that the general belief in human evolution is responsible for the New Age movement.[7] One link that the Hexhams made between evolution and the New Age movement is the belief that life must have evolved not only here but also on other planets. Therefore, some people claim that they believe in UFOs; after all, couldn't "beings" from other places travel to us? The Hexhams also claimed that in this movement, as in other new religions, people reach for godhood through human improvement; this desire also drives evolutionary belief. When the Hexhams claimed that the New Age movement could not exist without a prior acceptance of evolutionary theory, they might have overstated the case. But without doubt that prior acceptance plays an important role in the movement. (Many adherents of the "Gaia hypothesis"—described in Chapter 8—are also associated with the New Age movement.)

Economics. Economic theories preceded Darwin. Consequently, in the latter part of the nineteenth century, after Darwinism was well established, economists could look back and claim that their explanation of why people acted as they did in economic matters did not depend on Darwin. But the principles of *classical economics* were similar to those of social Darwinism. Thus, Richard Hofstadter contended that social Darwinism's emphasis on the struggle for existence did not impact economic theory because economic theory had already assumed the existence of such a struggle. Hofstadter quoted an 1890 statement of economist Francis Amasa Walker: "I must deem any man very shallow in his observation of the facts of life who fails to discern in competition the force to which it is mainly due that mankind have risen from stage to stage in intellectual, moral, and physical power."[8]

Now let us turn to the modern picture. In Chapter 12 I described the theory of many modern sociologists who hold that either for selfish or altruistic reasons individuals in a society—any society, human or animal—act to preserve the group. But if we ask people why they do what they do, they might give other reasons. Or, if they do not give straightforward answers, they might inadvertently reveal their motivations. What, then, do people actually believe about what motivates them?

Neoclassical economics, which is a school of economic thought that builds upon the classical economics of the nineteenth century, answers that question by saying that people do whatever they think is best for themselves. The theory holds that people always behave in economic matters in this way. Neoclassical economics is not merely a theory. The free-market economies of some countries, such as the United States and Canada, are largely based on neoclassical theory.

Since neoclassical theory is supposed to explain human behavior in one sphere of life, the economic sphere, it is not surprising that proponents of this theory have extended its application to other spheres as well. For example, James Buchanan won the Nobel Prize in Economics in 1986 for applying this theory to political science. Those who awarded the Prize seemed to be saying that political science is part of economics. In practical terms, this theory of human behavior says that in business arrangements, raising children, and any other activity of life, you do whatever gives *you* the best feeling. Anything that prevents you from acting to do what you think is best—for example, because of government interference—is bad.[9,10]

Those who hold to the neoclassical theory make one other assumption: human behavior approximates rationality. Even assuming the validity of the first point—that people act first of all in their own self-interest—there are two objections to the assumption of rational behavior. One objection is that people usually do not have enough information to make the best choices. The other objection is that even if they do have enough information, they tend to consider only local factors. As a result, they tend to benefit only in the short term.

These two objections are aspects of the fundamental point raised by R.J. Herrnstein.[11] In Chapters 4 and 12 I presented Herrnstein's argument that human behavior is not based on rational choice. Herrnstein argued in effect that this is not the best of all possible worlds because the behavior of organisms, including human beings, tends to maximize short-term benefits. This behavior is the "evolutionarily stable strategy." In rejecting neoclassical economics, Herrnstein said that postulating rational choice is like arguing for perfect design in the world:

> . . . the theological argument from perfect design is [parallel to] the model of rational choice at the heart of neoclassical economics. Modern economics depicts human behaviour as approximating rationality [and posits] that each person, left to his own devices and disregarding errors of calculation and the like, will tend to optimize utility . . . .

But Herrnstein considers both assumptions—perfect design and rational behavior—to be wrong:

> Lately, the theory of rational choice has been adopted by other behavioural disciplines, such as the optimal foraging models of modern biology. It is this notion of rationality that I hold to be as false a model of individual behaviour as special creation and perfect design are of the origin of the species.[12]

Thus, any behavioral theory that assumes rational choice is not satisfactory.
These two modern understandings of human behavior—neoclassical economics and the evolutionarily stable strategy outlined by Herrnstein—disagree. But both depend upon evolutionary assumptions. Neoclassical economics, just like Herrnstein's theory, is a form of social Darwinism and consistent with sociobiology.

Thus, according to neoclassical economics, individuals act in their own self-interest. But inevitably the actions of one person conflict with those of another. There is competition, and the stronger prevails. As a result, the species *Homo sapiens* progresses: even though there are ups and downs, the economic situation of the species is better this century than last century, better this millenium than the previous millenium, and so forth. All this is nothing more than a picture of the survival of the fittest by natural selection, say these social Darwinists. Neoclassical economics seems at first to be benevolent—explaining, as it does, not only harsh competition but also charitable acts and many characteristics of a gentle society—but it is similar to the social Darwinistic classical economics that provided the excuse for so many excesses, such as cruel oppression due to unbounded capitalism and, eventually, eugenics in some countries. Furthermore, according to neoclassical theory, the selfish individual does that which is most likely to preserve the species. Evolution proceeds as the strongest succeed.

But there are other economic schools of thought besides classical economics, neoclassical economics, and the modified view of neoclassical economics that invokes the concept of the evolutionarily stable strategy. I shall now describe one that led in a different direction.

Thorstein Veblen (1857-1929), of Norwegian descent, was raised on a farm in rural Minnesota, in a community where the leisure class was disliked and populism was an important factor of life.[13] Veblen linked his criticism of the leisure class to criticism of classical economics; he coined the phrase "conspicuous consumption."[14,15] Veblen vigorously opposed the social Darwinism of economist William Graham Sumner, perhaps the most prominent American leader of the social Darwinism movement. Because of what it had attained, the leisure class was the very class that social Darwinists claimed to be the most fit. Veblen equated the business class with the despised leisure class. Therefore, he distinguished between business and productive industry. Because business involved salesmanship and chicanery, it was partially fraudulent. But industry involved workmanship, not acquisition. The worker, not the businessman, is productive.[16]

Veblen's economic ideas were similar to those of Karl Marx. But there was a difference. For example, Marx spoke of class warfare between the propertied and the proletariat, but Veblen referred to conflict between large and small property owners. Veblen's compromise may have been only pragmatic.[17] In developing his economic theory, Veblen used Darwinism. But his use was different from that of classical economists, who were in effect social Darwinists. Hofstadter said of the classical economists:

> The dominant school of economists [i.e., classical economists] had said that the existing is the normal and the normal is the right, and that the roots of human ills lie in acts which interfere with

the natural unfolding of this normal process toward its inherent end in a beneficent order.

According to Hofstadter, Veblen wanted economics to be an evolutionary science but claimed that it actually was not. Here is the heart of the different path Veblen and his followers would take:

> Where other economists had found in Darwinian science merely a source of plausible analogies or a fresh rhetoric to substantiate traditional postulates and precepts, *Veblen saw it as a loom upon which the whole fabric of economic thinking could be rewoven.* (Emphasis added.)

Veblen wanted to make economics an evolutionary science because he held that human nature had developed over a long evolutionary span.[18] According to John P. Diggins, Veblen differed from other economists because he fixed his attention on primitive human behavior. Unlike classical economists, he linked modern aggressive behavior to primitive behavior. Barbaric, ancient predatory instincts lingered in the modern leisure class in its preference for fighting and dueling, its martial spirit, and its aggressive patriotism.

Veblen's views are important for this book, concerned with the impact of evolutionary thinking, because his evolutionary views had a long-term effect. By the 1920s he and his disciples were responsible for a large number of economists rethinking their own positions.[19] Furthermore, Veblen's influence, especially in the United States, continues up to the present time. After Veblen died in 1929, many people he influenced had an opportunity to help shape American economic policy during the Great Depression. Max Lerner stated that Veblen's influence was significant in President Franklin Roosevelt's New Deal of the 1930s and 1940s. The New Dealers, like Veblen, saw social Darwinism at work in businesses; businessmen were free to exert their coercions. Therefore, Lerner said:

> Given this theory of business enterprise, the New Dealers took a logical further step. They tried to set up a system of governmental counter-forces, to prevent the arbitrary acts of business power from wrecking the economy and making men and machines idle . . . . Thus Veblenism, in essence a theory of power in the economic sphere, led to a program of power in the governmental sphere.

Lerner stated that this governmental approach (which is *neoinstitutionalism*) is not due to Veblen himself. He added that within Veblenism there are two schools of thought: the one of the right, the New Dealers' approach; the other, of the left, which would abolish the price system and absentee ownership (reminiscent of Veblen's favoring small property owners in their conflict with large property owners).[20]

Others carried the torch for Veblen's ideas after the end of the New Deal. Diggins said that John Kenneth Galbraith, an influential modern economist, is a spiritual descendant of Veblen.[21] Galbraith is also a follower of the English economist John Maynard Keynes, who advocated government expenditure to counteract economic depression; obviously, this is the "logical further step" Lerner refers to in the quote above. Galbraith exhibited this synthesis as he concluded *The New Industrial State*:

> . . . We may, over time, come to see the industrial system in fitting light as an essentially technical arrangement for providing convenient goods and services in adequate volume . . . . [I]f economic goals are the only goals of the society it is natural that the industrial system should dominate the state and the state should serve its ends. If other goals are strongly asserted, the industrial system will fall into its place as a detached and autonomous arm of the state, but responsible to the larger purposes of the society.

Veblen would have been pleased. Galbraith would rid society of the evils Veblen saw by virtually fusing industry and the state; Galbraith said:

> We have seen wherein the chance for salvation lies. The industrial system, in contrast with its economic antecedents, is intellectually demanding. It brings into existence, to serve its intellectual and scientific needs, the community that, hopefully, will reject its monopoly of social purpose.[22]

Modern economic schools of thought are thus based on one of these three ideas: first, social Darwinism, which actually grew out of pre-Darwin thinking but is consistent with evolution by natural selection; second, some form of Veblenism, which takes into account evolutionary theory and calls for action to counteract the evolutionary process; and, third, some combination of these two extremes.[23]

Therefore, modern economies, as well as the schools of thought that analyze those economies, depend in one way or another on evolutionary theory. The choice is not good: accept natural selection and expect the best to happen, or expect continual economic betterment through human control of the evolutionary process, whether it is by governmental control or fusion of industry and government. The impact of evolutionary thinking is far more subtle here than, for example, in psychology, but it is present nonetheless.

Where does this leave Christian thinking? Should Christians transform economic ideas that are frankly pagan, much as Christians made Christian holidays out of pagan celebrations, such as the transformation of a winter festival to Christmas? Christians and non-Christians can, of course, work together because they do encounter the same creational law. But I doubt that there is some "right" blend of free market and government-control economics. Many Christians assume that seeking the right blend is the path to take. This tendency is dangerous; after all, both extremes rest on wrong principles.

The problem of economics is one of the great unsolved problems of the Christian community. Perhaps Christians, who seem condemned to live in a society that adopts non-Christian values until Christ returns, can function best by minimizing the competitive spirit, especially as manifested in the business world. Can this spirit be minimized simply by the exhibition of Christian love? Of course, it is one thing to prescribe Christian love and another to show how it defines economic theory in a sinful world. Nevertheless, Christian love should replace the struggle of the jungle that social Darwinists admire and that their opponents want to control.

How do we view ourselves? I shall answer that question in the next section by showing how some people have evaluated historical events and trends. Then I devote the following section to a discussion of how our self-perception is reflected in the arts.

Evaluation of Historical Events and Trends. Let us consider historical thinking in the United States during the nineteenth century. At that time the United States experienced almost unprecedented geographical expansion and rapid industrial growth. Both lent themselves to the evolutionary optimism of social Darwinism. The works of two American historians illustrate the use of evolutionary theory in understanding historical trends.[24]

John Fiske (1842-1901), a historian and popular lecturer, was an avid disciple of Herbert Spencer. He believed in Aryan race superiority. He rejoiced in the American victory over Spain—a victory of English methods over Spanish, he said—in the Spanish-American War. He formulated an "Anglo-Saxon thesis." Within a few centuries English people would fill Africa with teeming cities. Every nation on earth would become English; in fact, around 80% of the people of the earth would be of English descent.

This was an optimistic view, one entirely based on evolutionary theory.
One of Fiske's lectures on the eventual victory of Anglo-Saxon peoples bore the title "Manifest Destiny." It was initially given in England and because of its great popularity it was repeated more than twenty times in American cities. As a result, Fiske met with President Hayes and other high American officials, including the Chief Justice and the Cabinet.[25]

Frederick Jackson Turner (1861-1932), born in Wisconsin and educated at Johns Hopkins, thought that the American experience, by an evolutionary process, produced better institutions. For Turner,

> . . . the conquest of the American frontier was part of an evolutionary process. But as he argued in his immensely influential essay, "The Significance of the Frontier in American History" (1893), American democracy did not originate in the German forests but in the American forests. The European settler eventually conquered the New World wilderness, but during his long struggle the conqueror was himself transformed by his environment, stripped of his civilized garments, and forced to adapt himself to new conditions or to perish.[26]

Turner's argument was environmental, applied to the American scene: the society that survived the harsh environment of the frontier, that began on the Atlantic coast and moved westward for more than three centuries, would be a stronger and better society than one that never encountered that environment. The newer society would not be stronger because of the elimination of weak people; rather, it would be stronger because in order to survive people would teach the next generation what worked and what did not. The next generation would therefore be made up of stronger individuals; hence, *rugged individualism*. As a result, according to Turner, after many generations, American institutions were stronger than European. In contrast to European institutions, American institutions had more vigor. They were not worn out. America could certainly be independent of Europe.

Fiske's and Turner's ideas were very popular in the United States around the turn of the century. Imperialism, already popular in Europe, began to take hold in the United States. It was the duty of the white man to bear the burden of those not as favored as he was; in fact, "white man's burden" is a phrase taken from the title of an 1899 poem by Rudyard Kipling. So it was that President McKinley, who held office from 1897 to 1901, led the nation to war to "rescue" Cuba and the Philippines, both Spanish lands. Theodore Roosevelt, the personification of the rugged American spirit, was eager to fight in this war. A few years later, at the end of World War I, President Woodrow Wilson believed that the United States, the vigorous nation with the better ideas, could rescue Europe from itself.

But no one person, certainly neither Fiske nor Turner, typifies American historians. With these two, evolutionary theory was clearly influential. Evolutionary theory affected other historians less obviously. Some historians do not exhibit an overriding philosophy except for an antipathy to any interpretation of history that is not "scientific"; this feeling they share with adherents of an evolutionistic approach. Thus, a disbelief in anything but a closed universe appears in historical studies just as much as in the other human responses to Creation discussed in this book. Even so, many people believe that God cannot be ignored. But an attempt to combine a secular approach with a belief in a sovereign God is dualism, an attempt that will fail in this arena as well.

How We View Ourselves

The arts—including literature, the visual arts, and music—also tell us how we view ourselves. How has dualistic and evolutionary thinking affected the arts? What kind of self-image do we have? I shall look first at literature and then briefly at visual art.

Literature. In Chapter 2 I provided examples of the evolutionary mindset of some authors prior to Darwin. It was inevitable that Darwin's approach to life would strengthen the naturalistic trend that was already present. *Benet's Reader's Encyclopedia* described the situation:[27]

> [Naturalism is] a movement in fiction begun in France in the latter half of the 19th century. Revolting against the subjectivism and imaginative escapism that seemed to characterize the romantic school, the naturalist writers were influenced by the biological theories of Darwin and the social and economic determinism of Taine and Marx. The new movement sought to depict human society and the lives of the men and women who compose it as objectively and truthfully as the subject matter of science is handled.

Benet's listed over a dozen French, English, and American authors affected by this movement, spanning the time from the early nineteenth to the late twentieth century.

According to *Benet's*, evolutionary theory particularly affected the American authors. The effect of their work is still felt. Of course, one must not overstate the case: other factors besides the theory of evolution are at work with the authors of this period. But the impact of evolutionary thinking is present. I shall now demonstrate how evolutionary thinking affected three authors—one English, Thomas Hardy (1840-1928); and two American, Frank Norris (1870-1902) and Jack London (1876-1916).[28]

Hardy created characters who could not understand or control the forces of their environment. Affected by Darwinism, Hardy wrote novels in which his characters are defeated by chance and outside factors. In other words, Hardy was a cynical naturalistic materialist.[29] This view of life has an interesting consequence. In a discussion of the ideological origins of American environmentalism, Roderick Nash claimed that Hardy made an early contribution to the environmentalist movement. Nash said that Hardy took evolution to mean that human ethics were no longer to relate only to other human beings. The common origin of all species meant to Hardy that we are to extend the Golden Rule beyond "others"—that is, other human beings—to all animal species. This idea has obvious implications for human interaction with the environment.[30]

Norris exhibited the effect of evolutionary thought on his work by portraying characters who devolved, that is, who retrogressed from man to animal. In principle, if evolution to a higher state can occur because certain mutants are better fitted to an environment, then an environment changing in another direction could select "lower" mutants; devolution would occur. Of course, Norris's stories do not encompass the long periods of times such devolution would require. In *Vandover and the Brute* (1895; published posthumously in 1914), a Harvard-educated young man entertains his friends by howling like a wolf; eventually he retrogresses to a wolf-like character. In *McTeague* (1899) a dentist retrogresses; finally he roams the country like a wild animal.

London read voraciously and was influenced by Darwin, Marx, and the philosopher Friedrich Nietzsche. London was concerned with the brute within human beings in many of his short stories and novels. *Before Adam* (1906) is about prehistoric savages. *The Strength of the Strong* (1911) and *The Abysmal Brute* (1913) both exhibit his belief that human beings are animals. In *The Call of the Wild* (1903) the domesticated dog Buck retrogresses as he becomes the leader of a wolf pack.

Bert Bender, professor of English at Arizona State University, who writes from an evolutionary perspective, maintained that the Darwinian teaching of human descent from sea creatures particularly influenced sea stories.[31] Following is a summary of Bender's argument concerning five authors.

Morgan Robertson's (1861-1915) *Futility: Or the Wreck of the Titan* (1898) was an amazing prophecy of the wreck of the *Titanic* in 1912. The hero's troubles are, said Bender, "part of a great evolutionary principle, which develops the race life at the expense of the individual." But the hero is not worthy to survive. (Is this an early version of sociobiology?) In another sea story, Archie Binns' (1899-1971) captain in *Lightship* (1934) says, "... our blood is nothing but an ebbing and flowing tide of sea water, with one-celled animals."

Bender contended that evolutionary belief also influenced Ernest Hemingway (1899-1961). *The Old Man and the Sea* (1952) provides examples. Here, man is the brother of the bonito, the flying fish, and the marlin shark. When Hemingway's character Santiago eats sea food, it is like taking the Eucharist. When Santiago sees plankton he comes to know that "no man was ever alone on the sea."

The Log from the Sea of Cortez (1941) is the account of a sea voyage taken by John Steinbeck (1902-1968) and a marine biologist. They said they were engaged in a "search for that principle which keys us deeply into the pattern of all life." They wondered, "Why do we so dread to think of our species as a species?" It is often difficult to distinguish an evolutionistic outlook from pantheism; Steinbeck wrote:

> [A]ll things are one thing and ... one thing is all things—plankton, a shimmering phosphorescence on the sea and the spinning planets and an expanding universe, all bound together by the elastic string of time. It is advisable to look from the tide pool to the stars and then back to the tide pool again.

More recently, Peter Matthiessen in *Far Tortuga* (1975) told a sea story of turtlers in the Caribbean that has, according to Bender, evolutionary overtones. The turtlers, human beings but nevertheless a predatory species, are but another species: they disappear when the turtles disappear. Bender took up this theme in his conclusion. It is no longer enough to dramatize the fact that we evolved from the sea. Sea writers ought to ask now if life, our species along with the others, can survive. Bender suggested that literature ought to enter a new phase; romanticizing the evolutionary link between human beings and the rest of life should lead to the next step. After all, our species is no more than one part of the life of this planet. Bender concluded by suggesting the central question for writers in the next phase: "How can we—how can *life*—survive on earth?"

Lenora Ledwon, a specialist in nineteenth-century literature, contended that Darwinism affected ghost stories.[32] Ledwon used the term "ghost stories" broadly, including not only conventional ghost stories but also other "nonscientific" manifestations, some of which would today fall into the category of science fiction. For her purpose, Ledwon defined "ghost" as "that which haunts."

Ledwon said that the ghost stories of the late nineteenth and early twentieth centuries differed from earlier ghost stories in that they assumed the animal ancestry of human beings and the randomness of life's events. Consequently, the new ghost acts randomly and manifests itself in bestial form. The new ghost was no longer ethereal, but rather perceived by several senses. Ghosts could now be not only seen and heard (as before) but also felt and sometimes smelled. Ledwon said that this new attitude arose because, as Thomas Huxley contended in 1896, human beings had become aware of their relation "to the under-world of life," that is, to animals.

I shall describe four of Ledwon's many examples. In "Green Tea" (1872) by Sheridan Le Fanu (1814-1873), a scholarly minister meets a malign-looking monkey on a bus. Later, while the minister is preaching, the monkey sits on his Bible so that he cannot see the page to preach. Eventually the minister kills himself. The Darwinian monkey has killed religion.

In "The Great God Pan" (1894) by Arthur Machen (1863-1947), a doctor rearranges "a few cells" in a female patient. Devolution is the result. She goes mad and bears a child who later, in a single moment, reverses eons of evolutionary progress. An eyewitness says:

> The skin, and the flesh, and the muscles, and the bones, and the firm structure of the human body that I had thought to be unchangeable, and permanent as adamant began to melt and dissolve . . . . Here too was all work by which man had been made repeated before my eyes . . . . I saw the body descend to the beasts whence it ascended, and that which was on the heights go down to the depths, even to the abyss of all being . . . . [A]t last I saw nothing but a substance as jelly.

In his 1930 essay, "Tom O'Bedlam and His Song," Machen suggested that in the beginning an apelike mammal went mad and became the first man.

In Algernon Blackwood's (1869-1951) "The Willows" (1907), ". . . Nature itself is the ghost—entirely appropriate from a post-Darwinian viewpoint," said Ledwon. Blackwood's narrator says that the chattering of the willows "made me think of a host of beings from another plane of life, another evolution altogether, perhaps, all discussing a mystery known only to themselves."

These examples show that evolutionary thinking has been and still is a factor in literature. Even though it is not the only factor, the evolutionary influence is clear. Not many authors and literary critics protested the claim that human beings can look at plankton and see a brother. Perhaps the general lack of disagreement with such claims indicates more than anything else that evolutionary thinking permeates our lives. Evidently the way we view ourselves in Western societies is that we are but one more species, only one part of the biomass, as likely either to endure or to vanish as any other species.

The content of literature can be evolutionistic even without reference to the brotherhood of human beings, plants, and animals, or without any other remarks of the type cited above. For example, a common theme in modern literature is that early sex—without marriage—is not merely permissible, but even desirable. The unspoken assumption is that human beings may act just like animals because they are no more than animals.

With respect to human evolution, the contents of dramatic literature are similar to other literature: sometimes the assumption of human evolution is evident; sometimes it is not. But drama requires a theatre and so a new question arises: What about the *existence* of the theatre? Theatrical performance is a unique art form, a cultural phenomenon. It is not difficult to imagine how the invention of writing led to many forms of literature. But why the theatre? Why the formalized, sometimes stylized, acting out of a story? We can easily trace the modern theatre back to antiquity, principally to the Greek theatre. But going even farther back, how did the theatre begin?

Although understanding the history of the theatre is not strictly a matter of how we view ourselves, theatre's historical development is sometimes considered to be evolutionary. For that reason I discuss theatre here.

Theatre historians debate whether the universal principle of evolution applies to the history of the theatre.[33] Oscar G. Brockett discussed the origin of the theatre in *History of the Theatre*.[34] From about 1875 to 1915, said Brockett, the prevailing opinion was that of Sir James Frazer, who held that since all cultures go through the same evolutionary stages, the study of modern "primitive" societies will reveal the origin of the theatre. Then, said Brockett, one would arrive at this conclusion:

> In the beginning people gradually become aware of forces that appear to control their food supply and the other determinants of existence. Having no clear understanding of natural causes, they attribute them to supernatural or magical forces.

They try to appease these forces, eventually by formal means. They perform rites; the "audience" is the supernatural force. Stories or myths grow up around the rites. In the process of time, performers impersonate the mythical characters or supernatural forces. Brockett said that this impersonation is a major sign of a developing dramatic sense. The process of change continues: stories based on myth are acted out outside the rite; the religious purpose need not remain.

Brockett said that later, beginning around 1915, anthropologists began to reject the idea that all cultures evolve in the same way. According to them, cultural institutions develop differently in different societies. They rejected cultural Darwinism. They studied how specific societies function from day to day; they were *functionalists*, as are most modern anthropologists.

Even so, after World War II another school of thought arose. The *structuralists*, led by Claude Levi-Strauss, also rejected cultural Darwinism. Underlying patterns are important because all structures can be reduced to one of a few universal patterns. Myths are also significant because they indicate how the people of a primitive society thought. Brockett said that some structuralists extend their approach ". . . to the origins of theatre, as well as to today's drama and performance (seeking to discover a few basic structures to which all basic examples conform).''[35]

Brockett then summarized the present situation:

> [All anthropologists of the last century] agree on a fundamental point: that ritual and myth are important elements in all societies. Together, they reinforce the belief that theatre emerged out of primitive ritual. Thus, today most critics and historians agree that ritual is the source of theatre, although not necessarily the only one. On the other hand, most scholars now reject the idea that theatre has followed a similar evolutionary pattern in all societies.

No one doubts that the theatre has "evolved" in the sense that current theatre is the product of a long series of changes. But of course subscribing to that idea is not equivalent to accepting the inevitability of progress—in this case, in the theatre—by means of a Darwinistic, universally applicable principle of evolution. To assume that such a universal principle is valid is simply not justified. Whether it is proper to hold to evolution in a specific instance must be evaluated on a case-by-case basis; this is the same approach I have urged in the other disciplines discussed in this book.

With the theatre, just as with certain cultural phenomena discussed earlier, there is no consensus on the desirability of applying a universal evolutionary principle. Belief in cultural progress by means of such a principle is, however, in the air. Any realistic analysis of the impact of evolutionary thought on modern society must recognize the universal presence of the evolutionary idea, even though it is not universally applied.

One could make similar conclusions concerning the visual arts. First, some analysts conclude that art advances because of the inevitability of the universal evolutionary principle. Second, the content of art often reveals the assumption that human beings are only one more animal species. I shall discuss only the inevitability of the advancement of art.

Visual Art. Many Christians have made searching analyses of the foundations of art. They generally see human activity in the arts as a response to Creation, much as human scientific activity is a response to Creation. They analyze both the history of art and the content of artistic activity. It is not my purpose to discuss those efforts. Instead, I shall present one evolutionistic approach to one of the visual arts.

Sir Ernst Gombrich, an influential English art historian for several decades, has written many books and articles on the subject. Gombrich proposed that the history of visual art is similar to the history of life, that is, evolutionary. Although evolutionary thinking does not permeate this field, Gombrich's views are important.[36] Gombrich said that social Darwinism helps explain the development of aesthetics. He suggested that "evolution in the arts" is analogous to "evolution in nature." "What we call changes in style," said Gombrich, "can be interpreted as adaptations, on the part of the working artist, to the functions assigned to the visual image by a given society." Just as the outcome of the interaction between a species and its ecological niche is unpredictable, so is the outcome of the interaction between an artistic style and its ecological niche in society.

Accordingly, said Gombrich, a "need" produces a "result." The need to depict events in ancient Greece as if those events were taking place in front of the viewer so that the viewer could "see" historical events resulted in the development of photographic art. This development included the principle of foreshortening to present a sense of three dimensions.

During the Middle Ages, Christian art, both paintings and sculpture, had to accomplish several things, sometimes decreed by the popes, even as it had to avoid certain things. Artists—in their "niche"—responded to these demands. At one time, the purpose of their art was to tell the biblical story. But, said Gombrich, ". . . Italian artists had also to meet the demands of a very different task—the creation of cult images." There was to be no worship of images, but artists had to give attention to cults of saints, relics, and so forth.

Gombrich said that the decoration of the altar illustrates his evolutionary thesis. He said, "The emergence and evolution of this art-form demonstrates

Progress 247

to my mind the way a great variety of independent factors interact, ultimately to produce results which could never have been predicted at the outset.'' Throughout Gombrich's discussion, he compared the unpredictability of the outcome in both kinds of evolution: of a species interacting with conditions in its biological niche and of an art form with conditions in its societal niche. Thus, worshipers' need to see the priest meant that decorations could not be put on top of the altar. Only when the priest's position was changed could the top be decorated; and, in fact, such decorations became larger. The outcome was also unpredictable when Crusaders conquered Constantinople in 1204. The result was the temporary breakdown of the barrier between East and West and the appearance of imitation icons from the East in Italy.

One function of the altar decoration was to be symbolic; another, narrative. But the two modes of communication are separated in the altar paintings. Gombrich said, ''I believe that in nature hybrids often prove infertile, and in the history of art, too, this rather confusing mixture of modes was not granted a long life . . . .''

The sixteenth century saw an important step in the evolution of art. A painting could be too good for the altar and instead become a collector's item. Gombrich described an incident that occurred in 1520 in which Titian might have obtained more money by selling a painting to a duke than to the church. He said, ''The days of the collector had arrived. [The painting] was simply too good for a liturgical role and should be treasured simply as a work of art.'' Church artists such as Titian and Michelangelo created works appreciated for their artistic value itself. Gombrich said that there was a new standard of excellence and added:

> In other words art had created its own context, its own ecological niche, once more, as it had done in the ancient world, and it was this autonomy, this emancipation which led in turn to its survival in a new and hostile climate.[37]

Gombrich contended that this change took place just in time. The Reformation, which opposed liturgical art, was just beginning. Art had to make its way alone. Many paintings intended for the altar ended up in private collections. These paintings ''. . . had now become Art with a capital A, as it were, they had been cut loose from their roots and flourished in a new environment.'' The niche was not the same. Gombrich concluded by proclaiming that the modern artist ''. . . owes his predicament and his joy to the demands made on his predecessors some 700 years ago.''[38]

In summary, Gombrich emphasized that his thesis is not merely that change is response to the environment. After all, it is a truism that history consists of a sequence of causes and effects, with each event both an effect and a cause. That kind of "evolution" is so broad that it says nothing. Gombrich wanted to be much more specific; he used the Darwinian model for biological change. Thus, for him an artistic style is the consequence of interaction of artists with several external—environmental—factors: the style is the result of adaptation to the environment. Somehow the niche so filled *needs* the new style; a niche tends not to remain empty indefinitely. The factors responsible for change are sufficiently numerous and complex to make it impossible for an onlooker to predict the result: chance is important. If a niche disappears, a species or a style of art disappears. But if a new niche opens up, death is averted. Then the style that fills the new niche has, because of its long history, a demonstrated ability to adapt. These factors tend to make the style strong.

Gombrich even suggested a few specific analogies to biological evolution. Hybrids are not fertile and a style with a double purpose does not survive. Also, geographical isolation, so often cited as a factor affecting biological evolution, plays a role in the history of art (shown by the effect on art when for a short period East and West were not isolated).

The Problem of the Paradigm

What are we to make of Gombrich's analysis? What of his use of the biological evolutionary metaphor? What, in fact, of the assumption, made by so many scholars, that progress is inevitable?

I have cited two kinds of evolutionary applications in this book, especially in this chapter and Chapter 12. In one application, evolutionists apply their theory to the *content* of the subject; in the other application, they apply their theory to the *history* of the subject. Many authors—for example, Gombrich—claim that the two are related. For them the content of biological evolution provides a metaphor for the history of their subject.

But proposing an evolutionary model for the history of art or of any other subject does not actually depend upon the validity of biological evolutionary theory. Yet the primary assumption of Gombrich and evolutionists in other subjects is the validity of the universal principle of evolution. Progress is fundamental. These analysts function under the umbrella of the evolutionary paradigm. As a result, there is the problem of the paradigm: they simply do not consider what their analyses would be like if the assumed universal principle of evolution were not correct. Once the primary assumption has been made, it is a secondary matter to assume the relevance of this universal principle for the content of biology—or the history of art, or the content of economics, or for either the history or the content of any other subject. Now, for the analysis of the problem of the paradigm in specific cases:

History. Let us look first at the history of a subject. What happens if the assumed fundamental principle—the universality of evolution—is wrong? Where does that leave Frederick Jackson Turner's claims about the effect of the frontier on American history, James Frazer's evolutionary analysis of the history of the theatre, Gombrich's approach to the history of art, and similar evolutionary histories? Showing that the fundamental principle is wrong does not prove that the evolutionary analysis of a history is therefore wrong. But the burden of proof then rests on whoever makes such an analysis; whether these histories are in fact evolutionary must be decided on a case-by-case basis. Those who function within the evolutionary paradigm seem not to comprehend this point. Functioning within the paradigm, they assume use of the metaphor is justified. But using a metaphor actually proves nothing.

Suppose, then, that we do not assume the validity of the evolutionary paradigm as we examine Gombrich's argument. His insights into the cause-and-effect nature of events in art history—for example, the reason for Greek photographic art—are without question useful for the art historian. But leaning on the biological metaphor is going too far. For example, putting certain styles and trends in a niche prejudices understanding: it is difficult to see how "niche," a word associated so intimately with biological evolutionary theory, can be properly used in the context of art history. "Niche" has become a prejudicial word. In a similar way, when Frederick Jackson Turner used evolutionistic natural selection as a metaphor for the effect of the frontier on American history, he prejudiced his case. Wrong procedure led in his case to a wrong consequence: his ideas contributed to American chauvinism, now generally recognized to be an unhealthy attitude. When the shelter of the paradigmatic umbrella vanishes, the metaphor is seen for what it is: an illogical and sometimes dangerous tool used to "prove" a point.

Content. The discussion has already included several consequences for the content of a subject when one assumes the validity of the universal principle of evolution. Thus, assuming the inevitability of progress is an evolutionist's starting point in devising paths from nonlife to life, from animals to human beings, from an undifferentiated human society to one accepting the structures implied by kinship, from a society containing both weak and strong individuals to one of only strong individuals, from a society containing both weak and strong businesses to one of only strong businesses, and so forth.

Notice that these examples are all taken from previous chapters and the first section of this chapter, which discusses progress in human institutions. But when we consider the *content* of the various ways we view ourselves— that is, the content of literature, drama, and visual art—the picture is more complex. Thus, some art—Christian art, for example—is widely appreciated, even though its optimism is not based on an evolutionistic principle. However, some artistic expression is nihilistic, not based on faith in progress. This nihilism, while evolutionary, seems to be based on a pessimistic view of evolution: the human species, like all others, will eventually vanish, leaving no trace, lost in vast space and measureless time, with no more significance than a single grain of sand.

In the natural sciences, the evolutionistic interpretation of phenomena is dominant. Many investigators have brought this naturalistic, evolutionistic understanding of the origin and nature of the human family to the study of human behavior, human institutions, and the ways human beings view themselves. They have taken evolutionary theory from the natural sciences and applied it to human sciences and other human activities. But we have seen that an evolutionistic understanding of these activities is by no means universal. In fact, in some cases it is only a minority view; in others, it was once accepted but is accepted no longer. Yet its rejection by scholars in the human sciences never seems to be for the right reason, namely, the view of the human family presented by the Bible.

Many nonevolutionistic analyses of the human sciences and other human activities are, just like evolutionary analyses, based on a dualistic view of the world. In both cases it is assumed that for investigative purposes the universe is closed and that phenomena can in principle be explained by scientists assuming the definition of science adopted at the beginning of the era of modern science. Investigators seem to assume, "If I cannot use scientific methods to investigate it, 'it' is a nonfact." This view is dualistic because some people add a "spiritual" dimension which, however, they keep almost completely out of their analyses of the natural and human sciences. It is as if there are two worlds.

In spite of the lack of unanimity among workers in the human sciences, significant and dangerous trends are underway in that area. These trends will be considered in the next chapter.

Chapter Fourteen
Consequences

Without doubt the advent of evolutionary theory has made scholars more alert to the meaning of change in history. Such alertness is in itself a good thing. But the deeper idea, the idea that we must of necessity interpret every change using explainable scientific laws, is not good.

Dualists insist on the existence of "something else," which, however, can be contemplated quite apart from the operation of natural laws. Accepting the universal applicability of the evolutionary principle introduces problems into scholarly analysis. Those problems can be solved only when one abandons the naturalistic approach. But dualists cannot solve those problems because for all practical purposes they limit themselves to a naturalistic position. Thus, whenever dualistic Christians debate naturalistic non-Christians about origins and the evolutionary principle, they decline at the very beginning to make the one assumption they ought to make, namely, that natural laws will not always be sufficient to understand origins and the history of change. In any proper discussion of origins and the history of change, discussants must assume that natural laws cannot in principle explain all phenomena.

If one could show that all evolutionary explanations are wrong, the matter would be simpler than it actually is. But numerous examples of microevolution are valid. Extrapolation to macroevolution, to the origin of the human family, and finally to the explanation of a wide variety of human activities is not valid. In fact, such an extrapolation is usually mischievous. In *Macbeth* Shakespeare dramatized the human desire to go beyond the facts. Three witches speak to Macbeth: the first refers to him as the thane of Glamis, the second as thane of Cawdor, and the third as future king (Act I, Scene III). Macbeth is thrilled: he is already thane of Glamis; but what of thane of Cawdor, and, *especially*, what of *king*? Shortly thereafter messengers inform Macbeth that because of his successes the king has made him thane of Cawdor. Now Macbeth is certain the witches knew something he did not know. He is eager to believe the third witch's statement. But this extrapolation, the assumption that the correctness of the first two statements means the third is also true, leads to misery and murder in the case of Macbeth.

The Scope of Evolutionary Theory

During the last century scholars have been probing. Where, they ask, does Darwinism apply? People convinced that the evolutionistic principle is universally valid have an easy answer: it will be shown to apply everywhere. Listen to Russell Ruthen as he reported on the work of John Holland at the Sante Fe Institute:

> Holland and his colleagues at the Sante Fe Institute . . . are searching for a unified theory that would explain the dynamics of all living systems, be they groves of trees, colonies of bacteria, communities of animals or societies of people.

So, from bacteria to human societies. Ruthen stated that Holland's team—consisting of economists, biologists, physicists, computer scientists, and researchers from many other disciplines—have concluded that "living systems seem to evolve toward a boundary between order and randomness." Eventually, evolutionary theory will bind all the systems together: "Indeed, the Santa Fe group is trying to answer the question of evolution in the broadest sense of the word."[1]

In spite of this optimism, examination of the human sciences and how we look at ourselves indicates that the evolutionistic principle has been applied only here and there. Some scholars still look for nonevolutionary explanations of phenomena outside the natural sciences. Yet there are reasons to maintain that efforts to apply evolutionary theory in those areas will continue.

The first and most important reason is that many people still insist on a universe that is both closed and unified. If the evolutionary principle unifies the natural sciences, so should it also unify all the sciences. Dualistic Christians attempt to limit evolutionary theory to the natural sciences and allow for other kinds of explanation outside those sciences. But dualists provide little theoretical justification for placing a boundary line between the natural sciences and the other sciences—a boundary line whose position is, after all, arbitrary. Given that the closed-and-unified-universe and the dualistic positions still dominate the field of scholarly endeavor, many non-Christians now find the closed-and-unified-universe model attractive. For them, Richard Dawkins' claim holds: ". . . Darwin made it possible to be an intellectually fulfilled atheist."[2] Non-Christians who presently reject a suggested evolutionary explanation of, for example, the history of the theatre or the origin of human language usually do not deny in principle the universality of the evolutionary principle. There are many scholars who agree

Consequences

with John Holland in claiming that when we do fit everything together, we will indeed understand that the unifying principle is evolutionary.

Some people might contend that my claims are unduly pessimistic. I said that many scholars, perhaps most of the scholarly community, seem to say that evolutionary theory will eventually claim the areas not yet under its sway. Is that statement justified?

I claim that it is justified because there is still another reason for expecting a continuation of efforts to explain all life's activities by a universally applicable evolutionary theory. That reason is the vigorous, almost irrational insistence by a large number of scientists and other leaders that evolutionary theory must be taught in public schools. Their insistence goes far beyond a defense against advocates of creation as an alternate possibility. Educators teach—or are urged to teach—that biological evolution is a fact; it is not to be questioned. If students listen carefully, they will also hear the claim that evolutionary theory is useful outside the natural sciences.

Thus, many teachers want to "integrate" their evolutionary understanding of biology and human origins with other sciences. But how? A typical answer was provided by Martin Nickels, a biological anthropologist at Illinois State University, who offers the short course, "Incorporating Human Evolution Into Your Own Thinking and Teaching." The following is part of the course description:

> For most of the twentieth century, the scientific and intellectual community has accepted the idea that humans are animals with an evolutionary history. But to what extent has the idea that the human evolutionary past is important for understanding human nature today actually been incorporated into the thinking and teaching of social scientists, philosophers, health scientists, and even many biologists? What intellectual impact has knowledge of human evolutionary biology had on fields outside of anthropology?

Even though the application of evolutionary theory has not been universally successful, the assumption that the evolutionary principle has universal applicability is still pervasive and probably held by an increasing number of people as time passes. Many of those who do favor this principle are single-minded and dogmatic. They simply will not consider the counterarguments. Because of their single-mindedness, they often carry the day even when they are in the minority.

Two Modern Movements

I shall consider two important modern social movements in which evolutionists insist on the validity of the evolutionary principle. In each case, not everyone in the movement, but rather a dogmatic, zealous subgroup, insists that the foundation of the movement is the evolutionary principle. In each case, this zealous group may eventually dominate the movement. In each case, this insistence on the evolutionary principle may well be an indication of what the future holds for other movements and perhaps even for the public attitude toward all aspects of life.

Blurring the Difference Between Species. Christians throughout the world have become sensitive to ecological concerns. But the environmental movement, a movement close to the hearts of Christians because its goal is to preserve Creation, has not been free of evolutionary influence. The modern phase of this movement began when Lynn White maintained that the Christian ethic is responsible for destroying much of the environment that was once the home of many more species, both animal and plant. White ascribed the ecological problem to a neglect of Darwin's teachings:

> Our science and technology have grown out of Christian attitudes toward man's relation to nature which are almost universally held not only by Christians and neo-Christians but also by those who fondly regard themselves as post-Christians. *Despite Copernicus, all the cosmos rotates around our little globe. Despite Darwin, we are not, in our hearts, part of the natural process. We are superior to nature, contemptuous of it, willing to use it for our slightest whim.*[3] (Most of the emphasis is added.)

Roderick Nash and Joseph Sax are members of the rather large group of scholars and writers who have fleshed out White's ideas. In a discussion of the Judeo-Christian roots of the ecological movement, Robert H. Nelson, an economist, described the views of Nash and Sax and the religious roots of those views:

> The leading historian—an energetic advocate as well—of American environmentalism, Roderick Nash, recently described environmental views as deriving from a set of "ecotheologians" who propound a new "gospel of ecology." There is in the "recent concern for nature" what Nash describes as a "quasi-religious fervor." Joseph Sax, in making the case for reducing the human presence in the national parks, states candidly that he and other preservationists are in truth "secular prophets, preaching a message of secular salvation."[4]

Nash explained this religious fervor for ecological concerns by beginning with Darwinism:

> Darwinism took the conceit out of humanity by putting humans back into nature . . . . Darwin extended the boundaries of kinship to the limits of life. No more special creation in the image of God, no more "soul," and, it followed, no more hierarchy, dominion, or expectation that the rest of nature existed to serve one precocious primate . . . . The overarching concept that emerged from Darwin and his popularizers was the unity and continuity of life.

To emphasize the equal worth of species, Nash claimed that the species that were the prime movers of evolution may have changed many times.[5]

White claimed that a supposed human superiority over the rest of Creation, a Christian concept, is the reason for the widespread damage to the environment. But Nash said the environmental movement offers a cure: consider species continuous; then human beings will not have a preferred status. The essence of ecotheology is the demotion of humanity.

Belief in the continuity of species provides a theoretical basis for the modern animal rights movement. Of course, the Bible teaches it is wrong to torture animals. Also, for many decades the Christian Science cult has opposed medicine and therefore the use of animals in medical research. But in the last two decades, the situation has changed. In 1975 Philosopher Peter Singer wrote *Animal Liberation*, a book that urged people to be more aggressive in defense of animal welfare.[6] In 1983, Tom Regan in *The Case for Animal Rights* was more radical: he condemned any use of animals—for fur, for eating, for medical research, and so forth.[7] Animals have rights that we may not violate.

More recently, Philosopher James Rachels of the University of Alabama made an extremely important addition to the argument.[8] One reason for examining his argument is that he is not as extreme as some others: he allows for a hierarchy in the animal kingdom and urges that we give most of our attention to the top of this hierarchy, where he places "higher" animals and human beings. Because he is not as radical as activists who put all life—including plant life—on one plane, his argument will appeal to many people. Consequently, his approach is more dangerous.

Not only must we accept Darwinism, said Rachels, but our descent from animals has moral implications. In *Created from Animals: The Moral Implications of Darwinism*, Rachels explored what should happen to traditional morality now that we know we have animal ancestry. Rachels began by quoting Darwin: "Man in his arrogance thinks himself a great work worthy the interposition of a deity. More humble and I think truer to consider him created from animals."

Rachels asked, "What becomes of [traditional morality] if man is but a modified ape?" He then outlined his four-part answer. First, traditional morality says that human beings, as contrasted to animals, are in a special moral category because human beings bear the image of God and they are uniquely rational; human beings have dignity. Second, while Darwin does not of necessity remove human dignity, his work does remove its support—the image of God and unique rationality. Third, Rachels' suggested a new idea, *moral individualism*:

> According to moral individualism, the bare fact that one is human entitles one to no special consideration. How an individual should be treated depends on his or her own particular characteristics, rather than on whether he or she is a member of some preferred group—even the "group" of human beings . . . . [This] is the natural view to take if one views the world from an evolutionary perspective.

Fourth, abandoning the idea of human dignity has practical consequences. No longer will the thought of human life fill us with superstitious awe. No longer will the lives of nonhumans be a matter of indifference. He said:

> This means that human life will, in a sense, be devalued, while the value granted to non-human life will be increased. *A revised view of such matters as suicide and euthanasia, as well as a revised view of how we should treat animals, will result* . . . . *[This] leaves morality stronger and more rational* . . . . *[and] with a better ethic concerning the treatment of both human and non-human animals.*[9] (Emphasis added.)

Rachels then took up two tasks: first, to show that some animals are more important than we thought, and second, to show that human beings are less important than we thought. Thus, he welcomed evidence that rhesus monkeys exhibit altruism.[10] Rachels asserted that these monkeys and some other animals have more than *biological life*; they have *biographical life*, which is exhibited by their intelligence, organization into social groups, communications with each other, bonds between mother and offspring, and diversity among individuals. But these attributes appear less as we go down the biological scale, and so bugs and shrimp have biological, but not biographical, life.[11]

On the other hand, not all human beings have biographical lives. A genetically defective infant could be of less value than a healthy chimpanzee.[12] Moral individualism says that the value of a life depends upon the nature of the individual, not the species to which the individual happens to belong. That idea has some devastating corollaries. The lives of human beings are not necessarily of great value—certainly not of infinite value, as Christians claim. This reasoning led Rachels to arrive at the conclusion that there should be no absolute prohibition against either euthanasia or suicide; in a few cases they might be justified.[13]

Throughout his book Rachels attacked divine revelation concerning the nature of human beings. He repeatedly denied that human beings bear the image of God. In one reflection on the consequences of his position, he made the following revealing admission:

> It might be protested that this view [moral individualism] leaves the value of human life less secure than traditional views. Indeed it does. The abandonment of lofty conceptions of human nature, and grandiose ideas about the place of humans in the scheme of things, inevitably diminishes our moral status. *God and nature are powerful allies; losing them does mean losing something. But it does not mean losing everything.* Human life can still be valued, and we can still justify moral and legal rules to protect it. We will, however, have to acknowledge that these rules grow out of our own valuings, rather than descending to us from some higher authority. If that is a loss, it may be a loss that humans after Darwin must live with.[14] (Emphasis added.)

Finally, Rachels claimed that Darwin believed his theories of biological change and morality fitted together:

> ... Darwin was correct in thinking that all his work, from the theory of natural selection to the moral vision he articulates, is of one piece. It is one view, held together by a sense of how the elements of one's thinking must be mutually supportive, and how they must fit together, if one's outlook is to form a reasonable and satisfying whole.[15]

Not unexpectedly, Rachels' arguments led up to a defense of the animal rights movement. He described animals' pain and suffering in both medical research and the production of human food. He advocated vegetarianism.[16] In summarizing both what has happened and his vision for the future, Rachels claimed that once we erroneously thought that the earth is the center of the universe and that God provided the earth for a human home. But Copernicus showed the error of the first idea and Darwin showed that the second is wrong. Then people began to see that species membership is not important; only an individual's specific attributes can make that individual important. When we work out the consequences of this new idea, we will find "... a new equilibrium ... in which our morality can once again comfortably coexist with our understanding of the world and our place in it." We will come to agree with Darwin, who ". . . believed that our moral sentiments must eventually expand to include all mankind, regardless of nation, race, social status, or handicap," and, in Darwin's words, "and finally the lower animals."[17]

Two more points concerning animal rights are important. First, God has given human beings, created in his image, animals for their use. Human beings are to rule over animals (Gen. 1:26, 28). God used animals' skins to cover Adam and Eve after they sinned (Gen. 3:21). Human beings may use animals for food (Gen. 9:3). The Bible says that Christ ate meat (Luke 24:42-43). In the Old Testament, God demanded animal sacrifices. The Bible also indicates nothing wrong with certain occupations that involve the killing of animals, such as fishing or shepherding; nor does it condemn the use of beasts of burden. Given these biblical teachings about human beings and animals, could philosophers like James Rachels have it backwards? They claim that *since* human beings descended from animals, they may not kill animals. But God *does* allow human beings to kill animals. This permission is a strong argument that human beings did not descend from animals.

Second, belief in the evolution of human beings from animals—no matter how much people hedge by saying, "God did it," and by making other qualifications—leads to irrationality. Notice the step-by-step progression:

In the first step, at the philosophical level, many leaders in the animal rights movement freely blur the difference between species; they are taught by people like Singer, Regan, and Rachels. Thus, Michael Fox, a veterinarian who directs the Center for the Respect of Life and Environment, a part of the Humane Society, said: "There are no clear distinctions between us and animals. Animals communicate, animals have emotions, animals can think. Some thinkers believe that the human soul is different because we are immortal, and that just becomes completely absurd."[18] Ingrid Newkirk, co-founder and director of a large organization known as People for the Ethical Treatment of Animals (PETA), said "There really is no rational reason for saying a human being has special rights . . . . A rat is a pig is a dog is a boy." In their zeal to wipe out the difference between species, no wonder many animal rights advocates condemn *speciesism*, which they define as the preference for one species over another. For them, speciesism is as morally wrong as racism, the preference for one race over another.

The propaganda level is the next step. The philosophical ideas of the first step can become inflammatory. Thus, in July, 1991, Milwaukee police discovered the remains of a large number of grisly murders. Newspaper readers and television viewers had difficulty tearing themselves away from each day's new horror story. Then, on August 9, 1991, the following full-page advertisement appeared in some newspapers:

Milwaukee . . . July 1991

They were drugged and dragged
across the room . . .

Their legs and feet were
bound together . . .

Their struggles and cries
went unanswered . . .

Then they were slaughtered and
their heads sawn off . . .

Their body parts were refrigerated
to be eaten later . . .

Their bones were discarded
with the trash.

It's Still Going On

The advertisement continued, "Please remember that this scenario is reality for over 16 million sensitive individuals who lose their lives every day in this country for nothing more than the fleeting taste of 'meat.'" Later: "If this leaves a bad taste in your mouth, become a vegetarian." It was a PETA advertisement.[19] Such advertisements, along with television presentations and widely distributed literature, lead people to action.

The action level is the next step. Some animal rights organizations engage in terroristic acts. For example, in 1989 members of the Animal Liberation Front (ALF) broke into an animal research laboratory at Texas Tech University in Lubbock, Texas, destroyed a large amount of equipment, and generally interrupted experiments in progress. The ALF also took credit for similar university medical laboratory break-ins in Arizona in 1989 and in Oregon in 1986. David Foreman's book *Ecodefense*, a general defense of "Mother Earth," provides instructions for sabotage.[20]

Thus, many animal-rights activists begin with the belief that human beings descended from animals. With that starting point, they assert that a person who differentiates between species is as bad as a racist.

Blurring the Difference Between Genders. Another modern social phenomenon is the feminist movement. Here, too, zeal has sometimes replaced rationality. Just as with the environmental movement, reform was long overdue. Given that human beings have sinned so much both with respect to the environment and the domination of women by men, reform movements had to arise.

But with respect to gender, just as with environmentalism, scholars have often built on the wrong philosophical foundation. The secular mind maintains that this universe is closed; many Christians take a dualistic position and deny the relevance of special revelation for such a topic. Today the closed-universe model often implies an evolutionistic solution to problems, so some people approach the gender question in an evolutionistic manner. The evolutionistic approach to feminism is not as widely understood as in the animal rights movement but, as we shall see, such an approach is evident and dangerous.

If Darwinists ask about gender at the theoretical level, they encounter a gigantic problem: early evolutionists and others of the nineteenth-century scholarly community took it for granted that women are inferior to men. Darwin and others held that women are lower than men on the evolutionary scale.

The view of Carl Vogt, a Genevan scholar of the mid-nineteenth century, was typical of that period: "We may be sure that wherever we perceive an approach to the animal type, the female is nearer to it than the male."[21] Stephen Jay Gould quoted Paul Broca (1824-1880), professor of clinical surgery in Paris, who said:

> We might ask if the small size of the female brain depends exclusively upon the small size of her body . . . . But we must not forget that women are, on the average, a little less intelligent than men . . . . [T]he relatively small size of the female brain depends in part upon her physical inferiority and in part upon her intellectual inferiority.²²

According to Gould, Broca claimed that his data showed that the intellectual difference between men and women, as measured by brain size, is now greater than in prehistoric times. In other words, the difference between men and women is evolving. An *evolving* difference, but with a significance quite different from that intended by people like Broca, is extremely important in modern evolutionary theory. I shall return to that concept.

Evolution also fit into the scheme of Gustave Le Bon, a respected French scientist and one of the founders of social psychology, who said in 1879:

> In the most intelligent races, as among the Parisians, there are a large number of women whose brains are closer in size to those of gorillas than to the most developed male brains. This inferiority is so obvious that no one can contest it for a moment; only its degree is worth discussion. All psychologists who have studied the intelligence of women, as well as poets and novelists, recognize today that *they represent the most inferior forms of human evolution* and that they are *closer to children and savages than to an adult, civilized man.* They excel in fickleness, inconstancy, absence of thought and logic, and incapacity to reason. Without doubt there exist some distinguished women, very superior to the average man, but they are as exceptional as the birth of any monstrosity, as, for example, of a gorilla with two heads; consequently, we may neglect them entirely. (Emphasis added.)

Le Bon also said that women should not receive the same education as men; for, if women would leave the home, a social revolution would begin.²³

Modern Darwinists who investigate gender at the theoretical level have their greatest problem with Darwin himself. Concerning all animals, Darwin said in *The Descent of Man*, "Throughout the animal kingdom, when the sexes differ in external appearance, it is, with rare exceptions, the male which has been more modified."²⁴ Darwin also said:

> As with animals of all classes, so with man, the distinctive

characters of the male sex are not fully developed until he is nearly mature . . . . *Male and female children resemble each other closely*, like the young of so many other animals in which the adult sexes differ widely; *they likewise resemble the mature female much more closely than the mature male.* The female, however, ultimately assumes certain distinctive characters, and in the formation of her skull, is said to be intermediate between the child and the man.[25] (Emphasis added.)

Modern Darwinists simply cannot leave the matter of gender where Darwin left it. Feminists, who generally would be loath to discard something so foundational to modern thinking as evolutionary theory, are understandably upset at the sexist ideas promulgated by Darwin and other nineteenth-century scholars. Since Darwin's remarks about women were not simply offhand, but a part of his theory in his landmark *Descent of Man and Selection in Relation to Sex*, something had to be done. My purpose here is not to detail one more difficulty with Darwinism; I have described enough of those problems already. Rather, I shall show how this problem—Darwin's sexism versus Darwinism—has presented some modern thinkers with the opportunity to reconstruct the Darwinian foundation in a most sinister way. In particular, the problem makes it possible to justify deviant sexual behavior and dub "normal" that which is actually evil.

Lawrence Birken, who teaches history at New York University, attacked the gender problem in Darwin and found a way to defend him.[26] Birken formulated the problem as follows: Division into sexes, that is, *sexual dimorphism*, began early in the history of life. In fact, Darwin said that a remote ancestor of the vertebrate kingdom possessed organs of both sexes. Sexes emerged as a form of speciation. By now, many differences between the sexes have appeared; *sexual differentiation* is the accumulation of these differences. As human beings evolved, the extent of sexual differentiation increased.[27]

Birken said that according to the conventional or more "conservative" reading of Darwin, as sexual differentiation increased, males changed more than females. In the nineteenth century many people believed that a hierarchy existed in human society; they saw a middle-class society based on the nuclear family, in which women were subservient to men. The family structure was the ultimate purpose of the long history of the evolution of sexual difference. Birken said that Darwin's work seemed to provide a biological justification of middle-class gendered order. Darwin himself concurred; he said that a physiological division of labor is a good thing.

But, said Birken, a more radical idea emerged from Darwin's teachings. What is important is how well an organism is adapted to its environment, not whether it is "higher" or "lower." There is no hierarchy. Birken said, "... the Darwinian scheme of natural selection among chance variations implies a democratization of life in an amoral universe .... Species come into being and pass away into oblivion simply on the basis of their success or failure in adapting to an ever-changing environment." The key phrase is "democratization of life"; all life is fundamentally equal. Birken said that life was once unified, so the hidden meaning of evolutionary theory emphasizes the equality of all life. In fact, said Birken, "Darwinism indeed contained the seeds of a conception of life that threatened to abolish gender itself." Darwin actually said that every man and woman is both male and female.[28]

Birken showed how reading Darwin the conservative way could be a means to keep women subservient. Women who chose to leave the place assigned to females in the hierarchy could be accused of going back to a primitive, undifferentiated phase of human evolution.[29] Birken said that conservatives also claimed that homosexuals, transvestites, and transsexuals are abnormal, and that the existence of two sexes is normal.

But in the late nineteenth and early twentieth centuries Sigmund Freud and other sexologists discovered men who thought they were women and women who thought they were men. The sex categories then multiplied, so that one sex shaded into another. The "normal" situation, in which there were only two sexes, no longer existed. Abnormal sex (a "conservative" phrase) and the evolutionary principle finally combined to blur the lines between gender; Birken said:

The doctrine of natural selection among chance variations relativized sex by making any possible combination of structure, sexuality or desire potentially viable. (Emphasis added.)

Birken's argument can now be summarized. Life at the beginning was unified and it still possesses that basic unity. Sex differences, just like species differences, arise later to fill niches, but changes are by chance only. All life is democratized; there is neither higher nor lower. Proof that one sex shades into another is the demonstrated existence of transsexuality. What was once called abnormal—a person's change from one sex to another—actually reflects the superficiality of gender difference and the reality of unity. What was once called normal—sex differentiation in the nuclear human family—is "an unnatural condition of civilization." The final result is that any sexual desire and any combination of male and female will survive.

Birken did not specifically mention modern efforts to normalize sex outside of marriage. But if sex differentiation in the modern family is, as he said, "an unnatural condition of civilization," then permitting and even encouraging sex outside of marriage is probably a consequence of his position. Nor did he specifically mention the unisex movement, which allows for and probably encourages homosexual behavior, lesbianism, and, in fact, any kind of "sexual preference," a phrase close to Birken's "desire" that is "potentially viable."

Most people who advocate unisex or demand rights for various kinds of sexual preference probably do not consciously follow the scholarly reasoning of people like Lawrence Birken. But here, as in so many other areas of life, action follows theory even if the activists have little contact with theory and theoreticians. Male entertainers who present a female public image, or female entertainers who strive to be like men, probably know very little of the Darwinian theoretical basis of the unisex movement. But ideas, even when understood by only a few, have consequences. Furthermore, theorists do not theorize in a vacuum: some of their theorizing arises from observation of what has already happened—in this case, some of the actions of radical feminists and others advocating "new" sexual lifestyles. There has been a back-and-forth interaction between action and theory with respect to sexual lifestyles, so that the modern breakup of the nuclear family is related to a general acceptance of the evolutionary origin of human beings.

The Bible obviously condemns the concept of evolution of sex. The very first biblical reference to human beings (Gen. 1:26-28) states that God created man in his image, male and female. Of course, there is massive biblical evidence indicating the fundamental nature of both male and female. Sexual differences have always existed; they are fundamental in Creation. All efforts to blur the difference between men and women are wrong.

Conclusion

The Argument. When the modern scientific enterprise began in the sixteenth century, it was assumed for the purpose of doing scientific work that the universe is closed. A corollary assumption made by many Christians was that while scientific results can illumine the Bible, the Bible cannot contribute to scientific investigation; those Christians are dualists. As the scientific enterprise progressed, many phenomena were indeed explained by laws formulated by human beings, that is, descriptive laws. When serious problems arose, that is, when investigators encountered phenomena they could not explain, scientists continued to assume that all phenomena are in principle explainable. Very great problems arose in the nineteenth century, when natural scientists made serious efforts to explain all biological phenomena. In both the nineteenth and twentieth centuries, when closed-universe scientists attempted to answer questions concerning origins, their attempts to invoke the principle of all-encompassing descriptive law encountered the greatest difficulty.

Thus, by the end of the twentieth century, immense problems have arisen in many areas. For example, if a big bang or something like it occurred, what is the ultimate source of the universe? What scenario could possibly explain the origin of the simplest life from the inorganic substances present on the primitive earth? Given the calculated mathematical probabilities, how could other forms of life have possibly evolved from the simplest cells in the relatively short time available, a few hundred million years? Why are there vast gaps in the fossil record?

Finally, even though naturalistic scholars have made many suggestions to account for the obvious qualitative differences between animals and human beings, no suggestion is convincing. Even people with great imagination have not been able to suggest a pathway for the derivation of human behavior, the arts, and human scientific activity from animal characteristics. Positivists—those who insist that scientific methods can account for everything in the universe—cannot find scientific justification for bizarre propositions, such as the claim that animals and human beings have equal rights, and the claim that deviant sex is normal.

The Future. We can now examine two answers to the question of origins. Both present a vision of the future. One answer is that general evolutionary theory is correct. The other denies that this theory can be general, since human beings did not descend from animals.

(1) If general evolutionary theory is correct, then all life and even human behavior and human institutions arose from a space-time "point." Furthermore, even that point arose from nothing by a natural process. Biological evolution is then driven by natural selection from the results of random events, with well-adapted organisms filling ecological niches. General evolutionary theory states that all these processes are natural and describable. If this theory is correct, what does the future hold?

The scientific community would require explanations for the present difficulties in evolutionary theory. Very likely scientists would follow the path already taken by those biologists who accept punctuated equilibrium theory as their answer to gaps in the fossil record. It would be tempting to solve other problems in evolutionary theory using something analogous to punctuated equilibrium theory. After all, punctuated equilibrium theory possesses one particularly useful property: it is a natural scientific theory that is not falsifiable. It describes a means of crossing fossil gaps that makes it practically impossible to find fossils in the gaps, and so the postulated mechanism of crossing cannot be disproved.[30] An unfalsifiable theory can be very useful.

If biological evolution, including human evolution, actually occurred, then future scientific efforts will firm up the linkage from animal to human behavior. After all, some investigators already claim partial success in attempts to establish that linkage; previous chapters described those attempts. Those who cling to the idea that the human body descended from animals, but that the human soul, with all its attributes—altruism, faith in God, vision for the future, and so forth—is something different, will increasingly find themselves on the defensive. To the extent that they are willing to debate with materialistic evolutionists, they will continually be asked, "Why *shouldn't* human behavior evolve from animal behavior?"

If evolutionary theory is valid, then efforts to provide evolutionary explanations for individual and group human behavior will eventually be successful. For example, up to now use of evolutionary theory to explain music—such as John Cage's "random" compositions—has not been convincing. Likewise, the immense influence of professional sports and other athletics on modern life suggests that people—like some of the characters in a Steinbeck or a Hemingway novel discussed in Chapter 13—believe in their hearts that human beings are animals. As people fantasize about athletics, do they unconsciously think of themselves as animals, with powerful legs enabling them to jump great heights, or with strong arms, enabling them to throw a ball with great skill? But the case has not yet been made; it is only a suggestion, waiting for an evolutionary theorist.

In the popular mind, the theory of evolution is a theory of progress. But there is a pessimistic and an optimistic school of thought. The pessimists say that progress—as ordinarily defined—will not necessarily take place. If general evolutionary theory is valid, unprogressive changes could occur. For pessimists, general evolutionary theory does not necessarily call for an ever-onward-and-upward view of human progress. Consider their reasoning. Roderick Nash, as quoted above, said that we know from Darwin that there is continuity from species to species, but the prime mover of evolution probably changed many times. An individual species is not so important. This concept leads to the position of the animal rightists and their insistence that species membership is not important and that speciesism is wrong. Combine with that idea Lawrence Birken's discovery of the "true meaning" of Darwinism. Using Darwin's theory, Birken said (as quoted above), "In [an amoral, democratic] universe, species come into being and pass away into oblivion simply on the basis of their success or failure in adapting to an ever-changing environment." Thus, human beings are no more than one species among many; evolution is permanent but individual species are not; because the environment changes, species pass into oblivion.

If evolutionary theory is correct, a species could pass into oblivion by one of two ways. Literature often implies one way: the environmental niche occupied by a species disappears and consequently the species dies out. Here the environment includes possible predators. For example, passenger pigeons were hunted until the species disappeared. Even apart from human activity, species constantly disappear; *Homo sapiens* could also disappear—truly, from dust to dust. After all, many of our institutions are already decaying; the family is decaying as gender is being wiped out. Other species would also die. Arable land, already under siege, will erode and disappear. Lethal environmental changes suggested are global warming and the disappearance of the ozone shield.

But if evolutionary theory is valid, there is a second way a species could disappear. If evolution occurred, could not devolution also occur? Perhaps almost all the members of a species would have to die out—possibly because of a natural disaster—before the process of devolution could begin. If the few remaining members of the species were then forced to occupy a niche other than the niche they previously occupied, in time they would adapt to the new niche. This new niche could be like one they had once occupied on their upward climb. If it is possible to take one downward step, then, according to the principles used in evolutionary theory, it is possible to take any desired number of downward steps. Could not human beings eventually devolve to any animal in our supposed ancestry?[31]

The optimistic school of thought has traditionally been more popular among evolutionists. The ever-onward-and-upward theme appears in a wide range of evolutionistic writings. Many theologians have been influenced by Pierre Teilhard de Chardin, who combined evolutionary theory with the Roman Catholic faith in describing the future trajectory of human life. According to de Chardin, the next stage in evolution is the formation of a "mind layer" (the *noosphere*) on earth; man is evolving toward the "omega point," when God will be "all in all."

Other evolutionistic optimists approach the question in a different way. They predict that eventually the earth could become an inhospitable place. But, they say, technological developments suggest that some day human beings may be able to move to distant planets. Such a move could occur even if the earth remained habitable. Robert John Russell, of the Center for Theology and the Natural Sciences in Berkeley, California, described this position from a liberal Christian point of view. After describing his evolutionistic understanding of life, Russell said:[32]

> Finally, what about the future? . . . . [T]he single most important fact we face is that the universe will continue for an almost inconceivably long time. The future of the universe is immense . . . . The solar system should last for another five billion years, and beyond it *the universe will probably exist for at least one hundred billion years—if not forever.* (Emphasis added.)

Russell said human beings could have a surprisingly important role to play during that very long time span:

> [W]hat cosmic role will life spawned on this tiny planet have over the countless billions of years ahead? The Bible portrays a future of supreme fulfillment for humankind—though the path ahead includes an Armageddon of strife and pain. *How are we to think and rethink the biblical drama in contemporary cosmic proportions?* (Emphasis added.)

When Russell urged us to rethink the biblical drama, he wanted us—as he stated in the following quotation—to consider what our science means for the future:

> Somehow I believe we must start by conceiving human nature as intimately connected to the universe as a whole. We must let the reality of this universe which science has revealed [the reality of human evolution] reshape to the core our understanding of our destiny and our responsibility to a universal future.

Russell believes that we are clever enough to avoid extinction; life could "continue for countless billions of years into the far future." He suggested that perhaps we will colonize the stars and become the voice, mind, and spirit of the universe. Many other optimistic evolutionists have also claimed that we will continue to evolve, and that eventually our descendants will populate planets thousands of light years distant.

These considerations show us that with both kinds of evolutionistic scenarios—pessimistic and optimistic—there is no eternal hope for anyone

Consequences 269

now living. All will die. The most the optimists can say is that the *human species* will survive. That forecast is not true optimism.

(2) Another vision for the future is based on the belief that human beings did not descend from animals. Also, the present scientific evidence against macroevolution in the animal and plant kingdoms is overwhelming. People who accept human evolution and macroevolution have been improperly swept along by the agenda of the scientific community. They have been blinded because the prevailing paradigm is evolutionistic. The impact of this evolutionary thinking has been harmful. With this understanding, what can we say about the future?

First, Christian natural scientists not influenced by the evolutionistic paradigm have a task that is as yet only partially completed. They have, of course, insisted that human beings were created unique. But these scientists should teach not only the unique creation of human beings but also the uniqueness of their calling, namely, the responsibility to care for Creation.

Along with teaching care for Creation, Christian natural scientists should also show people the magnificence of Creation. In the past, many of those scientists taught that the discovery of great ages and distances glorified God; the magnitude of his Creation is far greater than had previously been supposed. In the same way, Christian natural scientists have a calling to show how the discovery of large numbers of species, including those represented only by fossils, constitute an hierarchical structure that glorifies God. Christian natural scientists have not done nearly enough to teach the public how the discovery of the vast intricacy of the genetic code reveals our God to have performed mighty acts about which our predecessors in the Christian community knew nothing. In short, Christian natural scientists need to show that many of God's acts can be joyously proclaimed to be miracles.

The primary purpose of all such teaching must be to honor the Lord. It is only because of the denial of God's honor that this teaching must also have a secondary purpose, namely, the refutation of cosmologies that deny God's work. In our day, it is necessary to refute any cosmology that rests on the assumption of a universal evolutionary principle. Christian natural scientists could show that modern data deal a deadly blow to the evolutionistic paradigm.

But dealing a blow does not mean it will be received as a blow. Up to now, evolutionists have been singularly unwilling to listen to anything that might undermine their position. They talk endlessly about the rational nature of science and particularly how the evolutionary principle represents the triumph of rationalism. But they protest too much. They seem to be increasingly irrational. Perhaps just before the Lord returns, the opponents of his people will become completely irrational.

Concerning refutation of the evolutionary principle, Christian scholars outside the natural sciences have a task that is for one reason easier, but for another reason more difficult, than the task of Christian natural scientists. It is easier because many efforts to provide an evolutionary explanation in the human sciences—with some obvious exceptions, such as in psychology—are contested. But belief in the universality of the evolutionary principle, even though its application has often not been successful, is still widespread. Certainly Christians in the human sciences need to be on guard.

Their task is more difficult than that of Christian natural scientists because of the diversity of human life. By contrast, good nonevolutionary suggestions have been made for unifying principles in the physical sciences, and—excluding biological macroevolution—for unifying biotic phenomena. But because of the complexity of the human sciences, unifying theories abound. If Christians in the human sciences do not accept the animal ancestry of human beings, they have an unbelievably large task to provide a Christian understanding of that area of life. Of course, significant efforts have been made. But Christian scholars do not agree on the usefulness of these efforts.

The principal task of Christian scholars outside the natural sciences is the same as the first task of Christian natural scientists: everyone should demonstrate to all the world the greatness, the magnificence, and the surprises we receive as our understanding increases.

This second way of looking at the world, emphasizing creation and not evolution, speaks of hope—hope for individuals and all God's people. All Christian scholars can look forward to the time when the effects of our sins against God, against each other, and against his Creation will be taken away. We do not know about life in distant parts of the universe, perhaps in other galaxies. But we do know that there will be a new heaven as well as a new earth. *Then* our work will not be preoccupied with, or even concerned with, refutation of a theory. Our work will then focus solely on praising God himself.

Notes and References for Pages 5 - 11

Chapter 2. Background

1. Peter J. Bowler, *Evolution: The History of an Idea* (Berkeley: University of California Press, 1983, revised 1989), p. 20.
2. Raymond Coughlin and David E. Zitarelli, *The Ascent of Mathematics* (New York: McGraw-Hill, 1984), p. 82; a quotation from an ancient papyrus whose author was Ahmes, an Egyptian.
3. Charles Alexander Robinson, Jr., *Ancient History: From Prehistoric Times to the Death of Justinian* (New York: Macmillan, 1967), p. 166.
4. Paul Davies, *The Mind of God: The Scientific Basis for a Rational World* (New York: Simon and Schuster, 1992), p. 36.
5. Michael Denton, *Evolution: A Theory in Crisis* (Bethesda, Md.: Adler & Adler, 1985), pp. 37-40.
6. David N. Livingstone, "Evolution as Metaphor and Myth," *Christian Scholar's Review*, 12 (1983), 111-25; p. 112.
7. Edward Grant, "Science and Theology in the Middle Ages," in *God & Nature*, eds. David C. Lindberg and Ronald L. Numbers (Berkeley: University of California Press, 1986), pp. 52-53.
8. Robinson, p. 167.
9. Robinson, p. 284.
10. Robinson, p. 426.
11. Robinson, p. 428.
12. David C. Lindberg, "Science and the Early Church," in *God & Nature*, p.31; quoted from *The Library of Christian Classics*, trans. Albert C. Outler (Philadelphia: Westminster Press, 1955), 7:341-42.
13. Lindberg, p. 31; quoted from *The Literal Meaning of Genesis*, in *Ancient Christian Writers: The Works of the Fathers in Translation*, trans. John Hammond Taylor, ed. Johannes Quarten et al, (New York: Newman Press, 1982), 41:42-43.
14. Grant, p. 52.
15. Grant, p. 53.
16. Grant, p. 54.
17. Richard S. Westfall, "The Rise of Science and the Decline of Orthodox Christianity: A Study of Kepler, Descartes, and Newton," in *God & Nature*, p. 222.
18. James R. Moore, "Geologists and Interpreters of Genesis in the Nineteenth Century," in *God & Nature*, p. 322; quotations from Francis Bacon, *The Advancement of Learning* (1605), 1.1.3, 1.6.16.
19. Moore, p. 323.
20. *The Philosophical Works of Descartes*, trans. E.S. Haldane and G.R.T. Ross (Cambridge: Cambridge University Press, 1911, 1975 rpt. with corrections); Part II of *Discourse on the Method of Rightly Conducting the Reason and Seeking for Truth in the Sciences*, I, 92-93.
21. Thomas S. Kuhn, *The Structure of Scientific Revolutions*. Second Edition (Chicago: University of Chicago Press, 1970), p.41.
22. Pattle P.T. Pun, *Evolution: Nature and Scripture in Conflict?* (Grand Rapids: Zondervan, 1982), p. 30.
23. Roger Lewin, *Bones of Contention: Controversies in the Search for Human Origins* (New York: Simon and Schuster, 1987), pp. 302-03.
24. Ernst Mayr, "The Nature of the Darwinian Revolution," *Science*, 176 (1972), 981-89; pp. 983-84.
25. In the nineteenth century, evolutionists, who postulated change instead of fixed species,

appealed to the highly successful Newtonian analysis of mechanics of the seventeenth century. Motion was at the heart of the Newtonian revolution. In the same way, said evolutionists, life is characterized by motion. This is their argument in modern terms: Throw a ball in a dark room; use a strobe light to illuminate the ball at various points in its trajectory. What one sees—the ball at different places at different times—is analogous to the appearance of a species, its disappearance, the appearance of a slightly different species, its disappearance, and so forth; here, as with the moving object, there is motion. Perhaps the appeal to Newtonian mechanics is weakened by the more recent understanding that physical motion is not absolute, even though the appearance of a new species does seem to represent an absolute change.

26. Denton, p. 22.
27. Denton, p. 100
28. S.J. Gould, "Eternal Metaphors of Palaeontology," in *Patterns of Evolution*, ed. A. Hallam (Amsterdam: Elsevier, 1977), p. 7. Quoted by Denton, p. 104.
29. Brook Hindle, *The Pursuit of Science in Revolutionary America, 1735-1789* (New York: W.W. Norton, 1956), p. 11.
30. Angelo Costanzo, "Editor's Notes," *Proteus*, 6, No. 2 (1989), v. These notes are an introduction to an entire issue devoted to the influence of Darwinism.
31. Edgar Allan Poe, "The Murders in the Rue Morgue," in *The Complete Tales and Poems of Edgar Allan Poe* (New York: The Modern Library, 1938), p. 141.
32. Pun, p. 28.
33. Pun, p. 29.
34. J. Steve Oliver, Ronald D. Simpson, and Wyatt W. Anderson, "Darwin, Science Education, and the Method of Science," *Proteus*, 6, No. 2 (1989), 5-9; p. 5.
35. Denton, pp. 70-71.
36. Quoted by Denton, p. 72.
37. David N. Livingstone, "Evangelicals' Encounter with Evolutionary Theory," Consultation on Evangelicals and American Public Life, Philadelphia, May 1989; p. 19.
38. Livingstone, "Evolution," p.122.
39. Public Broadcasting System, NOVA, "God, Darwin, and the Dinosaurs"; February 21, 1989.
40. Colin Russell, *Cross-currents: Interactions Between Science & Faith* (Leicester: Inter-Varsity Press, 1985), pp. 193-94.
41. The principal work by Moore on this subject is J.M. Moore, *The Post-Darwinian Controversies: A Study of the Protestant Struggle to Come to Terms with Darwin in Great Britain and America 1870-1900* (Cambridge: Cambridge University Press, 1979). Others agreeing with Moore's main thesis are David N. Livingstone, *Darwin's Forgotten Defenders* (Grand Rapids: Eerdmans, 1987); Richard Aulie, "The Post-Darwinian Controversies," *Journal of the American Scientific Affiliation*, 34, Nos. 1-4 (1982) (a four-part review of Moore); and D. Gareth Jones, "Approaches to Evolutionary Theorizing: Some Nineteenth Century Perspectives," *Journal of the American Scientific Affiliation*, 35 (1983), 72-79.
42. Livingstone, "Evolution," p. 124.
43. James Ward Smith, "Religion and Science in American Philosophy," in *Religion in American Life*, eds. James Ward Smith and A. Leland Johnson (Princeton: Princeton University Press, 1961), I, 402-42; p. 422.
44. Livingstone, *Darwin's Forgotten Defenders*, p. 160.
45. Livingstone, *Darwin's Forgotten Defenders*, pp. 118-19.

46. E.S. Cassels, rev. of *The Darwinian Revolution: Science Red in Tooth and Claw*, by Michael Ruse, *Journal of the American Scientific Affiliation*, 32 (1980), 239.
47. Livingstone, *Darwin's Forgotten Defenders*, p. 166.
48. Livingstone, "Evangelicals' Encounter," p. 13.
49. Denton, p. 74.
50. Lewin, p. 60.
51. Oliver, Simpson, and Anderson, p. 6.
52. Pun, pp. 225-26.
53. Oliver, Simpson, and Anderson, p. 7.

Chapter 3. Design
1. Pattle P.T. Pun, *Evolution: Nature and Scripture in Conflict?* (Grand Rapids, MI: Zondervan, 1982), p. 237.
2. James Ward Smith, "Religion and Science in American Philosophy," in *Religion in American Life*, eds. James Ward Smith and A. Leland Johnson (Princeton: Princeton University Press, 1961), I, 402-42; p. 418.
3. Peter J. Bowler, *Evolution: The History of an Idea* (Berkeley: University of California Press, 1983, revised 1989), p. 105.
4. Thomas Huxley, "Agnosticism," in *Science and Christian Tradition* (New York: Appleton, 1896), pp. 245-46. Quoted by A. Hunter Dupree, "Christianity and the Scientific Community in the Age of Darwin," in *God & Nature*, eds. David C. Lindberg and Ronald L. Numbers (Berkeley: University of California Press, 1986), pp. 362-63.
5. Alvin Plantinga, "When Faith and Reason Clash: Evolution and the Bible," *Christian Scholar's Review*, 21, No. 1 (1991), 8-32; p. 13. This is the lead article in an important symposium. Following are the responses to Plantinga: Howard J. Van Till, "When Faith and Reason Cooperate," pp. 33-45; Pattle Pun, "Response to Professor Plantinga," pp. 46-54; Ernan McMullin, "Plantinga's Defense of Special Creation," pp. 55-79. Plantinga replied: "Evolution, Neutrality, and Antecedent Probability: A Reply to Van Till and McMullin," pp. 80-109.
6. Smith, pp. 402-04, 413, 436.
7. Davis A.Young, *Christianity and the Age of the Earth* (Grand Rapids: Zondervan, 1982), pp. 52-53.
8. Richard H. Bube, rev. of Creation by Natural Law: *Laplace's Nebular Hypothesis in American Thought*, by Ronald L. Numbers, *Journal of the American Scientific Affiliation*, 29 (1977), 186-87; Charles E. Chaffey, rev. of Creation, *Journal of the American Scientific Affiliation*, 30 (1978), 93.
9. Donald Worster, *Nature's Economy: A History of Ecological Ideas* (Cambridge: Cambridge University Press, 1977), p. 37; quoted by Richard T. Wright, *Biology Through the Eyes of Faith* (San Francisco: Harper and Row, 1989), pp. 51-52.
10. Michael Denton, *Evolution: A Theory in Crisis* (Bethesda, Md.: Adler & Adler, 1985), p. 20.
11. Louis Agassiz, *Essay on Classification*, ed. Edward Lurie (Cambridge: Belknap Press of Harvard University Press, 1962), p. 137.
12. Pun, p. 226.
13. Pun, p. 27.
14. William Paley, *The Works of William Paley* (London: T. Nelson & Sons, 1853), p. 498. Quoted in David N. Livingstone, *Darwin's Forgotten Defenders* (Grand Rapids: Eerdmans, 1987), p. 4.
15. Livingstone, *Darwin's Forgotten Defenders*, p.4

16. Richard Aulie, "The Post-Darwinian Controversies, Part Four," *Journal of the American Scientific Affiliation*, 34 (1982), 219-24.
17. Glenn A. Remelts, "The Christian Reformed Church and Science, 1900-1930," *Fides et Historia*, 21, No.1 (1989), 61-80; p. 76.
18. David N. Livingstone, "Evangelicals' Encounter with Evolutionary Theory," Consultation on Evangelicals and American Public Life, Philadelphia, May 1989, p. 7.
19. David N. Livingstone, "The Darwinian Diffusion: Darwin and Darwinism, Divinity and Design," *Christian Scholar's Review*, 19 (1989), 186-99; p. 197.
20. Livingstone, "Evangelicals' Encounter," p. 10.
21. Denton, p. 306.
22. Gary Colwell, "Malice in Blunderland," *Journal of the American Scientific Affiliation*, 26 (1974), 99-101.
23. Denton, p. 96.
24. Denton, p. 290.
25. Kenneth W. Hermann, "Orthodoxy and the Challenge of Positivist Biology," *Journal of the American Scientific Affiliation*, 36 (1984), 169-76; pp. 171-72. Also, Neal C. Gillespie, *Charles Darwin and the Problem of Design* (Chicago: University of Chicago Press, 1979); see, for example, p. 88.
26. Aulie, p. 220.
27. Livingstone, *Darwin's Forgotten Defenders*, p. 5.
28. Charles Darwin, *The Origin of Species*, in *The Origin of Species* and *The Descent of Man* (New York: Modern Library, 1936), p. 149.
29. Richard Dawkins, *The Blind Watchmaker* (New York: W.W. Norton, 1986), p. 93.
30. Gillespie, pp. 83-85, 96-97.

Chapter 4. Objections to Design
1. David N. Livingstone, *Darwin's Forgotten Defenders* (Grand Rapids: Eerdmans, 1987), p. 5.
2. Richard T. Wright, *Biology Through the Eyes of Faith* (San Francisco: Harper and Row, 1989), pp. 57-58. This book, cosponsored by the Christian College Coalition, is one of a series designed to meet the needs of Christian college students.
3. Kenneth W. Hermann, "Orthodoxy and the Challenge of Positivist Biology," *Journal of the American Scientific Affiliation*, 36 (1984), 169-76; p. 173.
4. Some non-Christians have presented the most effective scientific arguments against evolutionary theory, theory that above all denies design. These objections have generally been among the most difficult for evolutionists to answer.
5. Livingstone, p. 4.
6. David N. Livingstone, "Evangelicals' Encounter with Evolutionary Theory," Consultation on Evangelicals and American Public Life, Philadelphia, May 1989; p. 19.
7. Richard Dawkins, *The Blind Watchmaker* (New York: Norton, 1986), p. 5.
8. Michael Denton, *Evolution: A Theory in Crisis* (Bethesda, Md.: Adler & Adler, 1985), pp. 39-40.
9. Dawkins, pp. 43-74. This is Chapter 3, "Accumulating Small Change."
10. Alvin Plantinga, "When Faith and Reason Clash: Evolution and the Bible," *Christian Scholar's Review*, 21, No. 1 (1991), 8-32; p. 18.
11. R.J. Herrnstein, "Darwinism and Behaviourism: Parallels and Intersections," in *Evolution and Its Influence*, ed. Alan Grafen (Oxford: Clarendon Press, 1989), pp. 35-61.
12. Herrnstein, p. 47.

13. Herrnstein, p. 41.
14. Although stating the problem this way neglects quantum mechanical uncertainty, it is a fair characterization of the optimism of those who hold to a closed universe.
15. However, Numbers 14:22 contains a *general* reference to signs (Hebrew: *othe*, usually translated as sign, but also as ensign, mark, miracle, and token) that God performed in the desert.
16. John D. Barrow and Frank J. Tipler, *The Anthropic Cosmological Principle* (Oxford: Oxford University Press, 1988), pp. 69-70.
17. David Hume, *Dialogues Concerning Natural Religion*, ed. N. Kemp Smith (Indiana: Bobbs Merrill, 1977). Cited in Barrow and Tipler, p. 71.
18. Immanuel Kant, *Critique of Pure Reason*, trans. J.M.D. Meiklejohn (New York: Dutton, 1934). Taken from the preface to the second edition (1787), p. 10.
19. Owen Gingerich, "Let There Be Light" (Montreal: Idea Series CBC [Canadian Broadcasting Corporation] Transcripts, December 26, 1988), p. 7.
20. Fred Hoyle in *Engineering and Science*, November, 1981; publication of the California Institute of Technology, Pasadena. Quoted in Gingerich, p. 7.
21. James Ward Smith, "Religion and Science in American Philosophy," in *Religion in American Life*, eds. James Ward Smith and A. Leland Johnson (Princeton: Princeton University Press, 1961), I, 402-42; p. 420.
22. John Wheeler, Foreword, Barrow and Tipler, p. vii.
23. Barrow and Tipler, p. 4.
24. Barrow and Tipler, pp. 6-8.
25. The "at rest" claim must be linked to time. After all, a particle such as an electron may have a velocity in one direction and then later in the reverse direction; since velocity in one direction is positive and negative in the reverse direction, the velocity of such a particle must pass through zero. But the principle says that we do not know at *what* time its velocity is zero. Thus, the argument presented here shows that its velocity does not remain zero, as it would were it at rest. We can make the same conclusion for any other velocity, say, 1000 meters per second: if we know the approximate position of an electron (for example, within the beaker), there is no way of saying that at a particular time its velocity is exactly 1000 meters per second, even though its velocity might pass through that value. One eventual objection to the pre-quantum mechanical Bohr model of the hydrogen atom was that the model permitted one to calculate an exact, constant velocity for an electron moving in a circle a known distance from the nucleus. The model provided more information than was justified.
26. Some physicists now maintain that assuming electrons have position and velocity is not valid, and that these quantities have meaning only for much larger objects. They claim that one cannot go beyond the uncertainty principle, that is, one cannot assume the reality of something unmeasurable. Their claim does not, however, invalidate my conclusion: because we are part of the systems we observe, physical things, space, and time are united in our perception. In addition, an entirely different, more sophisticated argument, one depending on relativity theory, also leads to the conclusion that physical things, space, and time are related; here, emphasis is not on our perception, but on our frame of reference.

Chapter 5. Scientific Consensus: The Scenario
1. If one uses evolutionary theory to explain *only* physical and biological phenomena, "natural" phenomena, then the dualistic division of phenomena poses a problem for Christians. Such a division suggests that everything human which is not characteristic of animals

(or conceivably derived from animal characteristics) is supernatural—a position that is, to say the least, awkward.

2. Davis Young, Daniel Wonderly, and Alan Hayward (a Christian physicist in England) have summarized much of the evidence concerning age presented in this chapter. These sources also provide considerable additional geological and astronomical evidence, discussion of the arguments of those opposed to the concept of great age, and numerous references to the original literature. See the following: (a) Davis A. Young, *Creation and the Flood: An Alternative to Flood Geology and Theistic Evolution* (Grand Rapids: Baker Book House, 1977); Chapter 7, "Radiometric Dating," in *Christianity and the Age of the Earth* (Grand Rapids: Zondervan, 1982), pp. 93-116. (b) Daniel E. Wonderly, "Non-Radiometric Data Relevant to the Question of Age," *Journal of the American Scientific Affiliation*, 27 (1975), 149-52; *Neglect of Geologic Data: Sedimentary Strata Compared with Young-Earth Creationist Writings* (Hatfield, Pa.: Interdisciplinary Biblical Research Institute, 1987). (c) Alan Hayward, *Creation and Evolution* (London: Triangle, 1985), pp. 69-157.

3. Wonderly, "Non-Radiometric Data," p. 149.

4. What about the small amount of argon in the atmosphere? Could it not diffuse into the rock and make it seem that the rock is very old? If diffusion occurs, one can determine how much argon diffused into the rock. Therefore, one can correct for the diffusion. Such correction is possible because atmospheric argon consists of both argon-36 and argon-40 in a known ratio; any argon-36 in the rock serves as a "tag," indicating how much argon-40 in the rock is not due to decay of potassium-40. Furthermore, potassium-argon dating of rocks on the moon, which has virtually no atmosphere to pollute the rock, yields ages of several billion years. See Young, *Christianity*, pp. 101-02.

5. D. York and R.M. Farquhar, *The Earth's Age and Geochronology* (Oxford: Pergamon Press, 1972), p. 75.

6. One of the better radiometric methods utilizes the decay of rubidium-87 to strontium-87. Both rubidium and strontium are metals which are parts of compounds found in igneous rocks, and so one cannot assume, as one could with the production of the gas argon, that no decay product was present in the initial molten material. In fact, for many years the question of the amount of strontium-87 present when a rock began to cool constituted a significant problem. What was lacking was confidence that the present ratio of strontium-87 to strontium-86 in the various sources of strontium is the same as the ratio when the rocks formed. The assumption was that the value has not changed, that is, that it always had its present value of about 0.71.

The newer, "whole rock" method solves that problem. This method depends upon the determination of the *present* relative amounts of three isotopes, rubidium-87, strontium-86, and strontium-87 in *different* minerals of the *same* rock. By a straightforward mathematical method, the method yields the initial ratio of strontium-87 to strontium-86. The initial ratio, no longer assumed, was between 0.71 and 0.72. This is one of the many verifications found among independent methods that determine the ages of rocks.

7. Owen Gingerich, "Let There Be Light" (Montreal: Idea Series CBC [Canadian Broadcasting Corporation] Transcripts, December 26, 1988), p. 3.

8. One unorthodox radiometric method addresses the question of whether the earth is young—say, ten thousand years old—as some people claim. To understand the method, first consider neptunium-237, the first member of a natural radioactive decay sequence. We cannot, however, find neptunium-237 in minerals or in any natural source. But we can synthesize it in nuclear reactors and measure its half-life. Those who claim the earth is very old maintain that we cannot find this isotope because its half-life, 2.2 million years, is

too short, Thus, if it were present at the beginning, in 2.2 million years only half the initial amount would be present; in 4.4 million years, only one-fourth; in 6.6 million years, one-eighth; and so forth. Obviously, if the earth is several billion years old, we could not find neptunium-237 today; the "missing" neptunium-237 could indicate the earth is very old.

Of course, a person who claims the earth is but ten thousand years old would very likely maintain that neptunium-237 was not present at the time of creation. Fair enough. But a problem arises because neptunium-237 is not the only "missing" isotope. Here is the critical piece of information: all 40 radioactive isotopes whose half-lives are between 1,000 years and 50 million years are *missing* in nature; all 17 radioactive isotopes with half-lives greater than 50 million years are *present* in nature. If the earth is several billion years old, then even for a 50-million year half life, many half-lives have elapsed since the beginning: one would not expect to find now in nature a substance with a half-life of as much as 50 million years. But if the earth is young—say, 10,000 years old—all 57 (40 plus 17) isotopes would be present in nature now *if* they were present initially. Yet, since we know of some of these isotopes only because we can synthesize them, it would not be necessary for all 57 to be present; on a random basis, some could have been present, others absent. In a young earth we would at the present time find whichever of the 57 isotopes were present initially. What, then, is the probability that the 40 short-lived isotopes would be missing and the 17 long-lived would be present at the beginning? Calculation shows that the probability of such a distribution at the beginning, compared to all possible random distributions, is less than one part in 100,000 billion; this is thus also the probability that the earth is young. [See Jerry D. Albert, *Journal of the American Scientific Affiliation*, 33 (1981), 253. Albert summarizes an article by Stanley Freske, "Evidence Supporting a Great Age for the Universe," in the Fall, 1980 issue of *Creation/Evolution*.]

9. For the distances to planets and stars, it is convenient to take a picture of the object of interest against the background of very distant stars. Then when two pictures are taken from different points on the base line, the pictures can be superimposed so that the fixed stars are in the same position. But the nearby object will appear in two places in the combined picture. The distance between the positions of the nearby object in the combined picture can be used to determine its distance from the base line. In all the examples given, the background pattern has but one purpose: it establishes direction. Thus, directing one's vision or pointing a telescope or a camera at the same point in the distant star pattern from the two points of observation insures that the first two imaginary lines will be essentially parallel.
10. Some cosmologists claim that the big bang could not have occurred as it has been described since the 1940s. I describe some of the alternate theory here, but the reader should be warned that some of the dissenters maintain that in a few years we will not even be discussing a big bang. The philosophical component of this new attitude has arisen partly because a big bang is too much in agreement with the Christian conception of creation; see John Maddox, "Down with the Big Bang," *Nature*, 340 (1989), 425.
11. Some of the material of the remainder of this chapter is a summary of part of the Appendix to "Report of the Synodical Study Committee on Creation and Science" to the Synod of 1991 of the Christian Reformed Church, held in Sioux Center, Iowa. The purpose of the Appendix is to present the consensus on origins in the natural scientific community.
12. For example, Henry E. Kandrup and Pawel O. Mazur constructed a specific mathematical model in which they postulated that the universe "tunneled into being" via a quantum

fluctuation. (Although "tunneled" has a technical meaning here, its common meaning conveys the idea intended in this description of the big bang.) [See Henry E. Kandrup and Pawel O. Mazur, "Generating a Hot Big Bang," 14th Texas Symposium on Relativistic Astrophysics, Dallas, Texas, December 1988; University of Florida preprint UFIFT-AST-89-6, January 1989.]
13. Stephen W. Hawking, *A Brief History of Time* (Toronto: Bantam Books, 1988), p. 141.
14. Bob Davis, "Beyond Big Bang," *Wall Street Journal*, Jan. 2, 1991, Sec. A, p. 1, col. 1.
15. Calculations based on this model predict that 25 percent of the nuclei in the universe are helium nuclei; the value found ranges from 20 to 25 percent, a reasonable agreement with prediction. [See Barry Parker, *Creation: The Story of the Origin and Evolution of the Universe* (New York: Plenum Press, 1988), pp. 162-63.]
16. J.C. Mather et al., "A Preliminary Measurement of the Cosmic Microwave Background Spectrum by the Cosmic Background Explorer (COBE) Satellite," NASA/Goddard Space Flight Center, Preprint No. 90-91, January, 1990.
17. James P. Ferris and David A. Usher, "Origins of Life," in *Biochemistry*, ed. Geoffrey Zubay (New York: Macmillan, 1988), p. 1126. Some of the material given later in this section is taken from this chapter and other parts of the volume.
18. Michael Denton, *Evolution: A Theory in Crisis* (Bethesda, Md.: Adler & Adler, 1985), p. 235.
19. Charles B. Thaxton, Walter L. Bradley, and Roger L. Olsen, *The Mystery of Life's Origin: Reassessing Current Theories* (New York: Philosophical Library, 1984), p.15.

Chapter 6. Analysis: From Inert Matter to Cells
1. For a discussion of the oxygen question and references to the original literature, see Charles B. Thaxton, Walter L. Bradley, and Roger L. Olsen, *The Mystery of Life's Origin: Reassessing Current Theories* (New York: Philosophical Library, 1984), pp. 76-93. Thaxton is a chemist and Director of Curriculum Research of the Foundation for Thought and Ethics, Dallas, Texas; Bradley is a professor of mechanical engineering at Texas A & M University; and Olsen is a geochemist with D'Appolonia Waste Management Services in Englewood, Colorado.
2. Thaxton, Bradley, and Olsen, p. 79.
3. Thaxton, Bradley, and Olsen, pp. 82 and 87.
4. Thaxton, Bradley, and Olsen, pp. 87-93.
5. James P. Ferris and David A. Usher, "Origins of Life," in *Biochemistry*, ed. Geoffrey Zubay, 2nd ed. (New York: Macmillan, 1988), p. 1128.
6. A.I. Oparin, *Origin of Life*, trans. Sergius Morgulis (1938; rpt. New York: Dover, 1953), p. 33.
7. Thaxton, Bradley, and Olsen, esp. Chapter 5, "Reassessing the Early Earth and Its Atmosphere," *Mystery*, pp. 69-98.
8. Richard M. Lemmon, "Life's Origin and the Supernatural," *Chemical and Engineering News*, July 1, 1985; p. 26. This is a review of Thaxton, Bradley, and Olsen, *Mystery*. Lemmon errs in his reference to creationism. In the context of this book, it is correct to speak of special creation [cf. Thaxton, et al, pp. 196-210], not creationism. The authors did not give evidence of holding other ideas characteristic of the creationism movement.
9. Thaxton, Bradley, and Olsen, pp. 99-110.
10. Michael Denton, *Evolution: A Theory in Crisis* (Bethesda, Md: Adler & Adler, 1985), pp. 254-57.
11. Denton, p. 258.

12. Jerry D. Albert, "New Insights into Thermodynamics," *Journal of the American Scientific Affiliation*, 30 (1978), 143.
13. Walter Bradley, Letter, *Journal of the American Scientific Affiliation*, 31 (1979), 127-28.
14. Ilya Prigogine, Gregoire Nicolis, and Agnes Babloyantz, "Thermodynamics of Evolution," *Physics Today*, 25, No. 11 (1972), 23-28; p. 28. For a discussion by the same authors of pre-biological evolution, see: *Physics Today*, 25, No. 12 (1972), 38-44.
15. Aaldert Van Der Ziel, "Random Processes and Evolution," *Journal of the American Scientific Affiliation*, 27 (1975), 160-64; p. 163.
16. Evolutionists, who maintain that more prolific species dominate and eventually replace others, ought to be consistent and contend that the more probable chemical reactions ultimately "take over."
17. Research continues on how the complicated molecules necessary for life first formed. Thus, in the 1980s many evolutionists held that at one time DNA was not needed; its role was filled by the much smaller, and therefore much simpler, RNA. People spoke of the early "RNA world." This approach still has its adherents, but formidable problems have arisen. In sum, this proposal seems not to solve the problems that biochemists have faced ever since the discovery of the DNA code in 1953. For a semipopular account of these developments, see John Horgan, "In the Beginning..." *Scientific American*, 264, No. 2 (1991), 116-25.
18. *Mathematical Challenges to the Neo-Darwinian Interpretation of Evolution*, eds. Paul S. Moorhead and Martin M. Kaplan (Philadelphia: The Wistar Institute Press, 1967).
19. John McIntyre, rev. of *Mathematical Challenges*, eds. Paul S. Moorhead and Martin M. Kaplan, *Journal of the American Scientific Affiliation*, 24 (1972), 70-72.
20. Jacques Monod, *Chance and Necessity*, trans. Austryn Wainhouse (New York: Knopf, 1971), p. 144.
21. Gordon C. Mills, "Hemoglobin Structure and the Biogenesis of Proteins. Part II. Significance of Protein Structure to the Biogenesis of Life," *Journal of the American Scientific Affiliation*, 27 (1975), 79-82; p. 79.
22. One of the greatest difficulties in constructing a plausible model for the formation of the first cells is that different substances in the functioning cell require separate evolutionary processes. Thus, T. Dobzhansky, F.J. Ayala, G.L. Stebbins, and J.W. Valentine [*Evolution* (San Francisco: Freeman, 1977) pp. 358-60], well-known evolutionists, said that natural selection, the accepted process for evolution, requires both proteins and nucleic acids, even though the origin of the relation of the two classes of substances surely required selection. [Cited in *Teaching Science in a Climate of Controversy: A View from the American Scientific Affiliation* (Ipswich, Mass.: American Scientific Affiliation, 1989), p. 32.]
23. Fred Hoyle and N.C. Wickramasinghe, *Evolution from Space: A Theory of Cosmic Creationism* (New York: Simon and Schuster, 1981), p. 24. For additional, but earlier, discussion of the concept that the first living cells on earth came from other places, see: Hoyle and Wickramasinghe, *Lifecloud: The Origin of Life in the Universe* (London: J.M. Dent, 1978).
24. Natural selection is the process whereby (a) species survive because they are more prolific than their competitors, and (b) they are more prolific because they are better suited to their environment.
25. Charles H.Townes, "How and Why Did It All Begin?" *Journal of the American Scientific Affiliation*, 24 (1972), 1-4; p. 2.
26. Peter Vorzimmer, *Charles Darwin: The Years of Controversy* (London: London University Press, 1972), p. 100; cited by Denton, p. 63.
27. George Gaylord Simpson, a noted American evolutionist, argued in this way. [See Simp-

son, "The Problem of Plan and Purpose in Nature," *Scientific Monthly*, 64 (1947), 481-95; p. 493.]
28. Denton, p. 186.
29. Harold J. Morowitz, "The Minimum Size of Cells," in *Principles of Biomolecular Organization*, eds. G.E.W. Wolstenhome and Maeve O'Connor (London: Churchill, 1966), 446-62; pp. 454-56.
30. Robert C. Newman, "Self-Reproducing Automata and the Origin of Life," *Perspectives on Science and Christian Faith*, 40 (1988), 24-31.
31. E.F. Codd, *Cellular Automata* (New York: Academic Press, 1968).
32. Christopher G. Langton, "Self-Reproduction in Cellular Automata," *Physica*, 10D (1984), 135-44.
33. John Byl, "On Cellular Automata and the Origin of Life," *Perspectives on Science and Christian Faith*, 41 (1989), 26-29.
34. Robert C. Newman, "Automata and the Origin of Life: Once Again," *Perspectives on Science and Christian Faith*, 42 (1990), 113-14. The debate about origins between Newman and Byl is refreshing for a reason quite apart from the content of the debate: both are Christian scientists and neither allows the impact of evolutionary thought on modern society to skew his thinking. For a discussion of computer-generated "life" forms based on a different worldview, see Paul Davies, *The Mind of God: The Scientific Basis for a Rational World* (New York: Simon and Schuster, 1992), especially pp. 110-16.
35. Denton, pp. 328-29.
36. Michael Polanyi, "Life Transcending Physics and Chemistry," *Chemical and Engineering News*, Aug. 21, 1967, pp.54-66; esp. pp. 60-61.
37. This summary is taken from Thaxton, Bradley, and Olsen, pp. 196-200. See Hoyle and Wickramasinghe, *Evolution*, esp. Chapter 8, "Insects from Space?" pp. 117-28.
38. Thaxton, Bradley, and Olsen, p. 194.
39. Pierre Teilhard de Chardin, *The Phenomenon of Man*, trans. Bernard Wall (New York: Harper and Row, 1965). (*Le Phenomene de l'homme*, the original French edition, appeared in 1955.)
40. H. James Birx, "Darwin & Teilhard: Some Final Thoughts," *Proteus*, 6, No. 2 (1989), 38-46; p. 39. But Birx contended that Teilhard would not have been a vitalist had he known of DNA.
41. The literature on Teilhard is extensive. For reviews by Christians of four books about Teilhard's approach, see *Journal of the American Scientific Affiliation*, 22 (1970), 23-27.
42. Henri Blocher, *In the Beginning: The Opening Chapters of Genesis*, trans. David G. Preston (Downers Grove, Ill.: Inter-Varsity Press, 1984), p. 223.
43. Birx, p. 39.
44. Birx, pp. 41-42.
45. William R. Fix, *The Bone Peddlers: Selling Evolution* (New York: Macmillan, 1984). Quotation from a review by B.J. Piersma, *Journal of the American Scientific Affiliation*, 36 (1984), 253-54.

Chapter 7. Analysis: From Cells to Humans
1. Michael Denton, *Evolution: A Theory in Crisis* (Bethesda, Md: Adler & Adler, 1985), p. 178.
2. Denton, p. 157 and pp. 178-80.
3. Denton, pp. 79-83.
4. Denton, pp. 88-90.
5. *Teaching Science in a Climate of Controversy: A View from the American Scientific Affiliation* (Ipswich, Mass.: American Scientific Affiliation, 1989), pp. 34-35.

6. George Gaylord Simpson, "The History of Life," in *The Evolution of Life*, ed. Sol Tax (Chicago: University of Chicago Press, 1960), I, 117-80; p. 149.
7. G.A. Kerkut, *Implications of Evolution* (Oxford: Pergamon Press, 1960), pp. 18-35, 49, 99-100, 111, and 151-53.
8. Pattle P.T. Pun, *Evolution: Nature and Scripture in Conflict?* (Grand Rapids: Zondervan, 1982), p. 53.
9. Denton, pp. 162-65.
10. N.C. Gillespie, *Charles Darwin and the Problem of Creation* (Chicago: University of Chicago Press, 1979), pp. 74-75.
11. Denton, p. 160.
12. Pun, p. 159.
13. A.S. Romer, *Vertebrate Paleontology* (Chicago: University of Chicago Press, 1966), pp. 347-96; data compiled by Denton, pp. 189-90.
14. Denton, p. 326.
15. Richard Goldschmidt, *The Material Basis of Evolution* (1940; rpt. New Haven: Yale University Press, 1982), pp. 6-7.
16. Denton, pp. 219-20.
17. For a more complete discussion of this evolutionary problem, see Pun, pp. 209-15; Denton, Chapter 12, "A Biochemical Echo of Typology," pp. 274-307; and Phillip E. Johnson, *Darwin on Trial* (Downers Grove, IL: InterVarsity Press, 1991), especially Chapter 7, "The Molecular Evidence," pp. 86-99. Richard T. Wright concluded that the molecular data provide evidence that human beings descended from animals; see Richard T. Wright, *Biology Through the Eyes of Faith* (San Francisco: Harper and Row, 1989), pp. 146-47. In the 1991 *Christian Scholar's Review* symposium described in Reference 5 of Chapter 3, McMullin defends the molecular method (pp. 67-68), while Plantinga presents evidence suggesting that the method is not reliable (pp. 105-109).
18. Roger Lewin, *Bones of Contention: Controversies in the Search for Human Origins* (New York: Simon and Schuster, 1987), pp. 121-22.
19. Pun (p. 207) described the method of determining the difference between DNA strands. Bring together single strands of DNA from two different organisms to make double strands. Isolate the new double strands and analyze to determine the extent of strand-to-strand bonding. Or, after the double strands have formed, raise the temperature until the single strands appear again; the higher the temperature of breaking, the more bonds that were broken. The more strand-to-strand bonds that form, the greater the similarity between the DNA of the two species.
20. Pun, pp. 207-08.
21. *Teaching Science*, p. 40.
22. Elwyn Simons, "The Origin and Radiation of the Primates," *Annals of the New York Academy of Sciences*, 167 (1968), 319-31; p. 330; quoted by Lewin (pp. 110-11).
23. Denton, p. 176.
24. Denton, p. 105.
25. Pun, pp. 137-38.
26. For discussions of punctuated equilibria by Stephen Jay Gould and Niles Eldredge and Roger Lewin's analysis, see the following: (a) Eldredge and Gould, "Punctuated Equilibria: An Alternative to Phyletic Gradualism," in *Models in Paleobiology*, ed. T.J.M. Schopf (San Francisco: Freeman, 1972), pp. 82-115. (b) Gould and Eldredge, "Punctuated Equilibria: The Tempo and Mode of Evolution Reconsidered," *Paleobiology*, 3 (1977), 115-51. (c) Gould, *The Panda's Thumb: More Reflections in Natural History* (New York:

Norton, 1980), pp. 177-213. (d) Gould, "Is a New and General Theory of Evolution Emerging?" *Paleobiology*, 6 (1980), 119-30. (e) Gould, "The Paradox of the First Tier: An Agenda for Paleobiology," *Paleobiology*, 11 (1985), 2-12. (f) Roger Lewin, "Evolutionary Theory Under Fire," *Science*, 210 (1980), 883-87.
27. Gould, *Panda's Thumb*, p. 181.
28. Wright, p. 129.
29. Two mechanisms, both extensively investigated in recent years, are thought by some to bring about a significant genetic changes in one generation. One involves sexual recombination: the genetically-different parents each make a significant contribution to the genetic makeup of their offspring. John Rennie ["DNA's New Twists," *Scientific American*, 266 (3) (1993), 122-32] summarizes work on the other mechanism, in which DNA can be affected by its environment, enabling acquired characteristics to be inherited.
30. Pun, p. 224. For a discussion of the term "hopeful monster" see Goldschmidt, pp. 390-93.
31. "The Search for Adam and Eve," *Newsweek*, Jan. 11, 1988, pp. 46-52. Since 1988, the date has been modified.
32. Many paleoanthropologists do not accept the "African Eve theory." Thus, at the February, 1990, meeting of the American Association for the Advancement of Science in New Orleans, Louisiana, David Frayer, Geoffrey Pope, and others maintained that fossil evidence indicates modern human beings evolved from several animal sources; this is the "multiregional origin" theory, as opposed to the "African origin" theory. The claim is made that human beings evolved separately in Europe, Africa, Asia (fossils from Hubei Province in China have been studied), and Australia.
33. Richard E. Leakey and Roger Lewin, *Origins: What New Discoveries Reveal About the Emergence of Our Species and Its Possible Future* (New York: Dutton, 1977), p. 91.
34. Since often cross-checks are not easily available, an analyst might not detect the error due to the loss of argon gas over long periods if the only determination is of the potassium-40/argon-40 ratio. If, however, an analyst uses an extremely sensitive method to determine this ratio and analyzes the center of a crystal and parts of the crystal which vary in distance from the center, it is possible to decide whether argon was lost. If the concentration of argon-40 (relative to potassium-40) decreases going out from the center, then argon was lost over the long periods involved; if not, the age obtained is far more reliable. To make this sensitive determination, the analyst bombards the sample containing potassium-40 and argon-40 with neutrons. This procedure converts potassium-40 to argon-39. The analyst can then use a very good method for the determination of the argon-40/argon-39 ratio. These results permit the analyst to deduce the potassium-40/argon-40 ratio in the various parts of the original crystal. See Lewin, *Bones*, pp. 192-93.
35. *Teaching Science*, p. 41; Pun, p. 266; Wright, pp.145-46; Leakey and Lewin, p. 125.
36. Leakey and Lewin, pp. 197-98.
37. Pun, pp. 112-17.
38. James M. Houston, "The Origin of Man," *Journal of the American Scientific Affiliation*, 34 (1982), 1-5. Reprinted from James M. Houston, *I Believe in the Creator* (Grand Rapids: Eerdmans, 1980).
39. Lewin, *Bones*, pp. 23-24.
40. Lewin, *Bones*, p. 173.
41. Selfishness is not new in this field. In the 1890s one man hid the fossils he had found under the floor boards of his house. See Lewin, *Bones*, p. 23.
42. Lewin, *Bones*, p. 132.

Notes and References for Pages 114 - 122   283

43. Lewin, *Bones*, p. 300.
44. From the television series, *The Making of Mankind*, 1979; quoted in *Teaching Science*, p. 42.
45. Lewin, *Bones*.
46. Often anti-evolutionists consider the notorious Piltdown hoax as evidence of a conspiracy on the part of the establishment. But refutation came from the establishment. In Chapter 2 I referred to an admission of Lewin (*Bones*, p.60), an evolutionist, namely, that because of the paucity of evidence the Piltdown "fossil" held the British anthropological community in its thrall for four decades. Such a situation is virtually impossible in other sciences.
47. From *Essays on the Evolution of Man* (Oxford: Oxford University Press, 1924), p. 55; quoted by Lewin, *Bones*, p. 19.
48. Lewin, *Bones*, p. 19.
49. Lewin, *Bones*, p. 85.
50. David Pilbeam, "Rethinking Human Origins," *Discovery*, 13 (1978), 2-9; p. 9; quoted by Lewin, *Bones*, p. 85.
51. Pilbeam, "Rethinking," pp. 8-9; quoted by Lewin, *Bones*, pp. 126-27.
52. Lewin, *Bones*, p. 95.
53. Loren Eiseley, "The Immense Journey," in *Evolution of Man*, ed. Louise Young (New York: Oxford University Press, 1970), pp. 266-75; pp. 271-72. "The Immense Journey" is excerpted from Loren Eiseley, *The Immense Journey* (New York: Random House, 1955).
54. For brain sizes of primates and human beings see, for example: Leakey and Lewin, pp. 198-99; Wright, p. 145.
55. Lewin, *Bones*, p. 314.
56. From a 1953 article by Raymond Dart, "The Predatory Transition from Ape to Man"; quoted by Lewin, *Bones*, p. 314.
57. Lewin, *Bones*, pp. 316-17.
58. John Durant, "The Myth of Human Evolution," *New Universities Quarterly*, 35, (1981), 425-38; p. 432; quoted by Lewin, *Bones*, p. 318. Durant is a scientist at Oxford University.
59. Lewin, *Bones*, pp. 318-19.

Chapter 8. Revelation
1. I am indebted to Professor Gordon Spykman of Calvin College for his insights concerning the two kinds of revelation.
2. This understanding of two revelations has been a part of the Christian tradition for more than four hundred years. The *Confession of Faith*, also called the *Belgic Confession*, written in 1561 by Guido de Bres and adopted by the Reformed Churches at the Synod of Dort in 1618-1619, meeting in Dordrecht (now a part of The Netherlands), states in Article II:

> We know him by two means: First, by the creation, preservation, and government of the universe, since that universe is before our eyes like a beautiful book . . . . Second, he makes himself known to us more openly by his holy and divine Word . . . (This text, a recent translation of the French text of 1619, was adopted by the Christian Reformed Church of North America in 1985, replacing the text adopted earlier.)

The "more openly" refers to the necessity of special revelation: for sinful people, general revelation is not enough. In the *Confession* the relation between the book of Creation and the divine Word is not the same as the relation between the two books of which Francis Bacon spoke (see Chapter 2). For Bacon, writing more than four decades after de Bres in *The Advancement of Learning* (1605), the book of general revelation opens the book of special revelation. But Bacon did not allow for the book of special revelation to open the book of general revelation. Although Bacon's emphasis is not correct, the question he raised is not simple. For, just because we are limited and sinful, our understanding of both revelations is incomplete. Thus, to help us cope with that problem, it is appropriate that we use not only special revelation to help us in our understanding of general revelation, but that we also use general revelation to help us with special revelation. This matter is taken up in Chapter 10 in connection with a discussion of the principles of interpretation needed in the discussion of origins.

3. Many theologians have emphasized that what we see in life and nature is God's general revelation and that it must be understood in the light of biblical teaching. For example, Abraham Kuyper (1837-1920) said in a speech concerning the work of a university: "Now, anyone who still believes in a God in any way whatsoever, admits with us that God has revealed Himself, and is still revealing Himself to us, and that we have to be guided by that revelation. Even the liberal theologian is on our side in that respect. Only, he states that God reveals Himself only in nature, including reason, conscience and history...[The liberal theologian] does not put Scripture aside, but he dissolves it in that general revelation of life." In the same speech Kuyper said, "There is a language of God in nature, there is a thought of God spoken in history, there is a word of God in our reason, there is a discourse of God in our inner consciousness of God." (Abraham Kuyper, "Binding to the Word, Answer to the Question: In What Way Is a University to Be Bound to the Word of God?" Trans. Jan De Koning. Address at Middleburg, The Netherlands, on June 28, 1899.)

4. Russell Maatman, *The Unity in Creation* (Sioux Center, Iowa: Dordt College Press, 1978), pp. 23-39.

5. Arie Leegwater, chemist and philosopher of science at Calvin College, commenting on Isaiah 45:18-19, noted the interdependence within Creation. Human beings are at home in Creation, which they are to develop, cultivate, and preserve. "This coherence and unity," said Leegwater, "are reflected, for example, in the interdependence of physical theories and in the relationships between sound scientific insights and an appropriate technology." (Arie Leegwater, "Creation: Does It Matter?" in *Life Is Religion: Essays in Honor of H. Evan Runner*, ed. H. Vander Goot [St. Catharines, Ont: Paideia Press, 1981], pp. 249-62; p. 260.) Use of *appropriate* technology, not just any technology, has become the hallmark of a truly Christian response to the effects of sin in a world badly scarred because of environmental damage, with billions of its human inhabitants living in misery.

6. Many persons take a position that mixes the second and third views: they concede that both "religion" and "science" are important to some people; however, they keep religion and science separate. Thus, in a discussion of the current controversy concerning science education, R.D. Simpson and N.D. Anderson made this claim: "To accept the position that special creationism does not qualify as science is not an attempt to indoctrinate students. Rather, it is a *recognition of the fact that religion and science are different ways of viewing phenomena* and that creationism does not qualify as science." (Emphasis added.) (R.D. Simpson and N.D. Anderson, *Science Students and Schools* [New York: Wiley, 1981]; quoted by J. Steve Oliver, Ronald D. Simpson, and Wyatt W. Anderson, "Darwin, Science Education, and the Method of Science," *Proteus*, 6, No. 2 (1989), 5-9; p. 9.) The position of Simpson and Anderson is therefore much more than a condemnation of "special creationism"; it is a decision *for others* that science (Simpson and Anderson refer to "true science") and the religion of *others* must be kept separate.

7. I am indebted to my colleague Professor Richard Hodgson for calling these examples to my attention.

8. For a semi-popular discussion showing how certain large systems tend to evolve to a state such that minor events can trigger a catastrophe, see Per Bak and Kan Chen (Brookhaven National Laboratory), "Self-Organized Criticality," *Scientific American*, 264, No. 1 (1991), 46-53.
9. John Calvin, *Institutes of the Christian Religion*, trans. John Allen (Grand Rapids: Eerdmans, 1949), Book I, Chap. VI, Part I; p. 80.
10. Many modern Reformed scholars use Calvin's concept of spectacles. See, for example: Gordon J. Spykman, *Spectacles: Biblical Perspectives on Christian Scholarship* (Potchefstroom, South Africa: Potchefstroom University for Christian Higher Education, 1985). This is Monograph No. 7 in the J2 Monograph Series, part of Series J, Potchefstroom Studies in Christian Scholarship.
11. Modern authors have often discussed de-deification and claims that the Christian understanding of the world made modern science possible. See the following: (a) for a detailed analysis, R. Hooykaas, *Religion and the Rise of Modern Science* (Grand Rapids: Eerdmans, 1972), pp. 67ff; (b) for the historical relation to evolutionary ideas, especially the evolutionary metaphor, David N. Livingstone, "Evolution as Metaphor and Myth," *Christian Scholar's Review*, 12 (1983), 111-25; p. 112; (c) for the view that the biblical text "charters" those called to pursue knowledge, John H. Stek, "What Says the Scripture?" in *Portraits of Creation*, ed. Howard J. Van Till (Grand Rapids: Eerdmans, 1990), pp. 203-65; p. 204.
12. Fritjof Capra, *The Tao of Physics* (Berkeley: Shambhala, 1975).
13. Terry A. Ward, "The New Baalism: God and Physical Theories," *Journal of the American Scientific Affiliation*, 34 (1982), 34-35.
14. John S. Hagelin, "Is Consciousness the Unified Field? (A Field Theorist's Perspective)," manuscript, 1987; 115 pages.
15. Richard T. Wright, *Biology Through the Eyes of Faith* (Cambridge: Harper & Row, 1989), p. 40.
16. For a discussion of some of Fredkin's ideas, see Paul Davies, *The Mind of God: The Scientific Basis for a Rational World* (New York: Simon and Schuster, 1992), pp. 121-23 and 128. For a popular account, see Robert Wright, "Did the Universe Just Happen?" *Atlantic Monthly*, April 1988, pp. 29-44.
17. Visualize the student section of a football stadium. Every student has a large card; one side is white and the other black. The students simultaneously hold up their cards, displaying, according to rules given to them, one side or the other to those sitting on the opposite side of the stadium. With a suitable arrangement of black and white cards, the students can form letters of the alphabet large enough to be seen across the stadium. With practice and a suitable set of rules, the students can, by simultaneously changing the side of the card that is displayed, send a message of several words across the stadium and perhaps to a television audience. Their instructions, their "set of rules," could enable them to send a second group of words; and so forth. This analogy shows that a set of rules could produce an interesting message. But it could also produce nonsense. What happens depends on the rules.
18. Robert Wright, p. 31 and p. 34.
19. Other examples are the following: Matthew 13:35, 24:21, 25:34; Luke 11:50, John 17:24; Romans 1:20; Ephesians 1:4; Hebrews 9:26; and Revelation 13:8, 17:8.
20. Other examples in which *kosmos* indicates everything on earth: in the parable of the sower, "the field is the world" (Matt. 13:38); one can gain the whole world but forfeit his soul (Matt. 16:26); if an account of the works of Christ had been written down, probably not

even the whole world could contain all the books (John 21:25); Christians shine as lights in the world (NIV: universe) (Phil. 2:15); the whole world sinned (I John 2:2). *Kosmos* can also indicate another kind of entity; thus, the tongue is a fire, a world of evil (James 3:6).
21. Other examples of *kosmos* having a negative connotation: woe to the world because of causing others to sin (Matt. 18:7); Christ has overcome the world (John 16:33); Christ's kingdom is not of this world (John 18:36); the wisdom of the world did not know God (I Cor. 1:21); the wisdom of this world is foolishness (I Cor. 3:19); the saints will judge the world (I Cor. 6:2); the world was not worthy of the heroes of the faith (Heb. 11:38); we must keep ourselves from being polluted by the world (James 1:27).
22. For a discussion of this passage see: John Calvin, *Commentary on the Gospel According to John*, trans. William Pringle (Grand Rapids: Eerdmans, 1949), II, 172-73.

Chapter 9. Science
1. In commenting on Hebrews 11:3, John Calvin said:

> Wherefore the author of the Epistle to the Hebrews elegantly represents the worlds as the manifestations of invisible things; *for the exact symmetry of the universe is a mirror, in which we may contemplate the otherwise invisible God*. (Emphasis added.) (John Calvin, *Institutes of the Christian Religion*, trans. John Allen [Grand Rapids: Eerdmans, 1949], Book I, Chap. V, Part I, p. 64)

2. That "grace restores nature" has been a central theme in Dutch Reformed theology and philosophy of the nineteenth and twentieth centuries. One of the most influential theologians was Herman Bavinck (1854-1921). E.P. Heidman observed "that grace does not abolish nature, but renews and restores it...may be called the central thought of Bavinck's theology." (*The Relation of Revelation to Reason in E. Brunner and H. Bavinck* [Assen, The Netherlands: n.p., 1959]; quoted by Jan Veenhof, *Revelatie en Inspiratie*, trans. A.M. Wolters [Amsterdam: n.p., 1968]).
3. Helmuth Thielicke, *The Evangelical Faith*, trans. Geoffrey W. Bromiley (Grand Rapids: Eerdmans, 1974), I, 281.
4. Owen Gingerich, "Let There Be Light" (Montreal: Ideas Series CBC [Canadian Broadcasting Corporation] Transcripts, December 26, 1988), p. 8.
5. Those who hold to this latter view define natural science as the study of matter and energy. This definition has its place. But when they go farther, to claim that whatever does not fall within the purview of natural science has no meaning, they are guilty of circularity. They say in effect that natural science includes studies of only matter and energy, and therefore anything related to matter and energy, including its behavior, must fall within the boundaries of natural laws, which human beings can understand. (Someone said, "That which my net can't catch ain't fish!")
6. Sometimes those who subscribe to the definition of science given here distinguish between the sciences in a different way: they refer to the normative sciences, in which the laws are moral imperatives, and the nonnormative sciences, where the laws are not of this nature. Thus, one is not free to respond either obediently or disobediently to the law of gravity, a nonnormative, physical law; but the choice does exist for the law of sexual purity, a normative law.
7. Quoted by Arie Leegwater, "Creation: Does It Matter?" in *Life Is Religion: Essays in Honor of H. Evan Runner*, ed. H. Vander Goot (St. Catherines, Ontario: Paideia Press, 1981), p. 256.

8. Richard M. Lemmon, "Chemical Evolution," *Chemical Reviews*, 70 (1970), 95-109. See Chapter 6 for additional discussion of Lemmon's views.
9. The description of the first four models given here is due to Glenn A. Remelts, "The Christian Reformed Church and Science, 1900-1930," *Fides et Historia*, 21, No. 1 (1989), 61-80. Remelts' first three models are from Ian G. Barbour, *Issues in Science and Religion* (Englewood Cliffs, N.J.: Prentice-Hall, 1966), pp. 238-70.
10. Remelts, p. 63.
11. Remelts, p. 64.
12. Remelts, pp. 64-65.
13. Remelts, p. 65.
14. Howard J. Van Till, *The Fourth Day: What the Bible and the Heavens Are Telling Us about the Creation* (Grand Rapids: Eerdmans, 1986).
15. Thomas Dozeman, "Stuck Between a Rock and a Hard Place," *Christian Scholar's Review*, 18 (1988), 173-81; p. 174.
16. Nicholas Wolterstorff, *Reason Within the Bounds of Religion* (Grand Rapids: Eerdmans, 1976), p. 66.
17. Wolterstorff, pp. 78-79.
18. In the discussion of scientific projects, I assume that "science" includes not only the basic disciplines but also those associated with the application of scientific results. Therefore, in this part of the discussion "scientific" includes "technical."
19. Henri Blocher, *In the Beginning: The Opening Chapters of Genesis*, trans. David G. Preston (Downers Grove, Ill.: Inter-Varsity Press, 1984), pp. 154-55.
20. Alvin Plantinga, "When Faith and Reason Clash: Evolution and the Bible," *Christian Scholar's Review*, 21, No. 1 (1991), 8-32; pp. 28-29.
21. Russell Maatman, *The Unity in Creation* (Sioux Center, Iowa: Dordt College Press, 1978), pp. 23-39 and 87-88.
22. A. D'Abro, *The Rise of the New Physics: Its Mathematical and Physical Theories* (1939; rpt. New York: Dover Publications, 1951), I, 28.
23. Maatman, pp. 35-36.
24. Ernst Mach, *The Science of Mathematics*, trans. T.J. McCormack (1883), p. 577; quoted by Marinus Dirk Stafleu, *Theories at Work* (Lanham, Md: University Press of America, 1987), p. 186.
25. Leegwater, p. 255.
26. John Byl, "Instrumentalism: A Third Option," *Journal of the American Scientific Affiliation*, 37 (1985), 11-18; p. 17.
27. Thomas S. Kuhn, *The Structure of Scientific Revolutions*, 2nd ed. (Chicago: University of Chicago Press, 1970).
28. Del Ratzsch, *Philosophy of Science: The Natural Sciences in Christian Perspective* (Downers Grove, Ill.: InterVarsity Press, 1986). I am also indebted to Professor Ratzsch for a personal communication concerning the structure of science. Richard T. Wright discussed Ratzsch's ideas in *Biology Through the Eyes of Faith* (San Francisco: Harper and Row, 1989), pp. 35ff.
29. Ratzsch, pp. 16-19.

Chapter 10. Genesis
1. Abraham Kuyper, "Binding to the Word, Answer to the Question: In What Way Is a University to Be Bound to the Word of God?" Address at Middleburg, The Netherlands, on June 28, 1899; trans. Jan De Koning.

2. Untitled introduction to "Song of Songs," *The NIV Study Bible* (Grand Rapids: Zondervan, 1985), p. 1003.
3. John Stek, "What Says the Scripture?" in *Portraits of Creation: Biblical and Scientific Perspectives on the World's Formation*, ed. Howard J. Van Till (Grand Rapids: Eerdmans, 1990), p. 261.
4. Stek, pp. 205-06.
5. That it is legitimate to compare the length of these days is indicated by Exodus 20:8-11, where God instructs Moses that the weekly human work-rest cycle is to follow the pattern of the divine work-rest cycle. God's six-one work-rest cycle of Creation Week was also the basis of Israel's agricultural six-one *yearly* work-rest cycle. The Year of Jubilee, culminating seven such seven-year cycles, was the fiftieth year; see Leviticus 25:1-14.
6. H.C. Leupold, *Exposition of Genesis* (Columbus, Ohio: Wartburg, 1942), p. 56; quoted by Davis C. Young, *Creation and the Flood: An Alternative to Flood Geology and Theistic Evolution* (Grand Rapids: Baker, 1977), p. 46.
7. For a more detailed discussion of "day" in Genesis 1, see Pattle P.T. Pun, *Evolution: Nature and Scripture in Conflict?* (Grand Rapids: Zondervan, 1982), pp. 254-60; Russell Maatman, *The Bible, Natural Science, and Evolution* (Sioux Center, Iowa: Dordt College Press, 1970), pp. 87-100.
8. For a detailed discussion of this selective and incorrect use of scientific results, see Alan Hayward, *Creation and Evolution: The Facts and Fallacies* (London: Triangle, 1985), pp. 135-57. Hayward wrote from a nonevolutionistic, evangelical perspective.
9. Pun, p. 261.
10. Pun, p. 260.
11. Pun, pp. 261-66.
12. Richard H. Bube, rev. of *Genesis One and the Origin of the Earth*, by Robert C. Newman and Herman J. Eckelmann, Jr., *Journal of the American Scientific Affiliation*, 30 (1978), 91.
13. Hayward, pp. 161-78.
14. Hayward, p. 171.
15. The question of punctuation is similar to questions about which words were emphasized or which gestures were made by a speaker whose words the Bible records. The matter of gesture has figured in the long debate over the nature of the Lord's Supper. Thus, when Christ said, "This is my body," what gesture did he make? Did he point to the bread? Or did he point to himself?
16. Robert C. Newman and Herman J. Eckelmann, Jr. (Downers Grove, Ill.: InterVarsity, 1977), pp. 83-88; Pun, pp. 261-62.
17. Newman and Eckelmann, pp. 85-86.
18. Among others, Henri Blocher cited Augustine, N.H. Ridderbos of The Netherlands, and Bernard Ramm and Meredith Kline of the United States (Blocher, *In the Beginning: The Opening Chapters of Genesis*, trans. David G. Preston [Leicester: Inter-Varsity, 1984], p. 49).
19. Blocher, p. 50.
20. Blocher, p. 33.
21. Blocher, pp. 52-53.
22. Blocher (pp.70-74) linked the order in Creation to the separations of Creation Week; hence, a creational hierarchy. I am also indebted to Professor Raymond C. Van Leeuwen of Calvin College for insights on God's boundaries and limits in Creation.
23. Some possible symbols are the tree of life, the tree of the knowledge of good and evil (both trees are mentioned in Genesis 2:9), the serpent (3:1), and the angel with the flashing

sword guarding the gate to Eden (3:24) Scholars have made many suggestions for these symbols. For example, Gordon J. Wenham said that the Garden of Eden was the archetypal sanctuary; see Wenham, "Sanctuary Symbolism in the Garden of Eden Story," *Proceedings of the Ninth World Congress of Jewish Studies* (Jerusalem: World Union of Jewish Studies, 1986), pp. 19-25; p. 19.
24. I am aware of modern research into the cultures of Middle Eastern nations contemporary with early Israel. Many scholars contend that the early readers of the Bible knew of those cultures and could easily perceive that Genesis is a polemic against contemporary pagan teachings on origins. Then, goes the argument, something is behind the symbol: the pagan teachings of those other cultures. I do not doubt that early Israelites did not take the book of Genesis to exist in a vacuum. Nor do I doubt that Genesis did answer contemporary pagan claims. If, however, the entire creation account is symbolic, then knowing what pagans claimed still does not reveal what is behind the symbol. Finally, God speaks in Genesis to his people of all times, most of whom had no knowledge of those long-gone pagan cultures, just as most of them did not know of modern scientific conclusions. Therefore, people who lived long after the early Israelites and long before the modern scientific period, say, in 1000 A.D., could derive very little from a symbolic creation account.

Chapter 11. Human Origin and the Evolutionary Paradigm
1. Some of this chapter is also part of my article, "The Origin of the Human Family," *Pro Rege*, 19, No. 3 (1991), 8-17. *Pro Rege* is a quarterly publication of the faculty of Dordt College, Sioux Center, Iowa.
2. I consider here only Christian theistic evolution, even though other kinds exist.
3. Richard T. Wright, *Biology Through the Eyes of Faith* (Cambridge, Mass.: Harper and Row, 1989), pp. 157-58.
4. R.J. Berry, "'I Believe in God . . . Maker of Heaven and Earth,'" in *Creation and Evolution*, ed. Derek Burke (Leicester: Inter-Varsity, 1985), pp. 100-01.
5. R.J. Berry, *Adam and the Ape: A Christian Approach to the Theory of Evolution* (London, Falcon, 1975).
6. Jesse De Boer, Letter, *The Calvin Spark*, 35, No. 4 (1988), 5. *The Calvin Spark* is the magazine of the Calvin College Alumni Association, Grand Rapids, Michigan.
7. One of those answers suggests that the Genesis passage refers to beginnings far more primitive than those discovered by anthropologists.
8. Richard Leakey, *The Making of Mankind* (New York: Dutton, 1981), p. 20; quoted by Wright, p. 148.
9. Roger Lewin, *Bones of Contention: Controversies in the Search for Human Origins* (New York: Simon and Schuster, 1987), p. 319.
10. Henri Blocher, *In the Beginning: The Opening Chapters of Genesis*, trans. David G. Preston (Leicester: Inter-Varsity, 1984), p. 79. Blocher devoted an entire chapter, "The Image of God," pp. 79-94, to a careful examination of the subject. He suggested that the commandment prohibiting the making of idols (Ex. 20:4), the biblical command to love our neighbors (Lev. 19:18), and John's instruction to love our brothers (I John 4:9) all rest on the image of God residing in human beings. He called attention to James' condemnation of those who "curse men, who have been made in God's likeness" (James 3:9). Blocher also suggested the possibility of a polemical thrust to the first biblical statement concerning the image of God in Genesis 1:27. Thus, God makes every person in his image; this teaching was contrary to some Middle Eastern teaching, which said that only the king bears the image of the Creator (pp. 86-87).

11. Wright, p. 153.
12. David W. Diehl, "Evangelicalism and General Revelation: An Unfinished Agenda," *Journal of the Evangelical Theological Society*, 30 (1987), 441-55; p. 451.
13. James M. Houston, "The Origin of Man," *Journal of the American Scientific Affiliation*, 34 (1982), 1-5; p. 5. Reprinted from James M. Houston, *I Believe in the Creator* (Grand Rapids: Eerdmans, 1980).
14. John Cooper, *Body, Soul, and Life Everlasting* (Grand Rapids: Eerdmans, 1989), pp. 52-53.
15. Although the conclusion of the argument does not depend upon the accuracy of the KJV translation, it is helpful to use it here because the modern reading of this translation may in part be the source of the problem alluded to above and because of consistency within the translation.
16. See, for example, Gen. 27:19, 27:25, 46:22, and 46:26; Ex. 1:5 and 12:4.
17. The close relation between the English words "woman" and "man" reflects the close relation in Hebrew: "Then the Lord God made a woman [*ishshah*] from the rib he had taken out of the man [*ish*]" (Gen. 2:22).
18. Blocher, p. 185.
19. Blocher, pp. 185-87.
20. Modern archaeological discoveries have revealed that Belshazzar ruled over part of the empire of his father, Nabonidus. Therefore, Belshazzar himself was second in command.
21. Thomas S. Kuhn, *The Structure of Scientific Revolutions* (Chicago: University of Chicago Press, 1970).
22. Michael Denton, *Evolution: A Theory in Crisis* (Bethesda, Md.: Adler & Adler, 1986), pp. 74-75.
23. Richard Dawkins, *The Selfish Gene*, 2nd ed. (Oxford: Oxford University Press, 1989), p.1.
24. At present, the situation has not been sorted out. The reason for the observation is not known.

Chapter 12. Human Behavior
1. Peter T. Hoffer, "Freud's 'Phylogenetic Fantasy': Poetry or Truth?" *Proteus*, 6, No. 2 (1989), 17-23.
2. Sigmund Freud, *Introductory Lectures on Psycho-Analysis, Standard Edition*, XVI, 370-71; cited by Hoffer, p. 18.
3. Sigmund Freud, *Totem and Taboo*, Standard Edition, XIII, 1-162; cited by Hoffer, p. 18.
4. Stephen J. Gould, rev. of *A Phylogenetic Fantasy*, by Sigmund Freud, *New York Times*, February 10, 1987, C4; quoted by Hoffer, p. 20.
5. Robert J. Richards, *Darwin and the Emergence of Evolutionary Theories of Mind and Behavior* (Chicago: University of Chicago Press, 1987).
6. Richards, p. 504.
7. Richards, p. 505f.
8. B.F. Skinner, *Beyond Freedom and Dignity* (New York: Knopf, 1971).
9. Skinner, p. 123.
10. Skinner, p. 124.
11. Skinner, p. 191.
12. Skinner, pp. 196-97.
13. Richards, pp. 509-10.
14. Richards, p. 512f.
15. The modern argument often presented in favor of abortion on demand is that the child would, if born, live in an inferior *environment*. In Nazi Germany, the argument for eliminating people, including unborn children, was that they were *genetically* inferior.

In spite of the fundamental difference between these two reasons, is it possible that the mentality that says that certain persons are unnecessary is the same in the two cases? Perhaps a historical link between the two positions can be shown.

16. Richards, p. 537f.
17. W.C. Allee, *Animal Aggregations: A Study in General Sociology* (Chicago: University of Chicago Press, 1931); cited by Richards, p. 537.
18. Hence, the title of Richard Dawkins' book: *The Selfish Gene* (Oxford: Oxford University Press, 1989).
19. Edward O. Wilson, *Sociobiology: The New Synthesis* (Cambridge: Harvard University Press, 1975).
20. Richard T. Wright, *Biology Through the Eyes of Faith* (San Francisco: Harper and Row, 1989), pp. 61-62.
21. R.J. Herrnstein, "Darwinism and Behaviourism: Parallels and Intersections," in *Evolution and Its Influence*, ed. Alan Grafen (Oxford: Clarendon Press, 1989), pp. 35-61; p. 38.
22. Richards, p. 542.
23. Richards, p. 548. Richards elaborates on the relation between morality and our animal past in his Appendix 2, "A Defense of Evolutionary Ethics," pp. 595-627.
24. Herrnstein, p. 59.
25. Herrnstein, p. 60.
26. Herrnstein, pp. 60-61.
27. Maurice Godelier, "Incest Taboo and the Evolution of Society," in *Evolution and Its Influence*, ed. Alan Grafen (Oxford: Clarendon Press, 1989), p. 63.
28. David Livingstone, "Evolution as Metaphor and Myth," *Christian Scholar's Review*, 12, No. 2 (1983), 111-25.
29. A.J. Cain, "The True Meaning of Darwinian Evolution," in *Evolution and Its Influence*, ed. Alan Grafen (Oxford: Clarendon Press, 1989), pp. 1-18; p. 14.
30. W.G. Runciman, "Evolution in Sociology," in *Evolution and Its Influence*, ed. Alan Grafen (Oxford: Clarendon Press, 1989), pp. 19-33; p. 27f.
31. Loren W. Dow, "The Theory of Social Evolution and the Concept of Entropy," *Journal of the American Scientific Affiliation*, 29 (1977), 91-93.
32. Runciman, p. 25.
33. Cain, p. 10.
34. John Tyler Bonner, *The Evolution of Culture in Animals* (Princeton: Princeton University Press, 1980).
35. Dawkins, p. 84.
36. Godelier, p. 71f.
37. Spencer's ideas on evolution developed slowly. But it seems certain that some of his main ideas preceded Darwin's *Origin of Species* of 1859. His first philosophical ideas appeared before 1860 in *Westminster Review*; in 1850 he published *Social States*; in 1855, *Principles of Psychology*; the first part of his ten-volume *Synthetic Philosophy* he sent out in 1860. He eagerly took up Darwin's ideas and was a leader in the Darwinian revolution.
38. Herrnstein, p. 36.
39. Runciman, p. 21f.
40. Thus, in 1986 the Herbert Spencer Lectures began at Oxford University. Since Spencer's influence spread across many disciplines, so do these lectures. Its announced purpose was "to survey the influence on various disciplines of 'the greatest intellectual revolution of the nineteenth century'—the Darwinian view of evolution by natural selection." (From Alan Grafen, "Preface," *Evolution and Its Influence* [Oxford: Clarendon Press, 1989].)

41. Although Spencer was English, his ideas had great influence in the United States. William Graham Sumner (1840-1910), not as well-known today but very influential during his lifetime, was his American counterpart. Greatly influenced by Spencer's writings while studying at Oxford, Sumner abandoned his supernatural beliefs and developed "a thoroughly materialistic interpretation of history and culture." From Stow Persons, "Introduction: Sumner's Science of Society," in *Social Darwinism: Selected Essays of William Graham Sumner*, ed. William F. Leuchtenburg and Bernard Wishy (Englewood Cliffs, N.J.: Prentice-Hall, 1963), p. 2.
42. Jarice Hanson, "Technology and the Social Sciences: The Triumph of the Darwinian Fallacy," *Proteus*, 6, No. 2 (1989), 47-51; p. 47.
43. Runciman, p. 24f.
44. Theodore Roosevelt, *The Works of Theodore Roosevelt* (National Ed.) (New York: Scribner's, 1926) XIII, 331; quoted in Richard Hofstadter, *Social Darwinism in American Thought* (Boston: Beacon Press, 1955), p. 180.
45. David N. Livingstone, *Darwin's Forgotten Defenders* (Grand Rapids: Eerdmans, 1987), p. 159.
46. Roger Lewin, *Bones of Contention: Controversies in the Search for Human Origins* (New York: Simon and Schuster, 1987), p. 306f.
47. Charles Darwin, *The Descent of Man*, in *The Origin of Species* and *The Descent of Man* (New York: Modern Library, 1936), pp. 542-43.
48. Carleton S. Coon, *The Story of Man* (New York: Knopf, 1954), pp. 187-88.
49. Coon, pp. 195-99.
50. Coon, pp. 200-12.
51. Coon, p. 213.
52. Coon, p. 214.
53. In my own experience in a city where racial integration of schools met with violent opposition, I observed that at least one local newspaper cited some of Coon's writings in defense of such opposition.
54. For discussion on the nature of language and its history, I am indebted to four of my Dordt College colleagues who are members of the Foreign Language Department: Professors Dallas Apol, Kornelis Boot, Abe Bos, and John Struyk.
55. Philip Lieberman, *On the Origins of Language: An Introduction to the Evolution of Human Speech* (New York: Macmillan, 1975), p. 6.
56. Lieberman, p. 2.
57. Marguerite Holloway, "Profile: Vive la Difference," *Scientific American*, 263, No. 4 (1990), 40-42.
58. Godelier, pp. 66-67.
59. Leonard Bloomfield, *Language* (n.p.: Holt, 1933).
60. Lieberman, p. 5.
61. "Evidence Accrues for Specific Female Ancestor," *Chemical and Engineering News*, Feb. 6, 1989, pp. 28-29.
62. Richard E. Leakey and Roger Lewin, *Origins: What New Discoveries Reveal About the Emergence of Our Species and Its Possible Future* (New York: Dutton, 1977), p. 205.
63. Lieberman, pp. 10-20.
64. Thomas G. Overmire, *The World of Biology* (New York: Wiley, 1986), p. 234.
65. I am indebted to Professor Albert M. Wolters of Redeemer College for suggesting this possibility.
66. Robin Fox, *Kinship and Marriage: An Anthropological Perspective* (Baltimore: Penguin, 1967), pp. 55-56.

67. Fox, pp. 27-28.
68. Fox, p. 29.
69. Fox, p. 30.
70. Godelier, pp. 63-92.
71. Godelier, p. 74.
72. Some people maintain that the incest taboo and the accompanying definition of "family" are natural. They claim, for example, that brother-sister mating often produces defective children. As a result, according to this argument, human beings would eventually become aware of this problem and avoid mating within what would become defined as the family. Suppose that the argument about defective children is correct; even so, societies include in the incest taboo mating between persons who are in the same family but not "blood" relatives. God prohibits such mating; an example is the mating of a man and his daughter-in-law (Lev. 18:15). Evidently the primary purpose of God's laws in this matter is to preserve the family, the God-ordained fundamental unit of society.

Chapter 13. Progress

1. Thomas S. Kuhn, *The Structure of Scientific Revolutions*, 2nd ed. (Chicago: University of Chicago Press, 1970), pp. 171-72.
2. W.G. Runciman, "Evolution in Sociology," in *Evolution and Its Influence*, ed. Alan Grafen (Oxford: Clarendon Press, 1989), 19-33; p. 33.
3. Colin Brown, *Philosophy and the Christian Faith* (Chicago: Inter-Varsity, 1969), pp. 141-42.
4. David N. Livingstone, "Evolution as Metaphor and Myth," *Christian Scholar's Review*, 12, No. 2 (1983), 111-25; p. 122.
5. Brown, p. 238.
6. F.Jappe, rev. of *Evolution and Guilt*, by J.L. Segundo, *Journal of the American Scientific Affiliation*, 29 (1977), 33.
7. Irving Hexham and Karla Poewe-Hexham, "The Soul of the New Age," *Christianity Today*, Sept. 2, 1988, pp. 17-21. The New Age movement is essentially the same as the earlier New Consciousness movement. For a discussion of the latter, see James Sire, *The Universe Next Door: A Basic World View Catalog* (Downers Grove, Ill.: InterVarsity Press, 1976), especially Chapter 8, "A Separate Universe: The New Consciousness," pp. 150-203.
8. Richard Hofstadter, *Social Darwinism in American Thought* (Boston: Beacon Press, 1955), pp.143-48; quote on p. 148.
9. Economist Milton Friedman of the University of Chicago advocates the removal of many governmental restrictions. For example, he maintains that the educational system would improve if people could, without financial penalty, freely choose among private and public schools. He would also allow unlicensed physicians: the market would determine which ones are qualified. For a popular exposition of many of Friedman's views, see Milton and Rose Friedman, *Free to Choose: A Personal Statement* (New York: Harcourt Brace Jovanovich, 1979).
10. For this reason, neoclassical economists advocate both a domestic free market and free trade between nations.
11. R.J. Herrnstein, "Darwinism and Behaviourism: Parallels and Intersections," in *Evolution and Its Influence*, ed. Alan Grafen (Oxford: Clarendon Press, 1989), 35-61.
12. Herrnstein, p. 44.
13. Editor's Introduction, *The Portable Veblen*, ed. Max Lerner (New York: Viking, 1950), p. 2.

14. John P. Diggins, *The Bard of Savagery: Thorstein Veblen and Modern Social Theory* (New York: Seabury, 1978), p. 17.
15. For a discussion of Veblen's views, see Paul T. Homan, *Contemporary Economic Thought* (Freeport, N.Y.: Books for Libraries Press, 1928), pp. 107-92; Lerner, pp. 1-49; David Riesman, *Thorstein Veblen: A Critical Interpretation* (New York: Scribner's, 1953); Hofstadter, pp. 151-56; and Diggins.
16. Hofstadter, pp. 152-53.
17. Riesman, p. 129.
18. Lerner, p. 23.
19. The above quotations concerning Veblen and Hofstadter's discussion of Veblen are taken from Hofstadter, pp.152-56.
20. Lerner, pp. 31-33.
21. Diggins, p. viii.
22. John Kenneth Galbraith, *The New Industrial State* (1967; rpt. New York: Signet, 1968), p. 406.
23. Lerner (pp. 37-38) commented that Veblen operated on two time scales, the one, dictated by his theory, that called for slow evolutionary change of habits and growth of institutions; and the other, the impatient time scale of the revolutionary. Concerning the latter time scale, Veblen was disappointed in the Russian Revolution, which at first attracted him, but later turned sour; the eventual failure of U.S. President Woodrow Wilson's postwar mission in spite of the outpouring of favorable sentiment for him among the common people of Europe; and the failure of the British General Strike of 1926.
24. For insights into the writing of American history I am indebted to my colleague Professor Louis Van Dyke.
25. Hofstadter, pp. 176-78.
26. Richard Hofstadter, William Miller, and Daniel Aaron, *The United States: The History of a Republic* (Englewood Cliffs, N.J.: Prentice-Hall, 1957), pp. 537-38.
27. *Benet's Reader's Encyclopedia* 3rd ed. (New York: Harper and Row, 1987), p. 683.
28. I am indebted to my colleague Professor Mike Vanden Bosch for insights on the writings of several English and American authors.
29. *Benet's Reader's Encyclopedia*, p. 425.
30. Roderick Frazier Nash, *The Rights of Nature: A History of Environmental Ethics* (Madison, Wisc.: University of Wisconsin Press, 1989), p. 43.
31. Bert Bender, "The Influence of Darwin in American Literature of the Sea," *Proteus*, 6, No. 2 (1989), 30-37. The quotations from works by authors cited by Bender are taken from his article.
32. Lenora Ledwon, "Darwin's Ghosts: The Influence of Darwinism on the Nineteenth-Century Ghost Story," *Proteus*, 6, No. 2 (1989), 10-16. The quotations from works by authors cited by Ledwon are taken from her article.
33. For insights on the history of the theatre I am indebted to my colleague Professor James Koldenhoven.
34. Oscar G. Brockett, *History of the Theatre* (Old Tappan, N.J.: Allyn and Bacon, 1987), pp. 2-4.
35. The various anthropological schools of thought have analyzed many cultural phenomena. For example, both Frazer and Levi-Strauss have been involved in the long debate over the origin of the incest taboo, discussed in Chapter 12.
36. E.H. Gombrich, "Evolution in the Arts: The Altar Painting, its Ancestry and Progeny," in *Evolution and its Influence*, ed. Alan Grafen (Oxford: Clarendon Press, 1989), pp. 107-25.

37. Gombrich, p. 124.
38. Gombrich, p. 125.

Chapter 14. Consequences
1. Russell Ruthen, "Adapting to Complexity," *Scientific American*, 268 (1) (1993), 130-40.
2. Richard Dawkins, *The Blind Watchmaker* (New York: Norton, 1986), p. 6.
3. Lynn White, Jr., "The Historic Roots of Our Ecologic Crisis," *Science*, 155 (1967), 1204.
4. Robert H. Nelson, "Unoriginal Sin: The Judeo-Christian Roots of Ecotheology," *Policy Review*, Summer 1990, 52-59; p. 52.
5. Roderick Frazier Nash, *The Rights of Nature: A History of Environmental Ethics* (Madison, Wisc.: University of Wisconsin Press, 1989), p. 42. This is taken from the chapter "Ideological Origins of American Environmentalism," pp. 33-54.
6. Peter Singer, *Animal Liberation* (New York: New York Review of Books, 1975). Because of the popularity of this book, a second edition appeared in 1990.
7. Tom Regan, *The Case for Animal Rights* (Berkeley: University of California Press, 1983).
8. James Rachels, *Created from Animals: The Moral Implications of Darwinism* (Oxford: Oxford University Press, 1990).
9. Rachels, pp. 4-5.
10. Rachels, pp. 149-52.
11. Rachels, p. 208.
12. Rachels, p. 209.
13. Rachels, pp. 203-04. On the jacket of Rachels' book the publisher advertises Rachels' *The End of Life: Euthanasia and Morality*, along with reviewers' praise to the effect that Rachels' analysis paves the way for voluntary euthanasia.
14. Rachels, p. 205.
15. Rachels, p. 223.
16. Rachels, pp. 210-12.
17. Rachels, pp. 221-23.
18. Quoted by Tim Stafford, "Animal Lib," *Christianity Today*, June 18, 1990, pp. 19-23; p. 19.
19. *Des Moines Register*, August 9, 1991, p. 9A.
20. K.L. Billingsley, "Watch Out! It's the New Fur Right," *World*, January 27, 1990, p. 12.
21. Quoted by Roger Lewin in *Bones of Contention: Controversies in the Search for Human Origins* (New York: Simon and Schuster, 1987), p. 305.
22. Cited in Stephen Jay Gould, *The Panda's Thumb* (New York: Norton, 1980), p. 154.
23. Gould, p. 155.
24. Charles Darwin, *The Descent of Man*, in *The Origin of Species by Means of Natural Selection and The Descent of Man and Selection in Relation to Sex* (New York: The Modern Library, 1936), p. 578.
25. Darwin, pp. 867-68. One of the sources for Darwin's "is said to be" in the last sentence is a lecture by Carl Vogt, who is cited above.
26. Lawrence Birken, "Darwin and Gender," *Proteus*, 6, No. 2 (1989), 24-29.
27. Modern evolutionists, as well as Darwin, hold to the evolution of sexual differences. See, for example, Marguerite Holloway's discussion ["Profile: Vive la Difference," *Scientific American*," 263, No. 4 (1990), 40-42] of the work of Doreen Kimura, a psychologist at the University of Western Ontario, London, Ontario. Kimura studied the roles of various parts of the human brain, especially with respect to sexual differences. Holloway said, "Kimura believes sexual dimorphism evolved as a result of task specialization in hunter-gatherer societies. Women stayed closer to camp and to their children, focusing on

immediate surroundings and developing fine-motor skills—the precursors of language . . . . Meanwhile men wandered afield, oriented more to external space, giving them an edge in specific spatial tests."

28. Birken, p. 27; quoted from Charles Darwin, *Metaphysics, Materialism and the Evolution of Mind: The Early Writings of Charles Darwin*, ed. Paul Barrett (Chicago: University of Chicago Press, 1980), pp. 97-98.

29. But how could evolutionists misinterpret their theory for so long? Two answers have been given recently. Sarah Blaffer Hrdy ["Raising Darwin's Consciousness," *Zygon*, 25 (1990), 129-37, reprinted from *The Evolution of Sex*, ed. Robert Bellig and George Stevens (San Francisco: Harper and Row, 1988)] maintained that researchers who investigated the social behavior of primates unconsciously introduced male bias into their conclusions; she offered documentation. Alice B. Kehoe ["Gender, an Organon," *Zygon*, 25 (1990), 139-50] contended that gender is no more than an organon, that is, an instrument of thought. Kehoe's thesis begins with the observation that in many Indo-European languages gender is a grammatical structure. Speakers of these languages are virtually forced to project this categorization into their experience of the world. Kehoe traced a process whereby this practice, not necessarily a part of non-Indo-European languages, has injected the concept of male dominance into Western thinking. Thus, both Hrdy and Kehoe provided what Birken's theory assumes, namely, the conclusion that males have not in fact evolved more than females.

30. About a decade after Stephen Jay Gould and Niles Eldredge proposed punctuated equilibrium theory, J. Steve Oliver, Ronald D. Simpson, and Wyatt W. Anderson could refer to the new theory as a new evolutionary *paradigm* ["Darwin, Science Education, and the Method of Science," *Proteus*, 6, No. 2 (1989), 5-9; p. 6.] The word "paradigm" carries freight; it is an umbrella that spreads easily. This is especially true if one part of this theory, its unfalsifiability with respect to the fossil gaps, is needed in other areas of study.

31. I realize that even an evolutionist would have difficulty finding the proper conditions for each of the large number of niche changes required. But devolution is not a new idea. The late Arthur Custance, a Canadian scholar, and the late Duyvene de Wit, a South African anthropologist, both maintained that aborigines, who seem to be more primitive than Adam and Eve, are actually their descendants; their "primitive" characteristics enabled them to survive under the harsh conditions of the wilderness better than the "civilized" characteristics of people living in settled regions. Custance contended that after the Flood some people were forced to move away from the settled, more civilized part of the world, Mesopotamia; only those who could cope with primitive living conditions could survive. [See Arthur Custance, *Genesis and Early Man* (Grand Rapids: Zondervan, 1975).] De Wit claimed that a process of "brutification and devolution" (his words) proceeded far enough so that there was morphological convergence with certain higher primates. He particularly mentioned the nonwhite races of southern Africa. (Although de Wit wrote many articles, his ideas on devolution are clearest in his address, "The Paleontological Record and the Origin of Man," presented to the Scientific Society of the Orange Free State, Republic of South Africa, on August 26, 1963; available only in mimeographed form.) Convergence, of course, produces only apparent similarity, not identity. But in my opinion, any devolutionistic theory applied to human beings does not do justice to the dignity that the Bible ascribes to them. Such theory can, in fact, be dangerous because it might be used to support racism.

32. Robert John Russell, "Christian Discipleship and the Challenge of Physics: Formation, Flux, and Focus," *Perspectives on Science and Christian Faith*, 42 (1990), 139-54; pp. 152-53.

Index of Subjects

aborigines
   descendants of Adam and Eve......296
abortion on demand................290
Abraham, call of..................179
absolute brightness.................61
acquired characteristics
   inherited......................209
Adam
   entire hum. fam., equate to........232
Adam and the Ape.................188
adamah, ground (Heb.).............194
adenine, letter of genet. code.........71
Advancement of Learning...........283
aesthetics and soc. Darwinism.......246
age of Creation.....................53
age of earth by. geol. methods........55
Age of Enlightenment...............23
Age of Reason.....................23
agnosticism
   a third option...................204
   Thomas Huxley's.................23
agriculture, first...............189, 192
Allende meteorite
   4.6-billion-yr. age................59
alphabetic structure in Bible.........181
altar decoration, evol. of............246
altruism
   evolutionary origin of.............210
   in rhesus monkeys...............256
   natural selec. accounts for.........217
American Scientific Affiliation...279, 280
American Sign Language
   and animal speech...............223
amino acids.......................73
   components of proteins............87
   description of....................69
   destruction by oxygen.............77
   in meteorites....................95
   laboratory synthesis of.............76
ammonia, for first life...............68
amphibians, appearance of...........74

angel guarding Eden...............288
Angiosperms......................173
Anglo-Saxon thesis
   English dominance in world.......238
animal ancestry
   allowing for possibility of.........187
animal culture and hum. cult.........216
animal cultures....................216
Animal Liberation..................255
Animal Liberation Front............260
animal rights movement.............255
   action level.....................260
   philosophical level...............258
   propaganda level.................259
animal suffering...................258
animals
   God's gift to human beings........258
   not disting'd from humans.........258
   treatment of....................256
Anthropic Cosmological
   Principle, The....................47
anthropic principle..............47, 65
   biblical.........................51
anti-evolution, responses to..........107
anti-evolutionists
   accept biol. diversity.............100
aphar, dust (Heb.).................193
apparent brightness.................61
apparition theory
   objects have spirits...............97
appropriate technology..............284
Archaeopteryx, bird-reptile..........107
argon
   atmos. Ar diff. into rocks.........276
argon-36.........................58
argon-40, K-40 decay to.............58
Aristotle, link to Aquinas.............8
artistic style
   interact'n with soc. niche..........246
Aryan race, superiority of...........238
assumptions, validity of.............154

Index of Subjects

astronomical methods
  age, distance detns. 59
  brightness 61
  distance of nearby objects 60
  distance of stars 61
  distance of planets, sun 61
atheist, intellect'ly fulfil'd 40
athletics 266
atmosphere of primitive earth 68
atoms, synthesis of 65
Audio Lingual Method 222
Australopithecines 107, 116
Australopithecus afarensis 113
Australopithecus africanus 113
  and the Taung child 115
Australopithecus robustus 113
autonomous man 211
Babylon 224
Baconian approach 9
barbaric instincts
  linger in mod. hum. beings 236
Beemerville igneous rocks, age 59
behavior
  and dualism 214
  and short-term goals 212
  controlled by environment 210
  evolutionary interp. of 213
  inherited from animals 209
behavior of human groups 214
behaviorism 210
Belgic Confession 283
belief, suspension of 38
beliefs, nonnegotiable
  from Genesis 1:1-2:3 186
Berkeley Physics Course, The 146
Bible
  and science 126, 127
  facts for science 131
  for "spiritual" only 128
  pre-scientific origin of 189
  tangential passages 129
Bible and general revelation
  not sepd. because of N.T. 131
Bible, specifics in
  God's witness in Creation 134
biblical interpretation
  principles of 166
big bang 48, 63, 98

before the 63
creation, agreement with 277
Bikita, Zimbabwe rock age 59
Binns's work 242
biogenesis
  linked to biosphere 96
biographical life
  and biological life 256
biology textbooks, probs. in 205
biopsychology, Darwinian
  English, American rejection 211
birth control for inferior 217
black backed gull 101
Blackwood's work 243
Blind Watchmaker, The 40
body-soul problem
  and holistic views 195
  three views of 195
bonding
  role in family formation 216
Bone Peddlers, The 97
Bones of Contention 190
boundaries
  created 179
  Creation and 30
boundary conditions, organisms 94
brain size 116
Bridgewater Treatises 29
burial sites and hum. fossils 200
calling, each person's 125
Cambrian explosion 75
carbon nuc. ener. lev. 28, 38, 46
carbon dioxide, for first life 68
carbon monoxide and first life 68
Case for Animal Rights, The 255
categorical complementarity 188
categories of mind impose ord. 45
cause
  Aristotle's views 6
  Pythagorean numbers and 6
cell
  complexity of living 92
  information bits in 83
  small probability of 88
  smallest possible 91
cells, first: evoln. beyond 73
cells, living: form. simplest 68
centipedes, appearance of 74

Index of Subjects

central dogma of molec. biol. 73
chance, blind, and design 39
chaos theory
   interrelationship of events 133
characteristics, inherited 17
chemical reactions
   probably "take over" 279
chimpanzee, rate of evolution 105
Chinese language, history of 222
chlorofluorocarbons
   and ozone layer 78
Christ
   active in creation 21, 97
   King of Creation 142
   not divided 195
Christian College Coalition 274
Christian community, students 206
Christian contribution
   to evolutionary problem 207
Christian influence on soc. 132
Christian nat. sci. task 269
Christian Reformed Church 148
   and the engagement model 147
Christian response
   to Darwin in 19th century 15
Christian Science 255
Christian synthesis
   with Aristotle by Aquinas 8
Christians and science
   according to Augustine 7
Christification of matter 96
chromosome 71
church scientific
   imitate estab. church 15
cities, hypothet.: appar. des. 33
Civil War, post
   anti-evol. in South 16
class struggle, Dar'n basis 217
classical economics 233
   consistent with Darwinism 235
   systematization of 216
classification
   according to Linnaeus 11
   and John Ray 11
closed universe 11, 97
codons
   functions of 73
   number of different 73

coelecanth, discovery of
   rel. fossil extinct species 100
community spirit
   natural selec. accounts for 217
competition, a force in hist. 233
computer program
   to mimic natural selection 40
Condemnation of 1277 8
Confession of Faith 283
conifers, appearance of 74
"conspicuous consumption"
   coined by Veblen 235
control beliefs 162
   and biblical teaching 163
   and Christian controversy 163
   and Creation Week account 183
   and miracles 152
   and the Bible 151
   changeable 164
   creation of human beings 186
   description of 151
   two kinds of 164
convergence 99, 296
conversation
   in broadest sense 203, 206
corals, age of 56
Cosmic Background Explorer
   and distribution of matter 66
   detn. of early radiation 66
cosmic sense, American loss of 24
cosmos, God's love for 138
Created from Animals 255
Creation
   age of 149
   and archetypal pattern 37
   Christ's redemption of 123
   development of 150
   human response to 121
   very good 120
Creation Week 169
   allegorical interpretation 183
   and work-rest cycle 288
   historicity of 180
   interpretations of 182
   literal interpretation 182
   numbers in account of 180
Creation, head of
   perfect human beings 140

Index of Subjects

Creation, order in
   according to Linnaeus 27
creation-evolution
   disagreem't among Christians 2
creationism, Lemmon's comment 278
creationism, special 284
creative synthesis
   linked to theosphere 96
Cretaceous period 173
Critique of Pure Reason 45
cultural evolution 214
   diff. from biol. evoln. 215
cultural institutions
   evolutionary legacy and 212
culture, evolution of 210, 213
cytosine, let'r of genet. code 71
Darwinian theory
   sociological context of 203
Darwinism
   and ecological movement 255
   and moral implications 255
Das Kapital 217
day
   changing length of 56
   use in Bible 170
day-age, interpretation 183
days of creation 182
de-deification 285
death as a result of sin 197
debate among Christians 280
deism and purpose 37
Descent of Man, The 261
descent with modification
   instead of design 13
design 22, 27, 52
   a creation of reason 45
   argue from God to design 30
   counterfeit 32, 42, 53
   illusory for Darwin 13
   objections to 37
   relation to human mind 50
design, poor
   according to Darwin 31
devolution 188, 241
   species disappear by 267
Dialogues Concerning Natural Religion 44
dinosaurs

appearance of 74
disappearance of 74, 75
discontinuities
   among living things 30
   in Creation 179
discovery
   improper predict. of future 205
disorder in social systems 215
Dispensationalists
   anti-evolutionary sentiment 16
divine command for sci. work 150
DNA 85, 88
   description of 70
DNA hybridization
   a molecular clock method 106
DNA molecules, complementary 71
DNA strands, difference bet. 281
documentary hypothesis 231
Dort, Synod of 283
double helix, DNA 71
dragonfly, str'ge behav. male 105
dualism 8, 120, 250
   and body-soul problem 195
   and Christians 52
   and natural law 251
   natural, spiritual 19
duck-billed platypus 108
dust
   only symbolic 194
   origin of human beings 193
earth
   early atmosphere 68
   early history 68
   use by John 140
earth-organism 136
Ecodefense 260
ecological movement
   Judeo-Christian roots of 254
ecological problem
   due to neglect of Darwin 254
economics 233
   Christian thinking, and 238
ecotheologians 254
electron
   diffraction 157
   motion of 49, 275
element
   synth. by neutron collision 67

Index of Subjects

synthesis by fusion 67
elements, periodic class. of 157
end of history 230
environment
    and synthetic theory 17
    relation to evolution 17
enzymes
    a class of proteins 88
    relation to polypeptides 69
ereb (Heb.), biblic. use of 171
ethics
    and paradigms 205
    relation to genetics 212
eugenics and races 211
euthanasia 257
    revised view of 256
evening, use in Bible 171
evolution
    and Creatn. Wk. interprtns. 184
    atheists' only choice 40
    by random change 18
    definition of 3
    mechanism of 17
    of animals 99
    of plants 99
    punctuated equilibrium 18
    sometimes a minority view 250
    universal principle of 248
    word used by Erasmus Darwin 12
evolution battle is over 15
Evolution from Space 95
evolution in the arts
    analogy: evol. in nature 246
Evolution of Culture in
    Animals, The 216
evolution of life, prob. of
    by new natural laws 93
evolution, biological
    by infinitesimal steps 90
evolution, general
    proposed by Maupertuis 12
evolution, reasons to accept
    in 19th century 14
evolutionarily stable strat. 216
    and economics 234
    and teleology 41
evolutionary ideas
    prevalent before Darwin 12

evolutionary paradigm
    and Christians 206
    like addiction 205
evolutionary principle
    assumed universal 209, 252
evolutionary scenario 63
evolutionary theory
    a new paradigm 296
    and behavior of individuals 208
    and human self-image 208
    and nature of hum. society 208
    and progress 208
    basis of modern economies 237
    binds together all systems 252
    certainty of 204
    dogmatism in unifying 253
    four applications of 208
    immense diffic. not grasped 206
    integrate disciplines with 253
    investigate for each case 203
    scope of 252
    summary of modern theory 14
evolutionary thinking
    a factor in literature 243
evolutionary thought
    and 19th cent. poets 12
    responsible for more evoln. 96
evolutionism 53
    definition of 4
exodus of Israelites
    importance for history 129
extrapolation, problem of 251
eye
    example of structure gap 104
    wired backwards 32
faith
    knows no boundaries 142
    never bows out 142
    role in scientific activity 149
family, def. by incest taboo 227
farmer taught by God 125
fatty acids in cell 72
fecundity problem
    evidence of poor design 31
female
    closer to animals than male 260
female evolution: Darw. ideas 261
female, human: brain size of 261

feminism and evolutionism 260
ferns, appearance of 74
fetishism 231
fiat interpretation 183
field 63
  energy levels of 63
  kinds of 49
first human beings
  and descent from animals 186
  death of 197
  microevolution since 188
first man
  a living being 169
  a living soul 169
  before first woman 197
first sin 20
fish, appearance of 74
Flood and typology 11
flux of matter
  creation by means of 40
  produces life 6, 20
food chain: evid. for design 28
fossil
  and arm surgery 113
  and fireplaces 113
  burial with bed of flowers 113
  dating by carbon-14 112
  dating by K-40 to Ar-40 113
  dating by U-238 decay 113
  dating methods 112
  evidence for a hunter 113
  radiometric dating methods 112
fossil evidence 113
fossil preservation
  affects the record 100
fossil record, gaps in 18
  examples of 102
  given by Denton 103
  given by Kerkut 103
  in spite of lrg. no. fosls 103
fossil record, use of 99
fossils and bias 200
fossils found: no. of old 17
fossils of living animals
  show record is good 103
fossils, human: number of 200
four dimensions
  and man's place in nature 117

Fourth Day, The 148
framework interpretation 183-85
frontier, American
  and Turner's thesis 239
functionalism
  and origin of theatre 245
fundamental constant
  relation to structure 45
fusion, nuclear
  cold 205
  the first 65
future of 100 billion years 268
Gaia hypothesis 136, 233
galaxies
  distance of 62
  formation of 66
Garden of Eden
  as archetypal sanctuary 289
  first sin 20
gases, viscosity of 157
ge, earth (Gk.) 140
gender
  19th cent. attitude toward 260
  a problem of Darwinists 260
  abolishing 263
  an organon 296
  blurring difference between 260
  evolving difference between 261
  theory and action 264
gene 73
  selfish 212, 213
general revelation 120
  and early human history 200
  Bacon's attitude toward 284
  definition of 121
  error in neglecting 122
  extent of 123
  infallible 121
  insufficiency of 134
Genesis, polemical nature of 289
genetic changes
  large amt. in one generat'n 282
genetic code 72
genetic theory repl'd grad'l'm 90
genetically-defective
  infant, value of 257
genetics
  founded by Mendel 17

Index of Subjects

relation to evol. theory 17
genome 72
geogenesis linked to geosphere 96
geology, beginning of 25
geometric analogy for discont. 31
Gethsemane, Christ's prayer 139
ghost stories, Dar. effect on 242
ghost story examples 243
God
   losing as an ally 257
   reveals himself 124
God and creation: Aristotle 6
God and matter: Plato 6
gods
   unnecc. for crn. (ancient) 6
Gombrich's examples 246
gradualism 90
gravitat'l energy forms stars 66
Great Bahama Bank, age of 55
Great Chain of Being 11, 18
   for living things 13
guanine, letter of genet. code 71
Hardy's work 241
helium
   nuclear synthesis of 65
   percent in universe 278
Hemingway's work 242
Herbert Spencer Lectures 291
herring gull 101
hierarchy
   in Creation 288
   struct. in nature (ancient) 6
historical trends, eval. of 238
historicity of Genesis 179
History of the Theatre 244
Holy Spirit, teacher 21
hominids, preexisting 187
Homo erectus 113
   and Adam and Eve 201
   appearance of 74
Homo habilis 113
Homo neanderthalensis 113
   and Adam and Eve 201
Homo sapiens 113
   appearance of 74
homosexuals 263
hopeful monsters 110
horse, modern

evolution from *Eohippus* 90
hot dilute soup 72
"how," "that": disting. betw. 189
human
   changing paleoanthrop. view 190
   definition of 113
human beings
   a species similar to 119
   and the image of God 198
   animal forebears 114
   arose in several continents 282
   behavior of individual 209
   changing self-image 118
   early history of 201
   holistic 196
   natural aggressiveness of 117
   nature of 189
   origin of 54
   peaceable nature of 117
   possible date of earliest 119
   unique 198
human death and the Fall 198
human dignity abandoned 256
human evolution 111
   belief linked to irrat'l'ty 258
   in the future 111
   reasons for considering 111
   relation to racism 220
human families
   conditions for formation of 216
human family
   age of 188
   fossils and the 199
human family, origin of 188
   and scientific results 199
human history, early
   and general revelation 200
human language 220
   and animal noises 220
   and clarification 221
   and human anatomy 223
   and image of God 225
   and naming 224
   artic'l'd: peculiar to hum. 221
   complexity and history of 222
   evolution of 220
   lack of evidence of evol. 222
   nonevolutionary origin of 224

reduction to mechanics...222
human lineage
   pal'nthrplgcl. construc. of...113
human mind, in tune with Crn....156
human nature related to univ....268
human origin, acc. to Bible...111
human race
   origin: purposeless process...40
human reason
   and praise for Creation...156
   and scientific activity...155
   effect of sin on...156
   triumphs in natural science...156
human society: supraorganic...214
human speech
   relation to human language...221
hybrids, infertile
   in both art and biology...247
hydrogen, for first life...68
"ideas": Plato's unchangeable...22
idols and image of God...289
image of God...289
   and the king...289
   created in the...190
   defines human...190
   denied...257
   meaning of...191
   removed...256
   treat with respect...190
immediate goals
   and Herrnsteins's theory...40
Immigration Restriction Act...211
immunological distance
   a molecular clock method...106
imperfection, object'n to des....40
imperialism, U.S....239
Implications of Evolution...102
incest taboo...210
   and defective children...293
   biblical origin of...227
   by regulation of sexuality...227
   Christian response...228
   effect of Gospel...229
   evolutionary explanations...227
   Godelier's explanation...226
   objections to explanat'n of...226
   simultaneous with kinship...227
incest, kinship and...225

individual
   reln. to group: selfish...212
   reln. to group: unselfish...211
industry fused with the state...237
inflationary theory: cosmol'y...65
insects
   appearance of...74
   higher intelligence...95, 135
instinct and evolution...209
instrumentalism
   definition...157
   laws as tools...158
   rejection of...158
interpretation
   masking the meaning of...179
   problems: historicity...168
   problems: translation...168
   problems: undrstndng. text...168
interpretation of Bible
   and ancient documents...167
interpretation of Gen. 1:1-2:3
   allegorical...171
   day-age...172
   fiat...175
   framework (literary)...177
   literal...169
   modified intermittent-day...176
   overlapping day-age...173
intersections bet. Bib., sci....129
invertebrates, appearance of...74
investigation
   by Adam...39
   Christian freedom in...155
   limitations on...150
Ionian philosophers
   mathematics and facts...6
"is" and "ought": confus'n of...217
ish, man (Heb.)...290
ishshah, woman (Heb.)...290
isotope...58
isotopes, missing: det. age...276
Israel, early: contemp. cult....289
Israel, history of
   for both spec., gen. rev....131
   miracles import. in history...130
Jehovah's Witnesses: anti-evo....16
jelly fish, appearance of...74
JEPD, origin of Pentateuch...231

Index of Subjects

Keystone, SD rock age 59
kind, according to its 179, 184
kinship
   and incest 225
   because of large brain 226
   origin and man's use of
     facts of life 226
   relation to evolution 226
kosmos (Gk.) 138
   designates earth or cosmos 138
   negative connotation 138
laboratory simulation
   chemical steps toward life 76
   guidance of 82
   problems with 82
Lamarckian mechanism of change 17
language: reln. to communic'n 222
languages, intermed.: dead 222
law, scientific
   a summary of observations 157
layers, alternating: det. age 55
Le Fanu's work 243
Leakey expeditions 112
leisure class: Veb'n crit. of 235
life
   chemicals necessary for 68
   democratization of 263
   evolution from nonlife 78
   inorg. matter to (ancient) 6
life, early, and UV radiation 78
life, multicell.: app'rance of 74
life, search for
   in other parts of universe 83
light
   diffraction by crystals 156
   in a magnetic field 157
   wave properties 156
limitations in Creation 179
lipids: reln. to fatty acids 72
literal interpretation
   and anti-evolution 206
literature, discussion of 240
living being became man 197
London's work 241
Lord's Supper and gestures 288
lottery: prob. of winning 89
love: role in sci. activity 149
lungfish 108

Lutherans, Missouri Synod
   early opposition to evol. 17
Macbeth 251
Machen's work 243
macroevolution 100
   barriers: nonbiol. examples 101
   reln. to punctuated equil. 18
magnetic particles, alignment 57
magnetic reversal, earth field 57
male superiority
   incorrectly assumed 296
Malthusian pressure on society 13
mammals, appearance of 74
"Manifest Destiny" 239
manna 43
marine organisms
   appearance of single-celled 74
Mars, search for life on 83
Marxist, Christian 232
mathematical conf. on evol. 86
mathematical r'soning for sci. 10
Matthias chosen by lot 44
Matthieson's work 242
maturation time: fam. f'mat'n 216
Mendel, genetics and 17
metal-working, first 189
metaphors and evolution 214
meteorites for starting mat'ls 68
methane, for first life 68
microevolution 100
   reln. to punctuated equil. 18
middle class society
   basis of greater male evol. 262
"might is right" 218
militarism, Bryan's view of 16
minerals, early earth, oxy. in 79
miracles 275
   and natural law 166
   by intervention 43
   some explained 151
   unnec.: 19 cent. scientists 12
mitochondrial DNA and "Eve" 112
modern art: evol. basis 248
modern science and Bacon 9
modified inter. day interp. 183
molecular biol.: central dogma 73
molecular clock
   and amino acid order 105

Index of Subjects

disagree with fossil evid. 107
discrep. in evoln. rates 106
   for dating 281
   for evolution rate 105
molecular methods: evol. rate 105
monkeys typing
   Encyclopedia Britannica 89
   works of Shakespeare 89
monotheism 231
moral individualism 256
morality
   and animal ancestry 256
   and animal past 291
   and our animal past 212
   "more openly" 283
mosses, club: appearance of 74
music 266
musicians, first 192
"must"
   about evolution of life 82
   for primitive atmosphere 81
   nonlife-to-life 80
mutation
   by shift bet. chromosomes 110
   by shifting piece of gene 110
   in genetic theory 90
myth
   and origin of theatre 245
   early chapters of Genesis 188
natural: sepn. from supernat. 97
natural explanation: anything 214
natural laws
   and origins 251
   explain everything 6, 53
   predictions by 156
natural science
   and closed universe 11
   and matter and energy 286
   birth of 23
   distort computer, ult. real 136
   distorted by Taoist thought 135
   distortions by unbelievers 134
   examples of distortions 135
   limiting evol. theory to 252
   other religions distort 135
   sepn. from other sciences 144
   structure in 126
   Thales, founder of 6

versus other sciences 144
natural selection 13
   and prolific species 279
   applied to Christianity 231
   does not produce optimum 42
   modif. by short-term goals 212
   req. nucl'c acids, proteins 279
natural theology 13, 27-28, 37, 147
naturalism in fiction 240
nature
   losing, as an ally 257
   restored by grace 286
Nature's Cathedral
   and Natural History Museum 15
Naziism and eugenics 211
Neanderthals
   appearance of 74
   like aborigines, Tasmanians 218
neoclassical economics 233
   and gov't interference 233
   and perfect design 234
   and rational behavior 233
   and surv. of the fittest 235
   progress by competition 234
neoclassical theory
   and information 234
   and local factors 234
neoinstitutionalism 236
neoorthodox 147
Neoplatonism: Copernicus's view 9
nephesh (Heb.)
   as a whole person 196
   summary concerning 196
neptunium-237 decay 59
neutrons, first appearance of 65
New Age 136
   link to evolution 232
New Deal and social Darwinism 236
New Industrial State, The 237
Newtonian mech.: life, motion 271
niche: a prejudicial word 249
nihilism in art 250
nitrogen, for first life 68
non-Christians and sci. work 154
nonequilibrium processes
   and life 84
   in social systems 215
nonevolutionary

Index of Subjects

explanations of phenomena 252
nonlife-to-life
   modifications of scenario 202
   time available for 86
nonnegotiable biblical ideas 199
nonnegotiable ideas in Gen. 1 182
nonnormative sciences 286
nonphysical forces 95
noogenesis
   linked to noosphere 96
noosphere 267
normal science
   paradigm, within the 202
normative sciences 286
Norris's work 241
nucleotide, definition of 71
numbers in Genesis account 178
numbers, ancient table
   calculations of fractions 6
observer a part of system 49, 275
oestrus, loss of
   role in family formation 216
Old and New Testaments
   unity of 172
omega point 267
On the Origins of Language 221
order
   imposed by mind 45
   in Creation 27, 126
organ gaps 104
   Goldschmidt's examples 104
Origin of Species, The 12, 14
origins
   control beliefs and 165
   miracles and 165
overlapping day-age
   interpretation 183, 185
oxidizing agent 77
oxygen
   and early atmosphere 68
   debate about early concn. 82
   in primitive atmosphere 77, 79
   nuclear energy level 46
oxygen nucleus, energy levels 28
oxygen, change in concentration
   in early atmosphere 80
ozone in primitive atmosphere 78
ozone layer: partial destruc. 78

paleoanthropologists
   and the Bible 201
   competitiveness among 114
   disagreement among 114
   gap problem 114
Palisades Sill rock age 59
palladium-107 decay to Ag-107 59
panspermia 95
   directed 95
paradigm
   before and after Darwin 17
   evolutionary 202
   problem of the 202, 248
paradigm, evolutionary
   and biological discoveries 202
   possible collapse of 202
Parrysound, ON rock age 59
peppered moth 101
perception
   binds space, time, physical 50
PETA 259
Phenomenon of Man 96
phosphate, source of 72
photons: early radiation 66
photosynthesis 79
   beginning of 73
physical evolutionary theory
   diff. from bio. evol. theory 98
physical laws, precedence of 8
physics and chemistry
   insuff. for living systems 93
Piltdown hoax 17, 283
planets
   formation of 67
   measurement of distance to 277
Poganophora, discovery of
   required new missing links 103
polypeptides, description of 69
polytheism 231
Portland, CT rock age 59
positivism 32, 231
positivist, inconsistency of 32
potassium-40, decay to Ar-40 58
potassium-argon
   method for loss of argon 282
practices, evolution of 215
pre-adaptation incomp. organ 104
pre-scientific orig. of Bible 189

prebiotic soup 86
presuppositions in sci. exam. 159
prime mover: a computer prog. 136
primitive atmos., reducing 76
primitive earth atmosphere 68
principles of interpretation
   authentic history 167
   infallible Word 166
   its own interpreter 167
   OT and NT closely linked 168
   science an aid 167
probability
   examples 88
   of forming cell components 86
progress
   change for the better 230
   in human institutions 230
   in religion 230
   in the eye of beholder 230
   toward a goal 230
proteins 87
   description of 69
   formation of 72, 90
proteins, useful: v. sm. frac. 87
protocell 72, 87, 91
protons, first appearance of 65
providence: 19 cent. approach 20
providential evol. and Darwin 31
psychogenesis: expl. of univ. 135
psychogenesis: objects, spir. 97
Ptolemaic system
   constant modifications of 202
   motion of planets 7
public schools, evolution in 253
punctuated equilibrium 149, 281
   evolution by 18, 108, 265
Pythagorean school, mathematics 7
quantum fluctuation 64, 277
quantum mechanics 275
   reln. bet. obsrvr. and phys. 49
quarks, first appearance of 65
rabbit, appendix not vestig. 108
race
   in NT church 220
   useful in maintaining order 219
   race extinction by nat. sel. 218
Rachels' four-part argument 256
racial history: controversial 219

racism
   effect of opposition to 211
   in nineteenth century 218
radio signals
   search for life elsewhere 83
radioactive multistep decays 59
radioactive props. of atoms 57
radiometric measurements 57
rationalism: dep. on reasoning 22
reason 22
   and image of God 24
   Christian view of 24
reasoning, deductive 22
reasoning, inductive 22
recapitulation
   history of ideas on origins 18
redemption
   includes cleansing 139
   is reconciliation 137
   of all Creation 137
   significance for Creation 122
   Triune God active in 123
redemption of Creation
   by Christ 21
   in special revelation 137
reducing agent 77
reducing atmosphere 76
reduction
   chemical 76
   of matter, genetic inform. 15
reductionism: biol. to phys. 94
reinforcement theory 212
   and controlling behavior 213
   and inherited behavior 213
   and learned behavior 213
relativity theory 275
   and the big bang 63
religion
   a competitor of science 212
   evolutionary history of 231
religious: all life 122
replication of cells
   by random events 91
   problem of 91
replication, simplest
   computer simulation 91
reptiles, appearance of 74
repunctuation of Genesis 175

Index of Subjects

revelations
  both are everywhere 122
  everyone interacts with 155
  God revealing himself 22
  integral relation between 162
  Kuyper's attitude toward 284
  no contradictions between 122
  not hidden 181
  purpose of 124
  relation between the two 121
riboses
  base-modified 72
  role of base-modified in RNA 70
ritual and origin of theatre 245
RNA 85, 88
  description of 70
  function of mRNA 72
  function of tRNA 73
  "RNA world" 279
Robertson's work 241
roles and institutions
  strengthening of 215
Romantic literature 23
rubidium-87 decay to Sr-87 276
rugged individualism
  and American frontier 239
sacrificial love: our calling 142
salvation, God's acts of
  integrity of all Creation 133
Sante Fe Institute 252
saphab (Heb.) 224
"save the phenomena," models 158
science
  and the Bible 126
  confusion with nat. science 127
  nature of 143
  result of human activity 144
science and theology
  interact. bet.: cat. compl. 148
  interaction bet.: contrast 147
  interaction bet.: derivatn. 147
  interaction bet.: engagmnt. 147
  interaction bet.: parallel 147
Science of Mechanics, The 157
science, nature of
  a non-Christian view 146
science, structure of
  component: data 159

  component: presuppositions 159
  component: theories 159
scientific activity
  and effect of sin 143
  and faith in God 143
  and love of Creation 143
  and love of God 143
  and rationality 143
  and redemption 143
  and the future 160
  as development of Creation 150
  definition 144
  in new heaven, new earth 160
  part of history 160
  related to God's image 154
scientific enterprise
  does not move backward 159
  exists because of order 134
scientific evidence, role of 199
scientific knowledge
  aid in interpretation 199
scientific results
  assuming future 149
  incorrect use of 288
scientists, Christian
  and scientific agenda 206
Scopes trial 16, 218
Scripture: epistem. supreme 158
sea slime, life from 6
sea stories, Darw'n effect on 241
sea-floor spread'g, const. rate 56
sermons on science 15
serpent as a symbol 288
seventh day, length of 170
Seventh Day Adventists
  anti-evolutionary sentiment 16
sex differences fill niches 263
sex differentiation
  accumulation of differences 262
  is unnatural 263
sex, evol. of, not biblical 264
sex, relativized 263
sexes, emergence of 262
sexologists 263
sexual dimorphism 262
  and the human brain 295
Shinar 224
Silurian Age 173

sin
    effect on natural science 152
    effects hum. reason. abil. 24
    sin, first: desire for auton. 152
Skull 1470 223
social Darwinism 216, 233
    and historical thinking 238
    modern revival of 217
    reasons for rejection of 218
social entropy 216
social evolution and order 216
social groups of animals 256
social organ. evol.: animals 216
social worker taught by God 125
social workers and environm't 218
sociobiology, conformer genes 212
Sociobiology: The New Synthesis 212
solar system: Laplace's theory 26
Song of Solomon
    nature of 164
    scholars and 183
Song of Songs: nature of 165
soul: confusion in Gen. 2:7 195
South, anti-evolution in 16
special revelation 120
    Bacon's attitude toward 284
    definition of 121
    two purposes of 163
speciation 100
    examples of 101
species
    blurring difference between 254
    pass into oblivion 263, 267
species membrshp. not impor't 257
speciesism 259
spectacles, Calvin's 134
speed of light 45
spiritual
    dualistic sepn. from naturl. 19
Spruce Pine, NC rock age 59
stability in species record 108
star clusters, distance of 62
stars
    colonizing the 268
    first, second generations 67
    formation of 66
    measurement of distance to 277
Steinbeck's work 242

stimulus-response, language 222
strong anthropic principle 47
strontium-87 from rubidium-87 276
structuralism: theatre origin 245
structure simil.: evol. evid. 99
subdue earth: divine command 150
subject, content of 249
    evolution in 248
subject, history of 249
    evolution in 248
sugars, description of 70
suicide, revised view of 256, 257
super-race, Nazi concept of 218
superintellect causes order 46
supernatural versus natural 52
survival of the fittest
    coined by Spencer 13, 216
symbolic numbers in the Bible 180
Synodical Study Committee 277
synthetic: new evoln. theory 17
Tao of Physics, The
    a non-Christian distortion 135
Tasmanian wolf
    skeleton sim. placental dog 100
Taung child 115
Taung skull 117
tectonic plates, movement of 57
Teilhard's synthesis 96
teleology
    and evol. stable strategy 42
theatre
    existence of 244
    theories of origin 244
theistic evolution 15, 186
    and origin of Adam and Eve 193
    arguments against 193
    Christian 289
    untenable 197
theological sci., bib. study 145
theories
    as useful fictions 158
    not perfect 159
Theories of Evolution 96
theories, scientific
    dep. on extra-sci. factors 159
thermodynamics 215
    and equilibrium processes 84
third option: agnosticism 204

Index of Subjects

thorium-232 decay 59
thymine, letter of genet. code 71
time zero, nonexistence of 64
TM 136
toledoth passages 192
tools, stone 113
Totem and Taboo 210
Tower of Babel
   a different explanation 224
   and language 223
   traditional understanding 224
trade secret of paleontology 109
transitional forms bet. gaps 107
transsexuals 263
transvestites 263
tree of knowl. of good, evil 288
tree of life 288
triads, Kepler's mystical 9
Triune God active in history 21
tuberculosis, stability of 108
tunneling, quantum 277
two books, Bacon and 9
two-domain theory of knowl. 8, 9
UFO and the New Age 232
ultraviolet radiation
   to the early earth 78
uncertainty
   in time of energy change 64
uncertainty principle 49, 275
unified field
   for phys. and consciousness 136
   quantized 63
uniformitarianism in biology 26
unisex movement 264
unity in physical sciences 156
universe
   closed 48, 52
   closed and unified 252
   no beginning 135
universes
   ensembles of 48
   existence of other 51, 65
uracil, letter of genet. code 71
uranium-235 decay 59

uranium-238 decay 59
variable star: distance detn. 62
Veblen's influence
   and American econ. policy 236
   and Galbraith 237
Veblen's teachings
   and evolution 236
   compared to Marx 235
Veblenism
   two schools thought within 237
Vedas 136
Vedic thought 135
vestigial organs 108
   not automatically assumed 203
viewing ourselves 240
Viking Lake, Sask. rock age 59
visual art, evol. history of 246
vitalism 95
   postulated driving force 135
volcanic exhalations 79
wakwak tree rumor: bears women 12
watchmaker and order in Crn. 39
water
   starting material for life 68
   photodissociation of 79
way station
   bet. two extremes interp. 174
weak anthropic principle 47
Wealth of Nations, The 216
"white man's burden" 239
whole rock method
   for Rb-87— Sr-87 276
wine from water 199
women subservient
   basis of greater male evol. 262
works of God: a continuum 43
world food supply
   Malthus' theory concerning 13
World War I, disillusionment 218
Worldview and creation-evoln. 1
yom (Heb.)
   use in Bible 170
Zoological Journal of London
   order in Creation 27

Index of Persons

Aaron, Daniel 294
Agassiz, Louis 28, 218, 273
Ahmes 6, 10, 20
Albert, Jerry 277, 279
Allee, W.C. 211, 291
Allen, John 285-86
Anaximander 6
Anderson, N.D. 284
Anderson, Wyatt 272-73, 284, 296
Andrews, Roy Chapman 218
Apol, Dallas 292
Aquinas, Thomas 8, 11, 19
Aristotle 6-8, 19, 28, 158, 202
Augustine 7, 19, 177, 288
Aulie, Richard 272, 274
Ayala, F.J. 279
Babloyantz, Agnes 279
Bacon, Francis 9, 11, 19, 271, 283
Bak, Per 285
Barbour, Ian 287
Barrett, Paul 296
Barrow, John 47-48, 275
Barth, Karl 147
Bavinck, Herman 30, 286
Bellig, Robert 296
Bender, Bert 241-42, 294
Berry, R.J. 187-88, 190, 289
Billingsley, K.L. 295
Binns, Archie 242
Birken, Lawrence . 262-64, 266-67, 295-96
Birx, H. James 96, 280
Bishop of Paris 8
Blackwood, Algernon 243
Blocher, Henri152, 177-78, 191, 280, 287-90
Bloomfield, Leonard 222, 292
Bonner, John Tyler 216, 291
Boot, Kornelis 292
Bos, Abe 292
Bowler, Peter 5, 23, 271, 273
Bradley, Walter 79, 81-82, 278-80
Broca, Paul 260-61

Brockett, Oscar G. 244-45, 294
Bromiley, Geoffrey W. 286
Brown, Colin 293
Browne, Thomas 143
Brunner, E. 286
Bryan, William Jennings 16, 218
Bube, Richard 174-75, 273, 288
Buchanan, James 233
Buckland, William 26
Buffon, George de 12
Burke, Derek 289
Byl, John 91-92, 158, 280, 287
Cage, John 266
Cain, A.J. 215-16, 291
Calvin, John 134, 171, 285-86
Capra, Fritjof 135, 285
Cassels, E.S. 273
Chaffey, Charles 273
Chen, Kan 285
Chuang Tzu 135
Codd, E.F. 280
Colden, Cadwallader 23
Colwell, Gary 31, 274
Comte, Auguste 231
Coon, Carleton 219-20, 292
Cooper, John 195, 290
Copernicus 254
Copernicus, Nicolaus 9
Costanzo, Angelo 272
Coughlin, Raymond 271
Crick, Francis 71, 95
Custance, Arthur 296
Cuvier, Baron George 12
Cuvier, Georges 26
D'Abro, A. 156, 287
Dart, Raymond 117, 283
Darwin, Charles 5, 12-13, 15, 17-20,
  22, 26-29, 31, 33, 39-40, 90, 102-03, 205,
  208, 210, 214-15, 217-18, 230, 233, 237,
  240-41, 252, 254-58, 260-63, 267, 274,
  281, 284, 291-92, 294-96

Index of Persons

Darwin, Erasmus 12
Davies, Paul 271, 280, 285
Davis, Bob 278
Dawkins, Richard 32, 40, 204, 206, 216, 252, 274, 290-91, 295
De Boer, Jesse 188, 289
de Bres, Guido 283
de Chardin, Pierre Teilhard 96, 232, 267, 280
De Koning, Jan 284, 287
de Lamarck, Chevalier 12
de Wit, Duyvene 296
Democritus 6
Denton, Michael .. 14, 31, 90, 92, 99-101, 103, 105, 203, 206, 271-74, 278-81, 290
Descartes, Rene 10, 11, 19, 271
Dewey, John 210
Diehl, David 290
Diggins, John P. 236-37, 294
Dobzhansky, T. 17, 279
Dooyeweerd, Herman 30
Dow, Loren W. 215, 291
Dozeman, Thomas 148, 287
Dunn, Robert 218
Dupree, A. Hunter 273
Durant, John 283
Eckelmann, Herman 176-77, 288
Edinger, Tilly 116
Einstein, Albert 63
Eiseley, Loren 116, 283
Eldredge, Niles . 18, 108-09, 149, 281, 296
Empedocles 6, 40
Epicurus 6
Euclid 7
Farquhar, R.M. 276
Ferris, James 80-81, 278
Fiske, John 238-40
Fix, William 97, 280
Foreman, David 260
Fox, Michael 258
Fox, Robin 225-27, 292-93
Franklin, Benjamin 23
Frayer, David 282
Frazer, James 244, 249, 294
Fredkin, Ed 136-37, 285
Freske, Stanley 277
Freud, Sigmund 209-10, 263, 290
Friedman, Milton 293

Friedman, Rose 293
Galbraith, John Kenneth 237, 294
Galileo 45
Gillespie, Neal C. 32, 53, 274, 281
Gingerich, Owen 142-43, 275-76, 286
Godelier, Maurice 216, 221, 226-27, 291-93
Goethe, Johann W. 23
Goldschmidt, Richard ... 104, 110, 281-82
Gombrich, Ernst 246-49, 294-95
Gould, Stephen Jay 18, 108-09, 149, 260-61, 272, 281-82, 290, 295-96
Grafen, Alan 274, 291, 293-94
Grant, Edward 8, 271
Hagelin, John 135-36, 285
Haldane, E.S. 271
Hallam, A. 272
Hanson, Jarice 292
Hardy, Thomas 241
Harris, George 231
Hawking, Stephen 64, 278
Hayes, Rutherford 239
Hayward, Alan 175, 276, 288
Heidman, E.P. 286
Hemingway, Ernest 242, 266
Hermann, Kenneth 274
Herrnstein, R.J. 40-42, 212-13, 234, 274-75, 291, 293
Hexham, Irving 232, 293
Hindle, Brook 272
Hitler, Adolf 212
Hodge, Charles 29
Hodgson, Richard 284
Hoffer, Peter 209-10, 290
Hofstadter, Richard .. 233, 235-36, 292-94
Holland, John 252-53
Holloway, Marguerite . 221, 223, 292, 295
Homan, Paul 294
Hooykaas, Reijer 285
Horgan, John 279
Houston, James 282, 290
Hoyle, Fred 46, 88, 95, 275, 279-80
Hrdy, Sarah Blaffer 296
Hume, David 40, 44-45, 47, 275
Hutton, James 25, 26
Huxley, Julian 15, 89
Huxley, Thomas 15, 23, 212, 232, 243, 273

314 Index of Persons

Jappe, F. 293
Johanson, Donald 114
Johnson, A. Leland 272-73, 275
Johnson, Phillip 281
Jones, D. Gareth 272
Kandrup, Henry 277-78
Kant, Immanuel 45, 47, 275
Kaplan, Martin 279
Kehoe, Alice 296
Kepler, Johannes 9
Kerkut, G.A. 102, 281
Keynes, John Maynard 237
Kimura, Doreen 221, 223, 295
Kipling, Rudyard 239
Kline, Meredith 288
Koldenhoven, James 294
Kuhn, Thomas 10, 159, 202, 230, 271, 287, 290, 293
Kuyper, Abraham 162, 284, 287
Langton, Christopher 280
Lao Tzu 135
Laplace, Pierre 26
Le Bon, Gustave 261
Le Fanu, Sheridan 243
Le Gros Clark, Wilfred 115
Leakey, Louis 114
Leakey, Mary 114
Leakey, Richard 114, 190, 223, 282-83, 289, 292
Ledwon, Lenora 242-43, 294
Leegwater, Arie 157, 284, 286-87
Lemmon, Richard M. 81-82, 146, 278, 287
Lerner, Max 236, 293-94
Leuchtenburg, William 292
Leupold, H.C. 170-71, 288
Levi-Strauss, Claude 245, 294
Lewin, Roger 114-18, 190, 223, 271, 273, 281-83, 289, 292, 295
Lieberman, Philip 221-23, 292
Lindberg, David 271, 273
Linnaeus, Carolus 11, 27
Livingstone, David 29, 214, 271-74, 285, 291-3
London, Jack 241
Lovelock, James 136
Maatman, Russell 284, 287-88
Mach, Ernst 157-58, 287

Machen, Arthur 243
Maddox, John 277
Maharishi Mahesh Yogi 136
Malthus, Thomas 12
Marx, Karl 215, 217, 235, 240-41
Mather, J.C. 278
Matthiessen, Peter 242
Maupertuis, Pierre 12
Mayr, Ernst 271
Mazur, Pawel 277-78
McIntyre, John 86, 279
McKinley, William 239
McMullin, Ernan 273, 281
Meiklejohn, J.M.D. 275
Mendel, Gregor 17
Michelangelo 247
Miller, Stanley 76
Miller, William 294
Mills, Gordon 87, 279
Monod, Jacques 87, 279
Moore, James R. 271, 272
Moorhead, Paul 279
Morowitz, Harold 91, 280
Nash, Roderick 241, 254-55, 266, 294-95
Nelson, Robert 254, 295
Newkirk, Ingrid 259
Newman, Robert 91-92, 176-77, 280, 288
Nickels, Martin 253
Nicolis, Gregoire 279
Nietzsche, Friedriche 241
Norris, Frank 241
Numbers, Ronald L. 271, 273
O'Connor, Maeve 280
Oliver, J. Steve 272-73, 284, 296
Olsen, Roger 79, 81-82, 278, 280
Oparin, A.I. 81, 278
Otto, Rudolph 147
Outler, Albert C. 271
Overmire, Thomas 223, 292
Owen, Richard 12, 37
Paley, William 28-29, 37, 39, 273
Parker, Barry 278
Persons, Stow 292
Piaget, Jean 210
Piersma, B.J. 280
Pilbeam, David 114-16, 283

Index of Persons

Plantinga, Alvin 24, 40, 155, 273-74, 281, 287
Plato 6, 7, 9, 19, 22, 158
Poe, Edgar Allan 12, 272
Poewe-Hexham, Karla 232, 293
Polanyi, Michael 93-94, 280
Pope, Geoffrey 282
Preston, David G. 280, 287-89
Price, George McCready 16
Prigogine, Ilya 84-85, 215, 279
Pringle, William 286
Ptolemy 7, 202
Pun, Pattle P.T. 103, 108, 110, 173, 271-273, 281-82, 288
Pythagoras 6, 19-20
Quarten, Johannes 271
Rachels, James 255-58, 295
Ramm, Bernard 288
Ratzsch, Del 159, 287
Ray, John 11
Regan, Tom 255, 258, 295
Remelts, Glenn 147, 274, 287
Rennie, John 282
Richards, Robert 210-12, 290-91
Ridderbos, N.H. 288
Riesman, David 294
Ritschl, Albrecht 147
Robertson, Morgan 241
Robinson, Charles, Jr. 271
Romer, A.S. 103, 281
Roosevelt, Franklin 236
Roosevelt, Theodore 217, 239, 292
Ross, G.R.T. 271
Runciman, W.G. 215-16, 230, 291-93
Runner, H. Evan 284, 286
Ruse, Michael 273
Rush, Benjamin 23
Russell, Colin 272
Russell, Robert John 268, 296
Ruthen, Russell 252, 295
Sagan, Carl 40
Sarich, Vincent 15, 107
Sax, Joseph 254
Schopf, T.J.M. 281
Segundo, J.L. 232, 293
Shakespeare, William 251
Simons, Elwyn 107, 115, 281

Simpson, George Gaylord 40, 102, 204, 206, 279, 281
Simpson, Ronald 272-73, 284, 296
Singer, Peter 255, 258, 295
Sire, James 293
Skinner, B.F. 210-11, 213, 290
Smith, Adam 216
Smith, Grafton Elliot 115
Smith, James Ward 15, 23-24, 46, 272-73, 275
Smith, John Maynard 41
Smith, N. Kemp 275
Smoot, George 66
Spencer, Herbert 13, 208, 214, 216-17, 238, 291-92
Spykman, Gordon 283, 285
Stafford, Tim 295
Stafleu, Marinus 287
Stebbins, G.L. 279
Steinbeck, John 242, 266
Stek, John 166-67, 285, 288
Stevens, George 296
Struyk, John 292
Sumner, William Graham 235, 292
Taine, Hippolyte 240
Tax, Sol 281
Taylor, John Hammond 271
Taylor, Samuel Coleridge 23
Tennyson, Alfred 12
Thales 6
Thaxton, Charles 79, 81-82, 278, 280
Thielicke, Helmuth 142, 286
Tipler, Frank 47-48, 275
Titian 247
Torrecelli 45
Townes, Charles 89, 279
Turner, Frederick Jackson ... 239-40, 249
Tye, Henry 65
Tyndall, John 14
Usher, David 80-81, 278
Valentine, J.W. 279
Van Der Ziel, Aaldert 85, 279
Van Dyke, Louis 294
Van Leeuwen, Raymond 288
Van Till, Howard 148, 273, 285, 287-88
Vanden Bosch, Mike 294
Vander Goet, H. 284, 286

Veblen, Thorstein 235-37, 293-94
Veenhof, Jan 286
Vogt, Carl 260, 295
Vorzimmer, Peter 90, 279
Walker, Francis Amasa 233
Wall, Bernard 280
Ward, Terry 285
Warfield, Benjamin 16, 30
Watson, James 71, 95
Watson, John 210
Wenham, Gordon 289
Westfall, Richard 271
Wheeler, John 47, 275
White, Lynn, Jr. 254, 295
Whitman, Walt 12
Wickramasinghe, N.C. 88, 95, 279-80
William of Conches 8
Wilson, Allan 223
Wilson, Edward O. 212-13, 291
Wilson, Woodrow 240, 294
Wishy, Bernard 292
Wolstenhome, G.E.W. 280
Wolters, A.M. 286, 292
Wolterstorff, Nicholas 151, 287
Wonderly, Daniel 56, 276
Worster, Donald 273
Wright, Richard 37, 187, 191, 212, 273-74, 281-83, 285, 287, 289-91
Wright, Robert 285
York, D. 276
Young, Davis 273, 276, 288
Young, Louise 283
Zitarelli, David 271
Zubay, Geoffrey 278

Index of Bible References

Genesis 1:1-2:3 ...... 162, 169, 174, 179-86
Genesis 1:2 123
Genesis 1:3-2:3 175
Genesis 1:21 196
Genesis 1:24 196
Genesis 1:25 120
Genesis 1:26 .. 51, 124, 258
Genesis 1:26-28 ..... 150, 190-91, 225, 264
Genesis 1:27 289
Genesis 1:28 .... 121, 124, 258
Genesis 1:31 ..... 120, 174
Genesis 2:2 170
Genesis 2:2-3 174
Genesis 2:4 .... 169-70, 170, 179, 182, 192
Genesis 2:4-3:24 186
Genesis 2:7 .... 169, 193-97, 200
Genesis 2:9 288
Genesis 2:15-17 224
Genesis 2:18 197
Genesis 2:19 ..... 196, 225
Genesis 2:19-20 197
Genesis 2:20 227
Genesis 2:21-23 197
Genesis 2:22 290
Genesis 2:23 225
Genesis 2:24 227
Genesis 3:1 288
Genesis 3:3 197
Genesis 3:19 .. 194, 197-98
Genesis 3:20 192
Genesis 3:21 258
Genesis 3:24 289
Genesis 4:20 192
Genesis 4:20-22 189
Genesis 4:21 192
Genesis 5:1 192
Genesis 5:4-32 188
Genesis 6:9 192
Genesis 9:3 258
Genesis 9:4 196
Genesis 9:5 196
Genesis 9:10 196
Genesis 9:12 196
Genesis 9:15 196
Genesis 9:16 196
Genesis 10:1 192
Genesis 10:5 224
Genesis 10:10 224
Genesis 10:20 224
Genesis 10:31 224
Genesis 11:1 224
Genesis 11:1-9 223
Genesis 11:2 224
Genesis 11:6 224
Genesis 11:7 224
Genesis 11:9 224
Genesis 11:10 192
Genesis 11:27 192
Genesis 12:1-3 179
Genesis 13:16 193
Genesis 14:10 131
Genesis 17:14 196
Genesis 19:17 196
Genesis 25:12 192
Genesis 25:19 192
Genesis 27:4 196
Genesis 27:19 290
Genesis 27:25 290
Genesis 34:3 196
Genesis 36:1 192
Genesis 36:9 192
Genesis 37:2 192
Genesis 46:18 196
Genesis 46:22 290
Genesis 46:26 290
Exodus 1:5 290
Exodus 6:12 224
Exodus 12:4 290
Exodus 12:15 196
Exodus 15:23-25 151
Exodus 16 43
Exodus 19:18 131
Exodus 20:4 289
Exodus 20:8-11 288
Leviticus 4:2 196
Leviticus 11:46 196
Leviticus 14:42 193
Leviticus 17:12 196
Leviticus 17:14 196
Leviticus 18:6-7 227
Leviticus 18:8-23 228
Leviticus 18:15 293
Leviticus 18:24 228
Leviticus 19:18 289
Leviticus 20:11-21 228
Leviticus 21:11 196
Leviticus 24:18 196
Leviticus 25:1-14 288
Numbers 1:46 129-30
Numbers 9:13 196
Numbers 14:22 275
Numbers 19:17 193
Numbers 21:4 196
Numbers 31:28 196
Deuteronomy 4:37-39 . 129
Deuteronomy 12:23 ... 196
Deuteronomy 31:18 ... 171
Deuteronomy 34:6 171
Joshua 10:28 196
Judges 14:5-6 131
I Samuel 14:15 131
I Samuel 17:34-37 131
I Kings 19:11 131
II Kings 23:6 194
I Chronicles 1:1 192
Nehemiah 4:2 194
Job 19:25 194
Job 38:8-10 ...... 30, 179

Index of Bible References

Job 38:22-35 43
Job 38:31-32 131
Job 41:21 196
Psalm 3:2 196
Psalm 19:1 ... 38, 124, 134
Psalm 37:13 171
Psalm 95:11 ..... 170, 174
Psalm 104:9 ...... 30, 179
Psalm 137:7 171
Proverbs 8:29 ..... 30, 179
Proverbs 31:10-31 181
Proverbs 31:11 181
Proverbs 31:16-19 181
Proverbs 31:24 181
Ecclesiastes 3:20 194
Isaiah 19:18 224
Isaiah 28:24-29 ... 125, 134
Isaiah 40:31 171
Isaiah 45:18-19 .... 27, 50, 126, 134, 284
Isaiah 61:2 171
Isaiah 66:22 140
Lamentations 1:4 181
Lamentations 2:9 181
Lamentations 5:2 181
Daniel 5:29 199
Jonah 1:17 151
Nahum 2:4 171
Zechariah 14:1 171
Zechariah 14:1-2 170
Zechariah 14:4-9 171
Zechariah 14:7 171
Matthew 4:8 138
Matthew 13:35 285
Matthew 13:38 285
Matthew 16:26 285
Matthew 17:27 43
Matthew 18:7 286
Matthew 19:4-6 228
Matthew 22:29 14
Matthew 24:21 285
Matthew 25:34 285
Matthew 27:51 131
Matthew 28:2 131
Luke 3:23 192
Luke 11:50 285
Luke 24:42-43 258
John 1:1-3 123
John 3:16 138-39
John 9:5 138
John 15:18-19 138
John 16:33 286
John 17:9 139
John 17:24 285
John 18:36 286
John 21:25 286
Acts 1:23-26 44
Acts 11:26 220
Acts 13:1 220
Acts 14:16-17 .... 124, 134
Acts 14:17 43
Acts 16:26 131
Acts 17:24 138
Acts 17:26 192
Romans 1:18 ..... 38, 134
Romans 1:20 ..... 38, 124, 134, 285
Romans 5:12 138
Romans 5:12-19 ..... 172, 192, 198
Romans 8:18-25 177
I Cor. 1:21 286
I Cor. 3:19 286
I Cor. 5:10 138
I Cor. 6:2 286
I Cor. 7:31 138
I Cor. 15:21-22 198
I Cor. 15:22 192
I Cor. 15:34-54 198
I Cor. 15:45 192
Galatians 3:28 220
Galatians 4:3 138
Ephesians 1:4 285
Ephesians 1:5 139
Ephesians 2:15-16 137
Philippians 2:6-7 51
Philippians 2:15 286
Colossians 1:15-20 51
Colossians 1:16-17 .... 21, 123
Colossians 1:16-20 137
Colossians 1:17 22
Colossians 1:19 123
Colossians 2:9 195
I Timothy 2:13 197
Titus 1:6 228
Hebrews 4:1-11 177
Hebrews 4:3-5 ... 170, 174
Hebrews 9:26 285
Hebrews 11:3 286
Hebrews 11:38 286
James 1:27 286
James 3:6 286
James 3:9 289
I John 2:2 286
I John 4:9 289
Revelation 11:15 139
Revelation 13:8 285
Revelation 17:8 285
Revelation 21:1 140
Revelation 21:23-24 ... 140